# Thought in Action

How does thinking affect doing? There is a widely held view—both in academia and in the popular press—that thinking about what you are doing, as you are doing it, hinders performance. Once you have acquired the ability to putt a golf ball, play an arpeggio on the piano, or parallel-park, it is believed that reflecting on your actions leads to inaccuracies, blunders, and sometimes even utter paralysis. Experts, accordingly, don't need to try to do it; they just do it. But is this true? After exploring some of the contemporary and historical manifestations of the idea that highly accomplished skills are automatic and effortless, Barbara Gail Montero develops a theory of expertise which emphasizes the role of the conscious mind in expert action. Along the way, she dispels various mythical accounts of experts who proceed without any understanding of what guides their action and analyzes research in both philosophy and psychology that is taken to show that conscious control impedes well practiced skills. She also explores real-life examples of optimal performance—culled from sports, the performing arts, chess, nursing, medicine, the military and elsewhere— and draws from psychology, neuroscience, and literature to create a picture of expertise according to which expert action generally is and ought to be thoughtful, effortful, and reflective.

**Barbara Gail Montero** is Professor of Philosophy at the College of Staten Island and the Graduate Center of the City University of New York.

# Thought in Action

*Expertise and the Conscious Mind*

Barbara Gail Montero

## OXFORD
### UNIVERSITY PRESS

Great Clarendon Street, Oxford, OX2 6DP,
United Kingdom

Oxford University Press is a department of the University of Oxford.
It furthers the University's objective of excellence in research, scholarship,
and education by publishing worldwide. Oxford is a registered trade mark of
Oxford University Press in the UK and in certain other countries

First published 2016
First published in paperback 2018

Published in the United States of America by Oxford University Press
198 Madison Avenue, New York, NY 10016, United States of America

British Library Cataloguing in Publication Data
Data available

Library of Congress Cataloging in Publication Data
Data available

ISBN 978-0-19-959677-5 (Hbk.)
ISBN 978-0-19-882242-4 (Pbk.)

*Dedicated to the memory of my parents, José and Dorothy Montero, who inspired my curiosity about the workings of the human mind and body while imparting their abiding belief in the value of effort.*

*All things excellent are as difficult as they are rare.*

*Baruch Spinoza (1632–1677)*
*The Ethics*

# Contents

# Preface

I remember how difficult philosophy seemed when I was an undergraduate at Berkeley. I was taking epistemology with Barry Stroud at the time and feeling a bit disheartened, went to his office and asked, "Does it ever get easier?" No, it doesn't, he told me, since as you grow as a philosopher you work on increasingly challenging problems. Although this was not the response I wanted to hear, it made sense immediately, for I was entering college directly from a career as a professional ballet dancer. Ballet, I knew, never gets easier; if anything, it gets harder, for as you advance as a dancer, you develop both higher standards for what counts as excellence and an enhanced ability to evaluate your skills, finding flaws that previously went unnoticed. Just as in Plato's dialogue the *Apology*, where Socrates is wise because he knows he is ignorant, it is the capacity to recognize where there is room for improvement that allows expert dancers to reach great heights.

The ability to see room for improvement, however, is not of much use unless one also has a strong and ongoing desire to improve. And it may be that, more so than talent, it is this desire to improve, an attitude the Japanese call "*kaizen*," that turns a novice into an expert. I certainly had *kaizen* in abundance; it was ingrained in my mind and body to the extent that every class, rehearsal, and performance was in part aimed at self-improvement. And improving, especially after having already achieved a high level of competency, requires thought, diligence, willpower, and prodigious effort.

Although practice may be hard work, it is widely supposed that great performances, in ballet and elsewhere, are intuitive and effortless: like water running downstream, once experts achieve mastery, their actions are thought simply to flow. Indeed, much of the research on expertise in philosophy and psychology avers that trying, as opposed to just letting it happen, interferes with expert skill. This book is about why that contention is wrong.

It was during the spring of 2003 that I began ruminating over the standard view of the relationship between expert action and thought. I was being interviewed for an assistant professor position at City University of New York and had just given a talk on how proprioception, which is our nonvisual sense of the positions and movements of our bodies in space, provides insight into the beauty, grace, power, and precision of one's own movements, and how dancers, by focusing on their proprioceptive experiences, can have such insight. The typical question-and-answer period ensued during which the faculty tries unrelentingly to test your mettle, whereupon the philosopher Bob Child (who happened to also be an avid golfer) asked, "but doesn't focusing on what you are doing interfere with performance?" Child, it struck me then, was right, for I had often heard the admonishment "you're thinking too much," coupled with the advice to just let it happen. So I ended up vacillating a bit, as philosophers are wont to do in the face of devastating objections, before timidly suggesting that perhaps a dancer on stage would need to settle for enjoying whatever proprioceptive experiences spontaneously bubble up to consciousness, rather than actively introspecting. Fortunately, Child seemed satisfied; I wiped the sweat off my brow, and I got the job. Yet I didn't stop pondering his question. And the more I thought about it, the more I reflected on my own experiences both as a professional ballet dancer and as a philosophy professor, the more I talked to others about their experiences of performing at their best in their area of expertise and read up on the psychology and neuroscience of expert skill, the more I realized that the correct answer to Child's question should have been *no*. These pages recount the journey I went through in arriving at this answer.

During the years of working on this volume, it has often seemed to me that the arduous process of writing should be an emblem of my view that expert action typically demands thought and effort. Although I have told myself time and time again to stop fretting and just get to work, this was more of a call to cease the needless lamentations over how I will never be able to accomplish my goal, rather than a command to ease up and let it happen; for me, letting it happen would have led to nothing happening. Of course, part of the reason the process has been so challenging is that it has required me to learn about new topics; although there are aspects of this work that I have been thinking about for over a decade, some inroads represent more recent sallies unto the breach. Be that as it may, writing, whether it is about topics new or old, is never easy for me.

In explaining what it is like to write a song, Billy Joel once said "I love having written; but I hate writing." I, too, relish the experience of having written. I write not because it engenders moment-by-moment pleasure—the kind of pleasure you get when putting on clothes straight out of the dryer or locking eyes with that winsome stranger across the room—but rather because it leads to the type of happiness that results from looking back over your life and accomplishments with a sense of fulfillment, a species of happiness the ancient Greeks referred to as *eudaimonia*. Nonetheless, despite the pain, it would be misleading to characterize the task of writing this book as all work and no play—all work and no pay, perhaps, but play has certainly been an element. Possibly, this is in part because philosophers and ballet dancers have something in common: they enjoy suffering. But more importantly, I think it is also because writing, like dancing, can sometimes occasion the exhilaration of learning, improving, and creating, and I hope that in the subsequent pages I have conveyed not only my view that expert action involves both thought and effort, but also some of this joy.

# Acknowledgments

Because this book has taken me so long to write, there has been ample time for assistance. In the beginning, however, there was Peter Momtchiloff, my editor at Oxford University Press. I thank him for his encouragement at the start of the project, his patience as the years wore on, and his unwavering confidence that I would eventually get it done. He was right.

I have been able to devote so many hours to writing in part because I have been blessed with a number of fellowships and supported leaves. The paper that instigated the entire project and which developed into Chapter 10, was supported by a 2004–05 National Endowment for the Humanities Research Fellowship; an American Council of Learned Societies Ryskamp Research Fellowship got the book going during the 2008–09 academic year; the following year, an Andrew W. Mellon Science Studies Fellowship at the Graduate Center kept it going as did both a 2012–13 academic year sabbatical from the College of Staten Island and release time from Dean Sussman during the spring of 2015; a second National Endowment for the Humanities Research Fellowship (2015–16) enabled me to wrap everything up; and three Provost's Travel Grants allowed me to present parts of the book in progress at conferences near and far.

While this project would not yet be finished without this time off from teaching, it would be much worse were it not for the comments, ideas, and corrections I have received from students. I discussed my incipient ideas about expertise in my Bodily Awareness course at the CUNY Graduate Center during the spring of 2009. Niels Bohr once said that an expert is a person who has made all the mistakes possible to make in a narrow field; attendees of that class, which included Professor Frederique Vingnemont, did a great job of correcting me as I began on this path towards expertise. In the autumn of 2013, my undergraduate students at the College of Staten Island read an early draft of most of the book. Two students in that course told me that they aspired to become writers and were taking my class for inspiration. If I inspired them even half as much as they ended up inspiring me, they are off to a good start. My undergraduates in 2014 read parts of the book and offered useful advice, as did the students in my honors class in the spring of 2015. Students at University of Puget Sound, where I gave a guest lecture on how to understand the concept of expertise, had great questions, which I hope to have now answered in the book. And, finally, Graduate Center Nursing doctoral students in my philosophy of science course in the 2010, 2011, 2013, and 2014 autumn semesters also read parts of the book; I knew when I had a draft that was not utterly torn apart by them, the book was ready to go.

I am additionally grateful for comments, criticisms, and suggestions from, among others: Lauren Alpert, Torin Alter, Stephanie Beardman, Dean James Beckwith, Martin Bingisser, Caroline Bollinger, David Brendel, Chris Brown, Sara Buss, Erin Carmondy, David Chalmers, Sam Chase, Jonathan Cole, Ursula Coope, Alex Craven, Amy DeBellis, John Doris, James Dow, Stuart Dreyfus, Anne Eaton, Cory Evans, Larry D. Evans, Rich Flannagan, Ellen Fridland, Shaun Gallagher, Mary Louise Gill, Elena Goldberg, Jon Hamkins, Monica Hamkins, SuEllen Hamkins, Simon Høffding, Amanda Huminski, Marilyn Inglis, Sean Kelly, Andrew Lambert, Rob Lovering, Brian Moen, Steve Monte, Steve Morris, David Papineau, Nick Pappas, Nick Parrott, Laurie Paul, Vasilious Petrados, Andrew Porter, Kevin Ryan, Tobias Schaeffer, Susanna Schellenberg, Henry Selvin, Jane Sheldon, Peter Simpson, Jason Stanley, John Sutton, John Toner, Violette Verdy, Ronny Wasserstrom, Mark White, Andrew Woodard, Christine Yang, Philip Zigman, Rachel Zuckert; audience members at the University of Munster, *The Philosophy of Expertise: What is Expertise?* Conference, the University of Memphis *Spindel Conference: Alternative Models of the Mind*, the Yale *Symposium on Skills and Practices*, the New York City *Night of Philosophy,* the *Philosophy Now* Lecture Series, the University of Leeds *Improvisation in Dance: A Philosophical Perspective,* the Delmenhorst *International Conference: Aesthetics and the Embodied Mind*, and the College of Staten Island *Philosophy Forum*; the two Oxford University Press readers; and, for her expert cover design idea, Ann Petter.

Beyond this, I am indebted to the many high-achieving Hunter College Elementary School and Brearley School parents—doctors, musicians, artists, actors, writers, graphic designers, lawyers, financiers, and even a former competitive surfer—who have not only generously offered their time to tell me about how they approach their professions, but, with their unflagging enthusiasm about the project (even when it must have seemed to them that wrapping up this book was my permanent occupation), gave me the strength to reach the finish line.

I also must express my gratitude to the crew at my appropriately named writing spot, the Fourth Avenue *Think Coffee*, for always knowing my order, occasionally making me laugh, and comping me whenever I forgot my wallet, which happened an embarrassing number of times. (What wasn't written at *Think Coffee* was completed on the X10 to and from the College of Staten Island—thank you NYC traffic.)

Søren Kierkegaard said that you live your life forward, but understand it backwards. This no doubt is true, however—as they know all too well at *Think Coffee*—since I tend to forget quite a bit along the way, let me conclude these acknowledgments by covering all bases and saying, as my then six-year-old daughter did one Thanksgiving, "I am grateful for the Big Bang."

# Introduction

## What Can a Philosopher Tell You About Expertise?

Science, Richard Feynman once said, is the belief in the ignorance of experts. If so—though I wouldn't put it in quite those words—then perhaps my project should be dubbed scientific, for it is my belief that a wide range of experts who have written about expertise have been mistaken. In particular, I believe that various psychologists, philosophers, neuroscientists, and other experts on high-level performance have erroneously concluded that expert action proceeds best when the mind is relatively inactive, when action occurs automatically, and when bodily movements are effortless. These expertise experts, I believe, are wrong.

If science is not the belief in the ignorance of experts, or rather, if it is not only this but also calls for creating theories that are both based on the results of observation and are capable of empirical refutation, then, perhaps, here too at least part of my present task should be seen as scientific. For although I have not recorded and analyzed my findings in the sort of systematic, quantitative way characteristic of what we typically think of as scientific investigation, my understanding of expertise is partially grounded in observations of hundreds of experts whom I have spoken with or read about and have sometimes also observed in action and, as such, my views are capable of being proven wrong by further empirical data.

However, if science requires performing controlled experiments of the sort found in much of the psychology of expertise and drawing conclusions based on their results, then this work is hardly scientific, for I have conducted no such experiments.[1] Indeed, I have no lab; I have no research staff; I am, as the old joke goes, one of those great bargains for the university. But philosophical investigation is only a bargain if it provides something worthwhile, and you might be wondering, "Of what use is a philosophical account of expertise?"

One answer to this question is to invite you to read the rest of the book and find out. However, for those who want some assurance that such an investment would yield a worthwhile return, let me try a different tack.

---

[1] Although in Chapter 11, I do discuss the results of some informal experiments I conducted on chess players.

## Obstacles to the Science of Expertise

When I told the mathematician Philip Welch that I was writing a book on the expert mind in action, he was puzzled: "But wouldn't an fMRI tell us whether experts think?" This comment surprised me, not because of its content—it is a reasonable question to ask—but rather because of its timing: he was just sitting down to a dinner I had pains-takingly prepared, and thus I would have expected him to merely nod his head politely and commence eating before the soup got cold. There are three rules regarding dinner-table conversation: no politics, no religion, and no questioning whether your host's lifework has any value. He knows this; therefore the possibility of the book being made obsolete by neuroscience must have really struck him. And since it has likely struck some of you as well, let me recount what I said that night in response (censoring expletives).

There is no doubt that we have learned a great deal about the mind of the expert in action from empirical research by cognitive neuroscientists, psychologists, physia-trists, psychiatrists, sports medicine physicians, and others. The experiments such researchers conduct, though occasionally carried out in the field—be it the baseball field or the Metropolitan Opera stage—typically take place in controlled settings. Controls are important since (at least ideally) they enable us to manipulate one varia-ble of a situation, such as an expert's attention to her actions, to see how it affects another variable, such as performance success. However, the nature of expertise makes it extremely challenging to study in controlled laboratory settings.

One reason for this is simply that experts are typically not willing to spend an after-noon as test subjects; they have better things to do and have become experts precisely because they make good use of their time. In this respect, the scientific study of con-scious experience, which is sometimes thought of as an empirically recalcitrant phe-nomenon, has an advantage over the scientific study of expertise. Consciousness, it is said, confounds scientific investigation since science can reveal only the neural or behavioral correlates of consciousness but never consciousness itself. Whether or not this is true, it is a trivial matter to find conscious college students—their typical blood-alcohol level notwithstanding—who are willing to participate in psychology experiments in exchange for a measly $10 or course credit; finding experts who are willing to trade in their time for such rewards is near impossible. If the question of how to understand consciousness scientifically is, as it is often called, "the hard problem," studying expertise is the really hard problem.[2]

Getting experts into the lab, though near impossible, may be feasible if one has a large enough grant or (more realistically) if one is in the right place at the right time. For example, the psychologist and master-level chess player, Adrian de Groot, who has been referred to as one of the founders of cognitive science, carried out much of his groundbreaking work on chess while he was ship-bound along with other members of

---

[2] See David Chalmers's (1996) discussion of the hard problem. (Of course, many other questions resist thorough study in controlled settings. For example, it would be useful to know how extreme pain affects behavior, yet we cannot subject participants to extreme pain in a study.)

the Netherlands national chess team on their way to the 1939 Chess Olympiad in Buenos Aires (de Groot 1946). Lashed to the deck waiting for the pelagic hours to pass, the chess players were not inhospitable to de Groot's requests; typically, though, psychologists do not have at their disposal such means to induce participation.

On those rare occasions when experts do make it into the lab (as well as when you bring the lab to them, as de Groot did), researchers trying to understand the expert mind in action via controlled experiments face a distinct obstacle, namely, that such experiments cannot capture the urgency of a trauma center, the excitement of opening night at the Paris Opera House, or the overwhelming aspiration, hunger, and yearning to beat your opponent at chess. Being asked to dribble soccer balls twenty-five times through a slalom course is not going to elicit quite the same drive as being asked to play for your country at the World Cup. It is somewhat analogous to studying sleep deprivation in a controlled setting: it's so boring in the lab that participants can't stay awake, yet on a mission, a fighter-jet pilot may be alert for days on end. One theme of this book, to put it baldly, is that controlled settings destroy expertise.

The psychologist Anders Ericsson suggests that since experts can perform in a wide range of conditions, they can perform their skills in the laboratory as well. And to a degree this is correct. Depending on their respective expertise, whether they are in or out of the lab, experts can putt a ball, play a sonata, or choose the next move in a chess game. But they will not be on their mettle; they will not be roused to perform at their best. Of course, it might be possible for them to perform optimally in a laboratory setting—a million dollar reward might do the trick—yet the typical incentives do not suffice to inspire excellence. With some investigations into expert performance, this might not matter. For example, if you are interested in where basketball players direct their eyes right before they shoot, a lack of motivation will likely not affect the outcome of your experiment. However, if you are interested, as I am, in whether experts exert significant amounts of effort during a performance or a game, a lackadaisical approach to a task in the laboratory does matter.

Another problem with some studies of expertise is that researchers sometimes ask experts to engage in actions that are quite different from those that occur during an actual game or performance. For example, soccer players may be asked to dribble a ball through a slalom course while reporting (at the sound of a randomly generated tone) which side of their foot had just touched the ball (Ford et al. 2005; Beilock et al. 2002); or baseball players may be asked to perform a batting task with a virtual ball while reporting (again, at the sound of a randomly generated tone) whether their bat is moving up or down. Yet these activities are not part of the professional athlete's repertoire. Research that fails to mirror real-life settings is sometimes criticized by psychologists as not being "ecologically valid" (Neisser 1976). What exactly ecological validity amounts to is an open question; nonetheless, if what an experiment tests differs significantly from the activity of interest, it is reasonable to question whether the results apply to performance out of the lab. And while some researchers trade in some of the control that exists in a laboratory setting for more ecological validity, finding the right balance between control and ecological validity is a challenge.

Moreover, in direct response to Philip—who was naturally ready to pitch into the dinner at this point—quite apart from the difficulty of performing a brain scan on a high-diver mid-air, brain imaging technology is not always useful in the study of expert action since, at least as things stand now, we do not adequately understand what areas of the brain underlie thought, effort, and attention. As Kielan Yarrow and colleagues (2009) conclude in a review article on neurological research investigating elite athletes, "clearly expert and novice athletes use their brains differently, but precisely interpreting these differences in terms of their functional roles seems some way off at present" (p. 589). And so, as I discuss in later chapters, although there are a number of neurological studies that are suggestive, there are none that are conclusive, and even what exactly they are suggestive of is frequently open to debate.

Finally (and I noticed Philip reach for the spoon on hearing this word), when we add to these challenges the fact that there is very little agreement among the expertise scientists about who exactly counts as an expert and what exactly expert action is, we are left with an area that is challenging to study scientifically, as well as one that has at least the potential to benefit from philosophical reflection. Philosophy, no doubt, faces obstacles as well (rather large ones). And I assume that the final answer—or, if there is no *final* answer, then something closer to the final answer—to the question of what goes on in the mind of an expert in action will be revealed in scientific inquiry, for I am very much of the opinion, as the philosopher of science Bas van Fraassen (1996) once put it, that "there are no science stoppers" (p. 80). Accordingly, I believe that if controlled experiments tend to destroy expertise, we ought to not give up, but to find a way to change the controls. Nonetheless, I think that at this point in the study of expertise it might be worthwhile to take a brief pause in the scientific investigation into the question of what goes on in the mind of the expert in action—if only long enough to read this book—and ponder it from, if not a strictly philosophical, then at least a philosopher's point of view.

## Methodology

Philosophy, as is well known, encompasses a wide variety of approaches, and it is sometimes difficult to find even a family resemblance among them. One philosophical approach I favor, however, is to see just about everything as open to question—not to question everything, of course, which would be impossible, but to hold very little as beyond reproach. In most walks of life, if someone were to doubt whether the sun will rise tomorrow, we would be inclined to see this as lunacy; philosophers, however, write long treatises about the topic. Though I am happy to assume that the sun always rises, I do question a view that, although not nearly as tightly woven into our mental fabric as our expectations about the break of day, is nevertheless widely assumed, and this is the view that thinking about what you are doing as you are doing it impedes performance.

Like anyone, philosophers are much better at questioning others' assumptions than at questioning their own, and in order to talk about expertise I shall, no doubt, leave innumerably many views unquestioned: not only basic beliefs such as the assumption that the sun will rise, but some views that are quite specific to my concerns, such as whether high anxiety can hinder performance, or whether being an expert is something valuable enough to justify research on expertise, or whether experts have minds, or whether experts exist at all. All that, I assume. What I question, however, and ultimately reject, is the maxim that expert action—whether of the more cognitive sort, such as chess, or the more physical sort, such as soccer—proceeds better with relatively less thought and less effort.

Part of my task is critical, as I aim to dispel various mythical accounts of experts who proceed without any understanding of what guides their actions. The chicken sexer that philosophers are fond of citing who can't explain why he makes his judgments—he doesn't exist (Nakayama 1993). And Coleridge's "Kubla Khan," which supposedly came to him fully formed in a dream, actually took nearly ten years to write (Schneider 1945). I also question research (in both philosophy and psychology) that extrapolates from everyday skills to draw conclusions about expert performance and argue that the type of extended analytical training that experts partake in, as well as the relatively higher stakes involved in expert action, make quotidian tasks (such as everyday driving) different enough from expert-level actions (such as professional race-car driving) so as to not warrant extrapolation from the former to the latter. It very well may be, as Bernard Williams (1985) points out, "that a practical skill can, in an individual case, be destroyed by reflection on how one practices it" (p. 167). However, as Williams also says, in "favorable circumstances," reflection may enhance expertise. Such circumstances, I argue, generally occur when an individual has undergone ten or more years of close to daily extended practice with the specific aim of improving, and, importantly, is still intent on improving. A theme of my research is that this manner of training enables experts to perform while engaging their self-reflective capacities without any detrimental effects; it allows experts to think and do at the same time.

I also present a handful of error theories that aim to explain why it is that so many have found the precept that thinking hinders high-level performance appealing, even though it is wrong. For example, some may accept the view that expert action is unreflective because, quite simply, expert actions often *appear* effortless. This is particularly true of ballet, where movements are often supposed to produce the illusion of effortlessness. Yet this illusion is difficult to create. The Renaissance writer Baldassare Castiglione (1528/1975), who was well aware of both the importance and difficulty of appearing spontaneous in one's actions, extols *sprezzatura*, which is a contrived effortlessness or as Wescott (2000) puts it, "the art of acting deviously" (p. 227). Though no contrivance may be involved in exercising other expert skills—a professional soccer player cares not about how her actions appear—in these cases, too, the apparent effortlessness is often merely apparent.

The central positive arguments that support my view fall roughly into three categories. First, I rely on case studies for in-depth explorations of specific examples of expert action, such as a head nurse's description of working in the emergency room, a tennis player's account of competing in a grand slam, or a chess player's experience of playing speed chess. Second, I examine and draw inferences from empirical research that identifies psychological factors experts themselves see as conducive to optimal performance in high-pressure situations; for example, a study by Adam Nicholls and colleagues (2006) suggests that professional rugby players regularly cope with pressure by increasing their concentration on the task. Third, I consider what we should expect would be true about expert action given what we know about experts and the way they train. What can we infer, for example, about expert performance given that experts practice in a thoughtful, analytic manner? How does the often-obsessive drive to improve affect the state of an expert's mind when she is exercising her skills? And what follows from the need to occasionally take risks in performance? Although no single line of argumentation is conclusive on its own, my hope is that, when taken together, these paths to my theory of effortful expertise lend it what William Wimsatt (2007) sees as a criterion for being the best explanation for the available data, namely, robustness.

The starting assumption of many researchers in this area seem to be that when experts are performing at their best, attention to what they are doing is harmful rather than helpful. Studies are then devised to test this preconception. Yet such studies sometimes seem better designed to substantiate it rather than to question it. If nothing else, I will consider my book a success if it creates a fissure in this approach.

## A Methodological Principle

Although for some purists, philosophy is and ought to be an entirely a priori pursuit, it should be apparent that this work is, in that sense, impure, for not only do I rely on empirical research to support my view, but anecdotes, or what I also call "case studies," based on data from experts whom I have spoken to or read about (as well as reflections on my own experience currently as a philosopher and formerly as a professional ballet dancer) play a role in the larger argument. Reliance on data is, of course, a cornerstone of science, yet I have not systematically recorded my data as would befit scientific inquiry. How, then, can anecdotes help me to make my point?

Anecdotes are not arguments, but there are many moves in the game we call "philosophy" that do not involve arguments. For example, philosophers are often happy to countenance theory construction. Many of the great philosophers were theory builders—Kant and Hegel, for example—and as long as such theories are internally coherent and do not contradict current scientific knowledge, many contemporary philosophers see theory construction as a worthwhile endeavor; but while these philosophers will happily countenance theory construction, as soon as an anecdote is brought in to illustrate what may have inspired such theory, they groan. Similarly, many philosophers, though not all, rely on intuitions. For example, some have the intuition that everything must ultimately depend on something fundamental; others have intuitions that allow for an infinite descent of ontological dependence (turtles all the way down, as it is sometimes put). Such intuitions, as they see it, can support a view; but my first-person report that I was thinking in action is suspect. And finally, it is often thought acceptable to make general claims about what everyone purportedly knows to be the case; for example, it is acceptable to write that "everyone knows that when you think about the details of your movements you mess up" or "when the soccer player is on the field, as far as he can tell, he is not thinking about what to do." But try to give even one actual anecdote in order to show that perhaps not everyone knows this or that perhaps not all soccer players attest to this, and you're under fire.

I think philosophers are a bit too trigger-happy here since examining individual cases can support one's argument in numerous ways: it can illustrate a view, reveal what inspires theory (and perhaps intuition), counter assertions to the effect that "all athletes claim x" or "all musicians do y," and (God forbid) add interest. Moreover, akin to how case studies can be relevant to medical research and research in the social sciences (George and Bennett 2005), I sometimes employ anecdotes to provide an in-depth look at a particular phenomenon. Of course, in medicine, the case study is presented out of necessity, for the condition is usually unique (or at least previously unseen), making a larger-scale study impossible. Expertise, however, is not unique; indeed, as we shall see, one can even perform large-scale statistical analyses of archival sports data in hopes of determining whether self-focus is deleterious to performance. Nonetheless, individual cases, like in medicine, though incapable of grounding generalizations, may also provide inspiration for further research.

In Plato's dialogue *Ion* (380 BCE/1996), Socrates presses Ion to accept that poets and rhapsodes (performers, like Ion, who recite and interpret poetry) are in some way guided by divine madness since they cannot have any understanding of the topics about which they speak. Ion responds: "[although your reasoning appears unassailable] I doubt whether you will ever have eloquence enough to persuade me that I praise Homer only when I am mad and possessed" (380 BCE/1996: 536d). This line is sometimes cut when the dialog is anthologized (for example, in Bychkov and Sheppard 2010), but it's important. Socrates not only doesn't take Ion's claims seriously, he apparently had never even observed Ion in action. Another leitmotif in the book is that it is at least sometimes worthwhile to listen to the experts themselves.

But is what experts say they are thinking a reliable guide to what they really are thinking? The questioners of assumptions will point out that we are frequently mistaken about the contents of our own minds and therefore neither introspection nor first-person reports can be trusted. However, although I believe that sometimes we are mistaken about what is going on in our own minds, especially with regards to the reasons we are acting in a certain way,[3] I shall assume throughout the book that, in general, as long as there are no good grounds to question any particular report about what someone says he or she is experiencing, first-person reports can be taken as defeasible evidence for what is actually going on in a person's mind. In other words, I accept the following:

*Methodological Principle.* First-person reports of what goes on in one's own mind should be accepted as (defeasible) evidence for the truth of the report unless we have good reason to question them.

For example, if you have good reason to believe that someone is lying or that some-one is likely self-deceived (based on, say, personal interactions), or that someone is making claims about his or her own mental states because they are responding to leading questions, or they have been reading a theory advocating the view, or that the results of a psychology experiment—or maybe even a philosophical argument (see Schwitzgebel 2011)—show that such type of introspection is more likely wrong than right, then we should doubt the reports of such an individual. However, barring any good reasons for doubt, I take first-person accounts of one's own mental pro-cesses at face value.[4] This methodological precept follows roughly from what Tyler Burge (1993) calls the "acceptance principle," which holds that "a person is entitled to accept as true something that is presented as true and that is intelligible to him, unless there are stronger reasons not to do so" (p. 467). Whether the acceptance principle is a fundamental principle that we know a priori, as Burge thought, or is justified through our experience of interacting with people, is a question I leave to the side. I state merely that in my reasoning about expertise, I maintain, in the form of the methodological principle, something very much akin to it.

I have occasionally heard it said that that experts' introspection can't be trusted since we have a glaring example of expert introspection gone wrong: expert batters in base-ball and cricket think that they are consciously aware of the ball in flight, yet eye-tracking experiments, which show that eye-gaze often lags behind the ball and is not on the ball when it makes contact with the bat, show that this cannot be so. However, that we should accept experts' claims about where parts of their bodies are moving (unless we have good reason to doubt this) is not the same as the position advocated in the meth-odological principle, which is that we should accept experts' claims about what is going on in their minds (unless we have good reason to doubt this). No matter where their eyes are, expert batters might still think that they are consciously aware of the ball in flight. Furthermore, although earlier studies found that the eyes of "club players" sometimes

---

[3] See, for example, Nisbett and Wilson (1977); Gobet (2009); Bilalić et al. (2008a; 2008b).

[4] Uriah Kriegel (2013) suggests that the introspection of expert athletes and others when playing in the so-called "zone," is highly questionable. He argues that because being in the zone precludes introspection, any attempt to introspect would disrupt its characteristic flow. This would be a good argument if optimal expert action did preclude introspection, however, if introspection is simply understood as having an awareness of the contents of your own mind, throughout the book I give many examples of how optimal expert action does not preclude such awareness. See also my 2015b paper, "Thinking in the Zone."

lag behind the ball and are not on the ball at the moment of contact with the bat (see, for example, Bahill and LaRitz 1984), a 2013 study by David Mann and colleagues of two elite cricket players found that players both track the ball as it approaches and also have their eyes on the ball as they hit it. Justin Langer (a retired international cricketer) claims to be able to see the markings on the ball as he strikes it; given Mann's research, we have no reason to doubt his introspective access to this (Mann et al. 2013).[5]

## What to Expect When You Are Reading

Though it may be easier, it is not much fun to argue against a position that is held by only a few individuals in a narrow field. With the view I am arguing against, there is fun to be had since, as I bring to the fore in Chapter 1, it is widely accepted that experts perform best without thinking about what they are doing—what I refer to as the "just-do-it principle," or for short, "just-do-it." People have held this view or something like it in many different forms and, in this chapter, galloping across time periods and intellectual traditions, I take the reader on a tour of some of its contemporary manifestations in popular culture, philosophy, psychology, and neuroscience, as well as some of its historical antecedents in Romanticism, Zen Buddhism, and Taoism. The aim here is neither to bury nor even less to praise the principle, but to show how ingrained it is in our psyche.

For ease of exposition, I often state the just-do-it idea as the view that "experts do not think," however, in Chapter 2 my pace slows down to a crawl, as I explain what I mean specifically by "the just-do-it principle," categorize the different takes on expertise encountered in the prior chapter, and pull apart the different kinds of mental processes that are proscribed by just-do-it advocates (which include conscious control, monitoring, analyzing, planning, deciding, and effort). Here, I also distinguish the descriptive aspect of the principle (the aspect that tells us what experts do) from the proscriptive claim about what experts ought not to do, and explain the widely held "principle of interference," which asserts, in short, that thinking interferes with expert action. Beyond this, I identify moderate forms of the just-do-it principle, which tell us that peak expert performance is free from certain sorts of mental processes, and contrast these moderate views with extreme views according to which experts, when acting at their best, do not engage their minds at all (the brain is working, of course, but the mind is absent). Finally, in this chapter, I present the "cognition-in-action principle," which captures the view that the book aims to defend.

---

[5] Given that the eyes of the two players do make predictive saccades—that is, their eyes quickly jump to the location where they expect to see the ball—do they "keep their eye on the ball?" Joshua Shepherd (2015) points out that since predicative saccades are part of what we think of as everyday continuous visual experience, if we were to say that such predictive saccades show that expert batters are not aware of what they are experiencing, we would have to say that such ignorance pervades all of our visual experience (see Shepherd 2015, section 4.2, especially fn. 15).

But what, exactly, is an expert? This is the question I tackle in Chapter 3. As I shall explain, although there are abundant investigations into the psychology of expertise, few researchers agree on who the experts are and how we ought to identify them. Are experts those who have amassed a great amount of knowledge about a topic? Or should we think of experts as individuals whose ability lies, say, two standard deviations above the mean? After addressing these and other proposed criteria for expertise (such as those by Edwin Ray Guthrie, Anders Ericsson, Alvin Goldman, Fitts and Posner, Dreyfus and Dreyfus, and Ericsson and Charness) I argue that for my purposes an expert should be understood as someone who has spent around ten years or more engaged in deliberate practice of their skill, which is practice with the specific aim of improving, and is still intent on improving. Such a definition might not match exactly what we call an "expert" in ordinary language, but, I argue, it comes close enough to warrant the appellation. Moreover, and more importantly, it identifies a group of individuals to whom, I go on to argue, the just-do-it principle does not apply.

With these clarifications in place, Chapter 4 begins an argument (which continues through the rest of the book) for the view that thought and effort do not interfere with but instead are integral to expert action. In this chapter and the next, I examine situations that many think clearly demand a just-do-it portrayal. Chapter 4 concerns performance under pressure. Athletes, performing artists, and others choke under pressure, according to the predominant theory of choking, the "explicit monitoring theory," because pressure is thought to induce attention to the details of a skill. This chapter scrutinizes some of the empirical studies and philosophical accounts of skill (including those of Richard Masters, Sian Beilock, Roy Baumeister, Wilson and Schooler, Goldman and Rao, and Hubert Dreyfus) that are thought to lend support to the so-called phenomenon of "paralysis by analysis," and presents an alternative account of the data that is in line with both the "distraction theory" of choking under pressure and the idea that monitoring and conscious control are beneficial even when performing under pressure.

Another situation commonly thought to support just-do-it is when actions must occur at lightning-fast speeds. Chapter 5, thus, addresses the question of whether there are skills—such as race-car driving, frontline warfare, and emergency-room nursing—requiring such quick responses that thinking, especially conscious thinking, is ruled out. Among others, I investigate cases where experts purportedly need to react to something before they have time to consciously see it, such as in professional tennis where, some claim, a player needs to strike back before consciously seeing the ball leave the server's racket. I argue that because it is an open question when a person becomes conscious of an event and because experts at interceptive sports (such as tennis, baseball, and cricket) detect clues before the ball leaves the pitcher's hand or their opponent's racket, conscious thinking in action should not be ruled out. Along the way, this chapter discusses work by (among others) Patricia Benner, Karl von Clausewitz, David Papineau, Jeffrey Gray, David Mann, Sian Beilock, Johnson and Raab, and Shakespeare.

Although proponents of just-do-it typically believe that a prodigious amount of thought and effort goes into making an expert, they nonetheless typically maintain that all the training aims at the final result of performing effortlessly, automatically, and with a minimal amount of conscious thought, if any. However, in Chapter 6, bolstered by research by John Toner and Aidan Moran, I argue that because experts practice thoughtfully, and that because the desire to improve and excel is so ingrained in experts, experts can think, without detriment, while performing (as long as they are thinking about the right things). The desire to improve involves increased attention to performance, yet a bedrock principle in psychology is that attention is limited. However, I conclude this chapter with a discussion of whether expert action may even give us reason to question that bedrock principle. In sports, the performing arts, academia, and elsewhere, when the pressure is on, or when the hunger to succeed is overwhelming—situations that never truly occur in laboratory settings—it is unclear what might be possible for an expert to achieve.

The next two chapters concern the role of effort in expert action. Beginning with a discussion of work by the philosophers Brian O'Shaughnessy, Jennifer Hornsby, and Robert Hanna and Michelle Maiese, who hold that trying is essential to all our intentional actions, I go on, in Chapter 7, to distinguish the various ways that trying or the closely related phenomenon of effort occurs in actions, and then identify the forms of trying that would reasonably occur in expert action. As consciously trying to do something, rather than just doing it, is effortful, expert action, as I shall argue (since it involves trying) is effortful. Moreover, though throughout most of the book I spotlight professional-level expert actions, this chapter also addresses an assumption about our social interactions, namely, that in one's quest to find a mate, trying isn't sexy.

Successful expert action, I argue in Chapter 7, involves effort. Nonetheless, such actions may appear effortless; they embody, it is sometimes said, what the Italian Renaissance thinker Castiglione refers to as "*sprezzatura*," or what ancient Chinese thinkers refer to as "*wu-wei*". How are we to understand this effortlessness, if such actions typically involve effort? By examining what it means for an action to be effortless and exploring—in light of both Henri Bergson's and Edmund Spencer's views of grace—what we find valuable about aesthetically effortless actions, such as those performed by ballet dancers, Chapter 8 provides an account of effortlessness with effort. Just as Castiglione's *sprezzatura* was more of a guise than an indication that an action was being performed without effort, I argue that the effortlessness of great athletes and dancers may also be deceptive. And our admiration of effortlessness, I suggest, is explained in part by the superfluity of fitness that effortlessness evinces.

In expert bodily actions, especially those that appear effortless, it is occasionally claimed that the self is lost: that when running a marathon, for example, the self dissolves into movement, that there is no self-awareness, no sense that you are exerting yourself. In Chapter 9, I explore this idea. Through discussion and analysis of the role of the self in expert action as it emerges from work by David Velleman, Mihaly Csikszentmihalyi (particularly his concepts of "autotelic" action and "flow"), Karl Reinhold, and others, I both revisit my work with the clinical neurophysiologist Jonathan Cole on affective proprioception and suggest that although certain types of thoughts, such as distress and worry, may at times be blissfully absent during expert action, thoughts about and proprioceptive awareness of relevant bodily movements are nonetheless often present.

As I mentioned in the preface, my initial motivation for questioning the just-do-it principle was prompted over ten years ago by an objection the philosopher and avid golfer, Bob Child, made after a talk I had given on the idea of proprioceiving aesthetic properties. I was arguing that proprioception—the sense by means of which we are aware of the positions and movements of our limbs via receptors in muscles, tendons, joints, ligaments, and skin—is an aesthetic sense; that is, a sense via which we come to experience aesthetic properties. Child wanted to know, how could a dancer on stage have an aesthetic experience of her own movements, if experts do not focus on their own movements but act intuitively and automatically? If experts are to perform at their best, he commented, they cannot focus on what they are doing, and thus they cannot have the sorts of aesthetic experiences I attribute to them. Chapter 10, at long last, provides my considered response to Child's objection. Countering forms of the just-do-it principle that proscribe bodily awareness, I argue that proprioception enables dancers to perceive the grace, beauty, power, and precision of their own bodies.

Because of its regimented ranking system, chess is a favorite area of investigation for researchers interested in expert performance, and I address the role of deliberation, rationality, and conceptualization in exemplary chess performance in Chapter 11. Chess, an endeavor sometimes referred to as "the gymnasium of the mind," might seem an obvious counterexample to the idea that expert action proceeds without thought. However, Hubert Dreyfus (2013) has argued that, because grand master chess players can play lightning chess (one minute per player games) so well without thinking, the truly great moves of a chess player are neither rational nor conceptual but are, rather, directed by "forces on the board" (p. 35). In contrast to Dreyfus's view, I argue for the conceptual nature of chess perception as well as for the view that high-level chess players deliberate even during lightning chess. And, as I explain, an experiment I conducted on chess players—the results of which conflict with a view of chess shared by both Hubert Dreyfus and John McDowell—suggests this as well. These ideas extend my work with the US national master chess player Cory Alexander Evans (Montero and Evans 2011), and address some insightful responses to this work by the cognitive scientist and international master chess player Fernand Gobet (2012).

Why do so many accept the just-do-it counsel given that, if I am correct, it is unsubstantiated? After summarizing the journey so far, in Chapter 12, I attempt to answer this question by, among other things, analyzing the "aha" moment, such as Archimedes' purported Eureka discovery. Here, I also explore the connection between expertise and life satisfaction. If leading a meaningful life includes cultivating what Immanuel Kant spoke of as our "predispositions to greater perfection"—a duty that often involves a struggle—thinking in action, I argue, is part and parcel of this pursuit (1785/2012, p. 42). On top of that, I address the questions of whether drugs can facilitate effortless creativity, whether rock musicians just do it, and whether thinking interferes with optimal sexual performance.

## Skipping Right Along

Finally, although I recommend reading each chapter in order (as well, of course, as reading each chapter), I endeavored to make the chapters more or less stand on their own so as to facilitate skipping around. But rather than talking more about the chapters and how you ought to read them, let us dive right in.

# 1

# "Don't think, dear; just do" and Other Manifestations of the Just-do-it Principle

A centipede was happy quite, until a toad in fun
Said "Pray, which leg comes after which?"
This raised his doubts to such a pitch
He fell distracted in the ditch
Not knowing how to run.

Katherine Craster (1841–74)
"The Centipede's Dilemma"

"How can you hit and think at the same time?" is Yogi Berra's well-known comment on baseball. Of course, since he also reportedly said, "I really didn't say everything I said," it is not clear that we should take this comment at face value. Nonetheless, both in academia and in the popular press, both in the psychology lab and on the baseball diamond, there is a widespread acceptance of the view that thinking about what you are doing, as you are doing it, interferes with performance. Once you have developed the ability to putt a golf ball, play an arpeggio, or parallel park, many believe that attention to what you are doing leads to inaccuracies, blunders, and sometimes even utter paralysis. As the great choreographer George Balanchine would say to his dancers, "Don't think, dear; just do;"[1] or in the words of the thirteen-time PGA Tour winner Dave Hill "a golf swing is like sex. You can't be thinking about the mechanics of the act while you are performing."[2] But why not? This book illustrates what is wrong with the view that thinking about what you are doing while you are doing it interferes with performance. Or in other words, it shows why, in fact, you can hit and think at the same time.

Let me refer to the idea that highly developed skills proceed best without thinking about them, without focusing on them, and without making an effort—an idea that I hope to elucidate as the book progresses—as the "just-do-it principle." Obviously, people use the phrase "just do it" to mean a variety of things, and some of these things do not exemplify the view I aim to question. Putting aside any racier interpretations,

---

[1] Quoted in Jowitt (1989).
[2] Attributed to Hill in, for example, <http://www.mulliganplus.com/dave-hill-dies-at-74.cfm>.

there is "just do it already," a venerable mandate against procrastination and making up excuses, as well as "just do it anyway," a mantra aimed at quashing inhibitions that may arise from thinking too much about the opinions of others. There is also the "just do it" command one tells someone who needs to conquer her fears and there is even the "just do it badly" counsel some writers follow when struggling to complete a draft and nicely summed up by a screenwriter I once met who has a sign written in large letters on his computer which reads: MAKE IT SUCK. Someday I'd love to write a book about these ideas. However, this is not that book. Rather, the view I aim to question is the idea that experts perform at their best when their actions are effortless, intuitive, and automatic, when they happen without deliberation, when they just flow without thought. The Olympic high diver, according to this principle, pushes off from the ten-meter-high platform, rapidly torques and turns, then enters the water straight as a pin, all without thinking about what she is doing or what she is supposed to do; it is effortless, as she doesn't even try, but rather lets her body take over. The physician, on this account, is thought to make her best diagnoses not by reasoning, but by going with her gut. More generally, experts are said to perform automatically or intuitively; their actions are simply done as opposed to being done as the result of thought and effort: experts do not know how they do their remarkable feats, the psychologist Paul Lewicki and his research team tell us, "all they know is that they 'just do it'" (Lewicki et al. 1992, p. 797).

Indeed, for experts—whether on the green or on the stage, whether in front of the classroom or in front of the boardroom—thinking about their ongoing actions and making an effort to perform them is seen as detrimental to their execution. For example, according to Asian Studies scholar Edward Slingerland (2014), "it is clear that conscious reflection has a negative effect on expert performance" (p. 226). Similarly, psychologist Sian Beilock (2010) maintains that a body of empirical research on highly developed athletic skills supports the phenomenon of "paralysis by analysis," telling us that "heightened attention to detail can actually mess you up" and that to prevent this, you need to "play outside your head" (p. 190). In a paper with Thomas Carr, we hear that phrase again: "when experienced soccer players kick a ball, for example, they do not think consciously about every component involved in kicking, they 'just do it'" (Beilock and Carr 2004, p. 310).

Of course, there is a cavernous gap between the view that experts don't think consciously about *every* component of a movement and the view that experts just do it without thinking at all, and I certainly do not intend to argue against the former. No one thinks consciously about *every* component of his or her actions. However, I do reject the extreme view that experts, in their domain of expertise, "just do it" in the sense that during expert action the mind is a blank, that, as Dreyfus puts it, expertise is "nonminded" (2007a, p. 355). And I also reject some less extreme positions that see a nonzero subset of mental processes as necessarily or even only generally detrimental to expert action. For example, I reject Beilock's view that experts, in general, ought not to monitor their actions (in their domain of expertise) as they perform. Yet I do not reject the idea that some mental processes tend to be detrimental to performance. An expert tennis player, for example, might be ill-advised to reflect on everything that has gone wrong so far during a match. But, on my view, monitoring certain components of one's movements or strategizing for the win might very well be useful.

Thinking, trying, and focusing on details are different types of mental processes. Moreover, public speaking, performing a high dive, and playing in a jazz band are all very different kinds of activities, and although much of the research into expertise proceeds with at least an ultimate aim of identifying characteristics that hold true of experts across all domains, it is not clear that this ambition can succeed. Nevertheless, I shall proceed with the assumption—one prevalent in the current scientific and philosophical literature on expertise—that there are significant commonalities across the various domains of expertise, and thus in formulating a theory of expertise, I'll shoot for a theory of everything, while being well aware that such a theory might not be feasible. In this chapter, however, to give you a sense of what I am up against, let me simply bring to the fore the widespread acceptance of certain views—some contemporary, others historical; some from popular culture, others from the groves of academe—that exemplify or at least are close relatives of the idea, roughly put, that expert action proceeds better when the mind recedes, the idea I call the "just-do-it principle."

## The Just-do-it Principle in Popular Culture

If you walk through the aisles of your local bookstore, or browse through one of the increasingly favored online substitutes, you will come across numerous titles that, at least on first glance, advocate the view that to perform at one's best, one must not try, but just do, and that one must proceed with a relatively blank, if not entirely empty mind. There are books on how to improve in golf, tennis, archery, and parenting by taking the conscious mind out of the picture. There are books on how to achieve mastery in poker, or cinch a business deal, or create high-impact web pages with nary a modicum of effort. There are books with titles such as *Unthink: Rediscover Your Creative Genius* (Wahl 2013), or *Trust your Gut: How to Overcome the Obstacles to Greater Success and Self-Fulfillment* (Walker 2004), or *Effortless Mastery: Liberating the Master Musician Within* (Werner 1996), as well as *Destined to Reign: The Secret to Effortless Success, Wholeness and Victorious Living* (Prince 2010).

Of course, sometimes the titles, perhaps chosen by publishers for their mass-market appeal, do not fully capture the book's content. A case in point is *Unconscious Putting: Dave Stockton's Guide to Unlocking Your Signature Stroke* (Stockton and Rudy 2011), wherein, despite Stockton's promise to introduce "an easier, more instinctive way to putt," one finds suggestion after suggestion about what to think about and how to concentrate on your stroke; indeed, as one reviewer put it, "the very reading of Stockton's book puts more stuff, not less, into the swollen, clogged chamber that is the golf brain" (McGrath 2012). And although jazz pianist Kenny Werner's (1996) *Effortless Mastery* emphasizes that the best playing is that which is "unobstructed by thought" (p. 11), many of the thoughts that obstruct playing, he tells us, have to do with insecurities; accordingly, he spends a great deal of time on explaining techniques that are aimed at boosting confidence (would that such a book existed for philosophers!). Nevertheless, one finds a good number of volumes that come down hard on thought, books such as *The Power of Habit: Why We do What we do in Life and Business* (Duhigg 2012), which showcases examples of actions that misfire because individuals "stop relying on their habits and start thinking too much" (p. 90). The book, *Incognito*, also cautions us against brainpower as it tells of a pianist who "discovers that there is only one way she can [play]: by not thinking about it" (Eagleman 2011, p. 8). And perhaps most explicitly—and here the title tells it all—we have: *Hare Brain, Tortoise Mind: How Intelligence Increases When You Think Less* (Claxton 2000).

A significant inspiration behind a number of these books is Eugen Herrigel's (1953) *Zen in the Art of Archery*, according to which an expert archer must become "completely empty and rid of the self" so that the release of the arrow occurs "automatically ... [without] further need of the controlling or reflecting intelligence" (p. 61). It is not the archer, Herrigel tells us, who shoots the arrow, but rather, when the master archer stands before the target, "it shoots." And riding on the coattails of the success of this book, you can find everything from *Zen and the Art of Information Security* (Winkley 2007) to *Zen and the Art of Anything* (French 2001). Regardless of whether such books have captured something correct about expertise, it seems clear that they, or at least their titles, have hit upon something that the public likes to hear.

Timothy Gallwey, who wrote the bestseller *The Inner Game of Tennis*, was also influenced by Herrigel's work, and he favorably quotes D. T. Suzuki's introduction to the 1953 edition of *Zen in the Art of Archery*: "as soon as we reflect, deliberate, and conceptualize, the original unconsciousness is lost and thought interferes" (Gallwey 1974, p. 15; quoting Herrigel p. viii). In the best expert performances, Gallwey says, "the mind is transcended—or at least in part rendered inoperative" (p. 7). People frequently tell me how much this book has meant to them and how it converted them to the just-do-it mentality.[3]

In addition to popular books chiming the praise of unreflective action at the highest level and warning against using the thinking mind to guide what is assumed to be done best without it, the just-do-it idea is also much-loved by the media, which not infrequently explains poor performance in terms of the mind interfering with the body. In the sports section of the newspapers, for example, one reads that the tennis player Venus Williams is off because she is "overthinking her tosses" (Vecsey 2010), or that football player Mark Sanchez's fumble is possibly a result of "trying too hard to make something happen" (Bretherton 2012), and a favorite accolade of sportscasters is that an athlete's playing is "simply unconscious," or as you'll read in *USA Today*, "the

---

[3] There are also numerous spin-offs of Gallwey's book, including *The Inner Game of Chess*, *The Inner Game of Trading*, *The Inner Game of Internet Marketing*, and so forth.

Rockies...[are] a delight, playing unconscious baseball, winning 21 of their last 22 games" (Brennan 2007).

The journalist David Epstein (2013), in a *Sports Illustrated* article about what makes great athletes great, writes that "*thinking* about an action is the sign of a novice, or a key to transforming an expert back into an amateur;" and in Jonathan Hock's (2013) short documentary "Play Without Thinking," the narrator tells us that the football coach "Kliff Kingsbury wants Texas Tech to play without thinking" (Hock 2013). And expressing what he sees as the cutting-edge sports psychology, journalist Jaimal Yogis, in a "Choking Issue" of *ESPN Magazine*, reports that "the most advanced mental trainers now discourage thinking" (Yogis 2012). Yet again, we have "don't think; just do."

In the arts pages, one comes across similar sentiments. For example, the dancer Robert Swinston is quoted in an article as expressing the view that "when you get on stage," you need to "stop thinking and give yourself to the dance" (Parris 2011). This is not the only vision of the road to excellence that one finds in the popular media, and Yogis also tells us that if you "ask 15 psychologists, psychiatrists or biologists [whether experts enter a zone of nonthinking] ... you'll get somewhere around three times as many answers" (2013). Nonetheless, it is a common one. Indeed, one could even say of just-do-it, as author Belleruth Naparstek said of the concomitant notion of intuition in an *Utne Reader* article about the profusion of books that sing its praises, "it's hot" (Naparstek 1998).

Baseball, perhaps because it leaves time open for long stretches of ratiocination, is seen by the media as especially beholden to the idea that thinking interferes with doing.[4] A particularly dramatic example of a situation in which thinking was seen as harmful to performance was the media's coverage of the tragic story of New York Yankee's former second baseman Chuck Knoblauch, a player who, in the middle of a brilliant career, developed severe throwing problems, sometimes being barely able to toss the ball, other times throwing it outrageously far out of play.[5] The media's analysis of the situation was in line with the just-do-it principle: Knoblauch was thinking too much. As Stephen Jay Gould (2000) sums up the popular press's take, "his conscious brain has intruded upon a bodily skill that must be honed by practice into a purely automatic and virtually infallible reflex." And David Brooks, a *New York Times* editorialist, explains why just-do-it is essential to baseball: "Over the decades, the institution of baseball has figured out how to instruct the unconscious mind, to make it better at what it does" and "has developed a series of habits and standards of behavior to keep the conscious mind from interfering with the automatic mind," for it is, "one of

---

[4]  See also Papineau (2015), who argues that having time for extended thought interferes with cricket bowling.

[5]  A more recent case is that of Rick Ankiel, who was a promising pitcher for the Cardinals, yet fell apart during his first postseason and became unable to find the strike zone. Although his pitching never recovered, after a few years of training, he returned to the majors as an outfielder. See, for example, Baumann (2013).

those activities in which the harder you try, the worse you do" (Brooks 2007). Professional baseball players, Brooks suggests, need to proceed without effort and without thought.

Though less physically demanding than baseball, and perhaps given the length of a sound bite, less open to prolonged stretches of ratiocination, one more example of an arena in which the just-do-it principle takes hold of the popular imagination is politics. A presidential candidate's poor showing, we are told, is due to his making "what appear to be laboriously studied moves rather than anything that comes naturally," and another candidate's success is due in part to his ability to exude impressive ease, "standing with a slight smile on his face and his hands resting easily in his pockets, looking on with calm amusement" (Fallows 2012). Of course, as it is often assumed that one's most heartfelt views come out naturally and without deep thought, some might see thinking during a debate as indicating that one is searching for words that will please the public. Socrates seems to accept the general idea that one's natural effortless discourse reveals one's honest views, for in the *Apology* he tells the jurors that, in contrast to his accusers who use "embroidered and stylized phrases to deceive, he will be expressing the truth ... [by using] the first words that come to mind" (2000, 17c). Whether extemporaneous discourse reveals one's true thoughts better than studied words can be debated (perhaps thoughtful speech can also provide an opportunity for revealing what you really think). And in any event, neither Socrates' comments about his accusers nor the analysis of the politician's poor showing decry thinking or effort per se, but rather allude to the idea that deep thought allows for duplicitous thought. Nonetheless, the admiration of effortlessness is apparent both in our present-day political climate and in the ancient Greek court of law.

During this stroll (or scroll) through the aisles, besides numerous paeans to the just-do-it principle, you will certainly also encounter popular books that, while they aim to teach you how to excel, do not even give it a nod: books such as Pepperdine tennis coach and former Davis Cup competitor Allen Fox's (1993) *Think to Win*, or Ben Hogan's (1957) *Five Lessons: The Modern Fundamentals of Golf*, and Michael Breed's (2011) *The 3-Degree Putting Solution: The Comprehensive, Scientifically Proven Guide to Better Putting*, all of which unabashedly aim at stuffing more guidelines into your head. Even Gallwey, though he uses phrases such as "playing outside your head," also emphasizes how important your head is in the game, indicating, for example, that as a tennis player, you should train in such a way so that you "get to know the feel of every inch of your stroke, every muscle in your body," so that when you play you can be "particularly aware of certain muscles" (1974, p. 90), which is quite contrary to the version of just-do-it that proclaims that experts should not focus on the fine-grained aspects of their movements.

Although there is something I relish about going against the grain, I probably wouldn't be writing this book if it weren't for the support I have found for my own views in works such as these, as well as autobiographical accounts of experts, such as that of the tennis player Rafael Nadal and Carlin (2011), who emphasizes the importance of thought in his playing, claiming that his ability to think in action, more than anything, helped him rise to the top. I have also found that my views resonate with much of Richard Shusterman's (2008; 2012) work on the importance of bodily awareness in correcting habits; with Jason Stanley's theory of skilled action according to which expertise and knowledge are inextricably intertwined (Stanley 2011 and Stanley and Krakauer 2013); with Anders Ericsson's theory of deliberate practice which involves focused attention and thought; with research by Daniel Kahneman and Amos Tversky (Kahneman 2011), which illustrates ways in which automatic or intuitive reactions lead us astray in certain situations; with studies of expertise by sports psychologists that suggest experts do think about what they are doing in action, such as Adam Nicholls's (2010) research on how expert athletes increase their attention to what they are doing in order to cope with stress during important tournaments, and Dave Collins's (Collins et al. 2001) studies of weightlifters suggesting that they use conscious control of their movements in competition; and also with certain statistical analyses of archival sports data, such as an analysis of "icing the kicker" that shows it to be ineffective.[6] ("Icing the kicker" is a practice in football whereby a time out is called right before an opposing team's kick in order to make the kicker start thinking about the kick and thereby blunder.) This piece of data crystallizes the point I hope to make, which is that although many believe that thinking is detrimental to expert performance, in general, it isn't.[7] However, I digress; the task of burying just-do-it is yet to come. The goal in this chapter is merely to illustrate its widespread acceptance, so let me return to it forthwith.

## Zen Buddhism and Taoism

Because we live in a world in which so much of what we need or, more accurately, want can be purchased with a tap and where instant gratification is measured in nanoseconds, one might be led to believe that the just-do-it principle is especially appealing in contemporary culture. How to do anything in no time or less seems to be our motto. But although the principle in its myriad forms is enormously popular today, it is not merely a fad, for it has been promoted by great thinkers of the past and is argued for today by philosophers, psychologists, and neuroscientists, among others.[8] I now turn to some of these contexts, beginning with a discussion of just-do-it in Zen Buddhism and Taoism. For those of you who crave distinctions, I counsel patience; you will get a flurry of these in the next chapter where I discuss stronger and weaker forms of

[6] The analysis at <espn.go.com/blog/statsinfo/post/_/id/34217/icing-the-kicker-remains-ineffective-practice> looked into the practice during ten years of National Football League games.
[7] And—though I was well into the writing process before I made these discoveries—there are numerous other researchers whose work supports my position. For example, Christiansen et al. (2014, 2015), John Sutton et al. (2011), and Toner and Moran (2009, 2014, 2015) all resonate with my view.
[8] Of course, academics, too, are susceptible to fads.

just-do-it and the different kinds of mental processes that are thought to be banned by just-do-it; indeed, so many distinctions arise in the next chapter that I shall need to counsel perseverance (and perhaps a good strong cup of coffee). But for now, let me paint with broad strokes.

We saw that in Herrigel's popularized version of Zen, the best actions of the expert archer are not even done by the archer himself: *it* shoots, not the archer. This particular aspect of Herrigel's view, however, may not express classical Zen teachings. As Yamada Shoji (2001) explains in his article, "The Myth of Zen in the Art of Archery," Herrigel did not speak Japanese and the translator whom Herrigel typically relied on during his lessons with Awa (the master archer whose teachings Herrigel claims to impart to the reader) was out sick when the crucial idea of "it shoots" was purportedly conveyed. Moreover, Shoji points out, the phrase "it shoots" does not appear in the first draft of the book at all. The conclusion Shoji draws is that the idea of "it shoots," the idea that it is not the archer performing the action, was either a misinterpretation of the Japanese "that's it," or simply invented by the author himself.

Shoji's dispelling of the "it shoots" myth notwithstanding, he sees some value in Herrigel's counsel, for he also posits that at the highest level of performance actions may very well just happen. Herrigel's view, he tells us, is not representative of any traditional Japanese archery practices only to the extent that it imparts the idea that from the beginning of one's practice the thinking mind, or self, should not be present. However, in what are referred to as "the secret teachings" in *The Book of Yoshida Toyokazu's Answers*, Shoji explains, we learn that once an archer has achieved a certain degree of expertise, the shot then does just happen without the archer doing anything. This is the doctrine of "nothing is needed":

as for the stance, the positioning of the body, the positioning of the bow, the grip on the bow, the grip on the string, the raising of the bow, the drawing of the bow, the draw length, the extension, the tension, the balance of hard and soft, the stretch, the rainfall release, and the morning storm release: I see that none are needed. (quoted by Shoji, p. 8)

It is not clear that these teachings advocate the view that the self dissolves entirely in expert action, however they do maintain that all of the technical advice that an archer has learned is abandoned when the archer becomes an expert.[9]

Taoism, in its two classic texts, the *Laozi* and the *Zhuangzi*, is also understood by some scholars as supporting a just-do-it mentality by advocating a way of acting in the world that is unfettered by trying and effort. Though there is controversy over exactly how to interpret these texts, Edward Slingerland (2003; 2014) sees them as advocating the idea that the pinnacle of skill involves a type of effortless action, an idea, as he sees it, that is captured by the Chinese concept of *wu-wei*, which is variously translated as

---

[9] For a more moderate view see Onuma et al. (1993), in which the authors explain the goal in Japanese archery as "not the elimination of thought... [but rather] the elimination of the remnants of thought: that which remains when thought is divorced from action" (p. 22).

the injunction to not act, or to act yet avoid action, or to act yet avoid purposeful action, or conceptualized action, or false action.

Because of their paradoxical nature, understanding these injunctions is fraught with difficulty. David Velleman (2008), however, building on Slingerland's (2007) interpretation, sees the *wu-wei* as "acting without deliberate intention or effort," which is a form of action which has at least a just-do-it flavor. Velleman questions whether the pinnacle of performance involves a reflective stance toward one's own actions and argues that in performing well, one need not "keep one's eye on an ultimate goal, or…follow the precepts of a method, or even…focus on one's actions themselves" (p. 184); rather, according to Velleman, we learn in the *Zhuangzi* that for the accomplished artisan, actions are not guided by the self but just flow. Indeed, Craster's poem—the epigraph for this chapter—might have been inspired by a story in the *Zhuangzi*, discussed by Velleman, about a mythical one-legged beast who asks a millipede how she manages to control all her legs, to which the millipede responds, "I just put my heavenly mechanism into motion. I don't know how it works!" Velleman does not advocate that we should be like the millipede, as he sees value in thoughtful training that involves self-reflection. However, he does proffer that ultimately, the ideal action leaves reflection behind. Experts, as he sees it, "have acquired their skills through training that involved self-scrutiny, self-criticism, and self-correction… [but this capacity to reflect] is no longer exercised after they have perfected their skill" (p. 188).

Closer to Velleman's conception of expertise is the story in the *Zhuangzi* of the butcher:

When I first began cutting up oxen, I did not see anything but oxen. Three years later, I couldn't see the whole ox. And now, I encounter them with spirit and don't look with my eyes. Sensible knowledge stops and spiritual desires proceed. (Ivanhoe and van Norden 2005, p. 225 and quoted by Velleman 2008, p. 183)

On this account, the action of the knife is guided, not by the butcher, but by "what is inherently so" (Ivanhoe and van Norden 2005, p. 225). Although there is some question as to whether the stories one finds in the *Zhuangzi* about individuals who perform their skill entirely effortlessly should be seen as providing a recipe for individual action rather than a metaphor for political rule (that is, as advocating the idea that leaders who govern their people apparently effortlessly will be more successful than those who govern by force), Velleman and Slingerland see them as illustrating how, when you are really good at something, you can perform amazing feats effortlessly.[10]

We see a sensationalized version of the butcher's effortless action in Herrigel's account of archery. In the same way that the butcher's knife proceeds without the butcher visually guiding it, Awa, as Herrigel describes him, is able to hit a bull's-eye

---

[10] For a criticism of Slingerland's interpretation of *wu-wei* see Fraser (2007), in which he also questions whether the passages about skill in the *Zhuangzi* are intended to express *wu-wei*.

without visually guiding his arrow. The apogee of the book occurs when, practicing in the dark, Awa hits a bullseye and then his second shot cracks the nock of the first arrow. According to Herrigel, Awa's explanation of this amazing feat is that he did not make the hit: "it is not 'I' who must be given credit for this shot"(1953, p. 59).

## Expertise as Openness to Divine Inspiration

Although Eastern ideas have inspired many in the West to see expert action as proceeding without thought and effort, just-do-it has a distinct lineage in Western thought, as seen, for example, in the ancient Greek conception of poets as conduits for the words of the gods. It was not a poet's thought and effort that gave birth to a great story or turn of phrase. Rather, poets were seen as merely expressing what came to them from above. When in the opening lines of the *Odyssey*, Homer proclaims, "Sing in me, Muse, and through me tell the story," he is, in line with this conception of poetic inspiration, giving credit where he thinks credit is due (1961).

Plato also saw poetry and the sort of poetic interpretation performed by rhapsodes (individuals who recited and sometimes interpreted poetry) as being divinely inspired. Such inspiration, however, he thought was a form of madness and ought to be guarded against. In the dialogue *Ion*, Socrates claims that "beautiful poems are not human, not even *from* human beings, but are divine and are from gods; that poets are nothing but representatives of the gods, possessed by whoever possesses them" (Plato 350 BCE/1996, 535e). Peter Kivy calls this "Plato's non-theory of poetic creation," according to which, as he puts it, "poetry happens to you; *you* don't *do* it" (Kivy 2001, p. 12).[11] On this view, Kivy says, "bright ideas are not generated by acts of will through the application of some 'method,' bright ideas just 'happen' to people ... [rather like an] infectious disease one succumbs to" (2001, p. 12). Plato's "non-theory" is an extreme position. It does not say merely that the poets refrain from certain types of thoughts when creating poetry, but that in a sense they do not do anything.

Since Plato decried rather than exalted such creation, he is not advocating the normative view that experts ought to just let it happen: expert poets, according to Plato, let the ideas come to them, yet this is not what they, or anyone, should do. However, ignoring the irony of Socrates' praises, the Romantic poet Percy Shelley embraces just-do-it wholeheartedly, interpreting the *Ion* as a tribute to otherworldly inspiration.[12] In Shelley's own translation of the dialogue, he has Socrates tell us:

[a poet is] a thing ethereally light, winged, and sacred ... [who cannot] compose anything worth calling poetry until he becomes inspired, and, as it were, mad, or whilst any reason

---

[11] Kivy also mentions that "of course it is a nice question where and how the gods get the ideas they impart to the poets and rhapsodes, but perhaps to consider thus is to consider too curiously" (p. 11).

[12] See Suzanne Stern-Gillet (2004) and Nickolas Pappas (1989) for arguments about why Shelley is misinterpreting Plato.

remains in him. For whilst a man retains any portion of the thing called reason, he is utterly incompetent to produce poetry or to vaticinate. (Shelley 1840/1965: 534b3–6)

Bringing this idea into the nineteenth century and interpreting "genius" as expertise, the idea of the expert's actions as originating not from the self but from some external force, is well summed up by the American Romantic poet James Russell Lowell's oft-quoted comment, "talent is that which is in a man's power: genius is that in whose power a man is" (for example, Brogan 1993, p. 550).

That divine inspiration is a conduit for great actions is also upheld by Hubert Dreyfus and Sean Dorrance Kelly (2011a) who, in their book *All Things Shining: Reading the Western Classics to find Meaning in a Secular Age*, argue that the most important lesson we can learn from the ancient Greeks, as they are depicted by Homer, is that meaningful lives are in part the result of individuals performing great actions for which, in the relevant sense, they are not fully responsible. Not going back to a polytheistic picture, nor even, at least explicitly, a theistic one, they argue, in a similarly themed article, that Homer shows us that "human beings are at their best when they hold themselves open to being called by the gods" (*Saving the Sacred from the Axial Revolution*, 2011b, p. 200). Recognizing the importance of this phenomenon in Homer, in the idea of being open to the call of the gods, they maintain, will help us recognize what is important about expert action today: "When human beings are acting at their best—in great feats of athleticism or in the composition of the finest poetry, in the activities of life in the everyday world or heroism on the battlefield... [they often feel as if their actions are] drawn out of them, as if they were called to act in the way they did" (2011b, p. 200). In their book (Kelly and Dreyfus 2011a), they describe the force that draws action out of someone in this particular way as the "whoosh."[13]

Dreyfus and Kelly also draw inspiration from the late nineteenth- and early twentieth-century phenomenologist Maurice Merleau-Ponty (1945/2005), who describes the "magical" efficacy of our unreflective bodily actions—actions which are such that, as Merleau-Ponty sees it, if we were to focus on them, they would degenerate into the absurd—as well as from Merleau-Ponty's contemporary, the German philosopher Martin Heidegger, who theorizes that when a lecturer enters a familiar classroom, the lecturer experiences neither the doorknob nor the seats; such features of the room, for the lecturer, are "completely unobtrusive and unthought" (Heidegger 1988, p. 164). Heidegger's views, inasmuch as they are about everyday actions, do not fall under the scope of just-do-it, which concerns expert action. Merleau-Ponty, however, has been interpreted as holding the type of injunction that I reject, for he extends his theory to cover actions such as those of the expert soccer player for whom "the soccer

---

[13] The movements of the butcher in the *Zhuangzi* are also described as proceeding with a whoosh (see Slingerland 2014, p. 29). (And, incidentally, another aspect of the Nike trademark, the swirly line, is called the "swoosh.").

field ... is pervaded by lines of force"; according to Merleau-Ponty, "the player becomes one with [the field] ... [and] at this moment consciousness is nothing but the dialectic of milieu and action" (1945/2005, pp. 168–9). The conscious mind, he seems to be saying, dissolves into a relation with the environment, which, like Homer's gods, calls forth actions. Or at least this is how Dreyfus understands the position, for in a recent debate with the philosopher John McDowell, he states the position like this: "for an expert to remain in flow and so perform at his best, he must let himself be merged into the field of forces and all monitoring must stop" (Dreyfus 2013, p. 31).

McDowell objects to such a picture, for he thinks that all action exemplifies rationality. Yet even McDowell holds a version of just-do-it, for, according to him, although an expert's actions are guided by reasons, these reasons are not on the forefront of an expert's mind as she proceeds. The idea that an expert "deliberates about what to do and acts in the light of the result," McDowell tells us, "should be rejected" (McDowell 2013, p. 47).

## Expertise as the Attainment of Automaticity

In thinking about how to explain expert action, the principle of inference to the best explanation does not typically lead psychologists to divine inspiration. In the psychology literature, the stand-in for divine inspiration is automaticity.

The term "automaticity," is far from univocal in this literature (for an overview of some of the different conceptions of it in the psychology literature see Norman and Shallice 1986; Wu 2013; and Fridland 2015), however, the conception of automaticity most salient to the just-do-it principle is that of an action performed with neither conscious control over nor explicit attention to the action (much like Schneider and Shiffrin's (1977) account). Fitts and Posner (1967), for example, in their urtext on the psychology of skilled performance, see an expert's performance as automatic and performed without attention. Thus they tell us that "if the attention of a[n expert] golfer is called to his muscle movements before an important putt, he may find it unusually difficult to attain his natural swing" (p. 15); this is, they explain, because expert performance is automatic or "autonomous," by which they also mean that it does not require control by the conscious mind. On their view, we develop expertise by passing through three phases. First, in what they dub "the cognitive phase," one aims at understanding and intellectualizing the task and what it demands. During this phase of skill learning, they say, "it is usually necessary to attend to cues, events, and responses that later go unnoticed" (p. 12). Next, in what they call "the associative phase," one acquires some mastery over the movement. And in the final, or "autonomous phase," one moves automatically and without consciously attending to the movement. Hence, as they see it, in the autonomous phase, conscious focus interferes with movement, or as Yarrow and colleagues (2009) sum up this view, "highly practiced skills become automatic, so performance may actually be damaged by introspection, which is characteristic of an earlier, consciously-mediated stage" (p. 591).[14]

Note how well Fitts and Posner's account of skill acquisition lines up with the story of the butcher. In the first stage, the butcher needs to think about where to draw his knife; three years later he develops a degree of mastery and the divisions become apparent to him; and in the final stage, the oxen are encountered with spirit, where the notion of spirit is opposed to conscious visual perception and deliberate action. Dreyfus and Dreyfus (2004), expresses a similar view, employing the term "awareness": [t]he expert driver, he tells us, "shifts gears when appropriate with no awareness of his acts. On the off-ramp his foot simply lifts off the accelerator. What must be done, simply is done" (p. 253).

The ability to verbalize what you are thinking about is often taken as an indication that an action is not automatic but, rather, is being guided by conscious thought. Thus, Fitts and Posner also castigate verbalization during performance: "verbalization," they tell us, "may interfere with a highly developed skill," (p. 15) and going further, Flegal and Anderson (2008) suggest that even after the deed, explaining an adept performance is counterproductive; turning an old motto on its head, they conclude that "those who teach, cannot do" (p. 931). Whether concerned with the mechanics of the movement or something at a higher level, one gets the feeling, in reading the literature on this topic, that thinking, at least consciously, is something we'd be better off without.

Fitts and Posner (1967) also maintain that experts are not consciously aware of their bodily movements and that such awareness can have deleterious consequences. So it is not merely verbalizable thoughts that they rail against, but also mere bodily awareness, which, as they seem to think, is not necessarily expressible in words: expert dancers, they tell us, "ignore kinesthetic information and visual information about their movements," and if an expert golfer thinks about, say, stabilizing her torso muscles during a swing, things may go awry (p. 16). Such thoughts about stabilizing one's torso muscles, and even more so, such awareness of kinesthetic and visual information about movements, might not be declarative or expressible in words, yet according to Fitts and Posner, they are deleterious nonetheless.

Fitts and Posner's theory that highly accomplished skill is automatic has inspired numerous researchers to devise experiments to test it. For example, in investigating the degree to which expert skill proceeds automatically, R. Gray (2004), Beilock et al. (2002; 2004), Ford et al. (2005), and Leavitt (1979) have looked at what happens when expert athletes perform their skill while directing their attention either to a specific aspect of their movement or to an extraneous task. Such experiments are seen as

---

[14] Following in Fitts and Posner's footsteps, Anderson (1982; 1983; 1993; and Anderson and Lebiere 1998) proposes that skill acquisition progresses from a "declarative phase," in which performance is guided in a step-by-step fashion by information about skill execution held in working memory to a "procedural phase," in which performance, rather than being guided in a step-by-step fashion, is thought to occur automatically.

supporting the just-do-it principle, since experts perform worse in the skill-focused condition than in the extraneous-task condition. Moreover, Beilock et al. (2004) and R. Gray (2004) found that the skill-focused condition produced worse results than having the experts perform as they normally do. When you are really good at something, focusing on what you are doing as you are doing it, these researchers conclude, is a bad idea.

The resulting conception of high-level skill is widely accepted by psychologists who work on expertise. As Gabriele Wulf (2007) tells us, "there is little disagreement that once an individual has reached the autonomous stage, in which movements are usually controlled automatically, paying attention to skill execution is typically detrimental" (p. 6). And in her own estimation, research on skill "clearly show[s] that if experienced individuals direct their attention to the details of skill execution, the result is almost certainly a decrement in performance" (2007, p. 23). Sian Beilock and colleagues (2002) have a similar perspective: "Current theories of skill acquisition and automaticity suggest," they tell us, "that well learned skill execution is 'automated'—controlled by procedural knowledge that requires little online attention and control and operates mainly outside of working memory"[15] (p. 1211). Some of this research is not on what I would refer to as expert-level performance, yet the results are often seen to generalize. As Beilock and colleagues claim, "this pattern [of skill development] suggests that whereas novel or less practiced performance may demand extensive attentional resources for successful implementation, such explicit monitoring and control may not be necessary at high levels of skill execution" (p. 1212).

## Tapping the Unconscious

Although some versions of just-do-it—such as the idea of "it shoots," the ancient Greek idea of divine inspiration, and Dreyfus and Kelly's "whoosh"—are "just let it happen" views, wherein the expert's mind absconds during peak performance and expert action is guided entirely by external forces, less extreme just-do-it views maintain that although experts' best actions involve thought, they do not involve conscious thought. Sometimes the specific type of consciousness inveighed upon is consciousness of the details—or, in line with Dave Hill's analogy between golf and sex, the mechanics of the act. Others disparage the conscious mind more generally, a view exemplified by the sportscasters words of praise: "She's playing unconscious." And still others do not so much disparage conscious thought, but elevate the unconscious, as does Goethe when, for example, he claims to have written his novella *The Sorrows of Young Werther* "unconsciously" and "like a sleepwalker." Summing up his stance on great achievement, he writes in a letter to Schiller: "What the genius, as genius, does, happens unconsciously," and "all our

---

[15] For example, Anderson (1982; 1983; 1993); Fitts and Posner (1967); Keele and Summers (1976); Kimble and Perlmuter (1970); Langer and Imber (1979); Proctor and Dutta (1995).

most sincere striving/succeeds only in the unconscious moment" (quoted in Bishop 2010, p. 30).

Proponents of this brand of just-do-it sometimes support the view that it is the effortless motions of the unconscious mind that are responsible for works of true genius by citing anecdotes about brilliant ideas arriving fully formed and unbidden, such as the nineteenth-century mathematician Henri Poincaré's account of a proof coming to him as he was clambering onto a bus: "at the moment I put my foot on the step the idea came to me, without anything in my former thoughts seeming to have paved the way for it" (quoted in Ghiselin 1952, p. 26); or Kekulé's description of the discovery of the structure of the benzene molecule by dreaming of a snake biting its tail (Ghiselin 1952, p. 237), or A. E. Housman's (1933) account of writing poems effortlessly—"two of the stanzas came into my head, just as they were printed while I was crossing the corner of Hampstead Heath between Spaniard's Inn and the footpath to Temple Fortune. A third came with a little coaxing after tea" (p. 91). Such are the miraculous, deliverances of the unconscious, or so proponents of this brand of just-do-it maintain.

The physician, zoologist, and physiologist W. B. Carpenter (1874/2011) introduced the term "unconscious cerebration" to describe this process, telling us that "[t]he act of 'unconscious cerebration'... is far more likely to lead us to good and true results than any continual discussion and argumentation," and that "the mind has obviously worked more clearly and successfully in this automatic condition, when left entirely to itself, than when we have been cudgeling our brains, so to speak, to get the solution" (p. 204). Henry James (1888/2010) wrote of the "unconscious cerebration of sleep" (p. 159), and Henri-Frédéric Amiel (1893) claimed that "the wise part of us, then, is that which is unconscious of itself, and what is most reasonable in man are those elements in him which do not reason" (p. 87).[16]

To be sure, as we will see in the final chapter, many accounts of ideas arriving fully formed are likely exaggerated, and Goethe himself later turned away from the extreme views expressed in his youth to advocate a view quite opposed to just-do-it; a musical composition arises, he writes, "through practice, teaching, reflection, success, failure, furtherance and resistance, and again and again reflection" (quoted in Frankl 2006, p. 30). Indeed, some have seen the Romantic veneration of the unconscious as a "pathology," with the poet and philosopher Friedrich Schiller at one point commenting that "classicism is health, romanticism is sickness" and emphasizing that unconscious inspiration must also be "accompanied by self-reflection and the capacity to bring such emotions within clear, formal boundaries" (quoted in Becker-Cantarino 2005, p. 29).[17] And, of course, the modernist poets break away from the Romantic tradition. According to Paul Valéry (1939/1954), for example, a poet must "struggle with inequality of moments, chance association, weak attention, and outer distractions"

[16] See also Maudsley (1867/1993), who summarized his ideas in *The Physiology and Pathology of the Mind*, saying "the most important part of mental activity, the essential processes on which thinking depends, is unconscious mental activity."

[17] See also David Hill (2003).

"DON'T THINK, DEAR; JUST DO"  29

and that to create a poem requires us "to recognize in ourselves and to choose in ourselves what deserves to be plucked from the very instant and carefully used" (p. 65).
Nonetheless, something very much like the Romantic adoration of the unconscious is
found today in the psychology of skilled performance, where some researchers claim
to have shown that consciously pondering what to do hinders performance. For example, the psychologists Flegal and Anderson (2008) claim that "[r]eflecting consciously
on what one knows about a skill often undermines its proper execution" and accordingly advise the expert to leave the conscious mind by the wayside (p. 927); Roy
Baumeister (1984) tells us that expert skills cannot be controlled consciously, because
"consciousness does not contain the knowledge of these skills" (p. 610); and, though
they have since turned away from this view, Toner and Moran (2011) at one point suggested that "it…appear[s] prudent for skilled performers to avoid consciously attending to their movement during competitive performance" (p. 682).[18] David Papineau
(2013) maintains this view as well: cricket batting, he tells us, is "automatic, not under
conscious control" (p. 177).

The contemporary take on the Romantic view of the unconscious, which sees the
unconscious as intelligent and sometimes more intelligent than the conscious mind, is
also brought out well by Stephen J. Gould, in his editorial on the media coverage of
Knoblauch's throwing problems. Gould (2000), whose summary of this coverage
I quoted above, goes on to criticize the press for expressing the idea that Knoblauch's
distress arises from "the imposition of…mind upon matter," telling us that this "represents the worst, and most philistine, of mischaracterizations." But Gould does not say
this because he thinks that conscious attention to movement is compatible with optimal expert performance. Rather he thinks that, for Knoblauch, an unwanted conscious
mentality is interfering with a wanted unconscious mentality. And it is this unconscious mentality, according to Gould, that reveals adept athletic performance as a
laudable intellectual endeavor and not merely brute bodily movement. As he argues,
"we encounter mentality in either case, not body against mind," but for expert athletes
it is unconscious mentality.

## Intuition

Closely connected to both the idea that expert performance proceeds best without
conscious interference and the idea that the expert's actions are automatic is the notion
that expert action is intuitive. As Dreyfus (2004) tells us, novices "make judgments using
strict rules and features, but that with talent and a great deal of involved experience,

[18] It might seem that research by Dijksterhuis et al. (2006) and Dijksterhuis and Olden (2006), which
suggests that for certain kinds of decisions, it is best to let the unconscious mind work for a period of time
before consciously deciding on a solution to a problem, illustrates the hazards of conscious thought. But it
only illustrates the importance of leaving time for unconscious cerebration, which I can accept. Also, it is
not clear that this research is relevant to the view I advocate since the subjects making the decisions in
these studies are not experts in the target domain.

the beginner develops into an expert who sees intuitively what to do without applying rules and making judgments at all" (p. 253). For Dreyfus and Kelly, who take the mind out of the picture entirely, this intuition is not even an unconscious process, for the unconscious is, after all, mental. However, for others, intuitive insight is a particular kind of unconscious process. It is not the slow-moving unconscious that Goethe sees as imbued with creative intelligence. Rather, it is more like what Daniel Kahneman (2011) refers to as 'System 1' thinking, which is fast and automatic. And such intuition is often seen as not rational. For Dreyfus (2004), experts proceed without attention to what they are doing; they do not calculate or compare alternatives but rather act spontaneously and without deliberation (p. 28; and throughout in Dreyfus and Dreyfus 1986).

Though he targets everyday types of decisions, Kahneman has written persuasively about how our intuitions mislead us and that at least at times better decisions occur when we employ more of our rational minds. However, there is also a large body of psychology literature about the superiority of intuitive ways of thinking over rational ones and about the superiority of intuitive action over thoughtful, deliberate action. Gary Klein (2003), for example, extols the intuitive powers of experienced firefighters. And in line with this view, it is sometimes said, perhaps almost exclusively by philosophers, that professional chicken sexers, without any understanding of how they arrive at their decisions, have an uncanny ability to determine the sex of day-old chicks at a glance with 99 percent accuracy.[19]

## Natural Talent

Some hold the view that experts perform effortlessly and without much thought because expert ability is, to a large degree, natural. The archetypical expression of this is found in a popular conception of the genius of Mozart, who was often thought to compose effortlessly: "the whole [composition], though it be long, stands almost finished and complete in my mind," he claims in a well-known letter of 1815 (quoted in Zaslaw 1994).

Though, as we shall see, the Mozart story is to a degree mythologized, the idea that Mozart composed without effort is extremely powerful, and it is this letter, perhaps via Aleksandr Pushkin's (1830) *Mozart and Salieri*, that likely played a role in inspiring the well-received movie (1984) and eponymous play *Amadeus*, written by Peter Shaffer (1979), wherein Mozart needed only to write out the music handed down to him by God. As *New York Times* critic Vincent Canby (1984) put it, Shaffer's film depicts genius "in a fashion that is simultaneously illuminating, moving and just."

The philosopher Stephen Schiffer (2002) seems to accept this picture of Mozart's effortless natural ability as well. In arguing against Jason Stanley and Timothy

---

[19] Almost exclusively, but not entirely: "But don't ask them how they do it," the psychologist David Myers says, "the sex difference as any chicken sexer can tell you, is too subtle to explain" (2002, p. 55).

Williamson's (2001) view that skill necessarily involves propositional knowledge—that, for example, knowing how to ride a bicycle at least requires knowing that this (where "this" refers to some way to ride a bike) is a way to ride a bike—Schiffer writes that even though "Mozart knew how…to write a symphony at the age of 8" he could not explain how he did so and therefore did not have the propositional knowledge Stanley seems to think is involved in skill (Schiffer 2002, p. 201).[20] Schiffer seems to think that Mozart just did it.

## Can so Many be Mistaken?

When one comes across an idea that appears in such a wide range of cultures, time periods, and intellectual traditions, it is hard not to conclude that the explanation for this agreement is that these diverse strands of thought are converging on the truth. This book is aimed at trying to shake you of that conviction.

My aim so far has been to illustrate the popularity of just-do-it. In the next two chapters, I aim to clarify the issue under consideration. In Chapter 2, I aim to specify the particular aspects of the just-do-it idea, encountered in so many different guises in this chapter, that I aim to question. And then in Chapter 3, I tackle the question of what it means to be an expert. In subsequent chapters, the shovel comes out in earnest, as I attempt to bury some of the views we have encountered and advance the cognition-in-action principle, which states that effort, thought, bodily awareness, and other such psychological factors are generally integral to the smooth, apparently effortless execution of expert-level skills. Contrary to the idea that expert action proceeds automatically, I argue that experts in fact present a model of Socratic rationality, exemplifying both conceptually grounded knowledge of their actions and self-awareness.

---

[20] Stanley and Williamson (2001) would presumably not be bothered much by this criticism since they do not think that having propositional knowledge of how to, say, ride a bike necessarily involves being able to explain how to ride a bike.

# 2

# Just-do-it Versus
# Cognition-in-action

Our discussion will be adequate if it has as much clearness as the subject-matter admits of, for precision is not to be sought for alike in all discussions, any more than in all the products of the crafts.

Aristotle (384–322 BCE)
*Nicomachean Ethics*

Presumably, when the sporting goods giant Nike used the phrase "just do it" in its advertising campaign, it was intended to mean, among other things, "stop procrastinating, get off your posterior, and get to work."[1] Interpreted as such, I'm in favor of "just do it." However, the sense of "just do it" I question is the idea that expert action, at its best, proceeds without a significant amount of thought, attention, or effort, or as the blues and rock musician Steve Miller purportedly would say, "when you're thinking, you're stinking."[2] As we saw in the last chapter, this view is embraced in diverse forms by philosophers, psychologists, journalists, and others. And it is this view that I think is a myth.

To be sure, Nike's "just do it" slogan also tells us that certain mental processes are detrimental to expert performance, for it tells us that if, rather than going to the gym, we spend our time thinking about all the other things we could be doing, our muscles will not get any stronger. However, this counsel is consistent with the conscious mind being present once you step on the treadmill. The presence of mind in expert action is my concern, and in this chapter I aim to clarify—to the extent the subject matter admits—both the position I advocate and the one I oppose.

Although Miller's "when you're thinking, you're stinking" adage might seem to imply that experts never think, or at least ought never to do so, most advocates of what

---

[1] They may also intend for the phrase to capture some of the other meanings of "just do it" that I write about in the Introduction, and which also stray from my intended meaning. Additionally, there is some reason to think that one of the intended meanings is *just get it over with*. According to the documentary *Art and Copy* (Pray 2009), Nike's inspiration for the slogan came from the last words of the murderer Gary Gilmore before he was executed by a firing squad: "Let's do it."

[2] Attributed by Chip Booth (chipbook.com) who owned a music store where Miller was a frequent customer.

I'm referring to as the "just-do-it principle" allow that online thought is sometimes useful for expert action. For example, psychologist Sian Beilock, who holds that focusing on or monitoring the details of movement interferes with performance, and philosophers Hubert Dreyfus and Sean Kelly, who hold that the best expert actions are drawn out of rather than done by the expert, accept that thinking might occur when something goes wrong, such as when a dancer encounters an unusually slippery spot on the floor or when a chess player's intuitions fail to identify the right move. So even according to just-do-it apostles, experts sometimes think in action. Now, as I claim that occasionally expert performance proceeds without experts at least being consciously aware that they are thinking, and that expert action invariably requires a large repertoire of automatic action, which seems to bypass any thought processes at all, one might wonder: wherein lies the difference between the view I advocate and the view I call a myth? This chapter answers this question.

## A Half Dozen Just-do-it Principles

I have been speaking of the myth of "just-do-it," but as we saw in the previous chapter, there are a number of very different positions that have something of a "just-do-it" flavor. Nonetheless, they have a common theme, namely, that experts are in some significant sense not entirely responsible for their actions. It is not just that sometimes their actions depend on factors outside their control—such as luck—which is something I accept as well, but also that the surprising checkmate, the game-winning hook shot, or the poetic flow of words, is rather like a gift. As such, we can sum up the various forms of just-do-it we encountered in terms of how they answer the question: Who or what ought we to thank for this gift?

1. *The divine or spiritual:* an expert's best actions are guided by divine or spiritual inspiration.

   Exemplified, for example, by the ancient Greek conception of divine inspiration and (on some interpretations) the Taoist account of skill attainment.
2. *An external force:* an expert's best actions are pulled out of her by some external force.

   Exemplified by Dreyfus and Kelly's idea of the "whoosh": when acting at our best, our actions are drawn out of us.
3. *The intelligent yet unconscious mind:* an expert's best action is guided by intelligent, often leisurely unconscious thought.

   Exemplified by the Romantic's view of creative inspiration and illustrated by anecdotal accounts of inspiration given by Goethe and Poincaré.
4. *Automatic processes:* an expert's best action is automatic or not guided by conscious control.

   Exemplified by Sian Beilock's work on athletic expertise and found in both Dreyfus's and Fitts and Posner's theories of skill acquisition.

5. *Intuition*: the best expert judgments are made, not slowly, deliberately, and rationally, but instantly.

What Daniel Kahneman refers to as "System 1" thinking, and exemplified by Gary Klein's and Hubert Dreyfus's work on expertise.
6. *Natural talent*: expert action, in certain domains, is primarily a product of natural talent.

Exemplified by popular accounts of Mozart's abilities.

The ensuing arguments in the book address forms 1 through 5—primarily 2, 4, and 5. However, since the categories readily bleed into one another, I often address more than one of these conceptions at a time, and indeed, most of the proponents of just-do-it whose work I discuss seem to hold a number of these views simultaneously. For example, although Dreyfus and Kelly may think of the external force that "pulls" actions out of experts as entirely this-worldly, the Zen notion of "nothing is needed" and the Taoist notion of nonaction, both of which have sometimes been interpreted as expressing the idea that certain actions are drawn out of an individual, imbue this phenomenon with a divine or spiritual component (though exactly how to understand this component, I leave to scholars of Eastern philosophy and religion to debate).

The unconscious and the divine variations of the principle sometimes overlap as well, since some see the unconscious as receiving divine inspiration; as the nineteenth-century German philosopher Eduard von Hartmann (1869/2002) put it in *The Philosophy of the Unconscious:* "The fruit of the Unconscious is as it were a gift of the gods, and man only its favoured messenger" (p. 40). Similarly, Goethe and others have expressed the view that it is through the unconscious that the divine speaks.

While Goethe's conception of the unconscious is thoughtful and highly intelligent in a very cerebral sense, working slowly in one's dreams, or during a leisurely stroll on a spring day, one finds another conception of the unconscious in the psychology literature on skill—the one in line with what Daniel Kahneman (2011) refers to as "System 1." This type of unconscious processing works instantly and is quite removed from any idea about higher powers. It is also sometimes referred to as "intuitive," in the sense that, without thinking, a grandmaster chess player can intuit the right move in chess, or an expert firefighter can intuit whether a building is about to collapse.

For Dreyfus, expert action, when all is going well, is intuitive (in the quick sense) yet entirely nonmental, which means that it is not even unconsciously mental. And intuitive expert action, for him, is automatic, in the sense that it is not being guided by, but is instead drawn out of the agent. However, in much of the psychology literature that supports just-do-it in athletic endeavors, athletes are described as acting automatically but not necessarily intuitively, and the idea of an external force is typically absent. Here, the "gift" metaphor does not readily apply, but perhaps we can say that the gift of expert athletic performance, on this view, is simply a result of having well-developed neural pathways; as such, somewhat like how you would not be responsible for what you would do were you to suffer a seizure, the expert is not responsible for her automatic action. (That said, even those who hold this view would likely claim that in the same way that an individual who fails to take her prescribed medicine would have some responsibility for actions during a seizure, an athlete, because she may choose to follow or not to follow a training regime, will have a level of responsibility for her athletic performance).

Finally, the view that expertise is due primarily to natural talent casts off the idea, accepted by many of those who uphold other just-do-it views, that one becomes an expert only after years of hard work. Although this conception of expert action stands more or less on its own, there are certainly those who see natural talent as having been bestowed upon an individual by the grace of God. My remarks shall be much less relevant to the 'natural talent conception' of expertise, and in the next chapter, I stipulate that the notion of expert that concerns me here excludes individuals, if any exist, who have achieved great heights not through hard work, but merely on the basis of natural talent.

## Clarifying the Just-do-it Principle

Although there are a number of different yet overlapping positions that I categorize as "just-do-it" views, I take the following to capture the more extreme versions:

**The just-do-it principle:**   For experts, when all is going well, optimal or near-optimal performance proceeds without any of the following mental processes: self-reflective thinking, planning, predicting, deliberation, attention to or monitoring of their actions, conceptualizing their actions, conscious control, trying, effort, having a sense of the self, or acting for a reason. Moreover, when all is going well, such processes interfere with expert performance and should be avoided.

Those who see the phenomenal feats of experts as being pulled out of them hold something like this extreme view. Indeed, on the most extreme just-do-it view, when we are awestruck by LeBron James's spectacular slam-dunk or Magnus Carlsen's surprising chess capture, we are witnessing an action that proceeds and should proceed without any mental intervention at all. Dreyfus's (2007a) view seems to fit this description: expert action, he says, is "direct and unreflective," which he takes to be the same as "nonconceptual and nonminded" (p. 355). On this view, expert action, at its best, is entirely bereft of mental processing: not just conscious mental processing, but any mental processing whatsoever; their actions are drawn out of them by external forces, at times without the experts even being able to recall what occurred.

My extreme just-do-it principle is somewhat more reserved, since it does not exclude *all* mental processes from the realm of expertise. Nonetheless, it covers a wide swath of them. It includes not only mental processes that are said to have a "mind-to-world direction of fit" (like belief, in which you aim to make your thoughts comport with the way the world is) but also "world-to-mind" mental processes (like planning and trying, in which you aim to make the world—be it your body or a basketball—comport with a conception in your mind); and it covers not just conscious mental processes, but many unconscious ones as well. Those who uphold this view (as well as Dreyfus's ultra-extreme view) still, of course, claim that the brain is involved in expert action. But not everything that goes on in the brain is correlated with something that goes on in the mind, and on the extreme just-do-it view, the expert's brain may be hard at work, save for those parts of the brain that subserve the mind (or at least the mental processes mentioned in the principle).

In order to refute the extreme principle, it would, of course, suffice to show that when an expert is performing well she employs merely one of the mentioned cognitive processes. However, I also argue against weaker forms of the principle that proscribe one or some proper subset of such mental processes. And often, I shall argue against still-weaker positions that claim that experts do whatever it is they do without some specific kind of conscious processing. For example, I shall at times argue against just-do-it with respect to conscious monitoring, which says:

**Restricted just-do-it (monitoring):**   For experts, when all is going well, optimal or near-optimal performance proceeds without consciously monitoring one's own bodily movements. Moreover, when all is going well, conscious monitoring interferes with expert performance and should be avoided.

At other times, I shall argue against just-do-it with respect to conscious trying:

**Restricted just-do-it (trying):**   For experts, when all is going well, optimal or near-optimal performance proceeds without their consciously trying to perform their actions. Moreover, when all is going well conscious trying interferes with expert performance and should be avoided.

And so on.

When context makes it unnecessary to specify that I am speaking of one of these restricted just-do-it principles, I leave off these qualifications. To further simply things, at times I refer to the just-do-it principle (whether restricted or unrestricted) as simply "just-do-it." And since talking about "just-do-it" over and over would be (and is most likely already getting) rather tiresome, I need another way to quickly sum up what it says. Thus, following Descartes (1641/1986), who uses the term "thinking" to cover doubting, understanding, conceiving, affirming, denying, willing, refusing, imagining and perceiving, I shall frequently refer to the retinue of mental processes the just-do-it principle excludes simply as forms of thought (or forms of thought and effort).

With this in mind, let us look at the components of the just-do-it principle, since some of the subsequent discussions will apply to one part but not another. The first part of the (extreme) principle, which is purely descriptive, can be expressed as follows:

**Descriptive just-do-it:**    For experts, when all is going well, optimal or near-optimal performance proceeds without thought.

I imagine that the idea of performance being optimal or near-optimal, though vague, is clear enough. But what about the qualification "when all is going well"? The reason for this qualification—a qualification I shall frequently omit when context makes it unnecessary—is that proponents of just-do-it don't maintain that experts, when doing their best, never think. On their view, if faced with an out-of-the-ordinary situation—an unusually slippery surface or an equipment malfunction—an expert may need to think to perform optimally (given the situation). The qualification "when all is going well," therefore, is meant to exclude circumstances that involve unusual problems or errors. If during a performance of *Giselle,* the ballerina's partner limps off stage with a torn Achilles tendon, this would be an unusual circumstance, and on anyone's view, she will need to figure out what to do. Although circumstances that involve unusual problems are not covered by just-do-it, some (if not many) expert actions normally proceed at a certain level of disaster. For example, during a chess game one player might be in a worse position than her opponent. This is a disaster for that player, yet it is in no way unusual. Or in the emergency room, a patient may arrive on the verge of death. In a good sense of the phrase, things are not going well! Nonetheless, this is par for the course. The qualification "when all is going well" is not meant to disallow such situations.

Advocates of just-do-it also hold that in certain situations when things are going drastically wrong, thinking interferes with performance. As they see it, however, this is precisely when things are going wrong because it is the thinking itself that is causing the disaster.

The second part of the just-do-it principle is what I refer to as the "principle of interference":

**Principle of interference:**    For experts, when all is going well, thinking interferes with expert performance.

This does not say merely that thinking about something highly distracting such as your impending divorce will interfere with your actions in your domain of expertise. That, I imagine, may very well be true.[3] Rather, it says that even some apparently skill-related thoughts, such as those included in the retinue of mental processes mentioned in the principle above, interfere with performance.

The last part of the just-do-it principle is proscriptive:

**Proscriptive just-do-it:**    When all is going well, experts should avoid thinking.

---

[3] See Andre Agassi's (2009) description of playing while distracted over thoughts about his impending breakup with Brooke Shields.

One might surmise that if thinking interferes with doing, then obviously experts ought to avoid thinking. I take the proscriptive element as a separate component, however, since someone who upholds the principle of interference might nonetheless accept that there could be times when thinking is recommended, such as when a tennis player has recently moved to a larger racket and needs to change her technique (and that such a situation could still count as a time when all is going well).

Some just-do-it proponents champion all three of these elements; others focus on only one or two.

## The Cognition-in-action Principle

What, then, is the position I advocate? First and foremost, I aim to show what is wrong with the extreme just-do-it principle and some of its less extreme variants, that is, to show why we should reject "I think, therefore I can't." However, throughout the book I also suggest a stronger view, not quite "I think, therefore I can" (*cogito ergo possum*), for I don't hold that mere thinking occasions the ability to act, but rather something close to its converse:

> **Cognition-in-action:**   For experts, when all is going well, optimal or near optimal performance frequently employs some of the following conscious mental processes: self-reflective thinking, planning, predicting, deliberation, attention to or monitoring of their actions, conceptualizing their actions, control, trying, effort, having a sense of the self, and acting for a reason. Moreover, such mental processes do not necessarily or even generally interfere with expert performance, and should not generally be avoided by experts.

Cognition-in-action, then, is a principle about specifically conscious mental processes. As such, it is not just a rejection of just-do-it, which, in its unrestricted form, takes many mental processes that are not conscious out of the expert realm; thus arguing for cognition-in-action requires more than simply arguing against an unrestricted just-do-it. This is not to say that the cognition-in-action principle implies that there is no unconscious thought in expert action. It allows for unconscious thought. However, the principle asserts the position that experts think consciously as well. In contrast, I formulate just-do-it to encompass both conscious and unconscious processing since there are some who see expert action as entirely "nonminded," and I want the unrestricted principle to cover even this extreme view.

Analogous to the different forms of the just-do-it principle, I also defend specific forms of cognition-in-action, some of which apply only to a particular type of expertise. For example, since on my view, dance, although not chess, frequently involves consciously monitoring one's bodily movements, the cognition-in-action principle for ballet dancers with respect to monitoring is as follows:

> **Cognition-in-action (monitoring):**   For experts, when all is going well, optimal or near-optimal performance frequently employs the conscious monitoring of one's

own actions. Moreover, such monitoring does not necessarily or even generally interfere with expert performance, and should not generally be avoided by experts.

For variety, I sometimes refer to the cognition-in-action principle as the view that expert action (frequently) involves thought (or thought and effort). This principle asserts only a tendency not an absolute feature of expert action, and one might object that this move rather handily enables me to take any counterexample to it as an occasional exception. Although the principle is indeed consistent with the odd counterexample, it nonetheless stands, as we shall see, in contrast to a number of just-do-it positions endorsed by various expertise experts.

To get a better sense of the position I advocate, let me list some specific claims that are consistent with it:

When all is going well, some professional tennis players may be able, without detriment, to pay attention to their shoulder muscles during a backhand.

Strategizing is a form of higher-level thought that occurs in a wide variety of competitive sports, without its hindering performance.

Employing the thought "just make the landing stick" can benefit certain gymnasts during a competition.

Some professional ballet dancers would perform better if they were to focus on positioning their heel forward when taking off for a leap.

Some professional pianists exert tremendous effort during even their best performances.

Top lightning chess players typically think (very quickly) about many of the best moves in their games.

A renowned poet may struggle, revise, and think extensively about what ends up as her best stanza.

A surgeon may, while performing very well, consciously attend to and experience pleasure in the precise workings of her hands.

An emergency room nurse should and will perform his best actions for a reason and with the ability to justify them.

An elite marathon runner may think about when to exert more energy and when to ease up, with beneficial results.

Traders on Wall Street sometimes make better decisions by deliberately acting contrary to their intuitions, or natural tendencies.

Some mathematicians come up with their greatest proofs through prolonged, effortful work.

For some experts (such as philosophers, mathematicians, writers, and scientists), the "aha!" moment is relatively insignificant; it is what they do with it that really matters.

I understand these as examples of when all is going well yet the mind is advantageous to expert performance. As such, they are all inconsistent with the ultra-extreme just-do-it principle, which takes the best expert action to be entirely nonminded, as well as with the relevant restricted forms of the principle. For example, the fact that a professional pianist may finish her best performance feeling exhausted indicates that her best performances are not necessarily effortless. The fact that a ballet dancer can focus on details of the movement indicates that the best performances are not necessarily ones in which the performer is not aware of the mechanics of her movements. And so on.

Let me also mention some specific views that I think are likely (or in some cases definitely) false and *do not* follow from the cognition-in-action principle, as well as, parenthetically, a related claim that I do accept. When all is going well:

Professional ballet dancers think about or attend to every detail of their bodily movements. (Professional performing artists and athletes don't focus on every detail, but they may beneficially focus on some.)

Professional tennis players consciously control all aspects of their movements. (Though much happens too quickly for conscious control, there is more time for conscious control than is often acknowledged; moreover, even in the quickest of movements, there may be time for conscious control at a high level, such as controlling where to hit the ball.)

During a marathon, an elite runner never feels that her running is effortless. (There are times during which experts might experience effortlessness, such as when they do not need to exert their willpower to go on. And perhaps even occasionally there are moments of utter effortlessness in the best performances. However, the best performances are still nonetheless effortful in a variety of ways. For example, they might involve arduous strategizing.)

Poets never experience an idea just bubbling up into consciousness. (Ideas do sometimes "bubble up," but such ideas are not necessarily good, and often require extensive revision. Moreover, their best ideas are not necessarily those that bubble up.)

Grandmaster chess players don't immediately see amazingly good moves. (They often do, but they will typically look for better moves and deliberate over which immediately seen move is best. Moreover, even the intuitively obvious move is conceptualized, so, contrary to the extreme just-do-it, it involves the mind in some sense.)

Surgeons never experience phenomenological blanks, about which, post-operation, they have no memory. (If this does happen, it is not characteristic of or at least not necessarily part of, the best expert performance.)

Traders never just go with an intuitive choice. (In a situation in which there is too much information to sort through, one might need to go with one's intuition and proceed from there. However, the intuitive choice might be reflected on and sometimes revised.)

Stopping the mind from thinking is never psychologically beneficial for an expert. (For some, this may be the only way to prevent extreme performance anxiety; however, increased focus and thought about what one is doing is another, possibly preferable way.)

There are no thoughts that interfere with expert performance. (Although I hold that experts frequently think when acting in their domain of expertise, I assume that highly distracting thoughts, such as—to pick an extreme example—thinking about the tree that was just struck with lightning and about to crash down before you, might distract you from doing well, unless it helps you to bound over it. And even other less intrusive thoughts, such as thinking about the details of a certain movement, might interfere if one has not practiced thinking about such things. Moreover, highly negative thoughts, such as, "It's hopeless; I'm going to lose," might for some be deleterious to performance.)

# The Retinue of Proscribed Mental Processes

I have described just-do-it as proscribing self-reflective thinking, planning, predicting, deliberation, attention to or monitoring of one's actions, conceptualizing one's actions, conscious control, trying, effort, having a sense of the self, and acting for a reason. But what are these processes? Since I take cognition-in-action to confront not only one or two just-do-it devotees, but the entire congregation, and since these devotees may understand these processes in slightly different ways than I do, I do not want to answer this question in a way that allows for some particular just-do-it position to remain unscathed simply because it precludes a very specific conception of thought and effort that I have simply failed to mention. Thus, my explanations in this section shall be somewhat general. (And when my argument against just-do-it does turn on a particular conception of one of these processes, as it does in Chapter 9 with "having a sense of the self," I aim to clarify the concept at issue during the course of that chapter.)

Aristotle points out that not all subject matters admit the same degree of precision. And certainly, in attempting to explain self-reflective thinking, planning, predicting, and so forth, my level of precision will be far less than what one might hope for in more mathematical disciplines. In fact, in my comments below I have not even attained what Aristotle saw as a criterion for adequacy, which is providing as much clarity as the subject matter admits; I could do more (one can always do more). Nonetheless, I hope what I say is enough to get us started and that if there is any doubt remaining, further and sufficient clarification will occur in context as the book progresses.

Again, just-do-it proponents differ as to which of these or to what extent these mental processes are allowable. The most extreme forms will say that experts, when performing at their best, engage in no mental processing at all, while less extreme proponents may allow for some but not others. And I hope that when I address the views of specific just-do-it advocates, the extent of their extremity will be reasonably clear as well. Furthermore, even though my concern is with these processes as they occur in expert action, to explain them here I also use examples from everyday actions.

**Self-reflective thinking,** as I see it, is thinking about what you are doing while you are doing it. You engage in self-reflective thinking, for example, if, while picking up a heavy box, you tell yourself: *Bend from the knees and not the back, keep the elbows relaxed,* and so forth; or when in the act of improving your posture you think, *I'm straightening my back,* while you are sitting more upright in your chair; or when you think, *I had better make that a tight turn,* while you narrowly avoid driving your car over the sidewalk; or when you think, *I'm going to move this pawn to take control of the center,* while you are taking such control. These examples involve thinking about your actions—mental or physical—while you are making them.

In addition to self-reflective thinking, which involves thinking about what you are doing as you are doing it, proponents of the just-do-it principle may inveigh against **planning**, which I understand as making decisions about what you should do, and **predicting**, which I understand as identifying what you think will happen and what you think you will do. You are planning your movements when, for example, you are walking down the street and, in the middle of the block, decide to turn left at the next corner. And you are making a prediction about your movements when you have the thought that, with this extra long stride you are taking, you'll be able to step over a puddle. Or, confronted with a patch of particularly jagged terrain, a mountain biker might, almost instantaneously, both predict a range of possible outcomes of riding over it at her current speed and plan accordingly (see Christensen et al. 2014 for a similar view). Some plans and predictions, however, look further into the future. Along with the prediction that this may allow for the best possible outcome, an athlete might notice that her energy is dwindling during a race and plan to take it easy during part of the course in order to conserve energy for the finish.

Now, simple short-term predictions and plans of action might be entirely unconscious and all but the most extreme forms of just-do-it accept that they occur (for the extreme forms there is no need to plan since trained reflexes can take over). In returning a tennis serve, for example, I think that most would allow that a player unconsciously makes a prediction about where the ball will land. However, more contentious—especially in activities where reactions need to be almost instantaneous—is the view that experts make conscious, declarative predictions and plans, especially those that involve **deliberation**, such as when a tennis player thinks about what she should do (a form of planning) in order to return a serve, by deliberating over possibilities. How much time there is for deliberation in such a tennis match, I am unsure, however, I do argue that in some activities that researchers have claimed do not allow for time to deliberate, deliberation nonetheless occurs. (Thinking about what you ought to have done, may, I admit, very well be detrimental to performance; though even this, I think, is not necessarily detrimental.)[4]

Declarative thoughts are something that Fitts and Posner (1967) warn against. They tell us that "there is a good deal of similarity between highly practiced skills and reflexes [since] both seem to run off without much verbalization or conscious content," and that "overt verbalization may interfere with a highly developed skill" (p. 15). In contrast, cognition-in-action allows for declarative thought. The clearest case of this would be when an expert thinks aloud. Of course, thinking aloud would be ill-advised in an activity like chess where you do not want your opponent to know your thoughts. However, a dancer might think aloud, even on stage, by counting the music, or telling

---

[4] See my description, in Chapter 6, of musician Alex Craven's thoughts about what he ought to have done.

himself "shoulders down," and expert tennis players, Andre Agassi tells us in his auto-biography, are always talking to themselves.

Some just-do-it advocates, however, do not see declarative thought as the only cul-prit. Fitts and Posner (1967), as I mentioned in the previous chapter, say that expert dancers "ignore kinesthetic information and visual information about their move-ments," and if an expert golfer thinks about, say, stabilizing her torso muscles during a swing, she may not be successful (p. 16). "In learning a dance step, one attends to kines-thetic and visual information about the feet," they tell us; yet on their view, once one develops expertise, such information is ignored. Such attention could be seen as a form of nondeclarative thought (though some might prefer to think of this as "less-declarative thought") about what you are doing, or one might classify such mental processes as **attending to** or **monitoring** of one's own actions.

The just-do-it principle proscribes attending to or monitoring one's actions. Although the terms "attention" and "monitoring" are sometimes used in different ways—when you are monitoring your movements, for example, this may be under-stood to mean that you are more actively watching for errors than you would be if you are simply attending to them—I shall, unless noted, use these terms interchangeably. And although I don't mention "awareness" in the principle, I sometimes use "being aware of" and "attending to" interchangeably. (The same goes for "focusing on.") Furthermore, although many of the cases I consider involve monitoring bodily move-ments, I am also concerned with the question of monitoring mental processes. Thus I pose the just-do-it principle as proscribing attention to (or monitoring of) actions, be it either the dribbling of a soccer ball or the proving of a theorem.

But what is attention? "Attention," as Elizabeth Styles (1999) points out is "a concept that psychologists find difficult to define" and, though I think that an expert ought not to shirk difficulties, one needs to choose them wisely, and defining attention is not for me a wise choice. This is in part because—along with De Brigard and Prinz (2010, p. 52) who comment that "idiosyncratic definitions [of attention] that settle crucial questions by fiat ... [typically do nothing to facilitate] the process of scientific investi-gation and discovery"—I feel that scientific investigation and the defining of terms progress together. But it is also because whatever your favored theory of attention is, the just-do-it principle in its most extreme form denounces it. For example, on the extreme view that Dreyfus holds, whether you equate attention with consciousness (as does Prinz 2012) or whether you allow for unconscious attention (as does Mole 2011), whether you see attention (or consciousness) as necessarily connected to action (as does Noë 2005) or whether you conceive of it as having the purpose of filtering infor-mation (Broadbent 1958; Treisman 1964), optimal expert action occurs, on the extreme just-do-it principle without it. (That said, in defending cognition-in-action, I aim to defend the stronger view that conscious attention—or attention as thought of as necessarily conscious—comes into play in expert action.)

Though it is exceedingly difficult to define attention, it is a relatively straightforward task to identify some of its forms. For example, we can distinguish 'top-down' endogenous attention—attention that you direct—from 'bottom-up' exogenous attention, which occurs when something in the environment captures your attention. You employ 'top-down' attention when you search for a matching sock in a pile of variously patterned black socks; you are directing your attention to the socks and the patterns. Conscious control of your movements often calls for top-down attention. For example, consciously controlling the action of gently lowering down to one's knee, involves, among other things, top-down attention to the standing leg. In contrast, 'bottom-up' exogenous attention might arise when the loud crash in the kitchen alerts you to the fact that someone has just dropped your crystal tumbler; you don't need to direct your attention to the noise; your attention is directed automatically.

Attention can also be divided into *focal* versus *peripheral* attention: when you look at your watch, your focal attention is on the watch, but your peripheral attention may provide information about your hand, arm, and so forth. When advocates of the just-do-it principle claim that, say, an expert rock climber should not be aware of the movements of her limbs as she scales the crag, they typically mean to proscribe top-down focal attention, as that is what a person has direct control over. However, one sometimes hears advice, such as, "keep your mind on other matters when performing," which, if followed, would seem to also preclude bottom-up attention to one's own bodily movements. Peripheral attention, however, is usually not inveighed against, except by the extreme just-do-it advocates such as Dreyfus ( 2005; 2007a; 2007b), who view expertise as entirely nonminded.

We can also distinguish *sensory* attention from *cognitive* attention. Whereas cognitive attention is more in line with what I referred to as "self-reflective thinking," sensory attention during action is awareness of your body through your senses, either because your senses are directed at your body (top-down), such as when you visually focus on your hands grasping the golf club, or because the sensory experience itself captures your attention (bottom-up), such as when you become aware of an unusual tactile sensation in your fingertips when hitting a chipped piano key.

You can't think about the mechanics of your golf swing, Dave Hill tells us. Putting aside the question of whether he is correct, let me note that such thought or attention to your swing can involve focusing on the sensory information you receive about your movement (the way it feels from the inside, or looks from the outside); it could also involve certain declarative thoughts, or it might (and perhaps typically does) involve both. Let us look into these forms of attention in more depth, highlighting the sensory side first.

As I'm understanding it, sensory attention is to a large degree nondeclarative—that is, not easily captured by words or articulated in sentences in our minds, but rather is more like the visual impression you may have of a sunset that leaves you speechless. You may, in seeing the scene, still conceptualize it as a sunset of brilliant oranges and reds, but there may be no particular sentences in your mind describing it. For example, you are not or at least need not be thinking *this sunset exhibits the most spectacular array of colors I have ever seen*. Nonetheless, you may be attending to the scene before you. This is not to say that language does not mediate sensory attention in some way. It might be that the way you experience a sunset depends in part on your conceptual understanding of sunsets and the words you have to describe it. (I leave the long-standing debate over this issue aside.) However, what I do intend to mean is that you can have a sensory experience without a verbal description of it being at the forefront of your mind and without any verbal description that you could readily give that would fully explain your experience of the sensation.

Sensory attention can be secured, of course, via any one of our senses. An opera singer might focus on her voice by hearing it. A gymnast might focus momentarily on his hands as he grips the rings by seeing them. A dancer might focus on her movements by proprioceiving them. Certain experts might even focus interoceptively on their heart rate or, maybe for long-distance swimmers, on their body temperature, and pain might be attended to (top-down) so as to prevent injuries, or it might capture an athlete's attention (bottom-up) after a fall. An expert wine taster might focus (top-down) on the taste of the Bordeaux, or a certain taste in an athlete's mouth might reveal to an athlete (bottom-up) that she has entered a state of ketosis.[5]

According to Dreyfus as well as a number of psychologists, the expert performs best when she does not **conceptualize** her actions. I take conceptualization roughly to be a process of understanding one thing as falling in a certain category, a process which can be, though is not necessarily, verbalizable. For example, in observing the table top at the café where I am working, I am conceptualizing it as being made out of marble. (Whether it actually is or not is another issue, though, alas, the more I think about it, the more the illusion shatters, for I am now conceptualizing it as some nondescript kind of cheap stone.) This conceptualization was expressed in words, but I leave open the possibility that we may have concepts that are not verbalizable. This is a somewhat controversial view, as philosophical theories of concepts generally understand conceptual content as declarative. Even José Lois Bermúdez (1998; 2007) who makes a strong case for nondeclarative thought, understands concepts to be necessarily linguistic (1998, 68–71). However, the disassociation is advocated by Christopher Peacocke (1992) and Peter Carruthers (1998), and Pessi Lyyra (2005) even sees it as the standard view among cognitive scientists outside philosophy. But is the disassociation reasonable?

Like many issues that philosophers assail, some of the debate over whether concepts are linguistic turns on matters of terminology. For example, a chess player might look at the board and see an isolani (an isolated pawn), while another player might conceptualize the board spatially as being of a certain type to which spatial or visual concepts apply. In the former case, the player's conceptualization is expressible in words. But what about the latter case? In one sense it is not, but in another sense perhaps it is if the player could say that she saw the board as being like "that," where the "that" refers to a visual image (a view suggested in Stanley 2011). Does this count as verbalizing her

---

[5] Ketosis is a metabolic state in which the body burns fat rather than glucose for energy, which can produce an odd taste.

conceptualization of the board? I leave this issue open, though I do return to it in Chapter 11, where I also take the ability to store a board position in long-term memory as a sufficient condition for conceptualizing it. In any event, whether or not concepts are necessarily declarative, many of the arguments I put forth in the book aimed at showing that experts conceptualize their actions, aim at showing that experts verbally conceptualize their actions.

**Conscious control,** as I see it, involves deliberately moving the body or deliberately engaging the mind; or, as the eighteenth-century philosopher David Hume (1888) put it much more eloquently, it is "when we knowingly give rise to any new motion of our body or new perception of our mind" (p. 708). Conscious control thus covers control of not only bodily movements, but also thought, so that, for example, in thinking over and analyzing a chess position, one could say that a grandmaster is exerting conscious control over her mental actions. There is a tight connection between conscious control and monitoring of or attending to what one is doing. It is possible to attend consciously to one's passive movements without consciously controlling them, at least when the passivity is absolute, as evinced by a type of spinal cord injury—anterior cord syndrome—that causes a complete loss of motor function below the injury while preserving proprioception (our sense of bodily position and movement). However, as Kimble and Permuter (1970) observe, "the act of paying attention [to what we are doing] or describing the steps as they occur tends to destroy the automaticity of such behavior" (p. 375).[6] Because of this tight connection and because it is sometimes easier to experimentally manipulate attention than control, some psychology research which intends to test whether conscious control interferes with performance directs subjects to monitor their actions.

There are different levels of control: you might control your movements by executing a low-level plan in tying your shoe: move my right hand over the left, lift my left thumb and grasp the right lace, and so forth. Or, more likely, you might control your movement by executing a high-level plan: let me tie my shoes now since it is time to leave. Or, consistent with my view, as shoe-tying for most of us is an everyday rather than an expert skill, you might while distracted by the fire alarm, just do it. (For much more in-depth discussions of the concept of control and the various kinds of conscious control Fridland 2014; Myopolous (2015); Shepherd (2015); and Pacherie 2007).

Just-do-it apostles also inveigh against **trying** and **effort**: "You're trying too hard" is a phrase you might hear after a poor showing. These two related concepts admit a variety of interpretations—for example, we can talk about mental and physical trying or

---

[6] It seems even less clear that one can consciously control one's movements without attending to them. The closest example of this occurring that I can think of is an incident described by Jonathan Cole (1995) in his book about Ian Waterman. Waterman suffered from a complete loss of proprioception from the neck down, and he typically needed to see his body in order to control what he was doing, otherwise he would collapse in a heap. However, once in an elevator when all the lights went out, he was able to maintain an upright posture by tensing all his muscles. Might this be an example of conscious control without monitoring?

effort, and within the mental category we can talk about trying as engaging our will to act or as engaging our minds in difficult calculations. And although much of what I say will concern both trying and effort, we tend to use the two terms in slightly different ways—for example, in some contexts we refrain from saying that someone tried to do something if she succeeds at it, but we still might think that the action was performed with enormous effort.

Some think of an action that is performed without effort as an action that does not require attention (for example, Bargh 1994). However, as I hope to make clear in Chapter 7 where I examine differing conceptions of effort, actions can be performed without effort or at least with reduced effort yet with increased attention. For example, an expert cellist might not work hard physically to move her bow, and so might be performing without effort in that sense, but might still be concentrating deeply on her playing.

What does it mean for the self to "dissolve" in expert action, for expert action, as David Velleman (2008) puts it, to exhibit "self-forgetful spontaneity" (p. 187)? Like all of the phrases that fall under the scope of just-do-it, the idea of having a **sense of self** is multiform (see, for example, Gallagher 2000; Blakemore et al. 2002; Pacherie 2007, 2008; Moore et al. 2012; Bayne and Levy 2006; Myopolous 2015). Nevertheless, one central idea which captures a position that just-do-iters rail against is that of having a sense of being the creator of the action being performed. This is not necessarily the sort of self that Hume (1888, pp. 252–3) claimed he was unable to find, upon introspection, something apart from any perception. Instead, it is the self you are aware of in having the experience that—rather than being carried away, rather than just letting the action happen to you—you are performing the action. As such, this conception of a sense of self is closely connected to the interrelated concepts of conscious control, trying, and effort, for in consciously controlling your actions, trying to act and making an effort to act, you have a sense that it is *you* who is acting.

José Luis Bermúdez (2010) argues that that there is no sensory component to agency. And I would agree that if one is looking for something over and above a sense of effort, trying, or conscious control, that any leftover sensation of agency is, at best, minimal. However, that expert action carries with it a sensory component of agency is less objectionable to just-do-it devotees than the idea that it encompasses a more reflective sense of the self. What is a reflective sense of self? Pacherie (2007) distinguishes a reflective conception of agency from what she refers to as a "minimal sense of agency" (p. 195; see also Marcel 2003; Gallagher 2007). The minimal sense is, as she describes it, nonreflective and "fully immersed," while the reflective conception comes in two forms: either taking a third-person stance toward one's own actions (perhaps what some people describe as "seeing oneself from above") or taking a first-person stance and being aware of the thoughts and experiences one has in action (Pacherie 2007, p. 195). I imagine many just-do-it proponents would likely be happy to accept that experts have a minimal sense of agency. However, I aim to illustrate that even first-person explicit awareness of being the agent of your actions is not incompatible with expert action. (I have little to say about the third-person sense of yourself as acting—and, as we'll see in Chapter 5, some experts warn against it—however, it seems to me that the sort of expert-induced time expansion that I discuss in Chapter 7 might incorporate this type of experience.)

Finally, as I shall use the phrase, to **act for a reason** is to act with some awareness of the reason for why you are acting; this, in turn, gives experts the ability to justify their action to some degree. This justification need not be complete; it might be simply "I knew that this method had worked before, so I presumed that it might work again." Neither must one's reason lead to the best possible action. A consummate chess player might make a move for a reason—*I could tell that it would lead to an even trade*—and might be able to justify it—*I was ahead so even trades are called for*—even if there were better moves that could have been made. Moreover, the justification might even sometimes be mistaken. In very complicated situations, even experts make mistakes: the move might not inevitably lead to an even trade. Nevertheless, I would still count this as an example of acting for a reason and having the ability to justify one's actions. And it stands in contrast to the idea that anything one might say to justify one's actions would be a mere retrospective rationalization.

## Are Everyday Actions Governed by Just-do-it?

For the sake of argument I shall assume that some everyday actions might be hampered by thinking about them as you are doing them.[7] Start thinking about exactly how to prevent spilling that full glass of water you are carrying and you may end up drenched. Or next time you are at your keyboard, think about which keys your fingers are supposed to reach for as you type in your password, and you may end up locked out of your account. How is it, precisely, that you are supposed to initiate a telephone conversation? Begin wondering, and before long the recipient of your call will notice your heavy breathing and hang up. Thinking, it seems about certain everyday actions does seem to interfere with them.

The just-do-it principle, however, as I explained it above, comprises a descriptive element (which tells us that the best expert actions are performed without thought), a claim about interference (thought interferes with performance) and a proscriptive or normative element (experts ought not to think in action). Part of the reason I do not want to count "everyday experts" as experts is that I do not want to question whether the principle of interference applies to everyday expert actions. However, as Richard Shusterman (2008) points out, even if the principle of interference applies to everyday expertise, it may not be proscriptively correct; it might not be that we should never think about everyday actions as we are performing them. The reason for this, as he

---

[7] See Rietveld (2010) for an argument and discussion of how our everyday-way-of-being primarily involves unreflective action.

explains, is that there are times when we need to think about our everyday actions in order to correct our movements. For example, someone might habitually walk with his toes slightly turned out; such an individual may walk proficiently, yet since walking in this way may lead to joint problems and is generally less efficient than walking with parallel feet, it would be advisable for this individual to change his habitual way of walking, and changing habits such as these, Shusterman argues, requires deliberate focused attention. Such deliberate focused attention, may impede the flow of movement; nonetheless, according to Shusterman one ought to employ this type of attention in such a situation. In such cases, we take one step back, in order to take two parallel steps forward.

If Shusterman is correct, our everyday actions may typically proceed without thought, and thought may tend to interfere with such actions. However, Shusterman doesn't follow William James's (1890/2007) advice to leave our daily actions "to the effortless custody of automatism" (p. 122). Rather, according to Shusterman, our everyday actions ought to proceed without thought "until they prove problematic in experience," and when this happens, "the unreflective action or habit must be brought into conscious critical reflection (if only for a limited time)" (pp. 212, 63). Perhaps it is reasonable to go further and say that even if such actions are not problematic, it may be worthwhile to reflect on them in order to improve them before the problem occurs, or to make efficient movements even more efficient. Additionally, the process of critically reflecting on your movements can be enjoyable in and of itself; thus, such reflection, even if it interferes with movement, might be recommended for the sheer delight of it. So even with everyday movements, there may be times when we ought to think in action.

There are many questions one could ask about the descriptive application of the just-do-it principle to everyday actions. Is it true that everyday actions typically do proceed without thought and effort? And if thinking about habitual, quotidian actions interferes with them, why does it? Do the answers to these questions depend on what type of self-directed thoughts one applies to everyday actions? Do they depend on what sort of everyday actions are being performed? And if thinking about quotidian actions interferes with their performance once one has become proficient, just how proficient does one need to be before such interference kicks in? I shall touch upon the topic of everyday performance again in Chapter 4, where I suggest that when our interactions with others are guided by stereotypes, thinking rather than just doing would be beneficial. Moreover, since some of the most influential theorists working on the topic of expert performance (including Dreyfus and Fitts and Posner) extrapolate an understanding of superior skills from our understanding of everyday skills, questions about habitual quotidian actions show up again in discussing their views. However, for the most part, I leave the everyday aside, for my concern is with the exceptional—or at least with the type of actions, as I go on to explain in the next chapter, that are to count as expert actions.

## A Matter of Emphasis

To a degree, the difference between my view and the positions of some of those whom I see as promoting just-do-it is a matter of emphasis. The Romantic poet Wordsworth (1862) tells us that "all good poetry is the spontaneous overflow of powerful feelings" (p. 662). My view does not eliminate the role of spontaneous ideas or actions, however, I downplay their importance. And even Wordsworth does this to an extent, for he continues "but though this be true, poems to which any value can be attached, were never produced on any variety of subjects but by a man, who being possessed of more than usual organic sensibility, had also thought long and deeply" (p. 662). On my view, one needs to start somewhere, but it is what you do with the starting point that makes a work great.

Consider this statement by the violinist Arnold Steinhardt, member of the long-standing Guarneri Quartet, about performing with the other members of the quartet:

When a performance is in progress, all four of us together enter a zone of magic somewhere between our music stands and become conduit, messenger, and missionary. In playing, say, the cavatina of Opus 130, we join hands to enter Beethoven's world, vividly aware of each other and our objective performance responsibilities, and yet, almost like sleepwalkers, we allow ourselves to slip into the music's spiritual realm . . . To label the stage a zone of magic sounds poetic, but it is also our work area. In the next two hours we will expend a significant amount of energy slaving over our individual instruments (Steinhardt 1998, pp. 10–11)

Steinhardt seems to be saying that his expertise involves a balance between thought and effort, on the one hand, and a magical just-do-it (or just-let-it happen), on the other. And ultimately, the true account of what is most conducive to expert performance might line up with Steinhardt's description of being both an effortless conduit of the music and also a hard-working agent who is vividly aware of and responsible for his own actions. That is, it might be that both the sacred and the sweat are equally essential to the best performances. The choreographer and dancer Z'eva Cohen once expressed a similar view: "When I was younger and starting out, I thought you couldn't do both, that the analytic mind destroys the intuitive; but then I learned" (pers. comm.). Though I shall be emphasizing the analytic mind and arguing for an account of expert action that sees the sweat as the real marvel, it is worthwhile to point out that Steinhardt's and Cohen's perfectly balanced positions still stand in stark contrast to the views of those who argue that the most amazing aspect of expert performance leaves the mind entirely behind.

# 3

# What is an Expert?

"They say that genius is an infinite capacity for taking pains," he remarked with a smile. "It's a very bad definition, but it does apply to detective work."

Sir Arthur Conan Doyle (1859–1930)
*A Study in Scarlet*

A study by the psychologists Timothy Wilson and Jonathan Schooler (1991) is frequently cited in support of what I'm calling the "just-do-it principle," which proposes that experts, when performing at their best, act intuitively, effortlessly, and automatically, that they don't think about what they are doing as they are doing it, but just do it. The study divided subjects, who were college students, into two groups. In both groups, participants were asked to rank five brands of jam from best to worst, and in one of these groups, participants were additionally asked to explain their reasons for their rankings. The group whose sole task was to rank the jams ended up with fairly consistent judgments, both among themselves and in comparison with expert food tasters's judgments (culled from *Consumer Reports*). The rankings of the other group, however, went haywire, with subjects' preferences neither in line with one another nor with the preferences of the experts. Why should this be? The researchers posit that when subjects explained their choices, they thought more about them. Thinking, it is therefore suggested, is detrimental to doing. The journalist Malcolm Gladwell (2005) puts it more colorfully: "[b]y making people think about jam, Wilson and Schooler turned them into jam idiots" (p. 181).

But the take-home message from Wilson and Schooler's experiment ought to be quite the opposite. Yes, it may very well be that when college students think about their jam choices, their ability to accurately identify the best jams declines. However, the expert food-tasters, who were a panel of trained individuals, were able to both justify their choices and, arguably, make the best choices. Indeed, the consumer report that Wilson and Schooler rely on is filled with such justifications (*Consumer Reports* 1985). Thus, the experiment does not support the idea that thinking is detrimental to expert performance. Rather, assuming that the food experts made the best choices, we should conclude from the experiment that poor choices come not from thinking, but from not being trained how to think.

To be sure, the difference between the experts' and the students' initial rankings was not great; the overall correlation was 0.55, and the discrepancy turned on the students simply preferring the slightly sweeter jams. Moreover, although I am a firm believer in "the less sugar the better," it must be admitted that jam ranking is not an exact science. Still, the conclusions drawn from this experiment—more so by journalists such as Gladwell than by Wilson and Schooler themselves—highlight what I see as a problem in some of the expertise literature, which is that the results of experiments performed on nonexperts are assumed to hold true of experts. It might be that thinking reduces the quality of preferences and decisions for ordinary college students, but I claim we overgeneralize when we assume that such a conclusion applies to experts.[1] It may be that in our everyday lives, we develop useful habits and fall into patterns that tend to deteriorate when we reflect on them, but experts have conceptualized their skills, and this enables reflection and action to occur simultaneously.

As I understand Aristotle, this is his view as well. Aristotle believed that we must become morally upstanding individuals through habit; through practicing the right actions, such actions become second nature and we are able to perform them without thought and deliberation. However, if you want to become an expert at ethical behavior, according to Aristotle, you need to develop a theoretical understanding of morality. His work *The Nicomachean Ethics* (2002) is aimed at providing such an understanding, aimed, that is, at proving a theoretical understanding of morality for those who have already developed the habit of acting ethically. Yes, Aristotle held that someone with expertise "does not deliberate" over his or her aim—a doctor does not deliberate over whether to cure—but he also held that experts deliberate over the means to achieve their desired end (*NE* III.3:1112b13).[2]

But what does it mean to be an expert?

Answering this question is the main goal of this chapter. Or, more accurately, the goal of this chapter is to answer the question of what I mean by "expert" when I claim that experts are not susceptible to just-do-it. What, for example, allows me to count the trained food-tasters as experts, yet not the college students? College students eat jam on a regular basis too—sometimes straight out of the jar. Why is it only after having developed a theoretical background that one should count as an expert in moral action? Aren't we all experts at this? Should we define expertise in reference to some sort of societal standard, perhaps saying that experts are those who have become "professionals" in their field? Or should we rely on a test of ability, saying perhaps that, regardless of whether they are recognized as such, experts perform in a relatively superior manner? Or might there be an objective standard against which we should measure expertise? Can we define expertise as the attainment of a certain calibre of skill, such as what on the Fitts and Posner (1967) model of skill acquisition counts as the highest level of prowess? Or should expertise be thought of as the accumulation of

---

[1] Later, in Chapter 4, in the section on verbal overshadowing, I discuss some empirical research that supports this view.

[2] A consonant position is found in Coope (2007), in which she argues that for Aristotle, action is guided by knowledge of general principles.

knowledge? Is having trained for a certain number of years a necessary component of being an expert? Or could an expert be born instead of made? Finally, should expertise be based on performance or ability, allowing for, say, someone with debilitating performance anxiety to still count as an expert? The truth of the just-do-it principle—since it is a principle about experts—depends in part on how we answer these questions.

There is a vast literature in the cognitive sciences on expertise, yet there is considerable disagreement in this literature as to what counts as an expert. Without a definition of "expertise," researchers can still conduct studies investigating what benefits and what hinders individuals with particular kinds of skill (regardless of whether we should identify such skills as those of experts). For example, Wilson and Schooler's experiment tells us something about college students, and this is informative and perhaps could be generalized to the lay population. However, the danger is that without a guiding definition of what is to count as an expert, conclusions formulated in terms of one notion of expertise might, without notice and without warrant, be applied to a very different conception of an expert. This might be behind what I see as the overgeneralization of the jam experiment; those who think that the conclusion applies to experts in the sense of trained individuals, may simply see the college students as experts themselves and thus see the generalization as warranted. I think, however, that the differences between individuals such as college-student jam-tasters, and trained food critics are significant enough that generalizations about how thinking affects action in the one group might not apply to the other.

Applying conclusions from research on everyday "expert" action to professional-level action also, I think, leads Dreyfus astray. Dreyfus applies his theory of expertise, which is arrived at in part by his phenomenological investigation into driving, to the actions of individuals who have trained intensively and studied for years. Indeed, in work with his brother, Stuart Dreyfus (Dreyfus and Dreyfus 1986), work which was funded by the United States Air Force, he generalizes from driving a car to piloting an airplane. As he puts it, though likely exaggerated for rhetorical effect, "once Stuart had worked out the five stages [of expertise] using his driving skills as his example, we just changed car to plane and driver to pilot and wrote a report for the Air Force" (p. 32). Yet as a lay driver, Dreyfus's position is similar to that of the college student tasting jam; he just does it and does it fairly well. Or rather, in contrast to expert drivers, Dreyfus's skill is actually significantly worse: although the judgments of college students did not differ much from the judgments of the expert jam tasters, Dreyfus's driving ability is presumably much less skilled than a professional race-car driver's. In brief, it is the Indianapolis 500 driver, rather than the lay driver, whom I refer to as an expert.

By what criteria am I to draw the line between the lay driver and the Indianapolis 500 driver or, more generally, between the "expert" and the "nonexpert"? Is there anything I can say that will illuminate this distinction? No doubt if God were an analytic philosopher, there would be a significant necessary and sufficient condition for what counts as an expert, as well as for a wide number of other weighty concepts. Yet, as will become clear as we make our way through various attempts to define expertise, God is not an analytic philosopher. (Indeed, it seems unlikely that She is a philosopher of any kind, else, rather than resting on the seventh day, She would have had to ask for an extension.) And if being an analytic philosopher means divining necessary and sufficient conditions for things, then neither am I: although in this chapter I shall criticize various extant accounts of expertise for failing to match up to either certain common-sense notions of expertise or how I would like to use the term (or both), my goal is not to come up with the one true conception of expertise, if there is such a thing, but rather to explain what I mean when I say that the idea that experts just do it is mistaken.[3]

That said, since defining the terms of a theory and developing the theory are interdependent, I submit that one effect of my theory of effortful expertise, if it is successful, might be a change in how we generally understand what it is to be an expert. Gertrude Stein once pronounced, "I don't read dictionaries; dictionary writers read me." I can't say this about my use of the term "expert." For one, I love to read dictionaries! For another, would that they were, but dictionary writers most likely aren't reading me. Finally, Stein said it already. Nonetheless, I do hold that living languages are evolving and so, in addition to arguing in this book that thinking is compatible with performing at an expert level, I may, ever so slightly, be pushing the evolution of the meaning of what it is to be an expert in my direction.

## The Expert as Someone Who Performs Automatically

There is one conception of an expert, found in both philosophy and psychology, that for my purposes I must reject forthwith and that is the idea that an expert is an individual who has developed her skills to the point where they have become effortless and automatic (in the sense that an automatic action is one that precludes some or all of the mental processes that are banned by the just-do-it principle, especially thought and effort).[4] This notion arguably plays a role in Guthrie's (1952) classic definition of expert skill as "the ability to bring about some end results with maximum certainty and minimum outlay of energy, or of time and energy" (p. 136; though he might instead mean that an expert uses energy efficiently not that she uses less of it); it is borne out in the accounts of skill acquisition proposed by Hubert Dreyfus and Stuart Dreyfus (1988; 2004) and Fitts and Posner (1967) whereby experts proceed without awareness of their actions; and it is expressed in Wulf and Lewthwaite's (2010) comment that "relative effortlessness is a defining characteristic of [expert] motor skill" (p. 75).

---

[3] For a crack at divining the necessary and sufficient conditions for expertise see Quast (forthcoming).

[4] Although I think this conception of automaticity suffices for my purposes and more or less captures Dreyfus's notion of automaticity, the concept is understood in myriad ways in the philosophy and psychology literature. For example, Sutton et al. (2011) argue that automatic actions themselves are thoughtful. See also Wu (2013) and Fridland (2015).

However, although this is a fairly common understanding of expertise, since my aim is to arrive at a conception of expertise that is germane for the purpose of arguing that expert action is often effortful rather than automatic, I must reject it.

## Accumulation of Knowledge

Everyone is familiar with the old joke that an expert is someone who knows more and more about less and less until they know everything about nothing. However, the idea that experts have accumulated extensive knowledge about a specific domain is not at all a joke, but is rather a central component of one common understanding of what it means to be an expert: a grandmaster chess player knows over one thousand openings, an expert cardiologist has amassed a great store of knowledge about medical problems related to the heart and the treatment thereof, and an expert on the history of the Spanish conquest of Mexico may know, among other things, by what percentage the native population decreased in Mesoamerica from the early sixteenth century to the middle of the seventeenth century, which diseases were transmitted by the Europeans, as well as the form of taxation imposed on and labor demanded of the natives.[5] On this view of expertise, as the psychologist Earl Hunt (2006) puts it, the idea of "an ignorant expert would be an oxymoron" (p. 31).[6]

Such a conception of expertise is more promising for my endeavor since if what makes an expert an expert is the great store of knowledge she possesses, then it is at least possible that reflecting on such knowledge is a component of expertise. However, there are objections to this view. Although experts often do seem to have copious amounts of knowledge about some topic, it is not clear that knowledge alone can be used to draw the line between the haves and the have-nots. Alvin Goldman (2001), for example, argues that even expertise in the cognitive realm (for example, in academic pursuits) is not just the possession of information but comprises various skills or techniques. Goldman distinguishes what he calls "an objective sense of expertise," which is "what it is to be an expert," from a "reputational" sense of expertise, which is what it is "to have a reputation for expertise" (p. 91). Since, for Goldman, "a reputational expert is someone widely believed to be an expert (in the objective sense)" (p. 91), the basic question, for him, is: What is it to be an expert in the objective sense? On his view, experts (in the objective sense) possess not only large amounts of information relevant to their domain of expertise but also have "the (cognitive) know-how, when presented with a new question in the domain, to go to the right sectors of [their] information-banks and perform appropriate operations on this information; or to deploy some external apparatus or data-banks to disclose relevant material" (pp. 91–2).

[5] I have in mind here the historian Woodrow Borah (1983).
[6] Presumably, it would not be an oxymoron according to Richard Feynman, whom I quoted at the start of the Introduction as saying that "science is the belief in the ignorance of experts."

One might ask whether such know-how is not simply part of what it is to possess the information about a topic or to have knowledge of something. If you say you have extensive knowledge of Edmund Spenser's *The Faerie Queene*, and I ask you what virtue the character Britomart represents, you had better be able to access the knowledge you have that provides the answer. Other examples, however, might better illustrate the idea that expertise is not merely superior knowledge. Outstanding chess players, for example, not only have knowledge in abundance, but they seem to have (or have developed) amazing cognitive abilities that allow them to excel, such as the ability to follow through long chains of chess moves. Because of the importance of such abilities, two people might in some sense possess the same knowledge about chess, yet differ as to whether we would want to call them expert chess players. (Fridland 2012 and Williams 2008 make a similar point.)

Although Goldman explicitly restricts his inquiry into what counts as an expert to the domain of cognitive expertise, the shortcomings of the 'mere accumulation of knowledge' definition of expertise may be more apparent in the arena of bodily expert endeavors. For example, one can know quite a bit about performing a gymnastics routine on the balance beam, yet not be able to do it even if one's life depended on it. And that ability to perform the routine, some will say, is essential to being an expert gymnast. Then, again, others might question this application of the term "expert:" sure, a gymnast might be able to perform on a balance beam but it is those with extensive knowledge of balance-beam technique that are the experts. As some of my undergraduate students vigorously argued, at a boxing match, the old coach in the ring, unable to throw a punch anymore, yet able to impart his great store of information to the boxer, is the expert. "Is the coach the expert at boxing theory while the boxer is an expert boxer?" I asked. "Not at all," they responded; on their view, the coach was the only expert in the ring. And my sense is that this conception of expertise while not universally accepted is not idiosyncratic. And perhaps now, if not before, you are beginning to see why I am hesitant to provide a necessary and sufficient condition for being an expert.[7]

Another route to defending the accumulation-of-knowledge definition of expertise might begin by asking whether we can even properly distinguish knowledge from skill. Jason Stanley and John Krakauer (2013) argue that skills (both professional-level expert skills and everyday skills such as riding a bike) at a minimum require some conceptual knowledge about how enacting the skill is begun. For example, if you have the ability to hit a baseball, you will at least know that you need to pick up the bat. And Carolotta Pavesse (2015) goes even further, arguing that skill is just knowledge. Of course, whether skill is or can be grounded in knowledge depends a great deal on what counts as knowledge. For example, must knowledge (that something is the case), be expressible in words? It seems that although I can ride a bike I can't explain very much

---

[7] Though for those, like Quast, who are interested in coming to understand what the term "expert" truly means, such disagreement is irrelevant, for some might simply be mistaken.

about how I do it. However, as Stanley (2011) argues, it is not at all clear in thinking about this issue what is to count as expressible in words. For example, I can say, "riding a bike is like 'this,'" where the "this" refers to the way I ride a bike. Have I thereby fully expressed my skill in words?[8]

Because I also think that the answer to this question is unclear, I grant the definition of skill in terms of factual knowledge (expressible in words) a reprieve. However, even assuming that knowing how to do something amounts to knowing certain facts, even assuming that skill can be entirely reduced to knowledge of certain facts, in order to arrive at a conception of expertise I would still need to specify how much knowledge is necessary to reach the level of expert skill. Goldman (2001) thinks that when someone is an expert in an objective sense, this individual possesses superior knowledge; and it is not just superior relative to others but superior from something like a "God's eye point of view" (p. 91). Yet how are we to attain a God's eye point of view? (It's hard enough for me to understand the point of view of other philosophers, let alone someone like God, who is not one.)[9]

## Peer Nominations and Reputation

Like George Dickie's (1969) "institutional definition of art," according to which something counts as art as long as it is acknowledged as such by the appropriate members of the art world, one might think that the best definition or account of what it is to be an expert is simply that an expert in a domain is someone who is recognized by peers as being an expert in that domain. Institutional definitions of art have been criticized (see, for example, Carroll 1994) yet it is interesting to note that the Wikipedia entry for

---

[8] Stanley (2011) thinks of the knowledge of how to ride a bike in this situation as represented by a "practical mode of presentation." And Pavesse (2015) provides an account of just what a practical mode of presentation is. For discussion and critique of this concept see Williams (2008); Koethe (2002); Noë (2005); and Rosefeldt (2004).

[9] Goldman's response to such an objection (pers. comm.) is that even if this idea does not help us to *identify* experts, it is what we *mean* by "expert" (in the cognitive realm). The meaning of a term "expert," and a criterion for how we identify experts arguably are different things, however, without some further clarification, it seems that the concept of a God's eye point of view (or an objective point of view) does not even help us understand what it means to be objectively superior. And then, if the question is whether this could be used as a necessarily and sufficient condition for being an expert, there are further issues: On Goldman's criterion, we can't all be experts at the ABCs since we (all cognitively healthy adults, that is) have basically the same knowledge of this sequence, yet someone of Dreyfus's persuasion might argue that we are all experts in this realm. How do we determine whether a correct application of the term should cover such individuals? Beyond this, some might say that expertise is in part a matter of social recognition and that if one has vast knowledge of P (and an ability to access and put such knowledge to use), but has not been recognized as a P expert, then such a person does not count as an expert. For example, if a medical doctor has great interest in philosophy and is as knowledgeable and able as a professional philosopher, this MD—because she is recognized as an MD and not a philosopher—would still not count as an expert philosopher. And then one might wonder whether simply having superior (in some sense) knowledge (plus the ability to access such knowledge) is sufficient for being an expert in a cognitive domain since besides having the knowledge might not one also need to do something with this knowledge? For example, you might have knowledge aplenty of medieval history and be able to access it, but to be an expert historian in this area, you need to be able to write books on the topic, or so tenure committees might aver.

expertise begins by telling us that an expert is "someone widely recognized as a reliable source of technique or skill whose faculty for judging or deciding rightly, justly, or wisely is accorded authority and status by peers or the public."

Peer nominations, however, are often used not so much as a way to define what it means to be an expert but as a way of identifying experts—something that is crucially important if one hopes to perform an experiment on experts. Yet the accuracy of this method of identification has also been questioned. For example, research by Shanteau (1988) shows that peers might be unduly influenced by others' "outward signs of extreme self-confidence" (p. 211). And a study by Elstein and colleagues (1978) indicates that diagnostic skills were no better in a group of physicians who were identified by peers as outstanding compared to a group of undistinguished physicians. To be sure, much depends on what standards are being used to determine that peer nominations are not an accurate way of identifying experts. Is it, for example, that the doctors identified by peers as outstanding produce lower mortality rates in their patients? This would seem to be a reasonable criterion, but one might argue that "bedside manner" also counts especially given that some physicians end up treating higher risk patients than others. Still, it might be that when there is little reason to think that peers have insight into their colleagues' prowess, it is reasonable to question the reliability of peer nominations. In medicine, for example, doctors typically aren't patients of very many other doctors, and therefore there is little reason to think that they would be able to make accurate judgments of their peers' diagnostic abilities.[10] Elstein and colleagues (1990) suggested as much in a retrospective analysis of their research into diagnostic performance. In other disciplines, this might not be such a problem. In philosophy, for example, we are more or less all each other's patients, inasmuch as we read the work of quite a number of other philosophers, and thus we have ample opportunity to judge our peers' work. Though, I would hazard a guess that Shanteau's conclusions apply to philosophy as well.

A definition or a criterion for identification of expertise in terms of the attainment of a certain degree or prize may need to contend with some of these objections as well (after all, prize winners may be chosen by peers). Moreover, one might think that such standards are either too lenient (right after getting a PhD are you an expert in the field?) or too strict (certainly there are more experts in physics, for example, than those who have won Nobel prizes). Relying on peer nominations might also be seen as too strict a criterion for being an expert since peer nominations are typically used to identify the crème of what might otherwise be thought of as an expert crop. Or at least, it is too strict for my purposes since I would like to identify a conception of expertise that allows me to say that, for example, there are many more expert physicians than those who are identified in *Castle Connoly Medical Ltd*. Of course, if just-do-it doesn't apply

---

[10] Though whether being a patient suffices for being an accurate judge of a doctor's diagnostic abilities is a separate question.

to experts in general, it would be true that it does not apply to the best of experts. However, a final reason why neither peer nominations nor the attainment of various prizes is a reliable means to arrive at the class of individuals whom I want to deem "experts" is that reputation may linger even when such individuals sit on their laurels and no longer care to improve. Yet I would like to allow for the just-do-it principle to apply to such individuals. Whether they should still rightly be called "experts," is not, as I have said, a question I can answer. My aim is to arrive ultimately at a conception of 'expert' that makes sense of my claim that just-do-it is a myth; of course, if this conception captures a good chunk of what we often mean by expert, all the better.

## Domain-Related Experience

Can expertise be determined by measuring the amount extensive practice someone has engaged in (or determined by measuring a combination of extensive practice and reputation, as in Michelene Chi et al. 1988)? One advantage of such a criterion is that it is relatively straightforward to determine how many years someone has spent practicing a skill. Although there may still be questions about exactly when the extensive practice began and just how extensive it has been, the idea that experts are those who have practiced their endeavors for a certain number of years is comparatively objective.

Ericsson (2006; 2008) rejects this approach since, as he points out, there are "numerous empirical examples...[of] 'experts' with extensive experience and extended education...unable to make better decisions than their less skilled peers or even sometimes than their secretaries" (2008, p. 989). For example, Camerer and Johnson (1991) cite a number of studies indicating that for clinical psychologists, after initial training, further years of experience does nothing to improve their ability to diagnose personality disorders, and research by Reif and Allen (1992) shows that physics professors at University of California, Berkeley, despite their long years of experience, are not significantly better at solving introductory physics problems than their students (though I hazard that they are much better at explaining them). And as Ericsson points out, there are many other examples of skills that do not seem to get better based on mere experience. After an initial learning phase, habitual actions such as buttoning and zipping up clothing are apparently like this. Apart from this issue, given that I do not intend to argue against the just-do-it principle with respect to everyday skills, and given that this criterion counts some everyday skills as expert skills, I shall not rely on merely the number of hours practiced as an indicator of expert-level performance.

## Reproducibly Superior Performance

In response to perceived problems with the prior definitions of expertise based on peer nominations and domain-related experience, Ericsson has come to understand the notion of what it is to be an expert in terms of *reproducibly superior* performance (Ericsson, Prietula, and Cokely 2007). For example, he tells us that "chess masters will almost always win chess games against recreational chess players in chess tournaments, medical specialists are far more likely to diagnose a disease correctly than advanced medical students, and professional musicians can perform pieces of music in a manner that is unattainable for less skilled musicians" (Ericsson 2006, p. 3). Experts, on this understanding of the term, are a cut above the rest of us in their domain of expertise, and consistently so.

Yet what is superior performance? Ericsson is not looking for a God's eye point of view, but rather for a relative one: an expert's performance, for him, is "at least two standard deviations above the mean level in the population" (Ericsson and Charness 1994, p. 731). On this definition, if your skill is two standard deviations above the mean (that is, assuming a normal distribution, better than approximately 97.725 percent of the population at a task), you are an expert at it. One might quibble that any criterion that draws a sharp line is ultimately unlikely to be satisfactory. The difference between being in the 97.72 percentile and 97.73 percentile should not make or break an expert. So the line needs to be fuzzy: it is not that one turns into an expert when one's abilities are at least two standard deviations above the mean, but rather that expertise occurs when one's abilities are around more than two standard deviations above the mean. Assuming that performance is measurable with quantitative data, this seems to be a simple fix, but I don't think that it is a complete one.

In defining expertise relative to the ability of others, we need to specify the population of comparison. Presumably, we do not want to end up saying that Olympic marathon runners of the distant past were not experts because many of today's serious amateur runners are comparatively faster; thus, it seems that the comparison class should be contemporaries. But does this mean that the comparison class should be the entire living population? It might not be very difficult to be in roughly the top percentile in an activity in which few perform. For example, since the vast majority of the world's population does not ice skate at all, having tried to ice skate for simply a few hours might place you in the 99th percentile. Perhaps one way around this would be to raise the bar for ice skating and other uncommon skills, and lower it for more widely practiced skills, such as running. However, we then need a prior criterion of expertise that tells us how high the bar should be for each activity.

Instead of making expertise relative to the entire population, should the comparison class be only those who have engaged in the activity? If we do this, then we could then take the expert ice skaters to be those that are two standard deviations above the mean with respect to ice skaters, which would lead to better results for skills in which ability is normally distributed. But how does this approach account for situations where there are extreme outliers? Imagine that the skills of chess players are distributed along a bell curve, which means that a small group of players are really good at chess. With the two-standard-deviations-above-the-mean criterion, such players count as experts. Now imagine that a chess super genius is born who was steeped in chess basically from birth, the result being that her ability soars so far beyond everyone else's that even the grandmasters are no longer two standard deviations above the mean. Have they ceased to be experts?

Here's a real-life example that, depending on how you look at it, either brings out another possible problem with the superior-performance approach or offers a defense of it. A nursing doctoral student once explained to me that a new technique, the "body-cooling technique," was introduced at her hospital to help infants who have reduced levels of oxygen in their brains. She was the first one to learn it. Right away, even after she had tried it only once, she became the floor "expert" on body cooling. Here natural language supports a relativistic view of expertise: she was likely better at the technique than 98 percent of the other nurses on her floor and her ability may have been two standard deviations above the mean. But did this suffice to make her an expert even on her floor? Maybe, but I know that she at least did not feel comfortable with the appellation.

A related problem arises in situations where everyone who does a certain activity is, we would want to naturally say, very good at it. For example, perhaps because period musical instruments are so expensive, most everyone who makes the investment is determined to work hard at playing them, leading to extraordinary prowess. If our comparison class is the general population, we do end up with all of these great period instrumentalists residing at the uppermost percentile of ability. However, if our comparison class is those who play these instruments, this standard would count the vast majority of such musicians as non-experts. And, just as students in an honors class hate grading on the curve, such musicians would likely balk at curving the concept of expertise in this way as well.

Furthermore, given that I aim to identify a conception of "expert" according to which someone who drives for her daily commute to work would not typically count as an expert while the Indianapolis 500 driver would, this relativistic criterion for expertise is inadequate since it might lead us to count someone with quite ordinary everyday abilities as an expert. Take the skill of shirt buttoning (among adults in cultures where button-down shirts are a common mode of attire). Perhaps if tested on some sort of time and accuracy trial (how many buttons can you fully fasten in five minutes) we would find a normal distribution with some people emerging in the top 99 percent, yet, for the purposes of arguing against the just-do-it principle, I don't want the ordinary shirt-buttoner to count since, as I've said, I want to leave open the question of whether everyday skills are subject to just-do-it. (I mention the "ordinary" shirt-buttoner, but is there any such thing as an extraordinary buttoner, someone whom I would count as an expert shirt buttoner? I'm not sure, but I've encountered some backstage dressers, the people who help performers in and out of their costumes, who would seem to fit the bill.)

Beyond this, on a relativistic criterion, we may be led to count people who have natural extreme abilities as experts. For example, there are savants who, with apparently no practice or training, can tell you what day of the week any calendar date lands on. With what is called "acquired savant syndrome," such abilities might even manifest themselves only after a head injury (Treffert 2013). Savant calendar calculators are certainly in the top 99 percent of the general population in terms of this skill. And in a good sense of the term, they are expert calendar calculators. However, since I do not want to necessarily say that the abilities of the savant are effortful, I need a conception of expertise that excludes them. (Though if you think that they should count as experts, you may think of them as exceptions to cognition-in-action.)

Apart from all this, is the question of how to determine whether someone falls into the top percentile of ability. In certain realms, such as the world of tournament chess, there are clear standards as to what counts as superior performance—roughly speaking, if one player is able to consistently beat another player, the one counts as superior to the other. But occasionally researchers on chess expertise take a chess player's ability to choose the better move (determined by a computer analysis) from a difficult position as indicative of better skill. And in typing, speed and accuracy have traditionally been identified as criteria by which we can judge expertise. Other areas are much more subjective. There is no direct test of mastery that can weed out the expert abstract expressionist painter from the novice. And there is no set of questions one can ask of individuals with philosophy training such that, if answered correctly, some of these individuals are revealed as experts. It is often more how they say it rather than what they say that matters, yet the how is less objective than the what (which is something that throws college assessment committees into a tizzy). Even in typing skills one needs to decide how much weight to give to speed and how much to accuracy, and in chess there is some question about the accuracy of the rating system (Moul and Nye 2009).

Ericsson (2008) would ideally like for all expert performance to be quantitatively measurable. And he points out that in addition to Olympic standards for athletic events, "more recently, there have emerged competitions in music, dance and chess that have objective performance measures to identify the winners" (p. 989). There is even such a thing as a philosophy slam competition; my ten-year-old son entered one.[11] Such competitions are not recent inventions; during Roman Emperor Nero's time (AD 67), competitive poetry reading was on the list of Olympic events. Yet do such competitions accurately identify experts?[12] The violinist Arnold Steinhardt, who himself won the Leventritt International Violin competition, sees competitions in music like this:

You were a nag in a horse race with a number on your back. There's nothing wrong with a real horse race—the first one across the finish line wins—but how does one judge a musical entrant in a competition? By how fast he plays, how few mistakes he makes? How does one grade beauty, after all? . . . The winners often triumph because of what they didn't do: they didn't play out of tune, they didn't play wrong notes, that didn't scratch, that didn't do anything offensive. Contestants who commit these sins are quickly voted out, but they may be the ones to turn a

---

[11]  See <http://www.philosophyslam.org/> Accessed March 15, 2013.
[12]  Obviously the philosophy slam competition does not do well at all, for my son didn't win!

beautiful phrase and play with great abandon, the ones who reach out to the listener's heart and mind (Steinhardt 1998, p. 37)

Finally, one might ask whether laboratory performance is indicative of the level of skill that an individual has attained. If a chess player can make superb moves when asked to choose the best move in a laboratory setting, yet wilts under pressure during a game, is she an expert? A researcher might calibrate subjects' level of golf expertise by looking at a golfer's ability to make a putt in the lab. But if someone performs spectacularly in the lab, yet abysmally during actual games because of performance anxiety, is this person still an expert? I cannot presume to answer such questions, but it is interesting to note that in some areas we allow for more leeway than others. In some areas of expertise, performance in the field is all that matters: for example, if a surgeon frequently gets nervous in the operating room so much so that her hands shake and she cannot perform her job well, she is not, I think we would want to say, an expert surgeon. With musicians, however, we might allow someone such as Barbra Streisand, who has severe performance anxiety, to count as an expert based on recordings.[13] And related to this, the use of anxiety-reducing drugs is banned in some arenas, such as the Olympics, but permitted in others, such as competitions in music. Does expertise in Olympic rifle shooting but not in music encompass an ability to control nerves?

## The Expert as a Quick Study

Ericsson (2008) also mentions that "it is part of the definition of an expert performer that they are able to perform at virtually any time with relatively limited preparation" (p. 989). However, although an emergency room nurse must be ready to act when the call comes in, it is arguable that sometimes the need to prepare for extended hours is irrelevant to whether we should judge that individual as an expert. If in getting ready to give a speech, let us say, one speaker must prepare for weeks and another just a day, it seems that the individual with the longer preparation should not necessarily be judged as an inexpert speaker, especially if it was widely agreed that her speech was outstanding. In the psychology of expertise, a musician's ability is sometimes determined by a test of how accurately an individual can play a piece without any preparation. But, given that musicians usually have time and take time to prepare for their performances, should this matter? I once observed a group of mathematicians at Berkeley's "math tea" discussing a problem: some were readily able to provide tentative answers, while another, when asked her opinion, said that she doesn't like to give her opinion off the cuff, but rather needs to spend some time pondering over a problem before making a judgment. If the ultimate solution to the problem is no less

[13] A further question is how to determine what counts as performance. Should playing in the family house with family members listening in as they go about their daily chores count as performance?

accurate and no less elegant, there seems no reason to deny her the honorific of "expert."

Sometimes it is not ability to prepare quickly, but rather one's raw speed in action that is seen as indicative of expert action. However, unless the action itself is one that requires speed, it is again not clear that this is a reasonable criterion. Imagine that two news writers have assignments that are due daily at midnight. And for the past ten years, one typically takes around eight hours to complete the assignment—and, at least based on her first-person experience of her job, has typically felt as if she needed this amount of time—while the other typically pulls it off in a couple hours. If the quality of the final output is the same, is there any reason to think that the quicker one is the expert writer, and the other one is not? Leonard Cohen took at least four years, he claims, to write the song 'Hallelujah'. And it wasn't easy for him: "I remember being in the Royalton Hotel on the carpet in my underwear, banging my head on the floor and saying, 'I can't finish this song'" (Light 2012, p. 3). Does this disqualify him from being an expert songwriter? Since I would like to count the first news writer as well as Leonard Cohen as experts at what they do, I do not take the ability to perform quickly as a necessary condition of expertise.

## My View: Deliberate Practice and the Desire to Improve

I have now questioned definitions of expertise in terms of automaticity, accumulation of knowledge, peer nominations, domain-related experience, reproducible superior performance, ability to perform with limited preparation, and performance speed. What, then, do I mean by "expert," when I say that "experts think in action?" Yarrow et al. (2009) explain that one can conceive of an expert as "a person who has had the motivation to practice one thing far more than most people could endure" (p. 588). And if the type of practice in question here is not mindless repetition, but activities done with the deliberate intent to improve, then this comes close to what I mean by the term "expert," with the additional requirement that experts maintain their drive to better their skills. To be more precise, I hold that *experts are individuals who have engaged in around ten or more years of deliberate practice, which means close to daily, extended practice with the specific aim of improving, and are still intent on improving*. I do not claim that this is the one correct definition of being an expert, the definition that arrives at the essence of the concept, for I am skeptical about whether there is such a thing. However, I do claim that not only do a significant range of individuals who are often dubbed "experts" fall under this conception, but also that this conception identifies the sorts of individuals I have in mind when I say that their performance is in line, not with "just do it," but with cognition-in-action. Therefore I refer to individuals who have engaged in (around) ten or more years of deliberate practice and who are still intent on improving as "professional-level experts" or more often simply "experts," and I use the term "expertise" to refer to the skills that such individuals have developed (see also Fridland 2014).

This conception of expertise is similar to Bereiter and Scardamalia's (1993) theory according to which expertise is not a static stage to be attained, but the continual striving to improve. They tell us that their view was inspired by studying writers, and it contrasts with the conventional view that expertise is effortless:

Conventional wisdom sees experts doing quickly and easily what novices do laboriously, if they can do it at all. Novices have to reason things out, whereas experts know what to do without thinking. [Yet] [t]he paragons of effortless performance were fifth-graders who, given a simple topic, would start writing in seconds and would produce copy as fast as their little fingers could move the pencil (Bereiter and Scardamalia 1993, pp. 2–3).

And simply doing more mindless practice, according to Bereiter and Scardamalia, will not lead these children to expertise; rather, as they put it, "for many, the effect of years of practice is simply [the ability] to produce increasingly fluent bad writing" (p. 2). The expert, for Bereiter and Scardamalia, is one who, through an ongoing practice of learning, continues to develop.

Although Ericsson's conception of expertise does not incorporate the idea of deliberate practice, his research supports the idea that experts have not only practiced for at least around ten years, but that they have engaged in deliberate practice for this time. That it takes a minimum of ten years to develop expertise (the "ten-year rule") has been known for a long time. It was perhaps first formulated by Bryan and Harter (1899), and although there may be some exceptions, it does seem that in many domains— such as sports, music composition, science, and chess—ten years does turn out to be the minimum necessary number of years it takes to reach professional status.[14] But, as Ericsson and colleagues (1993) have documented, those who excel in a wide variety of fields have not only engaged in at least ten years of practice, but have engaged in at least ten years of deliberate practice—that is, not mindless practice of merely doing actions over and over again, as might be true of our daily activities such as making coffee or driving to the office, but rather the sort of practice that encompasses working on aspects that are difficult and, after practice, analyzing one's own successes and failures.[15] As I use the term, experts have engaged in at least around ten years of

[14] Chase and Simon (1973a) apply the ten-year rule to chess. Ericsson et al. (1993) show that it extends to music composition, sports, science, and the visual arts.

[15] That experts analyze their mistakes as well as their correct actions is well illustrated in high-level chess, where it is de rigueur for players to carry out postgame analyses of how well they played. Compare this to Dreyfus's (2013) view that "in all domains, masters learn primarily not from *analyzing* their successes and failures but from the results of hundreds of thousands of actions" (p. 35). No doubt, those hundreds of thousands of actions are important, but so is the analyzing. The nurses I teach tell me about the practice of engaging in a "root cause analysis" after a "sentinel event," when something goes wrong unexpectedly, as well as after near misses. The aim is to figure out what went wrong and try to avoid it in the future. And, they "assure" me that sentinel events occur even with the best of nurses. The tennis champion Pete Sampras (2008) talks about training as a child, explaining that "I hit a million balls and that was important—I had to get that muscle memory, burn it in so it was a natural thing" (p. 14). However, he also explains that, together with coaches, he spent enormous amounts of time analyzing his games. And as Tiger Roholt (2015) explains it with respect to music: "[f]rom night to night—or from take to take while recording—musicians talk about what has worked and what hasn't" (p. 1).

deliberate practice and are still working to improve. Apart from the modicum of studying drivers do in order to renew their licenses, most everyday drivers don't aim to
hone their skills (that is, if the studying for the driver's test is to count as skill-building
at all). Most everyday drivers, for better or worse, just do it. Experts, as I define them,
engage in skill-building.

The idea of *practice*, however, is sometimes contrasted with *performance*, yet not all
experts perform. For example, in philosophy, although we give talks, it is not as if all
our work is leading up to the talk; indeed, the talk is often given in order to help
improve an article or book in progress. Similarly, a painter does not work on a painting
with the end of a performance in sight (though there are artists, such as Brian Olsen,
whose paintings are created in front of an audience). Nevertheless, there is a sense of
the term "practice" according to which a painter can spend ten years practicing (that is,
doing) her craft, whether she ever performs or not. Deliberate practice, in this sense,
covers any type of activity that is done with an aim, at least in part, to improve, or to
learn, or figure something out. This covers not only what we would call a period of
training (for example, either in graduate school or in art school, respectively), but also
the actions that such non-performing experts engage in when they are trying to get
better at their craft. In fact, although I don't usually give much credence to bureaucratese, it is a policy at the university where I work that all faculty must engage in
skill-building activities: quoting from an official CUNY document, "a full-time faculty
member is expected to . . . constantly [make] all efforts to improve his/her professional
standing through study and thought, and also through activities such as research, publication, attendance at professional conferences, and the giving of papers and lectures."[16] And even philosophers such as Dreyfus and Kelly, who hold that the best ideas
strike great thinkers like bolts of lightning, believe that some activities a professional
engages in are aimed at self-improvement. Experts, then, as I understand them, are
individuals who have for at least around ten years practiced their activity with the
intent to improve and are still going strong.

But what is it that needs to be practiced? As the conditions of performance differ
from situation to situation—for a tennis player, an unusually windy day might count
as a condition under which one has never practiced, while for a philosopher, each
new paper presents novel challenges—not everything will have been practiced.
Accordingly, my requirement for having practiced deliberately and extensively applies
to the general category of the activity. An expert pianist, for example, will have to have
deliberately practiced playing the piano for at least around ten years or more, though
she need not have practiced playing some particular piece, nor on a particular piano,
nor in a particular concert hall, nor with a specific interpretation for this amount of
time. (I shall discuss the notion of practice in expertise further in Chapter 6.)

---

[16] See the preamble (p. 6) of CUNY's "Statement of Policy on Multiple Positions," accessible at
<http://www.csi.cuny.edu/facultystaff/handbook/pdf/Appendix_J_Multiple_Position_Guidelines.pdf>
Accessed Nov. 1, 2014.

In his quest to understand what goes into making an expert, Ericsson needs an independent criterion for what counts as an expert. That is, he cannot define an expert as someone who is engaged in deliberate practice and then interpret his research as revealing that experts engage in deliberate practice. However, as my concern is not with what goes into making an expert but with what goes on in the mind of the expert in action, I can, without circularity, simply co-opt his findings and build them into my definition of expertise.

My view, then, is this: experts are those who have engaged in around ten or more years of deliberate practice and are still passionate about improving (that is, they aren't just resting on their laurels); expert actions are the domain-related actions of such individuals; and expertise is the ability experts have to perform such actions. And the rest of the book is aimed at showing that experts (in this sense) are governed, not by just-do-it, but by cognition-in-action.

## How Close is This Notion to Our Common Understanding of Expertise?

Even though this is primarily a stipulative definition, it is also a practical one. Here's why: 1) despite not having made a systematic analysis of how the term is used, it seems to me that many of those who are often referred to as "experts"—for example, many professional-level performing artists, athletes, chess players, experienced doctors, lawyers, and academics—are covered by my criterion; 2) my work engages with other researchers who write about individuals referred to as "experts"; and 3) it makes for a better reading experience than using a made-up word. (Mathematicians who talk about "blowing up planes" and physicists who tell us about "charm" and "strangeness" understand the importance of this. Not all philosophers do, however, and at a philosophy conference where I discussed my thoughts on what is an expert, a distinguished professor suggested that rather than employing the term "expert" I use the term "expert" written backwards: "trepxe.")

That said, I realize my conception of expertise conflicts not only with some of the other theoretical conceptions of expertise we've seen in this chapter but also with some everyday ways of thinking about what it is to be an expert. And although I am no doubt better at finding flaws in other people's definitions of what counts as an expert—and indeed, though I did not mention it in the Introduction, perhaps a particularly salient defining characteristic of a philosopher is the ability to criticize others' views—let me try to identify some of the ways in which my criterion might not line up with other notions of "expert." I once heard my cousin, the political scientist Gerald Rosenberg, explain that as long as you acknowledge that what you are eating breaks a kosher law, it's still kosher. I cannot comment on Gerry's counsel, however, I have no illusions that by owning up to some of the ways in which my definition of expertise diverges from ordinary understandings of it, I will have made my definition kosher. Nonetheless, in indicating some such divergences as well as possible objections to the view, I hope to help those who prefer to understand expertise in other ways to see where my theory would need adjusting. (For example, if you prefer a conception of expertise that counts the daily car-commuter as an expert driver, then such individuals might count as exceptions to my view that the cognition-in-action principle applies to experts.)

*Question 1*:    Could someone reach the status of professional athlete without much deliberate practice?

I leave this as an open question, however, if there are such individuals and one wants to count them as experts, then they may be an exception to the cognition-in-action principle.

*Question 2*:    Could there be individuals who have gone through approximately ten years of deliberate training yet have failed to develop what we would ordinarily think of as expertise?

Perhaps there are such individuals, though unless mastery appears within reach, it may be difficult to persist: what makes all the work endurable for the few is that they are achieving results. However, some might persevere out of sheer love of the activity, or perhaps blind ambition (blind, that is, to a lack of progress). If so, they would still count as experts on my criterion and, as such, think in action.

*Question 3*:    Could an expert, after years of deliberate practice, maintain expert-level skill without ongoing deliberate practice?

There probably are individuals who we would normally call "experts" yet who do not continue deliberately practicing their skills. On my use of the term, however, they do not count as experts. (Alternatively, I could count them as such, but would then need to acknowledge that they may be exceptions to cognition-in-action.)

*Question 4*:    Isn't everyday expertise still a form of expertise?

If one thinks that the notion of expert should cover everyday expertise, still more exceptions to my position may arise. For example, if tying your shoes or everyday driving (or, for us carless New York City denizens, navigating our way through a busy sidewalk) counts as expert action, then all of us expert shoe-tiers or drivers (or navigators) may be exceptions to cognition-in-action and may very well just do it. On my view, however, we are not *experts* at such things because after a brief initial learning period, we did not engage in deliberate practice of these things. For example, after the age of three or four (possibly later for the Velcro generation) we didn't work on getting better at tying our shoes. (Note that the view that we should understand expertise to cover such everyday activities also contrasts with the idea that expertise occurs at the far right of the bell curve, as we cannot all, by definition, be better than average.)

*Question 5:* My criterion for expertise specifies what counts as an expert in terms of what goes into creating a performance, rather than in terms of the performance itself. Yet, isn't it correct that, as Hegel (1807/1997) said, "the true being of a person is that person's deed" (§322)? Thus, shouldn't we define what it is to be an expert in terms of what the expert *does*, and call people who have practiced diligently for extended periods of time not experts (nor even "experts" written backwards), but workaholics?

There is, no doubt, something deeply right about Hegel's view that in judging others we should look at their actions and not at how we think that they might be on the inside. For example, if we need to compare two people's intelligence, we should compare what they have achieved or how they perform (given their circumstances) rather than comparing what we think they might "really" be like. If our perceptions of others come with implicit biases, as tests such as the implicit bias test seem to indicate, this is especially wise counsel since a judgment based on a mere impression (rather than a careful analysis of what an individual has accomplished) might lead us to perceive only certain groups of individuals as having innate or "inner" talent. And this, in turn, may lead us to treat such individuals in a way that facilitates the talents they have, while other groups of individuals with possibly equal abilities are ignored. To be sure, there are certain aspects about how you get there (as opposed to merely what is done) that matter. For example, if a writer plagiarizes, or if a scientist performs unethical experiments on subjects, this discredits their performances. Yet these means of performing are deeds, too, and therefore on Hegel's view, ought to be taken into account when judging a person's worth. Deliberate practice, too, is something someone does, rather than a hidden inner essence, and even my stipulation that an expert must still be intent on improving is behaviorally identifiable to a degree. However, one might object, although plagiarism should reveal that someone is not an expert at writing, the lack of deliberate practice should not. If so, this is another way in which my stipulated definition of what it is to be an expert does not line up with an ordinary sense of the term.

## How Can I Tell if Someone is an Expert?

As I am using the term "expert," whether you are an NBA basketball player or you have taken it as your life mission to darn socks with utmost precision, does not matter as long as your prowess is the result of extended deliberate practice and you aspire to improve. To contrast this view with everyday expertise, of the sort we all have in our daily ablutions, I sometimes refer to those whom I want to call experts as "professional-level experts," but this does not mean that they necessarily have become professionals in the sense of making a living from their skills. As I am using the term, the vast majority of us who have merely spent ten-plus years mindlessly slipping one lace over the other do not count as experts at tying shoes, but you would be such an expert if you spent more than ten years practicing with the intention of trying to perfect your knots and bows (making them more symmetrical, stronger, and so forth). This is the idea I have in mind, yet how can I tell if someone satisfies it? Indeed, in order to identify someone as an expert, I need to know not only that she has spent the requisite number of years training intensively, but also that she is still intent on improving.

How do I verify that the case studies I use to illustrate the cognition-in-action principle concern experts in my sense of the term? How, when I call someone an expert, do I know that this person has engaged in around at least ten years of deliberate practice and is still intent on improving? Typically, I reap this information from the individuals themselves, or from biographical information about them (or in my own case, of course, autobiographical information), though occasionally I might simply take professional status or recognized national status, such as being a member of an Olympic team, as indicative of having engaged in the relevant practice and having the requisite drive. This is far from a perfect indicator, yet I think that it is adequate for my purposes.

## The Generality of the Claim: Cognitive and Motor Expertise

I think that everyday expertise is sufficiently different from professional-level expertise so as to warrant my exclusive concern with professional-level expertise. However, within the category of professional-level expertise, there are some strikingly different kinds of expert actions that I plan to address in a more or less unified manner. In particular, I think that the just-do-it principle applies to neither motor nor cognitive expertise, that is, to neither the actions of an Olympic gymnast nor the grandmaster chess player; to neither the professional wrestler nor the polished poet. But if, as I claim, all sorts of professional-level expert actions involve thought, can I even distinguish cognitive or mental expertise from motor or bodily expertise?

Clearly, given my view that expertise involves thought, I cannot distinguish these two types of expertise in terms of one involving thought and the other being a mindless skill. No, I'm with the golfer Bobby Jones who purportedly said, "competitive golf is played on a five and a half inch course—the space between a player's ears." Yet I still think that there is at least a rough distinction we can make between these two kinds of skills. So let me conclude this chapter with a few comments about how I understand this distinction in light of my view of expertise.

Perhaps the first point I should note is that although I think there is a distinction between motor or bodily expertise and cognitive or mental expertise, the line between mind and body need not be that of Descartes's (1641/1986), where the mind is immaterial and the body material. Rather, it is the ordinary line we draw when we think of the mind as the part of us which, among other things, thinks, feels, emotes, wills, and attends (be it embodied as you like), and the body as the part of us which, among other things, jumps, runs, dances, and moves the fingers while typing. Whether dualism is true and the mind is immaterial—as well as, for that matter, whether idealism is true and the body and mind are both immaterial—is irrelevant to our concerns. Regardless of the truth of these metaphysical doctrines, we can distinguish mind, as what thinks and feels (among other things) from body, as what jumps and runs (among other things). Thus, when I say that my claims about expertise will apply to both bodily and mental expertise, the contrast between mind and body is in this metaphysically neutral way. But what, then, is this metaphysically neutral distinction?

One reasonable suggestion would seem to be that we can draw the line between gymnastics and tennis on the one hand and chess and poetry on the other in terms of how these activities differentially employ large muscle movements. That is, one might say that while both gymnastics and poetry involve hard mental work, gymnastics and golf also involve hard bodily work, as measured by strength of large muscle contractions, whereas chess and poetry—at least if you have good posture, are sitting in a decent chair, and take occasional breaks—are physically undemanding. Yet golf is not nearly as physically strenuous as gymnastics, and something like video gaming might be less physically strenuous in terms of large muscle contractions than even philosophy, which at a minimum often involves occasionally turning one's head away from the screen to take a sip of coffee and, perhaps in the best of situations, involves, in the peripatetic style, taking occasional strolls. So it seems that some of what we might want to call physical skills do not involve more large muscle movements than mental skills. And in fact, chess would be counted as a mental skill even if it were played with heavily weighted pieces. Perhaps such a game could count as both physical and mental expertise, yet if the strength it took to lift the pieces did not require special training, we might not think of it as involving physical expertise at all.

I think a better (though still not perfect) approach is to look at what counts as success in the respective endeavors. In gymnastics, for example, the success of an action seems intimately connected to the bodily movements the gymnast makes, whereas in chess the grandmaster's exact bodily movements seem incidental.[17] If a gymnast accidentally stumbles during a routine, it reveals something about her ability as a gymnast. Similarly, if the fingers of an expert at playing video games slip, this merits criticism. However, if a chess player's hand slips and accidently knocks over a piece during a game, she is not thought any the worse of as a chess player. In other words, for the gymnast (or video gamer), if her intention to act fails to produce the desired bodily movement, her performance is generally seen as flawed. Yet for the chess player, if her intention to move a piece accidentally knocks over another, this is generally not relevant to the quality of play. To be sure, if a chess player's hand slips during a tournament and accidentally pushes a pawn ahead, the player may very well need to accept the consequences of that move. It seems, however, that such slips have more to do with coordination than with chess expertise.

---

[17] In speed chess, this is less so, since the best players need to move exceedingly fast.

But this still might not give the results we want since one might argue that physical slip-ups are not necessarily more relevant to gymnastics than to chess, as long as they are mere "slip-ups." If a gymnast stumbles on her landing after a layout, this would seem to indicate that her actions are not as expertly performed as they would have been without the stumble. Or at least the judges may say so. But should a minor stumble count against her? In arts such as dance, I think it is arguable that even a large misstep should at times be irrelevant to the overall quality of the performance. Dancers sometimes fall, but I think that as long as they can pick themselves up and continue without letting the fall hinder the rest of the performance, the quality of the performance need not be affected: one hears, "it was just a fall." In philosophy-speak, one might say that although the quality of the dance *supervenes* on the individual movements, it is not *reducible* to them. In other words, although you can't change the quality of a dance without changing the dancer's movements, you can change the movements—even to a large degree—without changing the quality of the dance. This is true of chess as well: although you can't change the outcome of a chess game without changing the bodily movements of at least one of the players, large-scale bodily movements of the players can vary without altering the outcome of the game. (I'm simplifying here by ignoring the possibility that outcomes can change because of external factors. For example, two chess games might involve the exact same moves by the players, but if the rules of chess differ, then the outcomes of the games might be different as well. And the quality of two bodily identical dance performances might differ if quality depends in part on how observers perceive the performance.)

Nonetheless, there does seem to be a difference between the kind of movements done in chess or in writing poetry and those done in ballet and basketball, for the physical movements of a chess player seem to be irrelevant inasmuch as the board could be replaced with a computer screen without really changing the game. Those who can play proficiently on the physical board can also generally play well on the screen. But a dance created and performed on a computer is an entirely different kind of activity from one done in flesh and blood, and it is not the case that those who are good at physically dancing will be generally good at manipulating virtual bodies with a cursor.

So I think it does make sense to contrast mental and physical expertise, though not sharply (and certain forms of expertise, such as musical expertise and some types of electronic gaming expertise might fall on the fuzzy border between the two). Yet despite the differences between chess and poetry on the one hand and ballet and basketball on the other, many philosophers and psychologists working on expertise hold that the correct theory of expertise is going to cover all types of expert action, from overtly physical actions such as gymnastics to barely physical ones like chess. As Ericsson and his collaborators (2006) put it in their introduction to the *Cambridge Handbook of Expertise and Expert Performance*:

[Although i]t is not immediately apparent what is generalizable across such diverse domains of expertise, such as music, sport, medicine and chess…[t]he premise of a field studying expertise and expert performance is that there are sufficient similarities in the theoretical principles mediating the phenomena and the methods for studying them in different domains that it would be possible to propose a general theory of expertise and expert performance (Ericsson et al. 2006, p. 9).

Buskell (2015) also follows this approach. Whether the motivation for this classification is partly due to the human tendency to look for unified explanations, I cannot say; however, I too shall look for theoretically significant commonalities between mental and physical expert endeavors, and so, in talking about experts, be referring to those who have engaged in deliberate practice and are still intent on improving, whether athlete, dancer, chess player, or poet.

## A Theory of (Almost) Everything

Putting aside expert actions that are designed specifically to preclude effort or thought, if there be such activities,[18] my investigations into a wide variety of areas of expertise have led to me to think that Ericsson's premise in studying expertise and expert performance is a reasonable one, and I see this book as providing support for it. However, as befits theories in the so-called "special sciences," it may be that the most we can aspire to in this area is to identify principles that tend to be correct. And, indeed, this is as far as my aspirations go. For although I aim to propose a theory of many types of expertise—cognitive as well as motor, artistic as well as athletic, lightning-fast as well as snail-slow, open skill (where the environment changes in significant ways, such as in soccer) as well as closed skill (where the environment is relatively stable, such as in diving)—there may be significant relevant differences between these kinds of skills as well as among individual experts within domains. Nonetheless, I hypothesize and present arguments and evidence intended to support the view that experts, in general, think in action.

What type of thoughts do I permit? Although I claim that many types of thoughts are generally compatible with expert performance, I do not make an absolute ruling on any particular thoughts. Perhaps thoughts about things that are entirely irrelevant, or

---

[18] Slingerland (2014) uses mindball—a game where two players compete by trying to move a ball across a table to the other player by increasing alpha and theta brain waves, which are associated with a calm, intent focus and are detected by an EEG strapped to their heads—as an example of a skill that requires you to not try since, as he sees it, you win by being relaxed. I haven't played the game, so perhaps it is correct that you can't try, however, I'm not entirely convinced that it is a good example of an activity specifically designed to preclude thought and effort since one might be able to calmly exert effort. Moreover, the game also requires one to produce neural activity associated with being focused (though, not necessarily on the ball): Betsy Andrew explains on her blog (<https://betsyandrewsetchart.wordpress.com/2012/05/29/mindball-are-you-calmer-than-your-three-year-old/> Accessed Sept. 8, 2015) that she beat her three-year-old thinking, "I am sitting on a beach. I am listening to waves. I have a babysitter for the entire day." Might she be trying to think these thoughts and might it even be that in this situation focusing on those thoughts counts as focusing on what you are doing? Another example, however, might be contact improvisation, when it is practiced, as it sometimes is, with the goal as moving so fast that responses must be reflexive. But might one, even here, be trying to keep it moving?

about impending doom, or even about great success, might sometimes throw experts off, but some might thrive on this. Thus, rather than accounting for which specific kinds of thoughts are beneficial and which are detrimental, I instead suggest that the types of thoughts that have beneficially or at least unproblematically occurred during practice are compatible with performing well. Likely there are individual and domain-relevant differences that affect whether one or the other kind of thought will be beneficial or detrimental to performance, and it is the experts themselves along with their trainers, coaches, teachers, or mentors that are best suited to identify what works for them. Moreover, I presume there are differences within an individual from time to time. However, I do claim that, in general, thinking at the expert level does not hinder and at least apparently facilitates doing. And in the next chapter, the argument for this begins.

# 4

# Does Thinking Interfere With Doing?

We've pulled up from bottom to second place in two weeks against all those fellows on the ground here. That's because we play with our heads as well as our feet.

Rudyard Kipling (1865–1936)
"The Maltese Cat"

Sometimes, when it really matters, everything falls apart. A vivid example of this occurred during the 2011 Republican primary presidential debate, when Texas governor Rick Perry, while explaining how, if he were elected, he would eliminate three government agencies, couldn't call to mind the phrase "the Department of Energy." "The third agency of government I would do away with," the governor proclaimed, "the Education, the uh, the Commerce and let's see, I can't—the third one. I can't. Sorry. Oops" (quoted in Saenz and Friedman 2011). He curtailed his presidential campaign shortly after this.

Though other explanations are possible, it seems that Perry's monumental choke was in part due to his heightened state of anxiety over how well he was going to be perceived. His worry apparently interfered with his ability to bring to mind a phrase which in some sense he knew very well—after all, he had been railing against the Department of Energy nearly every day during the months leading up to the debate. But how does anxiety cause a choke?[1] How does anxiety cause one to bungle an action that would otherwise be a piece of cake?

No one fully knows the answer to this question, however, according to the predominant theory of choking under pressure—the "explicit-monitoring" theory of choking—anxiety can cause one to explicitly attend to or consciously control processes that would normally occur outside consciousness.[2] On this view, choking

---

[1] Does the phenomenon of so-called "choking under pressure" require explanation or does it merely describe poor performance that would be predicted statistically? Psychologists such as Beilock who aim to explain choking in terms of increased attention to movement, assume that it is a phenomenon that requires explanation; I do the same.

[2] See Baumeister (1984); Masters (1992); Wulf and Prinz (2001); Beilock and Carr (2001), (2005); Beilock and DeCaro (2007); Beilock and Gray (2007); Wallace et al. (2005); Ford et al. (2009); Beilock (2010); and Papineau (2015). Note that Papineau claims to explain why the yips are caused by self-reflective thinking rather than why choking under pressure is caused by this. Though I cannot now address this in

can occur in public speaking when individuals try to bring into working memory information they should be able to say automatically. For example, in explaining Chief Justice John Robert's fumbling of Obama's presidential oath, Beilock (2011) tells us that "when the pressure was on [Roberts] fumbled the well-learned set of lines likely because [he] was devoting too much working memory to monitoring the words he knew by heart" (p. 255). Presumably, she would provide a similar account of Perry's guffaw. Her advice: "Just go with it and try not to think too much about every word" (p. 275).

Explicit-monitoring theories are also employed to explain choking in expert-level athletics. The general idea is that at a high level of performance, many actions are proceduralized, that is, they run offline without conscious control, and so choking occurs when extreme nervousness causes one to try to monitor and control these actions consciously. Any conscious mental processes involved in guiding one's movement may be implicated in choking on this view. However, conscious monitoring and control are often singled out as the central culprits. These two processes are, of course, different, and although control might require monitoring, monitoring can occur during entirely passive bodily movements. (See the section on conscious control in Chapter 2.) However, proponents of explicit-monitoring theory typically see both as causally relevant to choking. Furthermore, the type of monitoring that is induced by the experiments that we shall go on to examine (experiments that are seen as supporting explicit-monitoring theory) is often thought to encourage control. I shall discuss both monitoring and control (and occasionally other related mental processes, such as focusing on your movements or thinking about your movements).

Explicit-monitoring theories of choking comport with the Fitts and Posner model of skill acquisition (1967), according to which performance at the highest level is "autonomous" or automatic. As Yarrow et al. (2009) explain, according to the explicit-monitoring theory, "highly practiced skills become automatic, so performance may actually be damaged by introspection, which [on the Fitts and Posner model of skill] is characteristic of an earlier, consciously mediated stage" (p. 591). Invoking the principle of interference, which is the part of the just-do-it principle that says that thinking about expert performance in action interferes with it, Sian Beilock (2010), a proponent of explicit-monitoring theory, tells us that in high-pressure situations, sports skills "are hurt, not because of worrying, but because of the attention and control that worry produces"(p. 193). In such situations, on this theory, pressure leads to worry and worry

---

detail, if what he means by the yips is what is typically thought of as the yips by sports psychologists and movement scientists, which is roughly involuntary jerks and twitches during highly skilled movement then the empirical results do not currently favor this position. See Klämpfl et al. (2013) who conclude that "reinvestment or the attempt to consciously control their own movements did not appear to be responsible for the occurrence of the yips." To be sure, like the experiments I addressed that supposedly show that monitoring interferes with expert performance, there are various questions one might ask related to the ecological validity of this work. In any case, Papineau seems to have a broader notion of the yips in mind as it includes cases such as Chuck Knobloch's. I address these cases later in this chapter.

leads experts to consciously monitor and control their actions. And it is the conscious monitoring and control that is thought to lead to the choke. Beilock (2011) tells athletes something similar to what she tells those preparing to deliver a public address: "distract yourself... don't give yourself too much time to think, focus on the outcome, not the mechanics... [and] just do it" (p. 232). In fact, "just do it," she says, seems to be "the key to high-level sports performance" (p. 185).

Beilock's ideas and the direction of her research are in part inspired by the psychologist Roy Baumeister's (1984) views on expert action under pressure. In high-pressure situations, according to Baumeister, "consciousness attempts to ensure the correctness of... execution of skill by monitoring the process of performance (e.g. the coordination and precision of muscle movements); but consciousness does not contain the knowledge of these skills, so that[,] ironically[,] it reduces the reliability and success of the performance when it attempts to control it" (pp. 610–11). Summing up what he sees as the conclusion of a number of studies on the relationship between pressure and poor performance, he says that "competition is arousing; arousal heightens self-consciousness [consciously monitoring and controlling one's movements]; and self-consciousness [consciously monitoring and controlling one's movements] disrupts performance of some tasks" (p. 610).

The psychologist Richard Masters's research on skill also fuels the idea that choking occurs because the mind interferes with well-practiced routines, arguing that performance is likely to decline when experts consciously think about and try to control their well-practiced skills. To do so is to "reinvest," which he defines as "purposefully endeavoring to run a skill with explicitly available knowledge of it" (Masters et al. 1993, p. 655). Anxiety, on his view, leads to problems because it causes reinvesting, and reinvesting, he thinks, degrades performance.

But are these views about the relationship between anxiety and skill correct? Does the experience of anxiety induce experts to focus on and consciously control or think about their movements? And does focus and conscious control cause poor performance at the expert level? Although the question of whether pressure causes one to think about one's actions will loom in the background of my discussion, my concern is with the question of whether consciously monitoring and controlling actions at an expert level is deleterious to performance. Or in slogan form: does thinking interfere with doing? And, as shall come as no surprise at this point, my answer is *no*: experts can and often do perform at their best while thinking—even consciously thinking—about what they are doing. Of course, since proponents of the explicit-monitoring theory of choking typically accept that experts do sometimes explicitly monitor and consciously control some of their movements without detriment (in, for example, novel situations), a more precise statement of the position I aim to argue for in this chapter is that experts can and often do perform at their best while explicitly monitoring and consciously controlling their movements. Moreover, the movements that they explicitly monitor and consciously control include those that proponents of the explicit monitoring theory of choking often think of as strongly proceduralized (that is, automatic in the sense of being neither consciously controlled, thought about, nor monitored).

At the risk of sounding like an analytic philosopher, let me go over the difference between my position and theirs a bit more carefully. If the just-do-it principle upheld by the explicit monitoring theorists were simply the view that explicit monitoring and thinking interfere with skills that are automatic (whatever skills those may be), the view they upheld would not only risk being trivially true (if it is also assumed that such skills, once proceduralized, are best done automatically) but also would be consistent with a position that goes much further than the cognition-in-action principle, for it is consistent with the position that no action ever proceeds without thought and monitoring (if no action, however fine grained, is fully automatic). However, Baumeister's and Beilock's views are not simply that explicit monitoring and thinking interfere with skills that are automatic (whatever skills those may be), for they also take a stand on which skills are automatic. And a conflict between their just-do-it position and my cognition-in-action view arises because some specific skills—such as hitting a baseball, returning a serve in tennis, dribbling a soccer ball—that on their view proceed automatically, on my view involve thought and effort. Moreover, in general, they hold that highly proficient skills, such as those of professional athletes in their domain of expertise, run automatically and without conscious interference, or as Beilock et al. (2002) put it, that "skill-focused attention benefits less practiced and less proficient performances yet hinders performance at higher levels of skill execution" (p. 14). This, also, is something I reject.[3]

"That skill-focused attention hinders expert-level skills" is an assertion of the descriptive component of the just-do-it principle. But, as should be obvious, the explicit monitoring theorists also uphold their version of what I referred to in Chapter 2 as "the principle of interference," for they hold that skill-focused attention hinders expert-level skills. And they also typically take what I identified as a proscriptive stance on the issue since they frequently offer their advice on what athletes should do, which—to sum it up again with those three words—is that they should "just do it."

There are legions of studies that purport to provide evidence for the view that attention to, monitoring and conceptualization of, and conscious control over one's well-practiced movements degrades performance. Although I cannot hope to address all of them, I shall discuss three central and distinct types of studies—the varied-focus experiments, the verbal-overshadowing experiments, and the statistical studies—that are seen as substantiating the principle of interference.

---

[3] Note that as Beilock and Carr explain their position in this quote, the idea that "higher levels of skill execution" have been proceduralized is assumed.

# Varied-Focus Experiments

Paring away the details, here is a description of the varied-focus experiments. Participants, usually college students, are divided into two groups, a more highly skilled group (usually of an intermediate level) and a novice group, where the division may be based on some type of team status, number of years playing, or institutional rating. (Golf, soccer, baseball, and other sports are commonly studied.) Both groups are then asked to perform a skill under various conditions: as they normally perform it (the *single-task*, or *control condition*); while directing their attention to a specific aspect of their own movement (the *skill-related supplemental task condition*); and while engaging in an extraneous task (the *skill-unrelated supplemental task condition*). And generally the results of such studies are that relative to the control condition, the more highly skilled athletes perform significantly worse in the skill-related supplemental task condition yet only marginally (or negligibly) worse in the skill-unrelated supplemental task condition, whereas novices, relative to the control condition, perform significantly worse in the skill-unrelated condition and, if anything, slightly better in the skill-related condition. In other words, the more highly skilled individuals, when focusing on what they are doing, do worse in comparison to when they are focusing on a skill-unrelated task. For the less skilled individuals, however, focusing on what they are doing does not seem to interfere with performance while focusing on a skill-unrelated task does.

Those who accept the explicit-monitoring theory of choking think that: 1) anxiety causes explicit monitoring, and 2) such monitoring causes one to choke. The varied-focus experiments aim to support the latter link. Now, one might ask whether the relatively small declines in performance that the higher-skilled experimental subjects experience tell us anything about the drastic flubs one typically identifies as a choke. But that is not my concern here. Nor, as I said, is it the interesting question of whether anxiety increases one's tendency to monitor and control what one is doing. Rather, my concern is with the relation between monitoring and controlling one's movement on the one hand and performance on the other.

To clarify the nature of the varied-focus experiments, let me explain a study by Ford et al. (2005). Subjects were divided into two groups (the more highly skilled and the less highly skilled) and were asked to dribble a soccer ball through a slalom course. In the skill-related supplemental task condition, participants were instructed to perform the dribbling task while continuously monitoring their feet (not necessarily visually), in order to be able to identify, upon hearing a randomly generated tone, which side of the foot had just been in contact with the ball. In the skill unrelated supplemental task condition, subjects were asked to perform the dribbling task while continuously monitoring a range of single syllable concrete nouns, in order to identify the target word "thorn." The results were in line with the general picture above: the more highly skilled soccer players performed worse under the skill-related condition than under the skill-unrelated condition, while for the less highly skilled players, the pattern was reversed or at least not present: they played worse (or at least no better) in the skill-unrelated condition than in the skill-related condition.

How do we account for these results? Wulf (2007) summarizes the research in this area by saying that the "findings clearly show that if experienced individuals direct their attention to the details of skill execution, the result is almost certainly a decrement in performance" (p. 23). The philosopher Ezio Di Nucci (2014) concurs: "these experiments suggest that more time to think, more attention, and more concentration worsen the performance of experts while they improve the performance of novices" (p. 19). Focusing on what you are doing, such research is taken to show, interferes with expert skill, or as Toner and Moran (2011) claim, "a practical implication...is that it would appear prudent for skilled performers to avoid consciously attending to their movement during competitive performance" (p. 682).[4] Thus the principle of (skill-focused) interference appears vindicated.

However, before we ask athletes to avoid paying attention to the details of their actions, let us take a closer look at this research, for I think that there are other reasonable interpretations of the data, which, when combined with results of diary studies of athletes' coping strategies, as well as various first-person reports—both of which we shall go on to examine—should lead us to reject Beilock, Wulf, and others' just-do-it conclusions.

Let me present three reasons to question the just-do-it conclusion of these experiments.

*Objection 1:*   The experiments are not ecologically valid.

An *ecologically valid* experiment captures relevant real-life conditions so as to make it viable to generalize the conclusions of the experiment beyond the laboratory walls and to the relevant population (which, for my purposes, is the population of experts). Though it is difficult to say exactly what it is for an experiment to be ecologically valid, there are a number of features of the varied-focus experiments that—though I think do not tell the whole story—intimate trouble.

One arguably ecologically invalid feature of these experiments that might seem significant to their outcome is that what subjects are asked to perform in the skill-related supplemental task is not something they would normally do. Christensen et al. (2015) explain this with an analogy. Asking players to continually monitor their feet, they tell us, is like asking a driver to continually monitor the rearview mirror while driving. On Christensen's view, just like a driver would perform suboptimally while doing this, even though it is important to *occasionally* monitor the rearview mirror, a soccer player would perform suboptimally while continually monitoring her feet even if occasional monitoring is part of typical play.

This seems reasonable, however, it may be worthwhile to ask whether it is actually known that even continually monitoring one's feet while playing high-level soccer would interfere with performance. I would like to see a study that looks into this, a

---

[4] However, see Toner, Moran, and Montero (2015).

study that simply asks players to continually monitor their feet, yet does not also ask them to report on what they have identified via such monitoring. As Stanley (2011) and Fodor (1968) point out, there is a difference between, for example, having the knowledge that you ride a bicycle in a certain way and being able to report how you do so, and it may be the reporting rather than the attention that hinders higher-level performance. And there would seem to be even more of a difference between monitoring an action and being able to report on what you have monitored. Of course, in such an experiment it would be more difficult to know whether subjects are complying with the request. Yet this cost might be offset by the greater ecological validity of the experiment because participants in Ford et al.'s study are not merely asked to monitor various aspects of their skills and report them, but they sometimes need to report on actions that have already gone by: individuals are instructed to attend to the side of the foot that *had just been* in contact with the ball. This makes it even less like real-life conditions since even if expert soccer players consciously focus on their feet in real-life situations and could report on such focus in real time without interference, it is highly unlikely that they reflect back on past foot action. Christensen's analogy, therefore, should be to a driver who is asked to continually monitor the rearview mirror to detect whether cars are receding or approaching, and also asked to identify (at the sound of a randomly generated tone) whether the car behind her has, most recently, been receding or approaching. (One can imagine that the experiment has been set up so there is at most one car visible in the rearview mirror and that that car is either receding or approaching.) If continually monitoring the rearview mirror interferes with performance, this would make one's driving performance all the worse. (Note, however, that the question of why performing the skill-focused extraneous task interferes with expert performance yet not novice performance remains—more on this later.)

Another way in which these experiments are, arguably, not ecologically valid is that they fail to produce the high-stakes situations athletes find themselves in when they are playing a real game. Because of this, it is very likely that an athlete will find herself in at least a slightly different psychological state during an experiment than during an actual game; significantly, it is possible that the controlled environment would not elicit the type of intense focus that is characteristic of expert-level performance in situations that matter.

Varied-focus experiments are often seen as supporting the view that, as Beilock et al. (2002) put it, expert skill is "governed by proceduralized knowledge that does not require explicit monitoring and control," and that a skill-unrelated extraneous task (such as listening to a recording of words and aurally identifying a target word) "should not degrade performance in comparison with skill execution under single-task conditions, as attention should be available to allocate to secondary task demands if necessary without detracting from control of the primary skill" (p. 9). But even if attention to a secondary task does not degrade performance in an experimental setting, it might degrade performance in the wild. In a psychology experiment, subjects may be motivated, but it is unlikely that they are as highly motivated as they are in an actual game. Thus they might not engage their full conscious powers while performing the requested tasks. This means that an extraneous task might not degrade their performance relative to a control condition (since performance in the control condition is already degraded due to lack of full attention and motivation). However, in a high stakes situation, this might not be the case.[5] Such considerations, I submit, leave us room to doubt the view that experts, when distracted by skill-unrelated supplemental tasks, perform just as well as they would in the wild.

That the varied-focus experiments fail to replicate real-life settings, however, cannot be the entire explanation for why such experiments appear to show that certain forms of expert action are harmed by self-monitoring, since both the less and more experienced participants perform ecologically invalid tasks, yet ability is differentially affected. Why is this, if not for the reason, as Beilock et al. (2002) conclude, that "well-learned performance may actually be compromised by attending to skill execution" (p. 9)?

*Objection 2*:   The skill-related supplementary task may be more distracting for those who are faster at performing a task or who are better at attending to their movements.

The more experienced soccer players are faster at the dribbling task than the less experienced players, and because of this, reporting on a past action may slow them down more compared to the less skilled players. When the faster players hear the tone, rather than focusing on their current normally fast-moving forward action, their reporting on their past action might draw their attention to the past—that is, to the most recent contact they had with the ball when the tone was sounded—which slows down their movement. Of course, the less-skilled (slower) participants also need to report on a past action, however, it could be that because they do not normally move through the slalom course as quickly as the more skilled participants, the effect, if any, is not as great as the effect on the faster participants.

However, although all of the varied-focus experiments involve reporting actions, not all clearly involve reporting past actions. For example, in one experiment, participants swinging at a virtual baseball are requested to report at the sound of a tone whether their bats are moving up or down at that moment (Castaneda and Gray 2007). But it still might be that the quicker you can perform such a task, the more detrimental it is to report on your movement, for reporting might slow you down to or pull you toward the tempo of the report, which is a greater reduction of speed for those who are quicker at performing a task than those who are slower at it.

---

[5] Moreover, it is interesting to note that some athletes claim that they take the drug Adderall—a drug often given to those with Attention-Deficit/Hyperactivity Disorder AD/HD—because it increases focus and eliminates distractions. I would like to thank Lorenzo Ruffo, an undergraduate student at the College of Staten Island, for drawing my attention to this issue.

Furthermore, it could be that experts are simply better at attending to their own movements; that is, it could be that because experts know how to direct their minds to their bodies while in action and can do it with a vengeance, the request to monitor an aspect of their movement that they normally would not monitor (or would not be the only thing they monitor) will be more distracting for experts than for novices. For example, if recalling which side of the foot was most recently in contact with the ball is not relevant to their skill, this focus may interfere with their performance more than with novices' performance, as novices are not able to monitor these details of their movements as well. And it could even be that since novices have not developed the ability to focus on their movements intently, the skill-related supplementary task, which encourages such focus, actually results in a better trial than one without any bodily focus.

Beyond this, if we assume that some type of bodily focus is beneficial at high levels of performance and that distractions closer to or more similar to your intended focus impede performance more than distractions dissimilar to your intended focus, the skill-related supplementary task may have degraded the skilled participants' performance more than the skill-unrelated supplementary task since it induced a type of focus that was close to, but not the same as that which the more highly skilled players have found beneficial. In other words, because the skill-related supplementary task brings about a type of focus that is close to but not exactly the type of focus most beneficial for experts, it distracts experts more than the skill-unrelated task. Again, for novices, who may not have developed this important aspect of skill, there is nothing to be distracted from, and any improvements could be explained in terms of the task prompting a beneficial type of attention.

*Objection 3*:    The "experts" are not experts.

In discussing whether the varied-focus experiments were ecologically valid, I suggested that in a controlled experiment, experts might not be motivated to perform in the highly focused way they would perform in situations where it really matters, and it might be because of this less intense focus, skill-unrelated distractions are not detrimental to their actions. And in discussing the idea that the skill-related supplementary task may be more distracting for experts than less skilled subjects, I suggested that experts, compared to the less skilled participants, might be more distracted during the skill-related task than the less skilled participants since they have something to be distracted from (the correct focus). I also suggested that experts are better able at complying with the request. But the fact of the matter is that controlled experiments rarely use experts as subjects. Or at least they are not experts in the sense I have in mind. (Recall, I stipulate that experts are those who have practiced their skill in a deliberate manner for at least around ten years and are still practicing such skills in this way.) But how does this relate to the outcome of the varied-focus experiments? Professional-level soccer players, for example, train with deliberate focus and conscious control and hence, since they are used to thinking while performing their actions, thinking should not interfere with performing their actions during a game.

The amateur mid-level soccer players (who fall into the more skilled group in the varied-focus experiments), however, might not be used to training in this manner—they train, of course, but not nearly as intensively as professionals. Because of this, monitoring their actions and consciously controlling them might interfere with their performance even if it does not interfere with the performance of professional athletes.

Let me take that a bit more slowly. Researchers such as Dreyfus and Dreyfus (1986) and Fitts and Posner (Fitts 1964; Fitts and Posner 1967) see the progression from novice to expert as leading to greater and still greater automaticity. However, on Anders Ericsson's (2008) theory of skill acquisition, falling into automaticity results in a plateau of skill, or what Ericsson refers to as "arrested development." On his view, once one achieves automaticity, merely repeating an action over and over again does little to improve it, and thus, as Ericsson sees it, "the key challenge for aspiring expert performers is to avoid the arrested development associated with automaticity" (p. 694). (Think again about tying your shoes and how stagnant your technique is; if you were to work diligently on increasing your speed, or the strength of the knot, or the aesthetic qualities of the bow, such as its symmetry, you might improve.) Those who move beyond automaticity by engaging their conscious minds during analytical, thoughtful, and effortful practice—the group I'm referring to as "experts"—might not, for all the varied-focus experiments show, be derailed by focusing on and reporting on skill-related tasks.[6] (Similarly, those of us who don't work on improving our shoelace-tying might be derailed by thinking about it while those who are working on improving can think about it to their heart's content.) In contrast, it may be that the more highly skilled subjects in these studies are at a level of ability that is both more proceduralized than a beginner's and less conceptualized than an expert's. If so, it would not be surprising that skill-related supplementary tasks interfere with their performance more than skill-unrelated tasks and, moreover, for the novices that this pattern would be reversed or at least not present. (Some studies, such as Beilock et al. 2002, show very little difference in performance for novices under the two conditions. This, of course, is what one would predict since with little skill to begin with there is little room for deterioration.)

In sum, there are a number of interpretations of the varied-focus experiments that do not support just-do-it. I have not shown that any of them are correct, but the mere existence of these alternate interpretations means that, even if high anxiety can cause athletes and others to attend consciously to their skills, such experiments leave room to doubt whether conscious attention (rather than some other effect of anxiety) interferes with performance. Besides, it is worth noting that not all varied-focus studies have shown that skill-focus interferes with high-level performance: Suss and Ward (2010), for example, asked expert shooters to monitor the action of their trigger finger while shooting. What these researchers found was that relative to a

---

[6] Sutton, et al. (2011) make a similar point: "In many distinctive domains," they tell us, "elite practitioners specifically resist the kind of automation which Dreyfus ascribes to the highest levels of expertise … [since these elite practitioners worry] that trusting the body alone to take over will lead to arrested development" (p. 95).

situation where they were asked to focus on a skill unrelated task, the shooters performed just as well.

## Verbal Overshadowing Experiments

While the varied focused experiments are supposed to show that highly skilled actions are hindered by skill-related attention, monitoring, or control during performance of the skill, experiments that elicit what is called "verbal overshadowing" (roughly speaking, where words get in the way of accurate decisions) are supposed to show that highly skilled actions are hindered by conceptualizing or thinking about them.

Research by Kristin Flegal and Michael Anderson illustrate this approach. In a 2008 paper entitled, "Overthinking skilled motor performance: or why those who teach can't do," they present an experiment which, as they see it, shows that for experts (as opposed to novices), even thinking retrospectively about a completed task hampers subsequent performance of the same task. In their study, one group of more highly skilled golfers and another less accomplished group performed a putting task. Each group then had to either explain from memory what they focused on during the task, or engage in an unrelated verbal task. All participants then performed the putting task again, and it was found that the more skilled golfers in the memory group performed much worse the second time around compared to the more accomplished players in the unrelated task group. Furthermore, the less skilled players performed no worse after the memory task than after the unrelated task.

Highly skilled golfers, Flegal and Anderson (2008) conclude, should not only just do it, but they also shouldn't think about it afterward. They take this to have a practical implication for sports coaches: "Whereas verbalization assists in the early stages of acquiring a skill, it may impede progress once an intermediate skill level is attained" (p. 931).[7]

But is this the correct conclusion to draw? Note that the participants in the study were asked, not just to record what they attended to, but to "record *every* detail" (italics in original) they could remember "regardless of how insignificant it may strike" them. This means that the golfers were recording the irrelevant and possibly distracting thoughts that might have occurred, thoughts that hindered rather than helped performance, and going into the second trial with these insignificant thoughts fresh on their minds may have in part been responsible for their performance decline. The less skilled players, of course, also may have had some insignificant thoughts, but, as I suggested in relation to the varied-focus experiments without much skill to begin with, there is little room from which to decline.

---

[7] See also Abernathy and Hamm (1995), who tell us that "the nature of expert [surgical] knowledge explains why it is difficult for the expert to explain accurately how he or she is able to make a diagnosis" (p. 172).

As with the varied-focus experiments, however, perhaps more important is that the highly skilled golfers were not experts, as they were not individuals who had trained seriously for at least around ten years and were still intent on improving. Rather, they are described as being of "intermediate level" by local golf experts based on the participants' self-reported score for a nine-hole course, and, indeed, of those who were classified as intermediate level players in the verbalization-task group, only 65 percent had ever taken a golf lesson. It may very well be that such players simply did not have a sufficient amount of training in conceptualizing their actions to be able to conceptualize them beneficially.

The detrimental effects of conceptualization on perceptual judgments (or 'verbal overshadowing') was also thought to play a role in the 1991 Wilson and Schooler experiment I discussed at the start of Chapter 2. Recall that in this study, researchers found that college students performed relatively well in ranking jams when they were asked only to make a list of rankings (as judged in comparison to the rankings listed on *Consumer Reports*), compared to when they were asked to make a list of rankings and also explain their reasons for those rankings. Their attempt to verbalize the reasons for their judgments apparently interfered with or overshadowed their perceptually accurate judgments. Yet, as I suggested, the expert jam tasters employed by *Consumer Reports* who served as a standard for accuracy were, presumably, not negatively affected by verbalizing their preferences.[8] And it may very well be that expert golf players would not be hampered by recording what they had focused on during the putting task.

Schooler's more recent work is in line with the possibility that experts are able to conceptualize their actions without interference. For example, Melcher and Schooler (1996) found that while wine tasters of an intermediate skill level were less accurate at recognizing a previously sampled wine after describing it, more highly skilled wine tasters were just as accurate after having described it. I spoke with the wine critic Peter Leim about this, who said—quite contrary to Beilock's (2010) advice to not "give yourself too much time to think"—that "typically you don't have much time with each glass to think...but the more time you have, the better your judgments are" (pers. comm.).

In another study, Melcher and Schooler (2004) trained subjects to identify mushrooms either entirely perceptually or conceptually (along with some perceptual cues). They then had each group either identify mushrooms without explaining their reasons for their identifications, or with explaining their reasons. What they found was that those who had conceptual training performed best when providing reasons for their identifications and, moreover, that when they did this, they performed best overall. Flegal and Anderson (2008) cite this study, yet nonetheless conclude that their own study "indicates that simply verbally expressing one's recent motor action may sow the

---

[8] See also Schooler and Engstler-Schooler (1990), who observed that participants who described a difficult-to-verbalize stimulus (the face of a bank robber) from memory were worse at later recognizing that face than were participants who did not put their memory into words. Again, people who have been trained to recognize faces, however, may not be similarly affected.

seeds of poor execution during later performance," and that "unless a concentrated effort is made to maintain one's procedural expertise, the verbalization necessary for teaching may hasten a decline in skill," which, as they point out, suggests "a new view of [the] old adage [that] those who teach, cannot do" (p. 931). Perhaps they see motor expertise as different in kind from perceptual expertise, but without an explanation for why the relatively little training their more skilled participants had should be irrelevant when it comes to golf yet not when it comes to perceptual skills, I think that their study gives us little reason to think that their conclusions hold for experts, for those who have trained hard and long to do what they do (Stanley 2011, p. 159 fn. 6 reaches a similar conclusion).[9]

## Those Who Do, Can't Teach?

Philosophers sometimes also extol the contrapositive of the old adage, arguing that those who do, can't teach. Kant, for example, comments in *Critique of Judgment* (2007, p. 132) that Homer cannot teach his method of composition because he does not himself know how he does it. Contemporary philosophers such as Robert Brandom (1994) and John McDowell (2010) are fond of citing the chicken sexer who can't teach anyone how he makes his judgments because he does not know himself. Stephen Schiffer (2002, p. 201) supports one of his arguments against Jason Stanley's view that know-how is inextricably connected to propositional knowledge by citing eight-year-old Mozart's apparent ability to compose a symphony without being able to explain how to do so. David Velleman (2008), in arguing that we achieve excellence only after we have moved beyond reflective agency, cites the *Zhuangzi*, in which expert wheelwrighting is described as proceeding without any understanding of how it is done:

You can't put it into words, and yet there's a knack to it somehow. I can't teach it to my son, and he can't learn it from me (p. 184).

In Plato's dialogue *Ion*, as I pointed out in Chapter 1, Socrates says that the poet's and the rhapsode's actions are a form of madness, since they have no knowledge whereof they speak.[10] And in illustrating how scientific hypotheses may be hit upon suddenly and unsystematically, Carl Hempel (1966) recounts the chemist Kekulé's story that in 1862 the idea for the ring structure for benzene came to him in a flash after dreaming of a snake biting its tail. (See also Wallis 2008 and Devitt 2011.)

What do I make of such views? One might say, in line with Stanley's (2011) and Fodor's (1968) distinction between knowing something to be the case and being able

---

[9] Wallis (2008) takes a set of experiments by Berry and Broadbent (1984) to show that expert skill is not conceptualized. However, Buchner, Funke, and Berry (1995) casts serious doubt on such an explanation of the data.

[10] Of course, it is generally accepted that Plato understands this as showing that *Ion* is actually not an expert at his craft.

to report it, that such experts have knowledge of their skills yet are unable to explain what they do. This seems reasonable and there are certainly cases of individuals who simply don't have the requisite social skills to teach anything, regardless of whether they excel at it themselves. And Stanley also points out that in some minimal sense experts can explain what they do: "I'm doing this." However, I would go further inasmuch as I think that in many of the cases put forth as illustrating situations in which experts can do things yet cannot explain how they do them, the experts actually can provide rather full explanations. For instance, although your everyday native English speaker might not be able to explain the five basic forms of English verbs, English-as-a-second-language teachers can, and their own ability to speak English will be none the worse. To return to the examples, Kekulé himself in his breakthrough 1865 paper claims that his theory was formed in 1858, four years prior to the dream. And the proverbial chicken sexer who has no understanding of how he is making his judgments simply doesn't exist. Tommy Nakayama (1993) makes this abundantly clear in an article explaining in painstaking detail just one of the intricate methods that chicken sexers learn. I also spoke with Tom Savage, who worked in the poultry industry for ten years prior to his academic career. As he explained it:

Poultry sexers learned the technique of vent/cloacal sexing from a trained individual...In the US that skill was learned by attending a school for poultry sexing. Sexing chicks is a very exacting technique that requires a high degree of accuracy in determining the sex of a day-old chick or turkey poult, etc....This technique (poultry sexing) is based upon the acquired ability to recognize/differentiate anatomic structures within the chick's cloaca (pers. comm.).

Even Aristotle had a theory of chicken sexing in his *On the Generation of Animals* (305 BCE/1990). (However, it wasn't correct: he thought males came from longer eggs. And neither was Pliny's view, some 200 years later, that females did (Nakayama 1993).)[11]

Though Mozart was no doubt incredibly gifted, there is little evidence that he had no understanding of what he was doing or that he composed without thinking about it. Eight-year-old children are often capable of detailed explanations of their skills—my seven-year-old daughter plays chess, and even though she's no Mozart, she can recount a game and explain the basic principles of the Four Knights Opening, the concept of checkmate, a back row checkmate, castling, en passant, the concept of a fair trade, a fork, a pin, a skewer, and so forth.

Moreover, the extent of Mozart's compositional genius at that age is also somewhat contested: handwriting analyses indicate that his father played a significant role in his compositions until Mozart was thirteen, and not merely as an amanuensis

---

[11] An interesting study by Biederman and Shiffrar (1987) showed that even without any training, subjects can identify whether a poult is male or female with more than 50 percent accuracy. The authors note that likely they were able to do this because the "presence of a prominent bead—which is the central singular structure—was interpreted as being male" (p. 644).

(Keys 1980).[12] So it may even be that the child Mozart was no Mozart. And as an adult, it seems clear that Mozart didn't compose without thinking. In Chapter 1, I also mentioned that the myth of Mozart's effortless abilities may have been inspired by a well-known letter, in which Mozart claims to see in his mind entire compositions finished "at a glance" and "all at once" and that all the inventing "takes place in a pleasing lively dream." However, this letter is now dismissed as a forgery, and his actual letters make no comments about sudden insights (Spaethling 2000). Moreover, his sister documented that he would spend endless hours mentally composing his music (though, after he had worked compositions out in his head, he did seem able to transcribe his compositions rather effortlessly and without thought; Stafford 1991). Furthermore, contrary to lore, Tyson's (1987) studies of the autograph scores reveal that some manuscripts contain numerous revisions.

We lack similar archival data about Homer's methods of composition and the ancient wheelwright's approach. Homer famously does say in the opening lines of the *Odyssey*: "Sing in me, Muse, and through me tell the story." Whether the authors of the *Zhuangzi* base their claims on what actual wheelwrights have said is unknown.

It is clear, however, that Socrates doesn't listen to Ion who begs of Socrates that if Socrates could only hear him speak of Homer, then he would understand that his actions are not a form of madness.

Of course, I am also neither a rhapsode nor wheelwright, nor have I spoken with experts in these domains (securing interviews is exceedingly difficult); however, based on my own experience in both philosophy and ballet, it is abundantly clear that, as with Savage's description of the art of poultry sexing, experts in these areas have a vast store of information that can be beneficially imparted to students and, moreover, that teaching generally helps rather than hinders performance. For example, as a philosopher, in teaching I need to make complex philosophical ideas both clear enough and engaging enough to garner the attention of my students, which helps me to better understand the ideas and devise ways of framing them in my written work. And after making writing suggestions on a student's paper, I not infrequently say to myself: why don't I follow that advice! And when I taught ballet, students' flaws would alert me to aspects of my own technique that needed work and their excellence would clue me into a form of movement I might like to imitate. Furthermore, and particularly relevant to the cognition-in-action principle, teaching would help me to conceptualize certain aspects of movement that might have become automatic. Conner Walsh, principal with Houston Ballet, comments on this in an interview:

When I'm teaching ballet, I see my own flaws in other people. It's a different way of understanding than catching yourself in the mirror. There are habits that we get from taking class day after day: often dancers face straight ahead without any epaulement [turning and inclining of the head], and we can get comfortable. Now I really pay attention to how I use my head and try to

[12] See also Stafford (1991).

find more quality to everything that I do in class.... I think that every dancer should try teaching to better understand their craft. (Rubin 2011)

And Walsh is not alone among dancers in thinking that teaching and conceptualizing movements benefits performance. Jennifer Kronenberg, principal dancer with Miami City Ballet, also comments on how teaching can help one break habits:

Often the things I end up explaining [when I teach] are the very ideas I've overlooked in my own dancing, like my habit of not bringing my shoulders with me. When I see it in my students, it registers. (Rubin 2011)

Julie Diana, Pennsylvania Ballet principal dancer tells us:

I give the very same steps I find difficult. When I break them down, I understand them better... Watching my students reminds me of the fundamentals and refreshes my own technique. (Rubin 2011)

James Whiteside, principal with Boston Ballet, says:

By verbalizing corrections, I understand key elements that I need to work on. I remember watching one student whose knees were facing the wrong directions during a forward *port de bras*. I really pay attention to my turnout now during that movement. (Rubin 2011)

And Caroline Rocher, a dancer with LINES Ballet, explains:

I just finished an anatomy for dancers class and now I apply all that I learned in my teaching and in performance. I like that I get a chance to analyze certain movements while teaching. (Rubin 2011)

Rocher is presumably exaggerating in saying that she applies *all* that she learned. Nonetheless, if these dancers are to be believed, dancing is not simply about just doing it. To be sure, they may be mistaken, however, I know of no psychological data that clearly shows that they are.

That said, it should be pointed out that teaching also hurts. In ballet, for example, it puts a strain on the body since one tends to demonstrate on one side more than the other, and one might end up showing a step without being properly warmed up; and in philosophy, it takes precious time away from writing.[13] However, there seems to be little reason to think that the conceptualizing involved in teaching hinders dancers' future performances. My friend Meg Potter, a former dancer with American Ballet Theater and Oregon Ballet Theater (where I met her), and current ballet teacher at Pacific Northwest Ballet School, recently lamented that she would have danced so much better if only she "could have had this mind with that body." This comment contained quite a bit, but I presume that one thing she meant by it was that her conceptual understanding of dance as developed through her teaching career would have helped her during her performance days.

---

[13] One colleague even advises abstaining from your own work for twenty-four hours after a session of grading so as to prevent any untoward stylistic influences.

Still, it is sometimes said, that the very best at doing are not usually the very best at teaching. This fact, if it is a fact, can be explained, however, in a way that does not require us to accept that being an expert precludes conceptualizing your skills: the very best dancers, musicians, athletes, and others have got where they are in large part because they have dedicated themselves so fully to their endeavors rather than to the art of teaching (which is its own skill). Similarly, individuals who are passionate about teaching both get better at teaching than their less passionate peers and spend less time practicing their discipline. Moreover, while the greats can risk being single-minded, those whose career paths are uncertain may be edged into teaching rather than doing.[14]

Be that as it may, sometimes retrospective conceptualizing of one's actions might lead one to perform something very differently from how one had performed it in the past; for example, a retrospective analysis might lead one to find a flaw that needs improving, which might lead one to try a new approach to a movement. In such a case, one might not be as proficient at this new way of movement as one was at the old way. But sometimes this is what improvement requires, and it is not a sign that conceptualization in itself hindered the performance. As I mentioned before, sometimes one needs to take a few steps back before moving forward. Ultimately, one wants to know whether it is best for an expert, when in the thick of things, to reflect on his or her actions. And I think that neither the varied focus experiments (where skill-focused attention is found to hinder performance) nor the experiments by Flegal and Anderson (which investigated the effect of retrospective conceptualization on skill) should lead us to think that it does.

## Analyzing Archival Sports Data

In a controlled setting, ecological validity, as we have seen, is sometimes elusive. But one can investigate whether skill-focused attention interferes with truly expert-level performance by statistically analyzing the outcomes of real-life games to determine the conditions under which experts perform dramatically worse than would be expected: do athletes perform worse than would be statistically expected in situations where they are presumed to be more skill-focused than they typically are? Does archival sports data support the idea that players perform suboptimally when they are thinking about what they are doing?

In a 1984 study, Baumeister and Steinhilber analyzed archival data from World Series baseball games between 1924 and 1982, and argued that the answer to this question is *yes*. What they found was startling, for the data showed that the home team, when they had the chance to win a decisive fourth game and clinch the Series,

---

[14] Some might explain why truly elite experts are generally not the best teachers as follows: "In an endeavor like ballet, the very best are likely those who not only have worked like dogs to be where they are but also those who start out with outstanding physical attributes (extremely arched feet, natural grace, and so forth). They learn what to do in order to improve their own elite bodies. And that because of this, they might be the best possible teachers for those lucky few who are similarly endowed, but perhaps not for the masses." There may be something to this as well, even if there are exceptions.

won only 39 percent of the time and made more errors than the visitors. This was surprising, since the home team had always been assumed to have a large advantage. The explanation, according the Baumeister and Steinhilber, for this apparent counterexample to "home-team advantage," is that such a situation encourages players to focus on their movements, and such focus interferes with performance. In their words, "the impending redefinition of self (as champions), particularly in front of the home crowd, engenders self-attention, which causes performance decrements" (p. 86). This finding became known as "the home team choke," and as it went counter to received wisdom, it quickly made its way into almost every social psychology textbook.

More recently, Matt Goldman and Justin Rao (2012), using a data set comprising 300,000 free throws, have argued that there is statistical support for the view that basketball players perform worse at free throws in clutch situations at home than when away, which, they claim, supports the explicit-monitoring theory of choking. As they see it, because home-team fans are absolutely quiet so as to not distract players at the free-throw line (while they will do everything possible to distract the away team), the home-team player at the free-throw line is likely to experience "increased self-focus, hampering the natural ability of [the] player to make [the] free-throw" (p. 8). In contrast, they found that players perform better in decisive offensive rebounds at home than at away, hypothesizing that the extra effort they put in when at home helps such a situation while the rapidity of the action leaves no time to reflect on the action. Thus, as they put it, "thinking about the details of how one should accomplish a goal, as opposed to 'just doing it,'" hampers performance (p. 1).

Both Baumeister and Steinhilber's conclusions and Goldman and Rao's are in line with the principle of interference. And Beilock favorably cites Baumeister and Steinhilber's results in her 2010 book.[15] However, Baumeister and Steinhilber's results are at best controversial, for—as Schlenker and colleagues (1995) later argued—when one expands the data base to include games through 1993, the home-choke effect fails to be statistically significant, and, importantly, errors were found to occur much more when the home team is behind rather than ahead. Therefore, contrary to Baumeister and Steinhilber, errors do not seem to result from the self-consciousness that arises as a result of players redefining themselves as champions. And the idea of a home choke has since largely disappeared from the psychology textbooks.

Goldman and Rao's results seem to be more statistically significant (all the statistical findings they rely on are significant at the 0.005 level or greater). Why does the home team do worse than the away team in clutch moments at the free-throw line? Goldman and Rao assume that because there are no external diversions, it must not have been because the players were distracted. However, it could be that other factors, including internal distractions—the worry about disappointing fans and family, the thought of so many out there rooting for you, the fear that you just don't have it in

---

[15] To be fair, Beilock does point out in a footnote that the statistical data are controversial.

you—are what really cause trouble (and this line of thought is perhaps bolstered by the fact that only the weaker free-throw shooters tended to suffer in these conditions). Indeed, it could be that the noise and wild arm motions the home fans make in order to distract the away-team might prevent all these worries and doubts from entering the away-team players' minds, as they may need to rivet their attention to what they are doing to prevent themselves from being distracted from the jeers.

Thus, I think that Goldman and Rao's data need not be seen as supporting the self-focus theory of choking since it need not be seen as supporting the principle of interference. And Schlenker and colleagues' (1995) reanalysis of the Baumeister and Steinhilber data defuses the idea that baseball players are more likely to choke when on the verge of victory in decisive games on the home turf than they are in earlier home games.[16] Interestingly, though Schlenker and colleagues argue that the data do not support the "kinder, more benevolent [choke] driven by visions of success, not fears of failure" (Schlenker et al., p. 634), they nonetheless claim that their analysis of errors support the darker form of choking, for they found that errors occur more frequently when a team is behind in the game. Thus they suggest that choking arises from the prospect of impending failure. But again, this is entirely consistent with the cognition-in-action principle, as it could be that the anxiety of impending failure leads to choking for reasons other than it causing players to think more about what they are doing; for example, the prospect of impending failure can cause a severe loss of confidence or it can cause the mind to fill up with irrelevant yet distracting thoughts, like those thoughts about how, if they lose, they will be perceived in the eyes of fans, friends, coaches, and family.

Moreover, high anxiety itself induces various physiological changes that appear to hinder performance. For example, the fight-or-flight response that accompanies anxiety shunts blood flow to the larger muscles at the expense of one's extremities, and thus motor skills relying on the hands or feet may be harmed. Anxiety can also increase perspiration and effects a loss of peripheral vision, both of which could hinder performance. It also produces tremors in some individuals. All of these physiological effects of anxiety could be detrimental to a player's performance regardless of whether the player is thinking about what he or she is doing.

The detrimental physiological effects of anxiety are well illustrated by the ways in which the class of pharmaceutical drugs popularly known as "beta blockers" affects

---

[16] In the ensuing debate between Baumeister and Schlenker et al., Baumeister (1995) attributed some of the disagreement over the existence of the home choke to the difficulty of working with messy archival data: "Should semifinal series be included? Should four-game sweeps be included? How far back in time should one go?" Although manipulation of such factors might move a finding back and forth across the magical .05 criterion, even the best intentioned researcher might find no solid a priori basis for making these decisions, and often it is difficult to make or even anticipate them all before knowing how they will affect the hypothesis. In contrast, the similar decisions regarding a laboratory experiment (e.g., whether to exclude a participant who seems intoxicated) are much rarer and can be made before data collection. He concludes that "archival data in general may be less than optimal for testing and building psychological theories" (p. 646). Schlenker et al. (1995), however, argue that archival data are not intrinsically more problematic than laboratory results, pointing out that "[a]ny data set, lab or field, can be good or bad" (p. 649).

performance. Beta blockers, in double-blind studies, have been shown to improve performance that relies on fine motor skills such as rifle shooting (Lieb 2010). Yet, although beta blockers appear to reduce some of the effects of anxiety (such as tremors), it is thought that they do not directly affect the *experience* of anxiety, indeed, certain beta blockers do not pass through the brain-blood barrier and therefore act exclusively on the autonomic branch of the peripheral nervous system. To be sure, knowing that you won't shake or (during a double-blind study) noticing that you are not shaking might have a calming psychological effect. So part of the benefit of beta blockers is likely psychological, yet its physiological benefits are undeniable. Thus, in some cases at least, even if the experience of anxiety causes some to think about what they are doing, performing poorly under pressure might not be related to the thinking, but rather to the physiological effects of anxiety.

Schlenker and his colleagues acknowledge that their "darker" form of choking might be accounted for in a variety of ways; however, they also at least leave open the possibility that part of the reason for the "dark choke" pertains to the principle of interference since they suggest that negative thoughts might induce athletes to consciously attend to the details of their movements and that such attention is detrimental to performance. "We agree with Baumeister (1995)," they tell us, "about many aspects of performance pressure, [such as the view that] focusing attention on the details of skilled performances can be disruptive (e.g. the expert pianist concentrating on precise finger movements)" (p. 634). So, although Schlenker and his coauthors reject the idea of the home choke in baseball, they apparently still assume the principle of interference. Yet, as far as the research we have just looked at, it seems possible that at least the right kind of self-directed thinking is compatible with performing at one's best. Again, it is likely that some "darker" mental processes, such as extreme confidence-undermining negative thoughts, may interfere with performance.[17] Moreover, even overwhelmingly positive yet distracting ones may be harmful. Indeed, any sort of focus that takes away from what the expert ought to be focusing on can be a hindrance. (This was the view espoused by an expert bus driver I once talked to: "The only time I miss a stop is when something breaks my train of thought, when someone cuts me off or something.") Yet, at least from what we have seen so far, there is no reason to hold that, in general, focusing on what one is doing—even focusing on the details of one's movements—is disruptive.

The view that thinking does not interfere with expert action, as I mentioned in Chapter 1, is corroborated by the ineffectiveness of "icing the kicker" in football. It is not uncommon for coaches to call a time-out right before the opposing team is to make a kick. They do this with the hope of inducing a choke by giving the kicker more time to

---

[17] Though I am often surprised by accounts of athletes and dancers who sometimes perform so well with so little confidence (see Agassi 2009). Could it be that the loss of confidence is sometimes beneficial since it increases anxiety, which increases adrenaline, which might help endurance and strength?

think. But a statistical analysis of ten years of National Football League games shows that there is no statistical support for the idea that iced kickers do worse than hot ones.[18] Of course, this doesn't show that thinking about what one is doing as one is doing it does not interfere with performance since it could be that the practice of icing the kicker never induced increased attention or thought in the first place. Nonetheless, it does seem to pull down one further pillar of support for just-do-it.

Baumeister, Goldman and Rao, Beilock, and Carr, and others hold that pressure induces self-directed, or skill-focused, attention, and that such attention is detrimental to performance that has become automatic. This is of course true, if being an automatic action means, in part, that it is an action that is hindered by conscious control. And I would agree that some components of expert action are automatic in this sense. For example, unless a basketball player has recently had knee surgery and has been spending long hours focusing on rebuilding the relevant muscles, concentrating deeply on the movements of her left kneecap might get in the way of her making a basket. However, I also hold that experts engage in skill-focused attention all the time. And, as we shall go on to see, rather than being the effect of anxiety and the cause of performance choking, skill-focused attention seems to be employed by athletes to help them cope with pressure.

## Distraction Theory and Qualitative Studies of Thinking While Doing

Although it is widely accepted that anxiety induces choking because it provokes experts to focus on or think about what they are doing, there is a competing theory about the relationship between anxiety and choking, which, far from supporting just-do-it, runs counter to it. On this view, sometimes referred to as "distraction theory," high pressure draws attention away from the task at hand and to irrelevant aspects of performance, such as worries over how performance will be judged and the possibility of failure (Wine 1971). Distraction theory is based on the idea that anxiety is thought to impair working memory and executive control, both of which are important components of, among other things, planning and strategizing. Although this theory doesn't entail that explicit monitoring and conscious control are components of highly skilled actions, it does provide an alternative explanation for why choking under pressure occurs, which is consistent with the view that experts explicitly monitor and consciously control their actions (and more generally, with the cognition-in-action principle).

---

[18] <espn.go.com/blog/statsinfo/post/_/id/34217/icing-the-kicker-remains-ineffective-practice> Accessed Nov. 20, 2013.

Researchers who explain choking under pressure in terms of "thinking too much" also accept that anxiety can distract performers and impair cognition, but since they see well-practiced sports skills as proceeding more or less automatically and without cognition, they feel the need to unearth another account. But if one holds, as I do, that thought is an important component of even well-practiced sports skills, it is possible that distraction could account for many such cases as well. To be sure, I accept that explicit monitoring and conscious control sometimes interfere with performance at an expert level, for sometimes experts do fall into performing automatically. And it might be that in such cases, conscious monitoring and control does hinder performance. However, the remedy in this case, I claim, is not to keep the mind out of the picture, but rather to bring the mind back into practice and performance. And, in fact, there is some evidence that expert athletes, rather than suffering because anxiety provokes them to focus on their skill, actually focus more intently on their skills in order to cope with anxiety.

That experts increase their focus on their tasks in order to cope with pressure is suggested by studies carried out by the sport and exercise psychologist Adam Nicholls and colleagues (2006) that asked elite athletes to keep a diary of stressors that occurred and coping strategies that they employed during games, as well as to rate, on a scale of one to five, how effective these coping strategies were. Though small-scale, the study indicates that a common method of dealing with stress involves redoubling both effort and attention and that such methods are perceived as more effective than other methods. For example, in a study of eight first-class professional rugby union players over a one-month period, during which they played four tournament games, Nicholls et. al (2006) found that, although the players dealt with the pressure in a variety of ways, "the most effective coping strategies that were used on a frequent basis were increasing concentration on task and increasing effort" (p. 327).[19]

How does this relate to the question of whether explicit monitoring and conscious control interferes with expert action? If "increasing concentration on task and increasing effort" involves monitoring and conscious control of one's actions, then Nicholls's results seem to run directly contrary to the view that choking occurs because experts "reinvest" their actions with such mental processes. And even if concentration and effort did not involve explicit monitoring and conscious control, this research finding would be consistent with the view that explicit monitoring and conscious control are conducive to expert action. Moreover, in line with cognition-in-action, it suggests that at least concentration and effort are conducive to expert action. Beyond this, Nicholls's research is in tension with the idea that at high levels of performance, nonskill-related distractions do not interfere with skills (an idea that researchers who perform the varied-focus experiments sometimes claim is supported by such experiments). To be sure, there are limitations to diary studies, as Nicholls points out. For example, as is common in longitudinal studies, diary studies typically have a high

[19] For studies that reach similar conclusions see also Nicholls et al. (2005) and Oudejans et al. (2011).

dropout rate, and some research suggests that diary methods inspire subjects to report only concrete and discrete events and ignore more complex problems (Folkman and Moskowitz 2004). Nonetheless, such studies fail to suggest that reducing monitoring and conscious control of one's actions is an effective strategy for an expert to deal with stress.

Nicholls's results are consistent with the findings of another sports psychologist Dave Collins (Collins et al. 2001), who, along with colleagues, measured kinematic aspects of elite weightlifters' performance during training and competition, and questioned these athletes about their conscious use of any movement change strategy in response to competitive pressure. Collins et al. examined movement variability in seven elite male athletes from the British Olympic weightlifting team, under both low-pressure situations (practice) and high-pressure ones (competition), and found that although the participants modified their movements as a result of competitive pressure—and claimed to do so consciously—such modifications did not diminish their overall performance. And such a view is further supported by Hill et al.'s (2010) study based on interviews with elite athletes wherein distractions, rather than self-focus, are seen as the main cause of choking (p. 227).[20]

Though I have been concerned with whether thinking about what you are doing as you are doing it interferes with expert-level skill, it is also worthwhile to point out that a study by Raôul Oudejans et al. (2011), suggests that high-pressure situations rarely induce explicit monitoring. In this study, seventy athletes, who compete at the national or international level, were asked to describe the thoughts that went through their minds in high-pressure situations, and in line with distraction theories of choking, high pressure, rather than leading to reinvestment, tended to lead to thoughts about such things as how poorly they are doing or on how they could have made a certain mistake. The study also asked the athletes to explain what they do to get back on track and, in line with Nicholls et al., they found that one common way in which these athletes would attempt to maintain performance was to revert to positive monitoring, such as focusing on their technique.

Beyond this, recent empirical evidence indicates that, irrespective of any changes in perceived performance pressure, skilled performers may deliberately monitor their movement to help them choose an appropriate course of action. For example, Nyberg (2015) found that elite freeskiers monitored their rotational activity during the inflight phase of a jump so as to ascertain "whether they will be able to perform the trick the way it was intended without adjustments or whether they will need to make adjustments during the flight phase." And research by Bernier et al. (2009) revealed that 60 percent of the elite swimmers they studied mentioned a heightened state of bodily awareness (e.g. a "tingling" sensation in their muscles) during optimal performance. (For further discussion see Toner, Montero, and Moran 2014; and for a theory that can account for such results see Sutton et al. 2011.)

---

[20] See also Ravn and Christensen (2014).

Of course, one may wonder whether athletes (or anyone, for that matter) have accurate insight into what goes on in their minds.[21] Even in the varied-focus experiments, it is difficult to know whether the participants in these studies are actually focusing on what they were supposed to be focusing on. Presumably, to be able to report correctly which side of their foot had just been in contact with the ball, subjects need some conscious awareness of their feet. And although we are not told how accurate the soccer players were at making such identifications, perhaps merely making the attempt to report this indicates that they were attending to their feet. The more qualitative work of Nicholls, Collins, and others, in contrast, depends on what seem to be less reliable post-performance reports. How can we tell that the rugby players or weightlifters were actually thinking about what they claim to have been thinking about? It seems that we can be less certain of this than of the occurrence of the relevant mental processes in the varied-focus experiments. Yet there is a tradeoff between reliability and ecological validity, and the work of Nicholls and Collins, while perhaps dependent on less reliable indicators of conscious thought in their participants, is more ecologically valid, because it looks at experts—veritable experts—in real-life settings, asking them to do nothing other than what they would normally do while playing.[22] In contrast, saying "stop" at the exact moment one finishes the follow-through of one's golf swing (Beilock et al. 2002, p. 10) is not something that expert golfers do in tournaments.[23]

What would seem to be correct is that although some thoughts could hinder performance, the expert engages in thoughts that help. "[W]inning the psychological battle," tennis champion Rafael Nadal tells us, "usually translates into you playing better than your opponent, because you're thinking more clearly" (Nadal and Carlin 2011, p. 57). And when you're thinking more clearly, you are thinking the right thoughts.

That experts think in action, but not about the wrong things, is precisely the conclusion of a study performed by Toner and Moran (2011). In this study, expert golfers were instructed to monitor their clubhead and report after each putt exactly where on

---

[21] Though I've mentioned this in the Preface, as people often object at this point that there is good evidence showing that we are sometimes unaware of what we are doing—such as the eye-tracking experiments that show that although athletes think that they are continually keeping their eye on the ball, they are not—it is worth mentioning again that the question of whether individuals have a good sense of what they are doing is distinct from the question of whether they have a good sense of what is going on in their minds. In fact, experiments that aim to show that we are sometimes mistaken about what we are doing assume that we have a sense of what we are thinking, for this is how the researchers detect a mismatch between what we think we are doing and what we are doing. What might show that we are mistaken about what is going on our minds? This is a difficult question to answer, however see Eric Schwitzgebel (2011) for some suggestions.

[22] Might their performance be affected by the fact that they knew that, after playing, they would need to record what was going on in their minds? It certainly might have been, however, although this would be relevant to the question of how much athletes think during games that don't require them to record their thoughts, I don't think it is relevant to the question of whether thinking interferes with performing. Even if the athletes end up thinking more than they normally would, if such thinking was beneficial, it tells against the principle of interference.

[23] For further criticisms of the ecological validity of such experiments, see Gucciardi and Dimmock (2008, p. 49) and Wilson, Chattington, Marple-Horvat, and Smith (2007, p. 454).

the putter face they thought they had struck the ball (and after every fifth putt they were reminded to maintain this focus). This interfered with performance. However, Toner and Moran (2011) also found that when holing balls while engaging in a think-out-loud protocol the golfers not only reported numerous skill-focused thoughts but also that they performed as well as when they simply holed balls without thinking aloud. The researchers conclude, not that experts should putt without thought, but "that golfers may need to choose their swing thoughts very carefully because focusing on certain elements of movement, such as the impact spot, could lead to an impairment in performance proficiency" (p. 680). This sounds quite reasonable, yet I wonder if experts actually do need to be careful about this. It might be, as the think-out-loud protocol analysis indicates, that the thoughts they have in the normal course of play don't interfere with performance. And, perhaps, if thoughts about impact spot are part of a golfer's normal routine, even these would not interfere with performance.

## Individual Cases Illustrating Cognition-in-action

Although the just-do-it principle, specifically the principle of interference, proclaims that thinking interferes with doing, diary studies, as we saw, suggest that increased attention and effort can be beneficial when anxiety is present. It therefore seems reasonable that in some situations, rather than causing choking or suboptimal performance, thinking actually helps experts to cope with anxiety, and thereby to prevent the poor performance that high anxiety may cause. Moreover, we also saw that protocol studies indicate that experts *do* think in action. Experts sometimes suggest this as well:

### Classical guitarist Tobias Schaeffer

According to the classical guitarist and mathematician Tobias Schaeffer (pers. comm.), he learned how to avoid choking during performances by thinking more not less about his actions. When he was younger, despite the most assiduous practice, he used to fumble and sometimes blank out during performances. It seemed to him that although he would rehearse to the point where he could play a piece more or less automatically, during performance he would end up thinking about what he was doing, which, he felt, precipitated disaster. So far, this sounds like support for just-do-it, but there is more. He consulted his instructor, the classical guitarist Andreas Koch, who advised him to start thinking about his movements during practice. At first, as Schaeffer explained it, this slowed down his playing, but eventually he was able to direct his attention to his movements and think about what he was doing while playing in tempo. And by maintaining this sort of attention during performance, he said, not only was he able to avoid the dreaded performance choke, but his playing improved.

Schaeffer, according to his own account, is thinking in action. Moreover, his account provides a reason why such thinking is important: if one's actions become so automatized that the conscious mind no longer knows how to do them, any glitch which brings consciousness to the fore could result in blanking out, which in a guitar performance means suddenly forgetting how to proceed and thus needing to improvise until one gets back on track.[24] One way to avoid this problem is to prevent the mind from entering the picture. However, another way—if Schaeffer is correct—is to follow the advice Koch gave him: keep the movements in the conscious mind. [25]

*Tennis player and coach Timothy Gallwey*

Schaeffer's account of focusing on the details of his movements is not so different from Timothy Gallwey's (1974) account of his best tennis-playing. In Chapter 1, I quoted Gallwey as a popularizer of the just-do-it principle, and to be sure, his "all time bestseller" *The Inner Game of Tennis* pays homage, particularly in the opening pages, to the idea that you are playing at your best when you are "playing out of your mind" (p. 7). Nevertheless, in the book Gallwey also emphasizes the importance of some very specific skill-focused monitoring in tennis. He advises that during practice you should "get to know the feel of every inch of your stroke, every muscle in your body" (p. 90). This will enable you, he says, to focus on a few essentials during a tournament. He explains that after practicing in slow motion so as to increase awareness:

when you increase your stroke speed to normal and begin hitting, you may be particularly aware of certain muscles. For instance, when I hit my backhands, I am aware that my shoulder muscle rather than my forearm is pulling my arm through...Similarly, on my forehand I am particularly aware of my triceps when my racket is below the ball. (p. 90)

According to Wulf, "if experienced individuals direct their attention to the details of skill execution, the result is almost certainly a decrement in performance" (2007, p. 23). However, if Gallwey's description of how he plays doesn't count as directing one's attention to the details of skill execution, I don't know what does.[26]

*Cellist Inbal Segev*

The cellist Inbal Segev also sees the importance of keeping one's actions in the conscious mind. As she explained to me:

My teacher [Bernard Greenhouse], who was a student of [Pablo] Casals would say, "don't let the music lead you; you need to direct it." [In other words,] don't just

---

[24] For an illustration of blanking out in a dance performance see Montero (2015).

[25] Arnold Steinhart, a violist with the Guarneri Quartet, who, as I suggested in the Introduction, advocates a balance between the intuitive and the deliberate and thoughtful during performance, talks about the importance of slow-motion practice that allows extended time for thought as well (1998). And Steinhardt's teacher, Ivan Galamian, also encouraged Steinhardt to focus on the details of his movements. Indeed, as Steinhart explains, Galamian wanted him at first to "concentrate on the finger motions of the bow hand by doing them without the violin" (1998, p. 29). During this time, his roommates, he said, wondered how he was going to become a musician since he never made a sound.

[26] Morgan and Pollock (1977) also report that world-class marathon runners almost invariably claim that they are acutely aware of their physiological condition during a race.

play as if the music will talk by itself; don't just go on automatic pilot; you have to be alert and thinking."

And when I asked her how she keeps focused, she said, "I keep hearing [the music] playing in my head and imagining how I want it."

The idea that you should get lost in the music and simply let it lead you is mistaken, she thinks, because it proscribes thought. Dreyfus and Dreyfus (2004) tell us that the expert (as opposed to someone who is merely proficient) no longer needs "to think about what to do" (p. 253). However, Schaeffer and Segev indicate that skillful playing involves extensive conscious thought about what to do and when to do it.

### Swimming coach Alan Varner

According to the swimming coach Alan Varner (pers. comm.), he trains his swimmers to not worry about the mistakes they have already made, but this doesn't mean that they should swim with their minds blank. Rather, each swimmer, he said, needs to think about what is going to produce the best outcome. Varner is a former competitive swimmer himself, and he said that when he was swimming competitively, he would focus primarily on his hips and how they were driving his stroke. Of course, a myriad of other aspects of movement needed to occur more or less automatically for him to be able to maintain this focus. But, as he sees it, that focus was an essential element of his success at his best meets.

### Tennis coach David Breitkopf

This delicate balance between consciously controlling certain aspects of movement while allowing certain aspects of movement to occur automatically is also emphasized by professional tennis coach (and former professional tennis player) David Breitkopf:

I encourage [my students] ... to have a mantra-like phrase that they can use over and over again to reach their calm, optimum level. This mantra isn't just a phrase that calms you, but also is integral to the stroke itself, and allows every other part of the stroke to work properly. Just as an example—"get the racket below the ball." This implies much more than the phrase itself. It means I'm watching the ball, it also means that I will likely sweep the racket head up to the ball and lift the ball above the net. But it also implies because of the way I grip the racket that I will put topspin on the ball to keep it in play. I can get all this in because I said this one phrase, and the rest follows. So in point of fact, I'm thinking, but I'm thinking efficiently (pers. comm.).[27]

Contrary to the Dreyfus's view of mastery, which illustrates just-do-it, Breitkopf's view illustrates cognition-in-action.

Given, then, that 1) the studies purporting to show that high anxiety is detrimental to expert performance because it increases skill-focused attention are open to alternative explanations and 2) there are a number of qualitative studies supporting the idea

---

[27] The importance of a mantra-like phrase, or a cue word for athletes, comes up again in Chapter 7. See also Toner, Montero, and Moran (2014) and Sutton, McIlwain, Christensen, and Geeves (2011).

that attention to movement (and sometimes even the details of movement) occurs at an expert level, and 3) there are at least a few anecdotes countering sweeping claims to the effect that all athletes attest to the fact that thinking interferes with performing at their best, I think we should reject the principle of interference. Rather than impeding performance, experts seem to improve by focusing on what they are doing.

## Steve Blass Disease, Steve Sax Syndrome

Though not specifically concerned with the relation between anxiety and choking, the philosopher Hubert Dreyfus supports the idea that at an expert level of performance, attention to and conscious control over one's actions degrades performance in part by citing the fate of New York Yankees' former second baseman, Chuck Knoblauch. As I mentioned in Chapter 2, Knoblauch, a Gold Glove-winning player suddenly, at what would seem to be the height of his career, developed severe throwing problems, sometimes being barely able to toss the ball, and at other times throwing it outrageously far out of play of bounds. What happened to Knoblauch? Dreyfus's (2007a) analysis of the situation is that Knoblauch was thinking too much, that he "couldn't resist stepping back and being mindful" (p. 354). Expert skill, according to Dreyfus, is "nonminded," hence Knoblauch's trouble was that he tried to think about what should be happening automatically (p. 354). The journalist Malcolm Gladwell presents a similar analysis. Akin to how the 2005 WTA Tour champion tennis player Jana Novotna who "faltered at Wimbledon . . . because she began thinking about her shots again," Gladwell (2000) tells us, Knoblauch, "under the stress of playing in front of forty thousand fans at Yankee Stadium, [found] himself reverting to explicit mode" (p. 85).

John McDowell, who challenges Dreyfus's view that when Knoblauch played at his best his actions were not conceptualized, agrees. On McDowell's view, even though in throwing efficiently to first base Knoblauch was "realizing a concept of a thing to do," he lost his ability because he "started thinking about 'the mechanics,' about how throwing efficiently to first base is done" (2007b, p. 367). More generally, McDowell (2007b) tells us, "this kind of loss of skill comes about when the agent's means-end rationality tries, so to speak, to take over control of the details of her bodily movements, and it cannot do as good a job at that as the skill itself used to do" (2007b, pp. 367–8).

Although Dreyfus and McDowell agree that Knoblauch's loss of ability was due to his attempt to explicitly analyze or think about his movements, there is little indication that Knoblauch, or any of the other major league players who have suffered similar fates—"Steve Sax Syndrome" for fielders, "Steve Blass Disease" for pitchers—believe that the cause of their throwing problems is related to their thinking about what they are doing. Rather, they tend to say that they don't know why they can't throw and, indeed, Knoblauch has criticized the media's claim to understand the cause of his condition.[28] Furthermore, the origin of Steve Blass Disease is very much an open question within the scientific community, and the few theories that do attempt to account for it do not attribute it to misplaced thinking. For example, Adler (2007) speculates that some cases of the disease could involve a focal dystonia, a neurological condition involving involuntary muscle contractions. And David Grand and Alan Goldberg (2011) argue that it is a form of post-traumatic stress and players who suffer from it are holding earlier traumas in their bodies, and they treat it by, in part, desensitizing them to the trauma.

Moreover, for some at least, the condition does not seem to have been brought about because of anxiety. Steve Blass, in his autobiography (Blass and Sherman, 2012), talks about being confident at first that the problem would work itself out:

It was not bad in the beginning by any stretch, and my struggles were more of a gradual decline. I had had slumps before and I didn't have any particular anxiety early in the season…so I thought, OK. It's not working now, but we'll get it straightened out. We'll be fine. Just keep throwing and it'll click. It'll take care of itself. (p. 10)

So his case, at least does not seem to fit Beilock's and others' models, according to which pressure causes skill-focused attention, which in turn impedes performance.

Nonetheless, things did get worse, and Blass found himself pondering what could be wrong:

There were a lot of nights when I would just come home and sit in the backyard wondering why all this stuff was going on and what was happening. I'd try to find out if in quiet times I could sort it all out, but I just couldn't. (pp. 12–13)

It would seem that if overthinking were part of the cause of his problems, this would have occurred to him, but although in his book he mentions numerous other theories about what was causing what he called his "control problem," never once does he mention that it might have been due to thinking too much about what he was doing. As he says:

I tried every possible remedy for my control problems. There were times when we had two projectors showing me pitching good and showing me pitching bad side-by-side, looking for clues on how to improve my mechanics. (p. 19)

He took part in a visualization process, where he visualized the ball going out of his hand to where he wanted it to go (p. 19); he tried transcendental meditation, which was popular at the time; and—after he received a letter from a hunter who claimed that the only time his aim was off was when his underwear was too tight—he even tried wearing looser underwear. All of these possibilities occurred to him, but nowhere in the book does he say that he tried to think less about what he was doing. It seems, however, that if over-thinking precipitated his plight, it would have at least crossed his mind to try to stop being so mindful.

[28] See Associated Press (2004). See also Montero (2010), p. 112.

What was he aware of during these games when everything would fall apart? Apparently, many things:

Before my control problem I had the ability to just concentrate on the immediate task at hand, which is a wonderful thing for an athlete. I could block out family, world hunger, or anything that was going on, because of that focus. That focus all went away and everything was occurring in my mind. I was like an antenna. (p. 23)

Although throughout the book he emphasizes that the disease named after him is inexplicable, this account, if anything, sounds like the problem has to do with not thinking too much about his actions, but rather with not being able to think enough about them.

His story does have a somewhat happy ending since long after his career ended, he did find a cure, which he briefly describes as involving stepping out of the certain type of pattern he had fallen into. Ultimately, though he doesn't go into detail about this, Blass claims that he came to see his problem specifically as "not a psychological problem" (p. 213).

## Do Similar Considerations Apply to Giving a Talk?

Flubbing a golf shot that one could normally perform well is a different kind of mistake from *blanking out*, or not remembering something one would normally know well. And one might wonder whether, even if conscious self-monitoring isn't implicated in the former, consciously trying to remember what to say is implicated in the latter.

According to Dreyfus (2013), "in total absorption, sometimes called flow, one is so fully absorbed in one's activity that one is not even marginally thinking about what one is doing" (p. 28). He cites Merleau-Ponty in support:

The orator does not think before speaking, nor even while speaking; his speech is his thought. The end of the speech or text will be the lifting of a spell. It is at this stage that thoughts on the speech or text will be able to arise. (Dreyfus 2013, p. 28, quoting from Merleau-Ponty 1945, p. 209)

This might seem to apply to dancing as well: it might seem that during a performance a dancer must remain under the spell of what her body has learned so well that the choreography is no longer in her mind but that her movements are her thoughts. Is this the right picture?

I think it suits neither the dancer nor the orator. Perhaps Merleau-Ponty was an exception, however, many excellent orators consciously review their talks beforehand, and at least claim to think productively while speaking. Saul Kripke is one example; he wouldn't write down what he planned to say, but he would think hard and long about it beforehand, telling me that once before a talk someone asked what his opinion was about a certain logic puzzle: "I had to tell him, 'I can't think about that now: I'm thinking about my talk'" (pers. comm.).

Thinking during a talk can, of course, take many different forms, depending on the task: if presenting a work-in-progress, one might actually be trying to figure out ideas as one is speaking; if presenting a well-rehearsed speech or fully worked-out ideas, one might primarily think about delivery and the audience's reactions. But even in this latter case, it seems useful to keep the content present in the conscious mind, and to facilitate this, one may consciously review the speech ahead of time. And dancers often review choreography beforehand—no matter how well they know it—and keep it present in their minds as they dance. Correlatively, to be 'under a spell' is dangerous precisely because it leaves one open to blanking out. If one is not even marginally thinking about what one is saying, then if all of a sudden one switched to consciously guiding one's words, the words may not be there to find. Heidegger (1988) tells us that when a lecturer enters a familiar classroom, the lecturer experiences neither the doorknob nor the seats and that such features of the room for the lecturer are "completely unobtrusive and unthought" (p. 163). All of such things would indeed seem to be beneficially unthought so as to leave plenty of mental space to think about the lecture.

Heidegger, Merleau-Ponty, and Dreyfus, and indeed most researchers in sports psychology all agree that thinking occurs when one runs into problems. John Dewey (1910/1997) puts it like this:

Thinking begins in what may fairly enough be called a forked-road situation, a situation which is ambiguous, which presents a dilemma, which proposes alternatives [yet]...as long as our activity glides smoothly along from one thing to another, or as long as we permit our imagination to entertain fancies at pleasure, there is no call for reflection. (p. 11)

However, experts are continually in forked-road situations: although their activities glide smoothly from the observer's perspective, they are always considering, trying, and reflecting on how to surpass what they have done in the past. Heidegger (1927/1988) says that "in our natural comportment towards things we never think a single thing, and whenever we seize upon it expressly for itself we are taking it out of a contexture to which it belongs in its real content" (p. 162). This may be generally true, but expertise is not natural; it involves pushing beyond what is natural.[29]

As I see it, there are also cases of ordinary action in which thinking rather than just doing would be beneficial. Merleau-Ponty (1945/2005) emphasizes that in our everyday actions we proceed unreflectively and that "the conventions of our milieu...immediately elicit from us the words, the attitudes, the tone suited to them" (p. 126). Unfortunately, however, what are elicited unreflectively are sometimes stereotypical reactions (for example, complementing a girl's looks and a boy's brains) built on

---

[29] See also Strawson (2003) who argues that although most cases of practical deliberation "simply happens" and that "the play of pros and cons is automatic," he does admit that "if the issue is a difficult one, then there may well be a distinct, and distinctive phenomenon of setting one's mind at the problem" (pp. 243, 231). And experts, on my view, revel in the difficult.

implicit biases that perhaps can, at times, be avoided only by explicitly thinking about what you are doing or saying.[30]

## "Don't Think" as a Last Resort?

The conclusion we should draw from the considerations I have canvassed is that even given the just-do-it results of the varied-thought experiments, the idea that, as Beilock put it, "skill-focused attention... hinders performance at higher levels of skill," lacks the type of support that would make it reasonable to accept what some see as its corollary: that experts generally ought not to engage in skill-focused attention during skill execution. What this means for the explicit-monitoring theory is that regardless of whether anxiety causes increased focus on, monitoring of, and conscious control over one's movements, there is room to question whether such mental processes are causally relevant to choking. We should therefore rethink the view that preventing experts from engaging in such mental processes can prevent a choke.

Could it be, however, that for those with overwhelming performance anxiety, the only way to cope is to revert to an automatic mode of performing? Perhaps. But let me indicate some reasons for why, unless all else fails, one should not attempt to perform automatically. One, quite simply, is that if thought is important for high-calibre performance, then an entirely automatic performance is one in which the performer is not thinking about what need be thought about and thus an even better performance might result from a more thoughtful approach. Moreover, as we saw, Nicholls and colleagues (2006) qualitative research suggests that one way to mitigate anxiety is not to act automatically, but actually to redouble focus and attention.

Another problem is that it is at least not clear that one can deliberately achieve a state of not thinking, and thus, eliciting automaticity is not as controllable as eliciting

---

[30] This is not to say that simply thinking about stereotypes helps avoid the detrimental effects of stereotyped discourse, for as Steele and Aronson's (1995) study on racial stereotype threat indicates, it seems that merely mentioning a stereotype can hinder performance on standardized tests (perhaps because the subjects will have this stereotype in mind while taking the tests.) However, I take it that the situation I am describing is relevantly different primarily because the person who might make stereotypical remarks about girls and boys is not the one who is overtly negatively affected by the remarks; rather, it is the little girls who are always complimented on their looks (or at least it seems reasonable to think that at least in our culture this could have a negative effect). Another difference is that what I think is useful to keep in mind is not just the stereotype, or not even just the idea that such a view is mistaken, but the idea that making remarks in accord with the stereotype should be avoided, the idea that you should not complement a girl's looks. (It might be interesting to test how girls' performance on standardized tests is affected by priming the idea that although there is a stereotype that they do worse than boys, there is no truth to it and that in taking the test they should overcome this and prove that they are just as (if not more) capable than boys.) Still another difference is that presumably making a casual remark to a girl takes far fewer cognitive resources than taking a standardized test and so diverting cognitive resources to the thought that one needs to say *this* rather than *that* would presumably not have a negative effect on one's ability to make such claims whereas diverting cognitive resources even to thoughts about avoiding stereotypes might have a detrimental effect on the highly demanding task of taking a test. For other ways in which focusing on and thinking about one's ordinary actions as one is performing them can improve those actions, see Shusterman (2008, 2012).

thoughtful, deliberate actions, a problem illustrated by the paradoxical command, "be spontaneous." I can deliberately focus my mind on various aspects of my performance, but it seems that achieving the state of letting things happen, a state of acting automatically, is something one can no more do than making oneself fall asleep. Indeed, Dreyfus and Kelly (2011b) point out as much when they argue that the type of relation the expert has to her actions is analogous to how we stand in relation to the process of falling asleep—more like something that happens to us rather than something we do.[31] So even if playing automatically is one way to avoid choking, if playing with increased attention and effort is another equally effective means, it might be better to go with what one can control.

Finally, when acting automatically, it seems that at any point the mind might jump back into the picture, and thus, as Tobias's example illustrates, it might be best to have the mind present all along. The high diver standing motionless on the board for a moment before she jumps, goes over the dive in her head, painting her body with thought, so that the conscious mind will also be present in the dive.[32]

Of course, it might be that when things do start to go wrong, extra attention is called forth. As such, poor performance might be associated with attention. This might lead one to think of the attention as causally detrimental—yet it may be that the choke causes the heightened attention, rather than such attention causing the choke. Again, one cannot attend to every detail, and thus some aspects of the performance will need to be automatic. But if Tobias's and Gallwey's examples are correct, the level of focus is at times much lower than promoters of the just-do-it principle have thought.

However, there is another danger a performer needs to prepare for and that is distraction. Sometimes, like the bus driver who only misses a stop when something breaks his train of thought, distractions occur: someone cuts you off when you are driving a bus, or someone is talking in the front row as you are presenting a paper. And it might be that the only way to cope with such distractions is to revert to automatic mode. If you know your talk so well that you can say it in your sleep, you can proceed while distracted by a loud conversation; if you know your route like the back of your hand, you will pull up to the stop whether you are thinking about it or not. So it seems that the expert ultimately wants to be capable of performing automatically, without needing to perform automatically. It's not that problems occur when the expert reverts to "explicit mode" as Malcolm Gladwell had put it. However, when in explicit mode, experts should retain the ability to revert to implicit mode, if necessary.

[31] To be sure, we can try to fall asleep: we can try to calm the mind in various ways, lie still, close our eyes, and so forth. But in this sense I think that Dreyfus and Kelly would also say that the expert can try to be spontaneous, for just as there are various activities that facilitate sleep, there may be various activities that facilitate spontaneity.
[32] For a popular overview of the practice of visualization that many athletes engage in see <http://www.nytimes.com/2014/02/23/sports/olympics/olympians-use-imagery-as-mental-training.html?_r=0> Accessed March 30, 2014.

Moreover, an expert who is forced to revert to implicit or automatic mode should retain the ability to switch back to a more conscious form of engagement. And bringing in the conscious mind, as I have been emphasizing, need not interfere with doing your best. As Daniel Kahneman (2011) points out—and as those who have read to their children well know—it is possible to read out loud without paying any attention to what you are saying. You can do it automatically, with your mind entirely on other matters so that pages fly by while you have no idea of what you have uttered. However, this ability in no way prevents you from being able to read with attention. And for philosophers who have delivered papers at conferences, you know that this is what you want to do; not only do you want to say the words, but you also want to understand what you are saying.

Therefore, rather than advising those who are, say, preparing for an interview or a talk not to think very much during the process and "just let it roll," lest the thinking causes them to blank out, a better piece of advice is to be like the high diver on the board prior to her plunge: before the event, they should consciously review what they have to say—no matter how well they know it—so that what could be done automatically is also imprinted in the conscious mind, and once conscious, thinking about it will not interfere with doing their best. Maybe Rick Perry would have done better in that presidential primary debate if he had followed this advice.

# 5

# Thinking Fast

The thought of the war, introduced the thought of delivering up the king to his enemies; the thought of that, brought in the thought of the delivering up of Christ; and that again the thought of the thirty pence, which was the price of that treason.... and all this in a moment of time; for thought is quick.

Thomas Hobbes (1588–1679)
*Leviathan*

It is nearing 7 a.m. when a call comes through to the triage desk of a large hospital in the New York City metropolitan area: a pregnant woman with multiple abdominal gunshot wounds is due to arrive in about three minutes. Activating a trauma alert, the head nurse on duty, Denise, requests intubation, scans, anesthesia, surgery, and, due to the special circumstances, sonography and the labor and delivery team. The emergency medical service team slides the gurney into the hospital and the trauma center staff starts in with Denise coordinating and overseeing the action. How is it possible to think about so much so quickly?

## Is There Time to Think in an Emergency?

Denise (not her real name) is a soft-spoken woman in her upper fifties who, when she recounted this story, had been a nurse for more years than she was willing to reveal. I met her because she had recently begun the doctoral program in nursing science at the Graduate Center of the City University of New York, and was enrolled in my philosophy of science course for nursing students. In this course, amid discussions of Karl Popper's criterion for demarcating science from nonscience and Thomas Kuhn's theory of scientific revolutions, I would hear stories from her and other students about nursing: about newborns in the critical care unit; about patients who would, against all orders, remove their EKG monitors to use the toilet; about the travails of discussing the benefits of blood transfusions with desperately ill Jehovah's Witnesses. These stories often reminded me of how little urgency exists in philosophy—one doesn't feel much time pressure to solve the problem of free will when it has been open for the past two thousand years—as well as how little tragedy: the nurses in my classes learned fairly quickly that they should bring tissues for me. However, more to the point of questioning the just-do-it principle, these stories also sometimes illustrated how much thought goes into even the quickest decisions.

When that call came in, Denise had to act instantly. Indeed, she told the class that much of what she does happens automatically. "After working in trauma for a few years, I could close my eyes; I didn't need to think about the steps," she told me, explaining that fast responses are essential in an emergency room: "this is why you do not have newly trained nurses in trauma." So far, we seem to have a defense of the just-do-it principle, specifically of the idea that expert action occurs automatically and without reflection. But although Denise didn't need to think about the steps—and what she meant in this case by "the steps," she later elaborated, was the series of requests she put out in response to the initial call—she could think about them if she had to, for she sometimes talks through her actions as she's performing them with nurses in training. Moreover, she typically thinks about other aspects of her actions. For example, as a head nurse she has to constantly monitor her staff: "you have to be aware of what everyone is doing; where other people are; looking at breaks, people's lunch breaks, additional bathroom breaks, smoke breaks," she explained. And she has her mind on the time. This is in part because in trauma, obviously, every second counts, for brain damage can occur within two minutes if someone has stopped breathing. Yet more surprisingly—or at least it was for me, though I did come to accept it as par for the course after hearing it time and time again from the nurses in my classes—the other seconds that seemed to matter were those on the time clock. That "it was nearing 7 a.m. and the staff was about to change shift" was the first thing she told the class when recounting this story. This was important, she said, since she needed to figure out how to maneuver that transition without interfering with treatment. Thus, even in an emergency situation, which seemed to leave so little time for thought, she was thinking, thinking about the complex social orchestration she would need to accomplish to get her job done. Surely what she was able to do automatically was amazing, but her ability to think in action was as well, and it seems that this, in line with the cognition-in-action principle, was essential for her to perform at her best.

The nurse researcher Patricia Benner's extensive investigations into the practice of nursing support this view (Benner 1982, 1984, 2004; Benner et al. 1992, 1996). Benner's studies, which are based on interviews of hundreds of nurses, are often seen as illustrating not cognition-in-action, but rather Dreyfus's account of expertise, according to which expert action is intuitive, in the sense of immediate action that, though successful, is not done for a reason and accordingly cannot be justified (save for by employing a retrospective rationalization, that is, save for providing a reason that would seem to justify your action but was not actually guiding your behavior in action). However, although Benner speaks of expert nurses' actions being "intuitive," the intuition that expert nurses rely on, according to Benner, is not the type of "arational," unjustifiable immediate insight that Dreyfus thinks is characteristic of expertise.[1] Rather, on

---

[1] Gobet (2012) points out that the term "arational" is an "etymological monster," as it combines a root from Greek and from Latin (p. 238). However, as precedent has been set, I shall stick with "arational."

Benner's view, nurses must always possess the ability to justify their actions. Pointing out how her account of nursing expertise does not quite fit the Dreyfus model, Benner (2004) explains the rational component of nursing practice as follows:

... whereas [according to Dreyfus] in some skill situations, such as playing chess or driving a car, experts would not need to articulate their perspectives before taking action ... [i]n emergencies, when there is no physician available, the nurse must be able to articulate clearly the reason for using a standing order or protocol or going beyond the usual boundaries of usual nursing practice. This is expected and defensible when it is critical for the patient's survival. (p. 190)

Moreover, she emphasizes that because "practice in the individual case is underdetermined ... the practitioner must use good clinical reasoning to intelligently select and use the relevant science," which, of course, sounds quite the opposite to "just doing it," or going with "gut instinct" (Benner 2004, p. 189). Of course, this is not to say that nurses never rely on instinct or intuition. Jane Cioffi (2000), for example, interviewed nurses and found that they claim to rely on "gut feelings," and sometimes "recognize deterioration or patients' problems prior to explicit changes in vital signs" (p. 31). However, are such gut feelings actually reliable? Or does one merely tend to remember the times when they are accurate, and forget the times when they mislead?

An affirmative answer to the latter question can be found in Ellis (1997). While Cioffi's research was based on nurses' memories of their past practice, Ellis interviewed nurses immediately after their shifts, and found that nurses rarely report acting on gut feelings or being guided by intuition; rather, both more- and less-experienced nurses report engaging in step-by-step reasoning. So it could be, as Ericsson, Whyte, and Ward (2007) suggest, the time lag in Cioffi's studies allows for a somewhat unfaithful "recollection of old memories" (p. 63). Nevertheless, there still may be some room for intuition in the sense of, say, occasionally entering a patient's room and knowing something is wrong, but not being able to pinpoint exactly what it is. I think that this phenomenon does exist, but it is not a magic bullet that leads the expert straight to the truth. "[Gut intuitions] shouldn't be ignored," one nurse in my class said, "but you can't always trust them, so you need to check if they are right." Beyond this, it may be that at the highest level of mastery, not only does one sense that something is wrong, but one can identify it as well. Expert nurses have a vast amount of experience seeing patients through both thick and thin, and can sometimes recognize when a patient does not look right. But they have not been trained to diagnose illness, or at least not in the way doctors have, so it is unsurprising that there may be situations in which they have a sense that something is wrong without being able to explain what it is (though even in such cases, it may be that something could be said: "his eyes didn't look right" or "her color was off"). Moreover, because they may spend more time with patients, this instinct might occasionally do more good than a doctor's judgment (and my nurses love to provide illustrations of this). However, the ideal diagnostician might be one who spends time with patients like a nurse but has the training of a doctor.

Benner also realizes the importance of nurses having a store of experience on which to draw. But the way she sees this experience guiding the nurse is also not quite the way Dreyfus sees background experience guiding the expert. On Dreyfus's view, once one has the experience, the mind need not guide one's behavior; as he sees it, thought and deliberation will step in if something goes wrong, yet if all is well, the mind of the expert lies dormant. On Benner's account, in contrast with Dreyfus and in line with cognition-in-action, acting on the basis of past experience leaves room for thought.

Consider the comments that Benner presents of a nurse in action:

I looked at his heart rate and I said: "O.K. he is bradying down. Someone want to give me some atropine?"...I was just barking out [what had to be done]. I can't even tell you the sequence....I needed to anticipate what was going to happen and I could do this because I had been through this a week before with this guy and knew what we had done. (Benner 2004, p. 196)

Here, actions, though based on past experience, do not merely occur out of habit; rather, there seems to be some awareness that the past experience would justify her present actions, for nurses do need to be able to justify their actions. Now it could be that the justification could have gone further, for when I discuss this example with my nursing students, I hear such things as, "the nurse had better be able to tell you the sequence," and "simply knowing that this had happened a week before wasn't sufficient for action." Was the situation actually similar? If so, in which ways was it similar? What has occurred to this patient during the intervening week? Answers to such questions, a number of my students have told me, would have to be part of the thinking process. Nonetheless, even with the description as it is, we do not have an example of simply "going with your gut," nor do we have an example of a nurse "just being drawn to act" without any understanding of why she is doing what she is doing. Experience guides her action, but it was justifiable: the action was done again because it had been done a week before and had worked. (And this is a justification, even if it is not a full justification.)

On my view of expert action, it is, of course, not only nursing excellence that employs thoughtful action; save for activities in which excellence is defined in terms of the mind being absent, they all do. For example, the physician Eddie Pont explained to me what he sees as the dangers of relying on gut instinct in medicine. I quote him at length:

As a pediatrician, I encounter this reflex [go with your gut] in medicine from time to time....Recently, another doctor in my medical group prescribed a medicine which I don't believe my patient needed. When I questioned her by email...[she claimed]—among other things—that her "gut" had saved her countless times from patient care misadventures. I found myself secretly wondering how many times that same gut, by circumventing a more reasoned consideration of her patient's condition, had gotten her into trouble.

In medicine, perhaps this reaction is somewhat understandable. We will never fully comprehend the human body in all its humbling complexity—practically speaking, it's impossible for a physician to master even the modicum of understanding we currently have. It all makes for an inherently insecure profession. So an almost magical belief in one's "gut" is perhaps a necessary talisman, a tonic to keep us from fretting constantly as to whether that headache really was in fact a brain tumor.

However, when I was in training, one of the finest compliments we could receive from our teachers was that we were "astute." The dictionary definition aside, we always felt it meant that, when faced with a challenging patient, rather than giving up or panicking, we put on our thinking caps, combined that with keen observation, and reasoned our way to a better understanding of the patient's problem. The compliment was so precious that I think I remember every time it was given to me. (pers. corres.)

In highly uncertain situations, one might try to assure oneself that one's decision was guided by "expert intuitions," and doing so may be reasonable, since without it, on Pont's view, one might worry oneself into a frenzy. However, the assurance might simply be empty.

## Social Coordination

I found an intriguing similarity between Denise's account of how, when she receives a call from the emergency medical technician, she focuses on coordinating the emergency room team, and rock and blues bass player Alex Craven's account of how, during a show, he keeps track of the audience and the other band members. Like Denise, he also started his explanation with a nod to automaticity: "I don't think," he said, "not in words, but I'm thinking in music all the time; it's making, making, making" (pers. comm.). But then he also explained that when he's in the groove, he has a pulse on the audience and is constantly reading the other members of the trio, so that he is ready "to give them what they need and take from them what's offered." Playing is, of course, not an emergency and, much like philosophy, no one's life will be endangered if you pause for a few minutes to consider the best course of action. But rather unlike philosophy, there are penalties for delays. To be sure, there is some expectation in philosophy that articles and books will make it to editors near their due dates; yet few editors are shocked when "near their due date" extends for years past the due date (and I thank Oxford University Press here, for its patience). However, putting one's instrument down during a performance in the middle of the piece in order to stop and think, whether playing with others or alone, would lead a musician to serious embarrassment, perhaps being fired, and disappointing or at least mystifying the audience. So there is pressure to keep things moving. Accordingly, as in the emergency room or on the tennis course, when thought occurs, it has to occur in the process of performing an action.[2] And such thought needs to be fast. Of course, in line with golfer Dave Hill's quip that golf is like sex, neither Denise nor Alex were focused on the mechanics of their actions; rather, they were thinking about social coordination. Denise was focused on

[2] Again, as the nurse practitioner Steven Baumann has pointed out to me, it is significant that nursing, as opposed to the other cases, involves true life or death situations.

coordinating everything from the nurses' shift change to grumpy doctors. Alex was concerned with the audience's mood and the other players' needs. The psychologists Joshua Ackerman and John Bargh (2010), however, tell us that "social coordination is highly automatized," and that effective and skillful engagement in group activities "requires a relatively high degree of automaticity from all of the interaction partners" (pp. 352–3). But although at a certain level, many interactions did occur automatically for both Alex and Denise, they put conscious effort into making this coordination occur at an optimal level. In our everyday social interactions, being good enough rather than optimal is often the goal, and so there is no need to effortfully employ conscious cognition; rather, the aim is automaticity so that one can focus on more important things. However, for Denise and Alex, there is nothing more important.

## Time Out

It is not surprising that in the field of medicine, where so much depends on one's actions, there is an ongoing discussion about what practices lead to the best outcomes. And in 2003 the Joint Commission approved the *Universal Protocol for Preventing Wrong Site, Wrong Procedure and Wrong Person Surgery*, otherwise known as "time out," which is a set of procedures that are aimed at getting doctors to relinquish their "automatic mode" of action and think before any surgery occurs in order to avoid errors such as amputating the wrong foot or performing an operation on the wrong patient.[3] The protocol, among other things, requires the surgeon to mark on the patient's skin where the incision is to occur, to certify that the correct patient is on the operating table, and to take a moment to have the entire surgical team agree on the procedure. In trauma, where time is of the essence and when it is obvious where the site of injury is, marking is not required, yet the team will still take a moment—a time out—to make sure everyone is in agreement about what is to occur. Thus, according to the Joint Commission, even in high time-pressure situations, all things considered, thinking is beneficial. The advantage one gains in speed when guided by the scalpel rather than the brain is not worth the risks.[4]

According to the psychologist Fernand Gobet, however, "one of the hallmarks of expertise is the speed and ease with which experts can recognize the key features of a situation, a phenomenon often called 'intuition.'" And to illustrate, he tells us that "a radiologist can diagnose a disease nearly instantaneously, and a chess grandmaster can literally 'see' the good move straight away," adding that "with routine problems, the decision will be correct most of the time" (Gobet and Chassy, 2009, pp. 151–2). I agree that experts often can do this. But the question is: should they do this, and when things matter do they do this? And it seems to me that the answer to this question

---

[3] See the Joint Commission (2014).

[4] Dr. Steven L. Lee (2010) reports that "the extended STO [surgical time out] before anesthesia induction improved communication among the surgical team members and did not disrupt work flow" (p. 19).

is "no," since although with routine problems, a nearly instantaneous diagnosis may very well be correct most of the time, "most of the time" is often not good enough. I'll return to chess in Chapter 11 where we'll see that Gobet's view is in many ways in line with cognition-in-action. Regarding radiology, it seems that deliberately slowing down the thinking process appears beneficial. The physician Jerome Groopman (2007) illustrates this with an account of the systematic manner in which the radiologist Dennis Orwig avoids making errors: it's not by near instantaneous intuition, but rather by "slowing his perception and analysis" (p. 182). When he proceeds in this way, Orwig says:

> My brain is forced to work in a...stepwise way. It is easier—certainly quicker—to simply look at the pneumonia in the right lower lobe of the lung...and not take the time to detail all of the other information. But this protects me...I am literally reading hundreds of x-rays, day after day, on different patients...I have to keep reminding myself to be systematic. The more experience you have, the more seasoned you are, the greater the temptation to rely on gestalt. (p. 185)

However, those who promote the just-do-it principle often claim that relying on gestalt is exactly what an expert must do.[5]

Gobet, though he thinks intuition is important, does not endorse unqualified intuition. Rather, as he makes clear in his work on chess, he thinks that intuition and deliberation must work together. Moreover, as he suggests above, it is only with *routine* problems that intuitive decisions will generally be correct. But what is meant by a "routine problem?" Certainly if we mean by "routine problems" those that generally can be correctly solved without thought, then, of course, routine problems generally can be correctly solved without thought. But if "routine" means the type of problem experts typically encounter on a daily basis, it is not clear, at least as Orwig seems to see it, that such problems *should* be solved without thought. Perhaps most of the images a radiologist looks at could be correctly evaluated without much deliberate thought; however, it is better to slow down and think so as to not miss a crucial feature.

The practice of dermatology is similar to radiology in this respect; that is, although fast and intuitive judgments would likely be right in simple cases, dermatologists I have spoken with say that they deliberately slow down in performing full-body scans so as to not miss key but subtle indicators of disease. Dermatology seems so effortless: with apparent nonchalance dermatologists observe a patient's skin. However, the nonchalance may be illusory. As Dr. Elizabeth Hale explained rather incredulously, when I asked her about whether she needs to think about what she is doing during a full body scan, or if the problems just pop out to her, "it's definitely conscious"; she went on to tell me that she not only thinks about a patient's various moles, but also consciously follows a set order of steps to make sure that she does not miss anything. Her sister

---

[5] Dreyfus and Dreyfus (1986), for example, make this claim.

Dr. Julie Karen, also a dermatologist, was in agreement, adding that it is never easy. Again, as I mentioned in the Introduction, anecdotal reports provide little evidence for the cognition-in-action principle. However, I take them to illustrate the view that I am arguing for and, as they accumulate, perhaps even append a question mark to the just-do-it principle.

Of course there is basically no cost for radiologists and dermatologists to slow down to optimize their judgments (save, of course, for that big cost: their exorbitant hourly fee). Yet could it be that in certain situations any amount of "time out" before action would be disastrous? If the choice is either do something immediately and possibly save a life, or wait a second to think and certainly lose one, then all other things being equal, one needs to act. The time-out protocol does not admit exceptions, though in certain situations the steps may be carried out less formally and in action. But might there be other actions that preclude a time out entirely?

## Should Soldiers Think Before They Shoot?

One activity that might seem to fall into this category is frontline warfare. In the heat of battle, it might seem that there is no time to think. But should soldiers or other military personnel ever shoot without thinking? Clearly much of what must occur in military action must be automatic. A marine once told me that because of the numerous drills he has been through, he reloads his weapons without any thought at all. Reloading, yes, but what about shooting? Somehow, perhaps because of the large M4 carbine in his arms, I was too intimidated to ask. According to the view I advocate, expert action generally involves and is not hindered by relevant thoughts. This is not to say that expert action does not also involve some level of automaticity. And reloading for soldiers may be one aspect of expert warfare that does occur at the automatic level. (Though even here I would imagine that the action should not become so automatic so that if one does stop to think that she forgets what to do; that is a situation a soldier never wants to find herself in.)

According to the stereotypical idea of military performance, soldiers are taught not to think about what they are doing, lest they end up humanizing the enemy. However, in contrast to this stereotype, standard military protocol rejects the idea that soldiers should just do and not think, as highlighted, for example, in "The U.S. Army Concept for the Human Dimension in Full Spectrum Operations" (*U.S. Army Training and Doctrine Command* 2008), which states that "soldiers must be able to recognize the moral implications in a given situation, reason through the situation to form a moral judgment, develop the intent to act, and finally, summon the courage and conviction to carry through with the intended behavior" (p. 19). Recognizing moral implications, reasoning through situations, making moral judgments, developing intentions, and exerting one's willpower to follow thought with those intentions is as good an invocation of the cognition-in-action principle as I can imagine.

Like the nurse, the soldier must also be able to justify their actions. As Navy SEAL Chris Kyle (2012) puts it in his autobiography, "I was always extremely aware of the fact that every killing might have to be justified to the lawyers" ( p. 171). And following standard military protocol prior to action facilitates justification afterwards.

The standard military doctrines that demand reflecting on one's reasons for acting prior to acting, however, have been questioned. As the military theorist Jorgen Eriksen (2010) points out, "intuition [which entails acting without preliminary thought] has started to find its way into military doctrines as a supplement to traditional deci- sion-making procedures, primarily in time-constrained situations" (p. 197). In fact, as Eriksen points out, the idea that thought is inimical to outstanding military perfor- mance is not new having been espoused by the nineteenth-century military philoso- pher Karl von Clausewitz in his book *On War.* Clausewitz (1976) writes:

During an operation decisions usually have to be made at once: there may be no time to review the situation or even to think it through ... [T]he concept [of being a military genius or expert] merely refers to the quick recognition of a truth that the mind would ordinarily miss or would perceive only after long study and reflection. (p. 102)[6]

According to Clausewitz, the military genius's characteristic decision is a "*coup d'oeil*"; he sees what to do at a glance or, literally, the stroke of the eye.

Eriksen wants to determine which view is correct: the view expressed in standard military protocol or the one found in *On War.* He wants to know, as he says, whether "soldiers [should] engage in deliberate and thoughtful processes before they respond to upcoming complex and ambiguous situations" (Eriksen 2010, p. 196). In particular, he is interested in the matter of discriminating between combatants and noncombat- ants, which may be extraordinarily difficult in situations where combatants with con- cealed weapons dress as civilians and mix in with the civilian population. Attacks from such combatants, Eriksen points out, "may occur at close range from seemingly non-combatant citizens and the soldiers' responses to such situations must be imme- diate to be successful" (p. 196).

Yet should such immediate action involve thought? Eriksen assumes that expert intuition (that is, the ability to see important features of a situation) arises out of the expert's background familiarly with the situation at issue. And, as he points out, on the Dreyfus and Dreyfus model of skill acquisition, it is only after years of involved experi- ence that such background familiarity is in place. Yet, based on information he culled from interviews and informal conversations with Norwegian soldiers and officers, Eriksen argues that when it comes to identifying combatants in civilian clothes, sol- diers never have enough opportunities for practice and so never reach the level of abil- ity that Dreyfus and Dreyfus characterize as intuitive (Eriksen 2010, pp. 204–6). Thus, it is at least not clear, he concludes, that they should proceed automatically.

[6] A different military classic, *The Art of War,* by Sun Tzu (513 BCE) emphasizes the deliberative side of warfare: "many calculations lead to victory, and few calculations to defeat: how much more no calculation at all!" (section I.26).

Putting aside the question of whether Eriksen is correct about the paucity of opportunities for soldiers to practice identifying combatants in civilian clothes, it seems that experts sometimes face situations for which their practice has not sufficiently prepared them. What, then, does this mean for the just-do-it principle? The (descriptive) just-do-it principle is a principle about what occurs in expert action: in normal circumstances, experts perform at their best without thinking in action. However, according to Eriksen, soldiers typically will not have much experience identifying combatants in difficult situations. As he puts it, "[although] it should theoretically be possible for them to develop into intuitive experts for that specific task,...it is questionable whether the soldiers are exposed to relevant situations enough times to develop any kind of intuitive response" (2010, p. 214). And the theory he relies on in order to support the idea that it is theoretically possible to develop intuitive expertise in this situation is Dreyfus's theory of skill acquisition, according to which the expert, after extended practice, acts intuitively. We have seen that the time-out protocol was introduced in order to encourage the members of surgical teams to deliberately slow down and employ conscious thought. And I suggested that in other medical specialties, such as radiology or dermatology, it may be beneficial to employ strategies that prevent one from falling into the automatic, strategies that, in a sense, prevent one from entering what some refer to as a state of "flow." The scenario Eriksen describes brings out another potential weakness of just-do-it, which is that experts may not have sufficient experience in a particular domain-relevant skill that would call for the type of automatic processing Dreyfus thinks is characteristic of expertise.

Does the inapplicability of just-do-it in such situations count in favor of cognition-in-action? It doesn't since, if we assume that Eriksen is correct about soldiers not having the requisite practice, it is still an open question whether soldiers without such practice count as experts (as I use this term) at identifying combatants in the relevant situations. Hence, Eriksen's insight appears neutral with respect to the truth of just-do-it, and indeed he does seem to understand his point as being neutral in this way, for his claim is that with respect to activities in which we are not given the opportunity to develop expertise, neither can we develop intuitive insight of the kind Dreyfus admires. What this means in the case of identifying combatants in asymmetric warfare, according to Eriksen, is that thinking is advised. (Of course, as I discussed in Chapter 3, if we were to individuate domain-relevant skills finely enough, we would be forced to say that there are no experts whatsoever, since it is never the case that one performs actions in exactly the same way even twice. I would like to avoid this conclusion, even though I cannot present guidelines for differentiating practiced skills from unpracticed ones. On Eriksen's view, asymmetric warfare falls on the unpracticed side of the divide.)

The philosopher Larry May (2007), in his book on military ethics, presents a different argument for the importance of soldiers engaging in rational reflection prior to action, which does seem to attack just-do-it. Also concerned with the soldier's ability to discriminate combatants from noncombatants, he argues that one important reason to uphold the principle that war tactics ought to discriminate combatants from non-combatants is that this principle, in his words, "force[s] soldiers to think before they shoot" (p. 108). And this ought to be encouraged, he tells us, because "this will nearly always mean that the soldier will shoot less, which is nearly always good in itself" (pp. 108–9).

Taking a time out is important in combat since, as May sees it, it tends to lead to less shooting overall. Whether less shooting overall is good in itself can be debated, however, it does seem that in a society such as ours in which killing noncombatants is seen as highly morally reprehensible, one must try one's best to minimize it. And thinking in action, I submit, might help one achieve this goal. But what about situations where one really does not have time to think, such as when one sees a gun being pulled? Eriksen presents a soldier's description of how this scenario differs from others:

I think the most important capacity to develop concerns how fast I manage to get an impression of the situation, and as a consequence, how alert and focused I have to be. I use a kind of leveled system which indicates different states of alertness; green, yellow, orange, red and black. Green is careless, not thinking of a threat at all. Yellow indicates a little suspiciousness; something does not fit the total picture. Orange, something has triggered me. I start to consider what to do if something happens. Red is action, based on the considerations made in orange. Black occurs because you are in green when you should have been in orange. If somebody suddenly points at you with a gun, out of the blue, that's black; no consideration has been made about how to respond. (Eriksen 2010, p. 13)

Black (a situation in which you need to react without thinking), according to this soldier, does occur. But on his view, if you are doing your best, you don't enter black. "Black occurs," he tells us, "because you are in green when you should have been in orange." Perhaps it is overly optimistic to think that it is humanly possible to never enter black. Nonetheless, on his view, at least ideally, the best performance never leads to black. That is, even if once in black, one has to act instantly, one ought never to have got to black in the first place.

## Striking Before Seeing

Athletic performance, like philosophy, is not typically a life-or-death matter, though great athletes sometimes see it as such; unlike philosophy, which typically allows ample time for thought, many forms of athletics do not allow for a chance to pause one's actions and consider what to do. For example, as David Papineau (2013) sees it, for the cricket batsman: "[t]here is not time to think once the ball has been released. You can only react" (p. 177). But is there really "no time to think" in such situations?

There is a line of reasoning, loosely based on neurological data, according to which, thought or at least conscious thought would arise too late for it to be relevant to certain types of athletic expert performance. Of course, when you are running a marathon, there is time to think; even for elite runners, the event lasts over an hour. But can a baseball player think when the ball is coming at ninety-five miles per hour or, with the best pitchers, sometimes even faster? The expert athlete, in such a situation, it is sometimes argued, cannot consciously control her movements, as she has to move before consciousness can kick in. The philosopher Jeffrey Gray (2004) uses grand-slam tennis as an example. He argues that in grand-slam tennis, the speed of the ball after a serve is so fast and the distance it needs to travel so short that a player must strike it back before she consciously sees the ball leave the server's racket (pp. 7–8). According to Gray, "consciously [the receiver] neither sees nor feels his arm move before the stroke is completed" (p. 8). The brain, of course, receives the information about the serve, but, says Gray, given that it takes about 250 milliseconds to become conscious of an event after it has happened, this awareness cannot be relevant to the return. Gray concludes that the idea that "conscious awareness should guide immediate behavioral reaction to them is—on the experimental evidence—impossible" (p. 9).[7]

The results Gray cites, however, are more controversial than he indicates. First, in contrast to the 250 millisecond time lag for conscious experience, experiments by David Eagleman and Terrence Sejnowski (2000) suggest an 80 millisecond time lag, with Eagleman emphasizing in an interview that this is only an average, commenting that for all he knows "perhaps fighter pilots live less in the past than the rest of us" (Salk Institute 2000). Furthermore, athletes talk about not only consciously guiding their movements, but also having the time, even in extremely fast actions, to make judgments and misjudgments. Here is Rafael Nadal's description:

[E]very time you line up to hit a shot, you have to make a split-second judgment as to the trajectory and speed of the ball and then make a split-second decision as to how, how hard, and where you must try and hit the shot back. And you have to do that over and over, often fifty times in a game, fifteen times in twenty seconds. (Nadal and Carlin 2011, p. 6)

And Pete Sampras (Sampras and Bodo 2008), emphasizes the importance of thought when he needed to move from grinder to attacker:

I had to learn to start thinking differently, and more. A grinder can lay back, waiting for a mistake, or tempt you to end points too quickly. An attacker has to think a little more. Flat serve or kicker? Charge the net, or set up a ground stroke winner? Is my opponent reading my serving pattern or shot selection? As a serve-and-volleyer, you attack; as a grinder you counterattack. The basic difference between attacking and defending is that the former requires a plan of attack and the latter calls for reaction and good defense. (p. 30)

Athletes also sometimes comment on how they experience the subjective lengthening of time. As Sampras puts it:

[A]t big moments, everything slows down a little—and if it doesn't, you have to make it slow down. That's one of the first and most important things you need to know if you want

---

[7]  Papineau (2013) makes a similar point, arguing that "batting performance is entirely under the control of the unconscious dorsal stream" (p. 180).

to close out matches. You need to be deliberate, because it takes great-self control to close matches. (p. 47)

And race-car driver Jackie Stewart explains the optimal race like this:

At one hundred and ninety-five mph you should still have a very clear vision, almost in slow motion, of going through that corner—so that you have time to brake, time to line the car up, time to recognize the amount of drift, and then you've hit the apex, given it a bit of a tweak, hit the exit and are out at a hundred and seventy-three mph. Now, the good driver will do this in a calculated way.[8]

This seems to be the opposite of just-do-it and stands in stark contrast to Dreyfus's claim that "the expert driver, generally without any attention....knows how to perform the action without calculating" (Dreyfus and Dreyfus 1991, p. 116). Such conclusions are based on the phenomenology of everyday driving, not expert race-car driving.

If the above claims are to be believed, thinking, conceptualizing, and judging seem to occur in athletic endeavors even at lightning-fast speeds. Thought, as Hobbes pointed out, is quick, and indeed, the upper limits of how fast it can travel have been on the rise.[9]

In asserting that thought occurs at these outrageously fast speeds, are such players guilty of "intellectualism," or what Charles Seiwert (2013) describes as "the vice of overstating the role of intellect in experience and action, of seeing reason (or inferences, or concepts) where they are not" (p. 194). My methodological principle, as explained in the Introduction, says that first-person reports should be taken as defeasible evidence for their truth. And perhaps, one might say such reports are defeated because athletes only say these things in order to make what they do seem like an intellectual endeavor. Moreover, the advocates of just-do-it will cite examples of experts who claim to act without thinking. Or perhaps one might be skeptical about first-person access to one's thought processes in general. One cannot discount such points. However, since one can also explain away comments about "not thinking"—for example, if a tennis player is interviewed right after a grand slam, she might be too exhausted to recount her thinking process and might say instead "I just did it"—and since there seems little reason to believe that we never have insight into our thought process, I do not see the scale tipping in favor of the just-do-it position.

Another consideration that might tell against the idea that there is no time to think in such situations is that—as Gray himself points out—top players anticipate the ball's

[8] This is quoted in Murphy and White (1995), which documents many other athletes who claim to experience the slowing of time. Experimental data also seem to support this phenomenon: see Yarrow et al. (2001); Haggard et al. (2002); Morrone et al. (2005); and Hagura et al. (2012).
[9] See Tovée (1994). See also Mann et al.'s ruminations in the final paragraph of their (2015) paper about how it may be possible that cricketers while batting could be consciously guiding their actions even after the ball bounces.

trajectory well before it leaves the server's racket. Such anticipation has been studied in many sports (see, for example, Balser et al. 2014) and although no one knows exactly how it occurs, Aglioti et al. (2008) hypothesize that the human mirror system, which is thought by some to produce an internal representation of movement on seeing movement in another, may allow athletes to anticipate the outcomes of even very fast actions in basketball players. And presumably the same would apply to tennis. According to Gray, however, this still does not allow time for consciousness to play a role in the game. And to support this view, he cites the science journalist John McCrone (2000), who tells us that top players do not claim to get their clues about the ball's trajectory prior to the time the ball leaves the racket, but rather seem to be conscious of the shots as they happen (J. Gray 2004, p. 8). This, however, falls short of showing that "on the experimental evidence," conscious guidance of such actions is "impossible" (J. Gray 2004, p. 9). Moreover, it is not clear that McCrone captures what at least some of the best players claim to notice. For example, Pete Sampras (Sampras and Bodo 2008) explains how when he would disguise his serve, other players would comment that they were not receiving the typical clues they rely on to determine where the ball is going: during lessons, he explains, his coach would have him "toss the ball in the air, and then he would call out where he wanted me to hit it, and with which spin, if any...Later, players would say that they had trouble reading where my serve was going, or what kind of ball movement it had" (p. 17). This suggests that players are at some level "reading" the body language prior to the serve.

Of course, it may be that all of the "reading" happens automatically as an unconscious process, and that such players are merely reasoning that since they are not able to return Sampras's serve, they must be missing something. However, if they have a sense of missing something with Sampras, it seems that with other players they generally have some conscious awareness of the bodily cues. If there is no conscious awareness of, say, a room suddenly turning pitch dark, you would not have a sense that you are missing anything (or at least, you wouldn't have this sense until you bumped into the wall). And similarly, if the players are never consciously aware of the bodily cues prior to the ball leaving the racket, they would not have a sense that they are not picking up these cues (or at least, they wouldn't have this sense until they repeatedly fail to return the serve).

Moreover, in some domains athletes do talk about explicitly reading such clues. In baseball, Charley Metro describes how it is done:

The good hitters get their tip-off from the pitchers. And there are many, many ways that a pitcher tips off his pitches. He grips it like that [fingers straight over top of ball]; there's your fastball. When he throws a curveball, he chokes the ball [wedges it between his thumb and forefinger, gripping it on the side so it sticks out]. Now see how much white of the ball shows on a fastball? And how much more white shows on a curveball?...Another thing is when they bring the ball into the glove, when they come in with a flat wrist like that, that'll be a fastball. When they turn their wrist like that, it's a breaking pitch. There are many, many ways, and the good hitters pick out these things.... facial expressions...human habits and characteristics will tell. (quoted by Carlson, 2004)

Such anticipation seems to occur in music as well. The violinist Arnold Steinhardt (2000), for example refers to it in describing how he was able to play together with the other members of his quartet. In chamber music, he tells us:

[Y]ou had to learn how to be both soloist and accompanist, often slipping quickly from one role to the other. Most often, the solo line ruled, with the others dutifully following it. But if, when accompanist, I merely listened to the solo line, my violin voice would tend to lag behind. We learned to watch carefully the motions of the solo voice's fingers of both hands (and any other body language), as an advance warning system for the sound that was to come. (p. 23)

## Those Who Hesitate Are Lost Versus Haste Makes Waste

Two popular and at least apparently contradictory aphorisms are "those who hesitate are lost" and "haste makes waste." This chapter can be seen in part as an attempt to support the second of these as it applies to experts in certain situations, such as when the surgery team goes into action, when a radiologist is reading scans, or even when a soldier is on the battlefield. However, there is some empirical evidence which is taken to suggest the former: as the psychologists Johnson and Raab (2003) put it with respect to thinking in athletic performance: "less is indeed more" (p. 224).They came up with this conclusion based on a study that might seem to challenge the idea that it is benefi-cial for experts to take time out to think before they act. In this study, researchers had handball players of various skill levels watch a video of high-level handball, and when the video was paused at crucial moments, they asked the participants to report their *initial choice* for a player's best course of action. The participants then took some time to indicate various other possible courses of actions and, subsequently, to choose the best one (their *considered choice*) among a list containing these further options and their initial choice. The researchers found that the initial choices, though not always identified by the subjects as their considered choice, were generally better than any of the possibilities generated later.

Sian Beilock and colleagues (2004) have also conducted studies which they see as leading to the view that "haste does not always make waste," and that "whereas novice performance benefits from enhanced attention to execution in comparison with con-ditions that take such attention away, expert skill execution excels in situations [such as time pressure situations] that limit, rather than encourage, attention to execution" (pp. 378–9). In this study, researchers asked more skilled and less skilled golfers to perform putts either accurately or quickly, and found that the more highly skilled group did better with speed constraints than when attending to accuracy, concluding that "the proceduralized performances of experts do not require, and appear to be adversely affected by, unlimited execution time—perhaps because that time affords them the counterproductive opportunity to explicitly attend to and monitor automated execution processes" (Beilock et al. 2004, p. 378). The philosopher Ezio Di Nucci (2014) defending the idea that "being mindless is, in short, a good thing" (p. x) sums it up like this: "more time to think, more attention and more concentration worsen the performance of experts while they improve the performance of novices" (p. 19).

What am I to say about such studies? Note that in the Johnson and Raab experiment, the true experts in the study—that is, the experts they brought in to judge which choices were the best (for none of the subjects who were college students, were "experts" in my sense of the term)—may very well have made their judgments by the relatively slow process of comparing a range of options. So it seems to me that, as in the jam experiment I discussed in Chapter 2, this experiment might be better understood as indicating that if you are trained to act with thought, thinking does not interfere with performance. But that is speculation. What isn't speculation and is quite suggestive of my cognition-in-action view is the fact that when Johnson and Raab calculated the time between the end of the video scene and the production of the first choice in milliseconds, they found that "longer latencies to produce the first decision also resulted in better decisions" (p. 226). So in that sense, less is *not* more since taking at least a bit more time before making an initial choice was beneficial. Does this mean simply that identifying one's initial choice relatively slowly is beneficial? Or is it also that the time lag allowed participants to screen a few options before naming what was supposed to be their initial choice (a possibility the researchers point out themselves)? In either case, the experiment does not present unqualified support for the view that the quick intuitive decision is typically better than the slower, deliberative one.

Beilock's study also revealed that experts in both conditions—that is, in the accuracy and in the speed condition—took more time to perform than the novices. This leaves open the possibility that it is not taking the time to think which is detrimental to expert performance, but rather the nature of the situation. For example, perhaps the request to try to land the ball on the target while taking as much time as is needed (they do not state explicitly what the instructions were, but this is basically how they paraphrase them), set the expert subjects up with too-high expectations for their performance and these expectations may have led to pressure that may have led to nervousness, and it was that which led to a decline in performance. In contrast, novices, because they are novices, presumably had little expectations of doing well.

I've certainly noticed how high expectations can interfere with my dance technique. In ballet, one of the most nerve-wracking moves is the pirouette. Since I stopped dancing professionally, I have occasionally returned to class for a time until life gets too busy, and I stop going. And I have found that after returning to ballet class after a long break, the first pirouette I do is often surprisingly good—an effortless, floating triple, perhaps—but then I start thinking, and the next one is invariably worse. What is going on? Since this phenomenon was most apparent after I stopped being an expert ballet dancer, I no longer was engaged in the practice of turning and analyzing, and turning and analyzing, and analyzing some more. And for this reason I may have lost the ability—which on my view goes along with expertise—to usefully think about what I was doing and do it at the same time. But perhaps the more salient cause was that after the first good turn, I got nervous. I would say to myself: can I do that again? That was lucky; what if I fall this time? And it may have been such worries that destroyed the later turns.[10] But the right kinds of thoughts, at least for an expert, can be beneficial. Consider the expert marksman. What type of situation is going to make for the better shot: the one where she has to draw the gun instantly and shoot, or the one in which she has time to aim? Experts, in many endeavors, at least, need time to aim.

Shakespeare's Hamlet laments how his delayed revenge of his father's death may be due to his "thinking too precisely on the event," and how "the pale cast of thought," which impedes "the native hue of resolution," makes "enterprises of great pith and moment...lose the name of action" (1603/1973, *Hamlet*, Act V, Scene ii). Does this pale cast of thought impede him from performing optimally? Putting aside the question of whether Hamlet should count as an expert murderer in my sense of "expert," one might argue that Hamlet's ruminations over killing his uncle Claudius (to avenge his father's death) illustrate how thinking interferes with doing. Of course, Hamlet is a fictional character; nonetheless, fictional characters, when produced by someone with insight as keen as Shakespeare's into the inner springs of human action, are often prey to the same psychological forces that govern those in the world outside of fiction. But does Shakespeare intend us to believe that Hamlet would have performed better if he thought less and acted more?

Though not universally held among scholars, a number of literary critics have argued that the answer to this question is "no." The poet Samuel Taylor Coleridge (1856/1973), for example, who himself is sometimes seen a proponent of just-do-it, comments that Hamlet is using his "pale case of thought" merely as an excuse for not acting: "let me impress upon you most emphatically that it was merely an excuse Hamlet made to himself for not taking advantage of this particular and favorable moment for doing justice upon" (pp. 193–4). It was much easier, according to Coleridge, for Hamlet to bemoan his overactive ruminations than to admit that he was a poltroon.

I also question whether Hamlet's failure to kill Claudius in the church illustrates just-do-it, though for a different reason: I think that Hamlet's decision to not take advantage of the moment may have been an optimal one. For, in contrast to Coleridge's interpretation, if Hamlet was not simply making up excuses and truly thought that murdering Claudius during prayer would likely send him to heaven, then it would seem that he followed the most reasonable course of action, since killing Claudius then would not have effected the revenge he was aiming to achieve. From the perspective of many of us today who believe neither in heaven nor in hell nor, *a fortiori*, in the idea that praying to God could affect which of these destinations one's soul might be sent to after death, we might want to scream out to Hamlet, "Get your revenge and just do it!"

---

[10] Does this type of thinking in part explain the "anti-hot-hand phenomenon," that is, the idea that after a successful shot a basketball player, for example, will be less likely than she normally is to make her next shot? Possibly, however, what might be more relevant is that after a player has made a successful shot she is more likely to make a risky shot and will be more avidly guarded (Attali 2013).

Yet from the perspective of someone who truly believes that prayer redeems the soul, Hamlet made the right choice. Of course, Hamlet is not fully committed to this perspective himself, and his uncertainty torments him. Still, assuming that Hamlet felt it was more likely than not that Claudius's soul would be redeemed, his thoughtful stance enabled him to act rationally.

Beyond this, it is worth pointing out that, contrary to the just-do-it principle, which admonishes experts to refrain from thinking while acting, Shakespeare seems to illustrate the importance of reflection in showing how instinctive behavior has disastrous consequences, such as when Hamlet impulsively stabs Polonius, who was hiding behind a curtain in his mother's room. Might not a moment's hesitation have made him realize that he had, on his way to his mother's room, passed his intended victim (Claudius) praying in the church? Perhaps at times Hamlet felt the dangerous attraction of just-do-it: he felt that if he could only stop thinking, all would go well. But Shakespeare does not advocate this view. The play, along with the other considerations I have addressed in this chapter, gives us no reason to accept the principle of interference.

True enough, sometimes even one moment's hesitation can lead to disaster, to losing a life that perhaps could have been saved. Yet even when performing something like CPR it may be important to stop, if only momentarily, and think. For example, according to the *American Red Cross Handbook for Professional Rescuers and Health Care Providers*, before administering CPR one must, among other things, "size up the scene," which involves checking for hazards, such as traffic, explosions, or toxic gas exposure, determining whether there are other victims, determining the nature of the injury, putting on barrier devices to protect from possible exposure to pathogens. And when one really does need to act without hesitation, one can still think in action. Indeed, one can think of CPR as the conscious attempt to restart a spontaneous process: the beating of a heart (Scarry 2011 makes this point and provides a compelling picture of thinking in an emergency.)

To train for an emergency, one needs to train so that those actions that one will definitely need to perform—like the soldier's reloading of his gun—can occur automatically, but not in such a way so that they must occur automatically, else thinking might interfere with doing. And for those actions that might be warranted in certain situations but not in others—like shooting—one must be especially careful to guard against absolute automaticity, else doing might lead to regret. There is yet another saying, and that is "look before you leap." But if there really isn't time to look beforehand, look while you leap and be ready to adjust plans mid-air.

# 6

# Continuous Improvement

To strive, to seek, to find and not to yield.

Alfred Tennyson (1809–1892)
"Ulysses"

To excel, especially in the face of hardships, takes determination. After an operation intended to improve her failing eyesight, the Cuban ballerina Alicia Alonso was required to spend an entire year flat on her back. The surgery was only partially successful, and her doctors predicted that she would never dance again. However, rather than giving up, she started practicing with her hands. Eventually, legs took the place of fingers, and she not only danced again but rose to the top of her profession where, relentlessly, she kept honing her technique and artistry. "I find that I am never happy with the way I dance," she said in an interview; "of course, the audience doesn't always realize it. It's you—that's the worst one—you, yourself" (quoted in Newman 1982, p. 98).

This drive to continuously improve, a drive Alonso had in abundance, is of paramount importance on the path from novice to expert (Ericsson and Smith 1991). One hears stories about child prodigies, for example, about how Mozart with hardly any understanding of the process, was able to compose symphonies, or about how the golfer Sam Snead basically emerged from his mother's womb ready to swing. Yet once one investigates such accounts, somewhat different pictures often emerge. Mozart certainly had amazing musical gifts, but his first symphony, composed at the age of eight, was achieved after years of strenuous musical instruction from his father, in whose hand the composition was written. And although Snead has been referred to as "the best natural player ever," he sees it rather differently: "People always said I had a natural swing. But when I was young, I'd play and practice all day, then practice more at night by my car's headlights. My hands bled. Nobody worked harder at golf than I did" (interviewed by Yocum 2002). Certainly nature plays a role, but for those who truly excel, nature is almost invariably coupled with a vast amount of hard work.

Are there ever exceptions to the idea that becoming really good at something is difficult? Perhaps there are, but, as I explained in Chapter 3, if so, they fall outside my purview; though such individuals may reasonably be called "experts," they are not the group of individuals to whom my arguments for cognition-in-action apply. Moreover, experts, as I conceive of them, are those who have not only worked to achieve mastery but are also still intent on getting better and better. In this chapter, I discuss what this ongoing desire to improve—what in Japanese is called *kaizen*—suggests about the role of the mind in expert in action. In Japan, the idea of *kaizen* is typically associated with a business model of ongoing improvement, aimed at such things as making production plants more efficient and manufacturing more cost effective. My concern, however, is with the drive to improve at an individual level, with the drive expressed by the tennis player Steffi Graf when she said that, for her, what mattered most was "always... striving to show the best that I could" (interviewed by Dickson 2009).

## Deliberate Practice

Arguably, the central way in which experts hone their skills is by deliberate practice, and by deliberate practice I mean near-daily extended practice with the intent of improving. As such, deliberate practice is not simply mindlessly repeating an action over and over again, since one can do this without aiming to improve. For example, a child might play *Für Elise* on the piano ten times in a row merely to get her required practice over, yet never intend to get better—and never get better—in the process. In contrast, when engaging in deliberate practice, the process is conducive to improvement and the practitioner aims at improvement.

The psychologist Anders Ericsson (2008), whose work has been instrumental in establishing the view that when one is already at a high level of achievement deliberate practice is necessary to improve, explains that deliberate practice involves "[d]eliberate efforts to improve one's performance beyond its current level [and] demands full concentration and often requires problem-solving and better methods of performing the tasks" (p. 31); it is, as Ericsson characterizes it elsewhere, "very high on relevance for performance, high on effort, and comparatively low on inherent enjoyment" (Ericsson et al. 1993, p. 373). For example, a dancer might engage in deliberate practice when she works time and time again on a certain step, analyzing what went wrong and trying to incorporate corrections (from herself and others). A chess player's deliberate practice might encompass, among other things, studying past games, exploring lines, and working on openings. In other words, deliberate practice involves pushing yourself beyond what you can already do.[1]

In contrast to deliberate practice is mere repetition, which leads to the type of automaticity that we attain in, say, opening our front door. Such automaticity, according to Ericsson (2008), leads to "arrested development" (p. 991). As he explains:

When performance has reached this level of automaticity and effortless execution, additional experience will not improve the accuracy of behavior nor refine the structure of the mediating

---

[1] For example, although all professional-level ice skaters practice an enormous number of hours every day, Deakin and Cobley (2003) have found that the best of them challenge themselves more by spending more time on jumps that they have not mastered, while the others spend more time on jumps that they have already mastered. See also Bereiter and Scardamalia (1993).

mechanisms, and consequently, the amount of accumulated experience will not be related to higher levels of performance. (p. 991)

Deliberate practice, however, according to Ericsson, prevents the attainment of automaticity and allows for ongoing improvement. "The key challenge for aspiring expert performers," he tells us, "is to avoid the arrested development associated with automaticity," and the way to accomplish this is by "actively setting new goals and higher performance standards, which require them to increase speed, accuracy, and control over their actions" (p. 991). Because deliberate practice aims to achieve goals just beyond one's reach, it precludes complete automaticity. And since an automatic action is one that is habitually performed the same way over and over again, honing your skills, as he sees it, requires you to retain some flexibility as to how your skill is executed.[2]

Deliberate practice is often effortful and analytical, yet deliberate practice is not itself contrary to the just-do-it principle. Proponents of just-do-it can (and for the most part do) accept the idea that experts engage in deliberate practice, since on their view it is not expert *practice* that is effortless and automatic, but expert *performance*. I want to suggest that something like deliberate practice, what I refer to as "deliberate improvement," is an ongoing activity that occurs not only during what we would normally think of as practice (such as what might occur during a rehearsal), but also during performance.

Ericsson (2008) claims that although deliberate practice is essential to honing one's skills, one cannot engage in it during performance: "In a professional environment with real-time demands, it is generally necessary to wait until the end of ongoing activity before one is able to reflect on how the mistake happened and what could be changed to avoid a similar, future problem" (p. 922). He elaborates:

When people are engaged in professional activities, public performances and competitions, it is difficult to engage in learning and training because it is not possible to stop the ongoing activity during a public music performance. Instead, the professionals need to proceed and make any necessary adjustments to minimize the perceptible effects of the disruption and maximize the chances for a successful overall outcome. (p. 922)

I agree with the idea that improvement requires one to step out of the automatic mode of acting. And I even understand "experts" as individuals who have engaged in at least around ten years of deliberate practice of their skill and are still engaging in such practice. Yet I did not stipulate that they are trying to improve during performance (for one can be intent on improving yet only work on improving during practice and not performance). The game would have been mostly up if I had since if experts are trying to improve, or at least if they are consciously trying to improve during performance, they

---

[2] Ericsson points out that for some skills, such as radiology, it is very difficult to improve by merely doing one's job, since one does not get immediate feedback. This stands in opposition to, say, surgery, where one receives some—and occasionally some very dramatic—feedback about whether one's judgment was correct. And so he suggests that radiologists practice with past cases and when they find that they have made a mistake, stop and try to figure out what went wrong in the process.

are not just doing it. Rather, the idea that experts, in at least many domains, deliberately try to get better during performance is something I shall argue for. To be sure, an expert may not be able to work to improve in the same way during a performance or tournament that she might during practice. In performance, musicians can't stop, analyze their mistakes, and try again (unless their "performance" is an open rehearsal), but they might actually analyze their mistakes in action. The blues and rock bass player, Alex Craven, who I mentioned in the previous chapter, told me that in his last performance he found himself coming up with a musical idea but at the same time, realizing that "the time for it had just passed." Although a dancer who makes a mistake in practice can stop and go over that one passage numerous times before starting the entire piece again, during a performance she cannot do this. Nonetheless, she might train her attention on a troublesome spot, trying to make it better than before, or notice that something could be done better next time, or even give herself a little lecture while performing as to what to do. If this type of critical analysis occurs in performance, these experts are not just doing it.[3]

## Improvement in Expert Actions That Involve Performance

Some types of expert actions have a clear divide between performance and practice. In both ballet and basketball, experts spend time engaged in deliberate practice as well as time participating in either a performance or a tournament. However, as I see it, deliberate improvement is typically an element of not only practice but also of a performance or tournament. There are roughly two ways in which one aims to improve during practice: with the short-term goal of honing one's immediate actions so that they are better than ever before and with the long-term goal of honing one's future performance.

An extreme case of improvement with a distant goal in mind is when an athlete or performing artist makes a major change to his or her technique aimed at future gains. For example, Tiger Woods, even while widely regarded as the best golfer in the world, did this when he decided to revamp his swing technique. The swimmer Michael Phelps did as well when, after winning eight gold medals, he decided to overhaul his freestyle technique. And the tennis phenomenon Roger Federer did so when he moved to a larger racket.[4] Such changes arguably require these athletes to increase their attention

---

[3] Bernier et al. (2016) investigate this type of deliberate focus by interviewing eight expert figure skaters as they watch a videotape of their skating. Their analysis of the skaters' comments shows that deliberate foci, which includes commands such as "think about your arm," "hop," "breath," or "keep my back leg very straight," compose 68 percent of the identified relevant comments, what they refer to as the "meaning units," spoken by the skaters.

[4] There have been numerous discussions in the media of Woods's, Phelps's, and Federer's new techniques. See, for example, Eden (2013); Harig (2010); Andersons (2009); van Valkenburg (2009); and Bishop (2014).

to and thought about what they are doing during practice. When Woods is working on his new swing with his coach, he is attending to and analyzing aspects of this new movement. And, presumably, while in the transition period, during which the swing is not yet mastered, he is working on it during tournament rounds as well. This does seem to be a case in which an expert in action is thinking about what he is doing and ought to think about what he is doing. Moreover, it would seem that thinking helped, that is, that the new swing would have gone worse without the thinking.

Whether this is in tension with just-do-it, however, depends on whether one counts such a situation as one in which things are going well. This can be debated, as can the question of whether the results of his action are optimal or near optimal—for the just-do-it principle is about not just action in general but optimal (or near-optimal) action. In one good sense, when Woods was working on his swing, he was not performing optimally since during one PGA Tour tournament he had what was for him a rather dismal string of rounds (McLean and Welty 2004). And Phelps and Federer suffered as well. So even though these performances were still better than what could be done by most anyone else in the world, you might say that since such experts are playing worse than they were before, they are not performing optimally or near-optimally. However, if we assume that in the middle of such a transition these experts could not revert easily to the old technique, they actually are performing optimally, for they are presumably performing as best as they can at the moment in the sense that there is nothing else they could have done to significantly improve their performance. Indeed, one might even say that Woods is a better player while in the transition process, because he is approaching what is ultimately a better swing for him. Or as Woods himself sees it, becoming a better player did not always mean winning more games (McLean and Welty 2004). As such, though it may not fall under just-do-it since it may be an unusual situation, it nonetheless exemplifies optimal performance that is and ought to be thoughtful.

Why, however, did Woods have a dismal string of games when he was working on his new swing? Could it be, in line with the principle of interference, that he was focusing on his new swing? I think the best explanation of this is not that the thinking caused the problem—as I suggested, most likely his performance would have been worse without thought—but simply that he had not yet reached the level of competence with this new swing that he had reached with his old swing. Attaining such a level and eventually moving beyond it would in part call for strengthening muscles, making many of the subroutines automatic to the degree that they could (though not necessarily must) be performed without thought, and, as I see it, acquiring a better understanding of the new swing.[5] All this took time to achieve.

---

[5] An analog to this in ballet is when a dancer changes the type of pointe shoes she wears. For female dancers, moving up and down from the tips of one's toes should be a roll, not a bump, and it is also considered important to not make a great deal of noise when running on stage. Some types of shoes (or the same type constructed by different "makers"—pointe shoes are made by hand, and professional ballet dancers usually order shoes from a particular maker) facilitate this more than others. I decided at one point during my career to switch to a type of pointe shoe that was very quiet and supple. It was very difficult to do, and

In fact, even though Woods's playing did suffer for a time, it could be that part of the benefit of adopting a new technique is precisely that it refocuses one's mind on one's activity. In ballet, there are numerous techniques, some of which provide contradictory advice. For example, in Balanchine technique, your weight is kept to a large degree on the ball of your foot, while in Maggie Black technique, your weight is kept more on the heel. I've worked sometimes for years in one technique and sometimes for years in the other. Both are remarkably effective! But why is this if they provide contradictory advice? Perhaps it is because both focus the mind on the movement and it is this that provides the primary benefit.

But is it actually the case that experts think in action when they are improving in action, or (as someone might object) is it that when such individuals are improving in action, they cease to be experts? For example, even if Woods's situation were deemed to be one in which all is going well, one might argue that it does not contradict just-do-it, since in learning a new swing, Woods became a novice again (at least with respect to his swing), yet the just-do-it principle is, as I've emphasized, a principle about experts. Thus, this objection continues, just-do-it is still correct: experts do not think about their skills in action; rather, Woods, in thinking about his new technique ceased to be an expert.

As I have already mentioned, however, I would suggest that we do not identify the skill that needs to be deliberately practiced at such a fine level of grain, at least not at such a level that any change an expert makes to her technique that results in at least temporarily worse performance downgrades her status to novice. Again, it is difficult to say how fine-grained we ought to make our identification of experts. However, even if one thinks that Woods's decision to change his swing did dethrone his expert status, such a decision is merely a dramatic example of the sometimes very subtle learning processes that experts are continually engaged in, during both practice and performance. For experts, to put it paradoxically, must always be novices, forever working on goals, as Einstein (1915/1998) put it, that they "can just barely achieve through [their] greatest efforts."

In their endless quest to improve, experts engage their minds. Moreover, no one, not even Woods, ever swings a golf club in exactly the same way twice. But it seems that even slight differences in movement may occasion thought. The tennis player Rafael Nadal comments on this:

You might think that after the millions and millions of balls I've hit, I'd have the basic shots of tennis show up, that reliably hitting a true, smooth clean shot every time would be a piece of cake. But it isn't. Not just because every day you wake up feeling differently, but because every shot is different; every single one. From the moment the ball is in motion, it comes at you at an infinitesimal number of angles and speeds; with more topspin, or backspin, or flatter or higher.

clearly at first my dancing suffered in rehearsal and in performance. But it seems to me that this was not because I was thinking about my feet, which I was nevertheless doing. Rather, I hadn't yet forged new automatic muscle movements that worked with this type of shoe, my feet were not strong enough to work with these new shoes, and I didn't fully understand what they would do.

The differences might be minute, microscopic, but so are the variations your body makes—shoulders, elbow, wrists, hips, ankles, knees—in every shot. And there are so many other factors—the weather, the surface, the rival. (Nadal and Carlin 2011, p. 6)

Even though Nadal hasn't ever practiced any shot exactly the same way more than once, he is an expert tennis player. Yet, as he points out, his shots don't simply "show up;" they don't just happen effortlessly and automatically.

If one has only the short-term goal of winning a tournament in mind, experts typically ought not to make any major changes to their technique. Unless the only chance you have of not losing a game is to try something utterly new, it is advisable to work basically with the technique you have and push that as far as you can, but no further. Miracles are, at best, rare, and one will not be able to develop amazingly new abilities during a tournament. As tennis coach David Breitkopf put it:

As a teacher, I will work with students on many different aspects of technique, but when they...[play in a tournament, they need to] trust their strokes....[Y]ou go to war with the military you have...[and] in a competitive situation, you go to war with the game you've developed up until that moment in time. (pers. corr.)

Certainly, you can't do something that you can't do. And trying to do something radically new and unpracticed is likely to lead to no good. However, it seems that although you go to war with the military you have, at war you might be able to bring more out of this military than you had previously realized. Moreover, as research by Toner and Moran (2009) seems to indicate, subtle refinements to technique with the intent of performing better than ever—not the kind that involve employing a new military, but ones you can make with your old one—are compatible with expert performance. In this study, golfers were asked to make technical adjustments to their movements, yet performance was not hindered. In other words, the adjustments along with the concomitant thinking, trying, effort, and control, which promoters of just-do-it spurn, had no negative effects on performance. The researchers sum up their results as follows:

First, technical adjustments had no significant influence on expert golfers' putting proficiency. This result is quite surprising as we expected that such a severe form of conscious control (i.e. making technical adjustments to a skilled action) would disrupt a normally automated movement such as an expert golfer's putting stroke....[I]n contrast to received wisdom, it would appear that conscious control (in the form of technical adjustments) may not inevitably disrupt task performance. (p. 676)[6]

Contrary to the principle of interference, this study gave no indication that conscious control disrupts expert-level performance.

Could it be that there are certain actions that an expert does not need to improve and, moreover, that apart from waking up feeling slightly different every day, do not

[6]  See also Collins et al. (2001).

come with much variation? The free-throw might seem to be an example of this. Are there some basketball players who are such good free-throw shooters that all they need to do is to maintain their skill? When I suggested this possibility to Larry Hunter, the head basketball coach at Western Carolina University, he corrected me: even with the best players, he said, "they're always striving for perfection." I then asked him how someone who already seems perfect could improve. "There's always the mechanics," he said, "you're always grooving the mechanics." And then he also explained the numerous psychological factors that come into play—nerves, distraction, loss of confidence, and so on—that can also be improved. Of course, as a coach, it's his job to groove the mechanics. Furthermore, even though Hunter's team is awesome, he's not working with world-class athletes and so might not have ideal insight into what it is like for some of the best NBA players at the free-throw line. However, if there are examples of expert actions where the expert is not bent on improving, they do not fall under my stipulated definition of "expert" and so it would be consistent with my view that such actions could be and ought to be performed without thought or even conscious bodily awareness.

## Kaizen in Nonperforming Expert Actions

I suggested that experts generally aim to get better not only during practice, but also during performance. Yet, as I also mentioned, many expert endeavors do not readily divide up into practice and performance. For example, although one could say that the philosopher's practice time occurred during the years of university leading up to the PhD, it would seem odd, at least to me, to say that now that I've been trained I am simply performing. Nonetheless, though one doesn't have performances in philosophy or painting, for example (or if one does, they typically do not have the same significance as they would in sports and the performing arts) one still may practice with the conscious aim, in part, of improving one's skill, aiming to make that very performance better than prior performances or aiming to make one's performance of the actions better not immediately, but in the long term.

What are the activities that writers, scientists, painters, and other such individuals engage in with the aim of improving? Such activities are not limited to occasional writing workshops or classes on how to use the latest version of EndNote. These can be useful—and I should certainly enroll in more of them myself—but they are not the only means by which nonperforming and noncompetitive experts aim to improve their craft. Rather, I would like to suggest that experts in these fields (as well as fields that do divide into practice and performance) at times also aim to improve while performing (in the sense of "doing") the activities that compose part of their daily work. For example, one aims to improve while reviewing a draft of a paper, trying not only to make the draft better, but also to fine-tune one's writing in general and deepen one's understanding of a topic. This is part of the idea (mentioned in Chapter 3) that is captured in the official CUNY document that I sign off on every year, which states that "a full-time faculty member is expected to...constantly [make] all efforts to improve his/her professional standing through study and thought, and also through activities such as research, publication, attendance at professional conferences, and the giving of papers and lectures." I typically don't think much of bureaucratese, and I would substitute "skill," or "craft," or "ability," or even "self," for "professional standing"—but the bureaucrats have, this time, got something right, or at least nearly right: such activities are not done merely in order to meet expectations. It may be that early on in an academic career one performs such activities with the goal of achieving tenure. But tenure, ideally, is only given to those who have internalized the struggle.

To be sure, in academia and elsewhere, the motivation to excel does not always come from within. In youth (as well as later in life), it may be supplied by a parent, teacher, or coach. And for many, excellence may not be an end in itself, but only a means to earn a higher salary or do better than the next guy. The mathematician G. H. Hardy (2012), one is somewhat disappointed to hear, explains that his primary motivation for study-ing mathematics was to outshine others: "I do not remember having felt, as a boy, any passion for mathematics...I wanted to beat other [children], and this seemed to be the way in which I could do so most decisively" (p. 46). And even someone like myself, who discounts the role of sudden inspiration in expert action, cannot help but feel a bit disheartened to learn through Mozart's letters the degree to which he appears moti-vated not by the music, but by the promise of fame or financial reward (Spaethling 2000). Nonetheless, whether one tries to ameliorate one's skills because one is internally driven, or whether it is in order to please one's father, or to achieve fame or fortune, most everyone who accepts just-do-it concedes that deliberately trying to improve involves thought and hard work. And, thus, for experts in disciplines that do not admit a performance/practice distinction, it would seem that as long as they are intent on improving, at least part of their ongoing activities within their domain of expertise will call for thought and effort. But not only that: even their best actions—their best mathe-matical proofs, their best lines of poetry, their best paintings—may be arrived at not via effortless intuition, but, as I shall argue in later chapters, as the result of conscious cerebration and travail.

## One's Own Worst Critic

Although experts exhibit *kaizen* for a motley collection of reasons, one salient cata-lyst for improvement, often present during both practice and performance, is that experts are frequently their own worst critics. Those who advocate just-do-it, such as Beilock and Carr (2004), Dreyfus and Dreyfus (1986) and Fitts and Posner (1967), all admit that during those occasions when something goes wrong, per-formers or athletes need to direct their attention to their actions. Yet they think that these occasions seldom occur. However, although from an audience's point of view things rarely go wrong, from the expert's point of view, things are going wrong all the time. Lynn Seymour, who was a principal dancer with the Royal Ballet, commented that when she danced with Rudolph Nureyev for the film *I Am a Dancer*, she was too cowardly to ever watch it: "Whenever I see myself dancing I practically die" (Gruen 1976, p. 135). And although being aware of one's own foibles while on stage may not be as viscerally unpleasant as watching oneself on film, during each and every performance dancers are aware of many aspects of their performance that have gone wrong. Indeed, as I said in the Introduction, just as Socrates claimed that he is wise because he knows that he is ignorant, it is at least in part the ability to recognize where there is room for improvement that allows experts to excel.

Improving, in the sense of doing better than before, involves effort. "Why isn't this getting any easier?" the violinist Arnold Steinhardt (1998) asks. "One might have expected," he tells us, "that after this long, [the] music would have settled comfortably into the muscles, tendons, even the synapses of the brain, and play itself" (p. 4). Is this, he asks, simply because "I am treading water as a musician," or is it because "my expectations are growing" (pp. 3–4)? The answer, based on his playing at the time, seems to be that his expectations are growing and thus, rather than merely being satisfied with the status quo, in playing he is striving to meet his ever growing expectations (p. 21). Alicia Alonso expresses a similar view: "I think every role is difficult to dance...I am never satisfied, there's always much more to do, always something you can find, technically and artistically" (Newman 1982, p. 98).

It may be that, as is often said, "great is the enemy of good," for if you are working toward perfection and refuse to yield until you get there, you may end up with nothing to show for your effort. Yet this doesn't mean that experts shouldn't strive for excellence. It is merely that, when the curtain rises, you go to war with the military you have.

## While Improving Experts Do Not Just Do It

Experts, as I have suggested, are driven to improve, and the attempt to improve, even according to just-do-it apostles, requires thought and effort. So, if experts are trying to improve during performances, thought and effort are involved. The descriptive component of the just-do-it principle, however, says that when all is going well, expert performance is neither thoughtful nor effortful. Thus it would seem that an expert's improving during a performance or tournament contradicts at least the descriptive component of just-do-it.

As I shall have quite a bit more to say about the idea of effort in expert action in the next chapter, let me here address other aspects of cognition in action and their role in improvement. However, since some of these other aspects, such as conscious control, are often effortfull, much of what I say about these mental processes applies to the role of effort in improvement as well. thinking (attending, controlling, and so forth) requires more effort than just doing, much of what I say about the role of thought (attention, control, and so forth) in improving for an expert applies to the role of effort as well.

Although experts are driven to improve, there may be some things that an expert should work on and aim to master solely during rehearsal. For a dancer, this might be learning the steps and becoming proficient at performing them. In all but unusual situations (such as when filling in for someone at the last minute while the director calls out instructions from the wings), you know your choreography before going on stage. Other aspects of dance are more fluid, and though they must be mastered to a degree before a performance, they also may be developed, played with, and refined during performance. Eric Dirk, a former dancer with the Joffrey Ballet and Oregon Ballet (where he was a frequent partner of mine), explains it like this:

It is usually pretty difficult to work on improving my ballet technique much during an actual performance. I had better have already done that in the rehearsal period before. But I definitely would work to improve my performance quality. If I was doing a leading role, say Mercutio [in *Romeo and Juliet*], then I would be constantly looking for more drama, playful[ness], trag[edy]—whatever that section needed. For a more generic role, say like [James Canfield's] *Equinox*: not so much personality to work on. My mind would be thinking of spacing, being together with my fellow dancers if I need to be in sync. Staying on the music, adjusting to injuries, if I had some pain going on. Watching out for someone who might be new to a part and needs help. This is not to say that if you were doing a run of thirty-plus *Nutcracker* [shows] and were stuck in the *corps [de ballet]* without much variety, you could probably space out a bit and just go through the motions. (pers. corr.)

Working on a character's personality is one aspect of what a dancer may try to hone, but so is musicality, as well as movement quality. Certainly, as Eric says, after performing the same piece over and over again, you could let habit take over and "simply spontaneously [do] what has normally worked" (Dreyfus and Dreyfus 2004, p. 253). But this is not going to be much fun, even for dancers in the *corps* (the ensemble, as opposed to solo roles). Moreover, performing the same piece in the same way day in and day out can result in an interpretation without any spark; and you never advance out of the *corps* without showing spark.

Eric claimed that it is often difficult to improve one's technique during performance. However, one way to keep those strings of *Nutcracker* shows alive is to work on improving technique. And, as coach Hunter said about basketball, the thing with ballet is that there is always room to groove the mechanics. As Lynn Seymour explains, "in ballet, everything is really technique. And what's so awful is that the technique is not always within grasp" (Gruen 1976, p. 134). When it's out of grasp, one can't just do it.

While I do not maintain that all thinking can be expressed in words, expressing thoughts in words as you are thinking them (unless one is lying or acting) is usually a sign that you are thinking those thoughts as you are expressing them. And experts engaged in domain relevant skills sometimes do express their thoughts. Fitts and Posner (1967) warn against thinking aloud during performance. They tell us that "there is a good deal of similarity between highly practiced skills and reflexes [since] both seem to run off without much verbalization or conscious content" (p. 15). Indeed, they tell us that "overt verbalization may interfere with a highly developed skill" (p. 15). Even Jason Stanley (2011), who has argued for the importance of propositional knowledge to skill, assumes that making this knowledge explicit impedes skill (p. 173). But it seems that at least sometimes overt verbalization is employed as a form of self-coaching and, rather than harmful, is beneficial. In dance, for instance, though thinking aloud may be more common during the early rehearsals of a piece, it sometimes continues on through performances. For example, to keep my mind and body on task, I might whisper something like "stretch-lift-whoosh" (the "whoosh" representing the sort of feeling that I am trying to embody in the movement and not Dreyfus and Kelly's whoosh of the external forces taking over), or even an occasional muted reprimand, such as "shoulders" (short for "shoulders down"), might be appropriate. And according to Agassi (2010), tennis players are constantly talking to themselves out loud during games (see also Sutton et al. 2011 and Toner et al. 2014).

Perhaps more as an attempt to not fail than an attempt to improve, dancers onstage may also count the music, either silently to themselves or aloud. Sometimes this is required because the music has no discernible rhythm or even landmark passages that can be used as guides. This was the case with Laura Dean's *Night*, choreographed for the Joffrey Ballet in 1980. Because the dancers' movements were very complex rhythmically, and because the music had no recognizable structure, dancers counted continually for the entire eighteen minutes of the piece for the several years they performed it. Eric told me that when he was not in the cast, he sat in the orchestra pit next to the two pianists, counting in order to ensure that the music finished exactly when the dancing did.

A proponent of just-do-it might say that the Joffrey dancers are evidently not experts at performing the piece. And, true enough, in most choreography, the counts become something you can feel (which is not to say that the counts are necessarily not consciously present—when I listen to music, especially certain classical pieces, it seems that to a large extent, I hear the counts). But doesn't the need to count a difficult piece (such as *Night*) during performances show that the dancers are not expertly performing the piece? Anna Kisslegoff (1981), the (sometimes biting) former *New York Times* chief dance critic didn't think so, for she called it "a smashing success."

## But Should Experts Aim to Improve During Performance?

I have suggested that at times experts aim to improve during performance—both in the sense that they might be working on a new technique and in the sense that they frequently try to do better than ever before. But should experts do this, especially if it is during a significant game or performance? When you have a long-term worthwhile goal, such as changing to an ultimately superior technique, as long as you are reasonably confident that such changes will lead to your goal, improvement during performance would seem to be called for (even if, as in Tiger Woods's case, this leads to losing more games in the short run). But what about the type of online improvement that involves, for example, making alterations to one's movements with the hope, though not certainty of doing better than ever before right there and then? Should that occur during the most important tournaments or games? Perhaps it depends on how high the stakes are. When an athlete falls in the Olympics, it results in a serious disadvantage, and so trying out something new might not be worth the risk. In the performing arts, the situation is different; the artistic quality of the whole performance—while perhaps supervening on the individual movements (roughly, you can't change the artistic quality of the performance without changing the movements)—is not reducible to the individual movements (an individual movement can go very wrong without marring the artistic quality of the whole). George Balanchine famously used to say that he liked dancers who fall (Karz 2011, p. 89). What he meant is that he wanted dancers to take risks. And since risks sometimes lead to falls, it would seem that Balanchine, too, was a nonreductivist about the relationship between artistry and movements. In sports, however, performance might not be so irreducible: they don't hold the clock for you during the *Tour de France* as you get back up on your bike.

Another reason to think that improvement should be an aspect of performance in dance (and other performing arts) is that dancers (and other performing artists) often perform the same piece over and over again, which allows some room for trial and error. Broadway dancer John Selya puts it like this: "You dance the same thing every night in a Broadway musical. That gives you a chance to really examine it and do something with it" (Nathan 2008, p. 54). Certain athletic events, however, may occur only one time per year so if things don't work out, it is not possible to simply try again tomorrow. Nonetheless, it might be that in order to win, one must risk breaking with the past, since sometimes to win one must perform not as one has in the past, but better than ever. Yet taking a risk seems to be the opposite of just-do-it, the opposite of "simply spontaneously [doing] what has normally worked" (Dreyfus and Dreyfus 2004, p. 253).

## Interlude on Making it Interesting

The ballerina Natalia Makarova who defected from the Soviet Union to dance with American Ballet Theater, illustrates another way in which the mind can be present during performance. In an interview with Robert Sherman she claims that for her, "it is physically impossible...to do the same performance twice" (Sherman 1980/1977). And what she means by "physically impossible" is not simply that, because the human body has so many degrees of freedom, one could never perfectly reproduce a movement even if one tried. (This is probably true, but beside the point.) Rather, what she means is that she cannot bring herself to try to reproduce it again. And the reason for this, I presume, has to do both with *kaizen* and her desire to think about what she is doing, to make decisions, to use her mind, to tinker, to play, and experiment. It may be that her need to be creative guides her approach more than her desire to improve because she also says that if something went well, even then she cannot reproduce it. Nonetheless, the tinkering, the experimenting, the play all involve an active mind. However, it could also be that even though something went well, she still tinkers with it because it might be possible to make it go even better.

Another reason why conscious awareness is important in the performing arts may be that it is often the case that relying on the same approach can, as I suggested earlier, drain the life out of a performance. Habits ensure that we get done what we need to get done, like brushing our teeth; they also free up cognitive resources to attend to more important matters. But then when there are important matters to attend to, one ought to use those available resources, for proceeding entirely by habit—as Vladimir puts it in Samuel Beckett's play *Waiting for Godot*—"is a great deadener" (act 2). However, that the glimmer of artistry one perceives in great performers, which seems to involve thoughtful creativity in action, is enlivening. To be sure, creative ideas on how to approach a piece sometimes arrive unbidden. For example, some choreographic ideas do not arise out of prior thought, but seem to happen almost automatically once the music is played or even once one is in the studio and begins to let the body find its way. And in performing set choreography, one might find oneself moving in a particular way within those constrains. But this does not mean that all artistry is and ought to be mindless. Rather, I submit that in the arts the best performances allow observers to witness some deliberate, conscious thought in action. Consider the difference between listening to someone lecture on her feet and listening to someone read a paper. The lecture is typically animated and fresh while the reading is typically, in Beckett's words, a great deadener.[7] The performance bereft of the mind would be, in certain respects, like watching a machine; although the output could be amazing, that most interesting of spectacles—the human mind—is lacking.

A further factor that counts in favor of engaging the conscious mind during performance is that automatic responses tend toward stereotypes more than well-thought-out ones. This is especially apparent in improvisational theater, where all but experts tend to portray, say, a caregiver as a woman, a scientist as a man, and so forth. It seems that the merely proficient performer proceeds spontaneously, while the expert thoughtfully guides a scene. This, I believe, is true of improvisational dance as well, since letting the body move automatically may result in patterns of movements that lack novelty. As the contact-improv dancer Romain Bigé explained, for him an important guiding idea is "make the second choice" (pers. comm.). The second choice is better because it is not the obvious one. And the unobvious move is

---

[7] This is not to say that speaking on one's feet is always preferable to reading a paper. If the literary value of the written words is high, this can be lost when one explains the ideas. Moreover, thought and animation can play a role in how one reads, in the expression one chooses to display.

better because it makes it more interesting for you, for your partner, and, if there is an audience involved, for the audience as well.

## The Importance of Aligning Practice and Performance

Promoters of just-do-it typically think that during practice, athletes and performing artists need to attend consciously to what they are doing, and that it is only during performance that actions ought to proceed automatically. But might it be important that one's focus during both practice and performance match up? Might it be that once one has begun training with a certain focus, the best course is to maintain that focus? No doubt, some performers like to "save something" for the stage. And of course, rehearsing or practicing full-out every time as if it were a performance might be exhausting. If there is a morning tech rehearsal (which allows the tech crew—lighting, scenery, and so forth—to practice and figure out what they need to do), followed by a full rehearsal with the orchestra for a performance that night, one might want to walk through the steps (what dancers call "marking") for the tech rehearsal. Nonetheless, too much of a change in mindset could throw one off; if the analytical mind is used to and comfortable with making choices and foreseeing possibilities, as it would be if the expert has been engaging in deliberate practice, letting it all go on autopilot might not work. Similarly, if one sustains an automatic mode of processing through practice, maintaining automaticity in performance might be the best option. However, in that case, one misses out on the benefits of deliberate practice. That said, it might be that the best practice routines allow for both practice without thought or much thought and practice that is highly thoughtful, as that would prepare the performer or athlete for both contingencies.

Schaeffer's example of playing the guitar, which I discussed in Chapter 4, seems to indicate that a consistent approach may be important: since one may not be able to control exogenous factors that lead to mindedness during performance, it would be best to practice mindedness during rehearsal as well. Perhaps the best athletes, artists, and experts in a variety of fields can handle such changes of focus. Perhaps Makarova could practice until her movements were automatic, and then all of a sudden start thinking about choreography on stage without missing a step. Yet, the sage advice might be that if all other things are equal, one should proceed in performance with the same type of focus and energy that one has used in rehearsal, giving it, if anything, a little bit more. Again, though during a performance a musician cannot stop and repeat a section of a piece, performing while engaging the conscious mind is advisable, I submit, since it is not thinking that messes one up, but, rather, moving from an attentive, thoughtful engagement in practice to a performance mode where the body simply takes over.

Ericsson, as I noted, emphasizes the importance of avoiding automaticity during one's training routine because automaticity leads to a plateau. Rather, in training it is important to develop strategies for engaging the conscious mind. This allows performers and athletes to notice, analyze, and work to remedy their weakness rather than merely promoting their ability to perform just as they have been doing before. Deliberate practice is important since, not only does it lead to improvement during practice, but it also encourages thinking during performing.

## Practicing for an Emergency

There is an old and well-supported theory in psychology, so old and well-supported that it has come to be known as a law—the Yerkes–Dodson law—that says that there is an ideal level of anxiety or arousal for different kinds of performance; too much or too little leads to suboptimal results. And according to this law, cognitive tasks suffer at a lower level of anxiety than do motor tasks. Thus, it would seem that in emergency situations, one will be at a cognitive disadvantage. But does this mean that emergency workers shouldn't think in action? Or does it mean that training ought to aim at producing individuals who are capable of thinking under pressure?

The view I have been arguing for—the idea that thinking is beneficial to expert action—indicates that if training can succeed in producing such individuals, then thinking would be preferable. Can training succeed in this way? And what would the essential components of such training be? Gary Klein (2003), who investigates the use of intuition in emergency and other situations, argues that we can train people to be better intuitive decision-makers by giving them as close as possible to real-life extensive and deliberate practice in making decisions. And this seems to me to be good advice for training to make reflective decisions as well. But I wonder if there is anything more that can be done to develop instant responses, for although I emphasize the role of thought and effort in expert action, I do not deny that sometimes one may need to make a decision without—or at least with greatly reduced—deliberation and reflection.

Kenneth Hammond (2000) presents two examples of successful decisions being made in emergency situations. The first is of the naval commander P. X. Rinn, captain of the USS *Samuel B. Roberts*, who on April 14, 1988 averted disaster when his vessel caught fire after striking a mine and subsequently began to sink. Rinn, realizing that the ship would go down before the fire could be extinguished, acted contrary to Navy protocol and focused primarily on staying afloat before addressing the fire. According to Hammond, "[h]e is on record as having arrived at his decision analytically, based on available information, training and operational experience." But sometimes there is nothing in one's background that one can call on to guide a judgment. Hammond's other example illustrates this type of situation: when a United DC-10 lost its hydraulic fluid, the captain and his crew flew the plane by using the throttles. As this is something they had never done and as it provided few of the normal cues pilots usually rely on, Hammond suggests that their ability "to land with minimal loss of life may be attributed to intuitive decision-making under stress." Although these are only two examples, I think they point to two importantly different types of situations that we may face in an emergency: one which provides sufficient information upon which to base your choice, and another which doesn't. And it seems that only the former allows one to choose a course of action based on explicit, conscious reasoning.

What might these examples reveal about practicing for an emergency? From the first we can infer the importance of practicing working consciously with the available information: setting priorities, managing conflicts, delegating responsibilities. And if emergency workers typically encounter situations where information is available, this should be the brunt of the training. But, given that sometimes there is very little to go on, as in the second example, it is prudent to prepare for such situations as well: to practice making decisions that are guided only by whatever subtle or nondeclarative or unconscious clues one may have of a relatively unknown situation (which is, as I understand it, what Hammond's attribution of intuition amounts to and which may still count as rational). Beyond this, it might even be useful to practice making guesses in unknown highly stressful situations where one does not even have any of these sorts of clues, even if the guesses are entirely arbitrary. One can't get better at making random choices; however, practice might mitigate incapacitating anxiety.

Playing the guitar is, of course, not typically called for during emergencies. However, performance anxiety can, for some, trigger an internal emergency alarm. And, because fine motor skills are liable to deteriorate when a performer is overly anxious—the musician and dancer Alison Clancy, for example, told me that although she avidly composes music on the guitar and plays the guitar with her band for recording sessions, she had to give up playing the guitar with her band because of anxiety but is still able to sing and dances during performances—musicians sometimes ask me how one can overcome incapacitating performance anxiety. I always respond by saying that the question is beyond my expertise. Yet I also don't refrain from making some suggestions. Practice in a way that makes you feel as if you are under stress. For example, practice with an elevated heart rate (say, after running up a flight of stairs). If anxiety makes your hands cold, practice with cold hands. If you can find a way to make your hands tremble, practice while trembling. In performance, your heart rate might still rise and your hands might still shiver, but you may be able to avoid the additional stress of not knowing how you are going to be able to perform in such conditions. Besides this, it would seem reasonable that one should practice techniques that can be used to keep oneself relatively calm. There are many such techniques (see, for example Green and Gallwey 1986), and even if the technique is not effective per se, the placebo effect may still obtain even if you know it's a placebo (Kaptchuk et al. 2010). Then there are also anxiety-reducing drugs. But, even if such drugs were fully effective, the pharmaceutical route is not for everyone. (It's a complicated topic.) Of course, the various techniques and practices might not prepare one sufficiently. Thus, it might be important to have all routine actions down pat so that if the mind is overcome with anxiety, the actions can still occur.

Nonetheless, it is preferable to practice these actions in such a way so that, although they could be performed automatically, they do not need to be performed automatically—one doesn't want to forget what notes to play or how to open the emergency door, if one all of a sudden tries to think about how to do so. Be prepared; but be prepared to think in action.

## Limitless Attention

On the classic understanding of attention, attention is limited, in the sense that attending to one aspect of your environment or your internal thoughts impedes your ability to attend simultaneously to another. "Everyone knows what attention is," William James (1890/2007) said: "it implies withdrawal from some things in order to deal effectively with others" (p. 424). Different theories of attention aim to account for this limitation in different ways. For example, according to Donald Broadbent's (1958) "bottleneck" theory, our brains are flooded with information and we prevent overflow by attending to only a small portion of it (what makes it into the bottleneck), which is selected on the basis of physical characteristics (such as which ear the input enters) as opposed to semantic ones. Later experiments (for example, Gray and Wedderburn 1960) cast doubt on the idea that information is selected solely on the basis of physical characteristics since subjects appeared to process some nonconscious information in a semantically meaningful way. And subsequently, for those researchers who interpreted these experiments as showing that we also attend to this nonconscoius information, the bottleneck widened a bit. Whether we should apply the term "attention" to both conscious and nonconscious processes or reserve the term "attention" for conscious processes is an open (and perhaps in part terminological) question (see Montemayor and Haljiadan 2015 for a defense of the former approach and Prinz 2012 for the latter). Nonetheless, most researchers agree that conscious attention, especially conscious attention in a single sensory modality, is a scarce resource.

Expertise, however, may give us reason to question the degree of this scarcity. The research showing that skills deteriorate when attention is divided, such as the research on driving, investigates everyday type of abilities rather than professional or expert-level ones: the everyday driver rather than the race-car driver. And it also looks into irrelevant (rather than relevant) channels of attention, like focusing on texting while driving (Salvucci and Taatgen 2008, for example). On my view, however, although distractions, such as, thinking about a shopping list during a performance, degrade expert action comparatively more than they degrade automatized, everyday action, relevant thoughts and channels of attention are unlikely to interfere with optimal expert-level performance; thus, expert actions may incorporate more skill-relevant foci than everyday action. But how many thoughts and different foci can experts have at the same time?

As we have seen in this chapter as well as the previous two chapters, when the pressure is on, or when the hunger to win is present, experts sometimes do seem to attend to numerous different targets. Schaeffer, as we saw, was able to think about the fine details of his technique and his artistry; the emergency room nurse I discussed in the previous chapter seemed able to focus on doctors, nurses, and patients, and, of course, the time-clock all at once; the ballet dancer Eric Dirk appeared simultaneously to make sure that he is in the proper space on the stage, check that he is moving together with other dancers, that he is staying on the music, and that he is adjusting to injuries; and, at one hundred and ninety-five mph, race-car driver Jackie Stewart seemed to think about braking and lining up the car while also monitoring the amount of drift, as he rounds the corner. Furthermore, Wiersma's (2014) interviews with elite big-wave surfers found that they claim to be simultaneously aware of both what is happening in front of the board (by attending, for example, to the contours of the water) and to what is happening behind the board (by attending, for example, to the sound of the waves). Perhaps it is the expert's multiple foci that accounts for the expertise-induced expansion of time that I discussed in Chapter 5: perhaps, as Pete Sampras put it, "at big moments, everything slows down a little" (Sampras and Bodo 2008) because what experts are able to focus on in such moments, would, in the normal course of things, be attended to only sequentially (Merino-Rajme's 2014 theory of our experience of the passage of time may account for this). Do all or at least some of these foci actually occur simultaneously and with equal (conscious) attention? Experiments that fail to inspire the type of hypervigilance one experiences when either closing out matches or working in an emergency room, might be unable to shed light on this question.

# 7

# You Can't Try Too Hard

Nature commonly lodges her treasure and jewels in rocky ground. If the matter be knotty and the sense lies deep, the mind must stop and buckle to it, and stick upon it with labour and thought, and close contemplation.

John Locke (1632–1704)
*The Conduct of the Understanding*

We've all experienced times where our seemingly best efforts lead to suboptimal or even disastrous results. You are cooking dinner for your in-laws for the first time, and despite sticking to tried and true recipes, the pie crust falls apart, the sauce doesn't thicken, and the crispy kale comes out of the oven burnt. Or consider the business executive on his way to clinch that all-important deal. Why, on this morning alone, does he appear with a shred of toilet paper on his chin sopping up the blood? What went wrong in these situations? Chance plays a role: occasionally ovens malfunction, and a chin might develop a bump overnight. Moreover, such situations could provoke anxiety which, as I highlighted in Chapter 4, could cause tremors (making that razor shake) or impede working memory (explaining why you forgot to turn off the oven). However, one explanation you might hear from your spouse after your in-laws have left is that you were trying too hard. Trying too hard, it is often thought, is detrimental to performance. "Ease up," the advice goes, "and you'll be fine." But can one really try too hard?

Somerset Maugham purportedly once said, "in each shave, lies a philosophy" (quoted in Murakami 2008, p. vi). And, for any logicians who may be reading this, I should mention that this isn't an allusion to Bertrand Russell's paradox of the barber who shaves all and only those who do not shave themselves.[1] Rather, as Maugham's writing itself well illustrates, in even the most mundane of actions, there are depths to explore. My concern, however, as I've emphasized, is not with everyday actions, but with expert-level actions, with how trying affects not the executive's quotidian shave, but rather the shave done by the expert barber (who exists, as opposed to Russell's paradoxical one). Part of the impetus for the idea that highly skilled action is intuitive, unreflective, automatic, and effortless—what I've been calling the

---

[1] To be more inclusive, rather than the "barber paradox," I teach my students what I refer to as "the paradox of the barista": if there were a barista who makes coffee for all and only those who do not make coffee for themselves, would she make coffee for herself?

"just-do-it principle"—comes from examples of situations where trying too hard seems to hinder performance. And it is not merely trying *too* hard that is proscribed. Rather, according to some, the best performances do not involve trying or effort at all. "Relax, don't even try, and the words will flow from your fingertips," or "your arms will take over your swing and the ball will go straight in" or "you'll end those thirty-two fouettés in the coda of *Swan Lake* with a triple." Clearly, expert writers, athletes, and dancers need to work hard to attain their prowess; however, once attained, it is thought that trying interferes with the smooth, automatic flow of their best performances. Indeed, as we saw in Chapter 3, skill, according to the classic definition in psychology, "consists in the ability to bring about some end results with maximum certainty and minimum outlay of energy, or of time and energy" (Guthrie 1952, p. 136).

Trying is related to the type of conscious control over movements that Beilock and others warn experts to avoid. When you are consciously controlling the movements of your shoulder as you swing a golf club, you are trying to move in some particular way. As such, I have already addressed and ultimately found wanting some of the relevant research that purports to support the idea that trying interferes with expert performance (what I call "the principle of interference"). Trying, furthermore, is a component of improvement, and so in discussing the expert's drive to improve, I have also proffered that experts try in action. If experts are striving to improve, they are trying. However, let me make use of this chapter to delve explicitly into the relation between trying and doing, to present my reasons for thinking that expert performance is generally compatible with and typically benefits from trying, and conclude with an explanation of the sense in which you can't try too hard. I shall not present a definition of what trying is; this term is used in numerous ways in various situations and my intention is to consider a good sampling of such uses and to let the context of my discussion clarify (to the degree, as Aristotle puts it, that the subject matter admits) what notion of trying is under discussion.

## Don't Try as Hard as You Can ... Don't Even Try

The sports psychologist Robert Rotella (2012, p. 65) tells us that a career-making or -breaking golf putt requires a relaxed, almost lackadaisical state of mind. This, he thinks, is true not only of golf, but of a wide variety of skilled performances. Indeed, in a somewhat frightening analogy, he tells of a surgeon he observed performing a life-or-death cardiac bypass who, according to Rotella, was able to perform well in part because she was *not* trying as hard as she could. As Rotella explains:

While performing the very fine, precise motor skills involved in surgery, [the surgeon had] to avoid getting too careful and trying too hard ... [T]he truth is that being very careful and trying as hard as you can are not the best ways to perform surgery. [Rather,] when it comes to performing complex physical tasks, human beings do best when they learn the task, practice it diligently, then go unconscious and rely on subconscious memory to perform the movements under pressure. If the conscious mind becomes involved in the process, the body proceeds less gracefully and efficiently... We have to get out of our own way. (p. 66)

Though the philosophers Hubert Dreyfus and Sean Kelly take their inspiration more from Merleau-Ponty and Heidegger than from clinical observations, the conclusions they arrive at resonate with Rotella's. For Dreyfus and Kelly, true excellence doesn't occur when we are trying; rather, it is something that happens to an individual. Should the chess player try as hard as she can to win the game? Should the tennis player, in the last match of a grand slam, try harder than ever? Not according to Dreyfus and Kelly, since, like Rotella, they think that experts need to 'get out of their own way.' Indeed, on their view, the expert is so far removed from trying that the closest analogy Dreyfus and Kelly (2011a) come up with to performing a great move in chess, pushing off a ten-meter-high diving platform, or coming up with a profound and unbelievably beautiful line of poetry, is falling asleep. In a discussion of excellence as exemplified by the ancient Greeks described by Homer, they explain:

...going to sleep is...not something achieved by the force of one's individual will, as if one could go to sleep simply by deciding to do so. Indeed, going to sleep is neither something one is caused to do by an outside force, nor something one achieves by dint of effort and control...and so it is in general for human beings at their best in Homer's world. Just as one cannot go to sleep by trying harder, so too one cannot act at one's best—in war, love, marriage, or adventure—by taking direct and complete responsibility for oneself. (p. 199)

But what is it about trying that is supposed to hinder performance? Why, according to these very different thinkers, must experts get out of their own way?

## Trying in Basic Actions

Wittgenstein (1953) observed, "[w]hen I raise my arm, I do not usually *try* to raise it" (p. 623). On his view, trying occurs when, for example, you want to raise your arm, yet someone is holding it down, or it's numb, or you want to be called on to speak but are enormously nervous at the prospect and thus need to exert your will to get that arm up—but not when you reach for the shampoo, hail a taxi, or catch a ball. And more recently, Robert Audi (1993, p. 92) has argued that although agents may try when they encounter resistance, agents need not exert themselves or try to act in ordinary situations.

Other philosophers, however, such as Brian O'Shaughnessy (1981), Jennifer Hornsby (1980), and Robert Hanna and Michelle Maiese (2009) argue that trying is an essential element of all intentional actions. If this is correct, it would follow directly that expert actions involve trying in this minimal sense as well: not necessarily trying your best, as Rotella warns against in the quote above, but in contrast to falling asleep, they would involve at least *some* measure of trying. Now, most advocates of just-do-it can accept this since, like Rotella, they are more concerned with proscribing effortful trying. Nonetheless, the arguments on each side of this debate are worth addressing since they will help us to differentiate various senses of trying. Furthermore, the arguments for the idea that all of our actions involve a minimal, effortless type of trying, seem to conflict, at least at first glance, with the strongest versions of just-do-it, such as those proposed by Dreyfus and Kelly, that understand expertise as not even unconsciously mental. So let me address the question of whether all of our actions involve trying in at least some minimal sense before returning to the question of whether expertise typically involves a more vigorous form of trying.

Clearly, we normally do not say of someone who is, say, toasting her daily bagel that she is *trying* to toast a bagel. Perhaps cutting the roly-poly thing, we might say, involves trying. But it would be odd to say that you try, in the typical situation, to toast it. You just toast it; you don't try to toast it. Yet what can we conclude about trying from the mere fact that it sounds odd to attribute trying to our quotidian tasks? Some think that the move from what sounds odd to how things are is invalid (Grice 1989; Hanfling 2000). On this view, how we ordinarily speak is one thing; how things are is another. This is likely true, however, I think that in philosophizing we should not entirely disregard our ordinary manners of speech, since manners of speech sometimes embody common sense, and while common sense shouldn't be the last word on a matter, it is often reasonable to take it as the first. In other words, I see it as reasonable to ask of any theorist whose views are contrary to common sense for an explanation of why common sense or ordinary language is wrong on this account.

O'Shaughnessy (1981) seems to take a similar stance since his first line of business, in arguing for the view that all of our actions involve trying, is an explanation of how true claims can sound odd. He reminds us that the statement, "the president is sober this morning," sounds odd, yet is (presumably) nonetheless true. And he thinks that the oddity of imparting trying to everyday actions can be discounted for the same reason that we discount the oddity of asserting the president's break-of-day sobriety. If so, he will have taken care of what he sees as his first line of business. Yet, does this particular analogy help us to understand why it sounds odd to impart trying to everyday actions?

Although the statement "the president is sober this morning" provides an example of a true sentence that sounds odd, it is not clear how relevant it is to the case in question, since it seems that the sentence "the president is sober this morning" sounds odd because it suggests that on other mornings he is not, which would, of course, be shocking.[2] But the same analysis does not account for the oddity of "he tried to toast his bagel," since it would not be shocking to hear that on other mornings he does not try to do this, but just does it. Or to go back to O'Shaughnessy's example, "he tried to walk across the road" does not sound odd for the reason that "the president is sober this morning" sounds odd, since it would not at all be shocking to hear that sometimes (or

---

[2] One might even question the truth of "the president is sober," if one understands "sober" to mean not just *not drunk*, but *not currently drunk, yet having a tendency to drink*.

even often), O'Shaughnessy's rural-dwelling bloke doesn't try to cross the road, but rather—much like the notorious chicken—simply walks to the other side. Instead, the oddity in O'Shaughnessy's example seems to arise precisely because we simply do not think that such an activity involves trying at all. That is, common sense tells us that although we need to try to cross, say, East 57th Street in New York City, and in fact may sometimes fail at our attempts—just for your information, every thirty hours a pedestrian is killed in New York City—we don't need to *try* when we want to cross a familiar road in a rural setting.

O'Shaughnessy, however, is thinking of the analogy rather differently. As he sees it, we understand that "the president is sober" is true because it makes sense to say that the president is sober in response to someone who insists, as O'Shaughnessy puts it, that the president was "blind-drunk at his breakfast" (p. 365). If so, because this would be the correct answer to the question were it to be asked, O'Shaughnessy claims that it is true, despite the oddity of the statement. Having diffused the oddity of the president's sobriety, his second order of business is to show how a similar line of reasoning indicates that even though the comment that, for example, we try to tie our shoes every time we tie our shoes sounds odd, it is nonetheless true.

For O'Shaughnessy, even though it might normally sound odd to impart trying to everyday actions, we can see that trying is nonetheless involved in such actions, because we can imagine certain situations in which the trying is revealed. Hornsby (2015) agrees with this: "[B]y way of seeing that we can often envisage a person [who sees the action as involving trying], we should be persuaded (defeasibly perhaps) that 'He tried to φ' is not merely compatible with a man's success in φ-ing, but integral to his having φ'd intentionally" (p. 85).

O'Shaughnessy (1981) elaborates with another example:

Suppose a man sets out to start a car…and suppose [another] person witnesses the spectacle; and suppose he knows the putative car-starter to be a fantastic pathological liar and this car to be a grossly unreliable instrument; and, to complete the picture, let us suppose him to know that the car starter has a truly urgent reason for making a quick getaway. The pathological liar gives vent in an absurdly complacent voice—as it happens on a sound factual basis, having just had the car completely overhauled and tuned—to the announcement that he is "now about to drive off." The skeptical onlooker has excellent reasons for doubting the truth of this evident boast. But, because he knows of the urgent reason for making a quick getaway, he does, I suggest, know one thing: namely, that the pathological liar is at least going to try and start the car. It follows that it is true that he is. (p. 368)

The skeptical onlooker, according to O'Shaughnessy, reveals that even though the agent does not conceive of himself as trying to start the car, he is nonetheless trying; "such onlookers," as O'Shaughnessy (1973) puts it, "act unwittingly as separator agencies, rather like magnets that one draws through a fine mixture of iron and copper filing. They draw to themselves an item normally concealed from view" (p. 368). And this item, as he sees it, is an event of trying. Moreover, the skeptical onlooker, for

O'Shaughnessy, need not even be present, since all action brings with it the possibility of failure. "Of no situation," he tells us, can it be said:

> This situation bears a charmed life…Therefore the totally aberrant can never be guaranteed not to happen. Now it is precisely this refusal of empirical reality ideally to match our mental representations, it is this special brand of uncertainty hanging like a question mark over everything, that gives trying a permanent foothold in intentional action. (p. 366)

What are we to think of this line of argument? The argument, I take it, is supposed to show that because an onlooker could know that the agent would try to start the car, the agent *did* try to start the car. That knowing *p* implies *p,* is a truth universally acknowledged (among philosophers at least), and here we have knowledge of trying. Thus, we have trying. That said, there may be reason to doubt this "universal truth." Think, for example, about scientific knowledge. We know so much; but alas, some of what we currently know—as future generations will discover—is false. So if you think that science is our best example of knowledge, perhaps it makes sense to say that we can have knowledge of falsehoods. But let us leave that aside, since even if the implication from knowledge to truth holds—that is, even if it is the case that if the onlooker knows the agent tries, then the agent does try—I think it is at least an open question whether the onlooker does *know* this, as it seems reasonable for the onlooker, after seeing the pathological liar drive off, to retract his knowledge claim, saying "well, look at that; I guess I was wrong." Because the skeptical onlooker did not have the relevant information about the car's tune-up, there seems to be at least one reasonable use of the word "try" (where trying involves some sort of effort or at least action with a goal in mind) according to which he did not know that the pathological liar is going to try to start the car. In contrast, when we imagine someone truly answering that the president is sober at breakfast, we imagine that all the relevant facts are known.

But perhaps the key to understanding O'Shaughnessy's argument is not the skeptical onlooker, but rather the "hanging question mark." Here, then, is a variation of the argument that maintains the question mark, yet does away with the onlooker. Imagine Jane is ready to set off to her office and, as she always does, she goes to her car and puts the key in the ignition; yet today, unlike other days, the car does not start, for, unbeknownst to her, the battery is dead. It seems, then, that she tried to start the car, but failed. Yet every other day she has done the same thing, so if she tried in the former case, she tried in the latter one as well. And, since all our actions bring with them possibility of failure, since there is that giant question mark looming over all of them, all action, whether successful or not, involves trying. If so, then not only Jane's starting of her car, but also expert actions such as Bubba Watson's apparently effortless swing (supposedly arrived at without ever having the assistance of a swing coach) involve trying in this minimal sense. Or do they?

If they do, then Dreyfus and Kelly are mistaken about true excellence; however, even with Jane, it is not clear that when her car's battery is dead, she should be described as *trying* to start the car when she does exactly what she would do if the car were to start, which would be turning the key once. Genuinely trying, in such a case, one might argue, should involve at least a few more attempts.

A similar point applies to an example of Arthur Danto's, which Hornsby (2015) cites favorably.

I dial Jones's number.... If I fail to reach Jones, I say I will try again, meaning that I will again dial that number, and if I reach Jones, I will have succeeded, even though I did nothing differently on that occasion than on the one before. (Danto 1966, p. 57)

Must we say, though, along with Danto and Hornsby, that you are trying to reach Jones every time you dial Jones, whether you succeed or fail? It is not clear that we must. Let us say that Jones is your son's third-grade teacher, and that your spouse has told you to call Jones today to apologize for the fact that you won't be able to volunteer for the cupcake sale to raise money for the school's "just say no to sugar" campaign. If you call only once and don't get through, you are going to be in deep water: "you didn't even try," your spouse will complain. And a reasonable response for you to make in such a situation would be, "true, but I wasn't motivated." Of course, another reasonable answer would be: "yes I did, but not very hard." The difficulty or perhaps impossibility of determining which of these responses captures what was really going on indicates that appealing to what it makes sense to say in such situations is not going to take us very close to answering the question, "Do all actions involve trying?" And thus, it is not clear that we have made any progress toward refuting the extreme just-do-it by arguing that trying occurs in all of our actions.

There may be another problem with the idea of ubiquitous trying. Doing such things as dialing a telephone and starting your car are typically effortless; thus if such actions involve trying, it would need to be an effortless sort of trying. But does the idea of effortless trying makes sense? Don't trying and effort go together? That is, isn't it the case that if you are trying to do something, you are making an effort to do it? If so, this may be another reason to reject the idea that all of our actions involve trying.

Hanna and Maiese (2009) think that the two concepts of trying and effort can come apart. Wittgenstein's comment that he normally doesn't need to try to raise his arm, they tell us, merely indicates that he usually need not make an effort to raise his arm, not that he wasn't trying to raise his arm. As they see it, "effortless trying" is present in all of our actions, and "manifests itself as the subjective experience of *flowing forward right into intentional body movement,* as in Yeats's dancer *becoming* her dance" (p. 179).[3] So on their view, a special kind of trying, an effortless trying, pervades all of our actions. But, as some actions are nonetheless also effortful, this, they are aware, leads to the question of how an action can be effortful and effortless at the same time. In

---

[3] Referring to Yeats's poem "Among School Children":

O body swayed to music, O brightening glance,
How can we know the dancer from the dance?

response to this difficulty, they present an example of an action that encompasses both effort and the lack of effort: if you have a sore arm, raising it would require effort, however, "as you effortfully try to raise your sore arm, you also effortlessly try to balance and orient the rest of your body" (p. 179). But is this an instance of trying to do something both effortfully and effortlessly? Or is it an example of an action composed of two (or more) sub-actions: one effortful, the other effortless? And if the latter, what is one to say about these sub-actions taken individually. In particular, would the arm raising, itself be both effortful and effortless?

I think it is unlikely that we are going to be able to defeat the extreme form of just-do-it, which precludes even unconscious mental processing in expert action, by arguing that all action involves trying. Neither the example of the skeptical onlooker, nor the idea that the very same actions occur in situations in which we would ascribe trying and in situations in which we would not, clearly lead to the desired conclusion, and even if they did, we would still be left in the uncomfortable situation of needing to make sense of an action being both effortful and effortless. Of course, those who hold that all of our actions embody trying have more to say in defense of their view. For example, they might be able to make sense of effortless and effortful action by appealing to different levels of description whereby an action might be automatic and thus effortless at a relatively lower level of description while at the same time being intentional and effortful at a higher level of description.

However, it seems that no matter how much is said, proponents of the extreme form of the just-do-it-principle, such as Dreyfus and Kelly, will be unmoved. True enough, Dreyfus and Kelly think that expert action is nonminded, and thus does not involve trying; yet they will be unmoved because O'Shaughnessy, Hornsby, and Hanna and Maiese take their arguments to apply only to intentional actions, while Dreyfus and Kelly think that the actions of the expert, when she is doing her best, are not intentional.

According to O'Shaughnessy (1973), actions such as occasionally moving your toes while reading a book are idle bodily movements, which he counts as actions—"one can hardly telescope them into mere spasms on the part of the toes"—yet nonintentional ones that occur without trying (p. 366). Such nonintentional actions, according to O'Shaughnessy, are merely "afterthought[s] in the scheme of things"; they relate, he tells us, "to standard examples of action somewhat as do objects that are mere lumps of stuff, say rough diamonds, to objects that are both lumps of stuff and more, e.g., artifacts" (p. 367). In contrast, Dreyfus and Kelly see many expert actions—for example, typical cases of shaving, reaching for doorknobs, and starting of cars, as well the truly great actions of Homer's heroes or today's heroes, such as, on their view, Lou Gehrig and Roger Federer—as nonintentional. They are nonintentional, but on their view they are more like finely faceted diamonds than lumps of stuff since they provide not merely the mainstay but also the meaning of our existence.

## Trying in Professional-Level Expert Actions

I am unsure whether our everyday actions proceed with some type of effortless trying, at least in the sense of being done with an aim—a sense that may capture at least to a degree what the theorists who advocate that all of our actions involve trying and which may also be compatible with effortful trying. However, it does seem that not all of our actions are performed with effortful trying since effortful trying would seem to be at least at times phenomenologically salient, yet there is no experience of effort in such action. Moreover, I leave open the possibility that effortful trying tends to interfere with routine activities. Indeed, it may very well be that we classify routine activities as routine in part because such actions are performed without effort. However, do expert actions typically or at least sometimes call for effortful trying?

The idea that effortful trying is part of expert performance conflicts, at least at first glance, with Bob Rotella's coaching—which by any measure is quite successful, helping seventy-four golfers win major professional titles (Rotella 2012). Moreover, it would seem to conflict with much of the psychological research on expert action, which, as Gabriele Wulf and Rebecca Lewthwaite (2010) sum it up, leads to the conclusion that "as a result of practice, movements are produced with less muscular energy—or physical effort" and, moreover, that "the mental effort associated with movement production lessens with practice and the movement is thought to become automated—that is, able to be generated without the conscious control of the mover" (p. 75).[4] And the idea that trying interferes with performing at one's best seems clearly demonstrated by Dugdale and Eklund's (2003) findings that accomplished dancers demonstrate more unwanted movements on a static balance task when instructed to try not to wobble than when they were simply asked to hold the board they were standing on steady. So does the expert athlete, musician, or dancer, in line with the cognition-in-action principle, try when she performs at her best? Or, in line with just-do-it, does it all flow out of her, like water moving downstream? Does she strenuously exert maximum effort, either physical or psychological? Does the task of coordinating her movements with others require work, or does it happen naturally? And if expert action is effortful, what type of effort is it? And, no matter what else, isn't it nonetheless true that trying "too hard" is detrimental?

## Kinds of Effort

To begin to answer these questions, we need to understand some of the different ways in which an action can encompass effortful trying. First off, we should distinguish *mental effort* from *physical effort*. Though they have many commonalities—for example, prolonged effort of either kind induces fatigue, they co-exist in various clinical

---

[4] Here the authors cite Lay et al. (2002), Sparrow et al. (1999), and a review by Sparrow and Newell (1998).

disorders such as Parkinson's disease and multiple sclerosis, and increases in either lead to increased pupil size—they are different types of effort: the former involves boosting cognitive load and the latter muscular contractions. (See Zénon et al. 2014 for discussion as well as an explanation of the experiment that led them to conclude that increased physical effort results in pupil dilation; that increased mental effort does so has been long known.) But this is only a start: within the categories of mental and physical effort, we can also talk about effort as observed—objectively, subjectively, and from a third-person subjective perspective. For example, measurements of muscular activity, oxygen consumption, and heart rate can be *objective* indicators of increased physical effort; your experience of effort is a *subjective* indicator of mental or physical effort; and when others who know you observe your performance and judge that you were exerting yourself mentally, this is a *third-person subjective* indicator of effort. And these different indicators do not always line up: for example, with physical training one might not perceive an increase in muscle contraction as (subjectively) effortful and sometimes what seems effortless from a third-person point of view is effortful in the subjective and objective sense. (And some measurements have both objective and subjective components, such as measuring the strength of muscle contraction relative to a subject's maximum level (identified subjectively) of muscular contraction, or the volume of oxygen used compared to one's maximal oxygen uptake (identified subjectively), what is referred to as one's $VO_2MAX$.)

I'll return to some of these distinctions in the next chapter (especially the last one, which I shall not say much more about here); however, we are already set up to ask, do professional-level experts perform with less effort than novices?

## Physical Effort in Expert Action

Many just-do-it enthusiasts would accept that expert athletes are, at least in an objective sense, exerting great physical effort. Obviously the amount of force an expert weightlifter applies to the barbell is more than what you or I could manage (unless, of course, you are an expert weightlifter) and for this reason most just-do-iters rail against mental trying more so than physical trying. However, it is sometimes thought (in line with one interpretation of Wulf and Lewthwaite's (2010) comment that "as a result of practice, movements are produced with less muscular energy—or physical effort") that when you are very good at something, the physical effort it takes to do it is lessened. In one sense, this must be correct: because an expert swimmer, for example, has learned to swim efficiently, she can, if she so desires, glide through the water with much less objective physical effort than a novice. Subjectively, too, it might seem quite effortless for the expert to make it from one side of the pool to the other. However, during a competition, an expert swimmer, presumably, will be extremely motivated and thus measured objectively and subjectively may exert more energy than an average recreational swimmer, for one of the things an expert swimmer has learned to do is maximize energy expenditure to the point at which any further expenditure would be detrimental to performance. A Division One swimmer I spoke with once put it rather alliteratively: "During a race I am constantly cognizant of every ounce of energy expenditure." (Of course, if one is trying not to drown, maximum effort will be exerted by expert and recreational swimmer alike.)

For an activity such as playing the cello, however, even during performance an expert may move the bow with less subjective muscular effort than someone who is picking it up for the first time and is (without much success) trying to correctly position it. After years of practice, her muscles have strengthened so that holding the bow in the correct position is not fatiguing; nor will she need to keep readjusting the position to try to get it right. This is not to say that an expert cello performance is never physically exhausting: Jacqueline du Pré seems to have expended tremendous physical effort and likely experienced this effort as well. Presumably, certain physical components that fatigue the novice are not experienced by her as effortful, yet overall, from an objective and presumably subjective point of view, she is going for broke.

That said, experts do sometimes claim to experience times when everything is easy, or at least times when, all of a sudden, things get easier. In marathon running, this may be explained in terms of your body switching from using one type of fuel (glucose) to another (ketones) (some research suggests that ketones are a more efficient source of fuel than glucose; see, for example, Prince et al. 2013). However, when you are trying to do more than anything to reach that finish line as fast as you can, once that switch occurs, you are not going to relax and take it easy. Rather, after perhaps a moment to revel in the feeling of no longer being on the brink of death, you are going to, like the swimmer I mentioned, be constantly cognizant of your energy expenditure and push yourself to the point at which any further expenditure would be detrimental to performance.

## The Experience of Effortful Trying in Expert Action

I have already argued that thinking is often present in expert action. Thinking in action can help one avoid the dreaded choke; it allows for a consistency between practice and performance; it is important for improvement during performance and for avoiding stereotypical responses; and it makes performing interesting for the performer (and perhaps for the audience, by revealing thought in action, which, I speculated, might be an essential element of artistry). These are all examples of mental effort. And they would seem to be examples in which effort is at least at times subjectively apparent.

Of course, introspection is an imprecise instrument and our experience of mental and physical effort in activities such as swimming, tennis, and marathon running is likely jumbled together. Perhaps what we at times experience might be best described in more general terms as the experience of overcoming a resistance. Tim Bayne and Neil Levy (2006) explain the subjective experience of effort as "[feeling] as though one is exerting a power of one's own against a force" (p. 17). And this might be a good way to understand the experience of effortful trying in general: to swing that tennis racket harder, to see the right move in chess, or to balance on the toes of one foot without a wobble, you need to push against a force.

Part of the reason for why introspection might lead to a jumble of the experience of physical effort and mental effort is the imprecision of the tool. However, I think that another reason is that difficult physical activities require both great physical and mental exertion. When you experience your elevated heart rate while running or muscle strain while weightlifting, you are experiencing (that is, you are subjectively aware of) the physical effort you are exerting to achieve your goal. However, in such cases it is likely that this is not all you are experiencing; if the argument I have made so far in this book is correct, experts are also using their mental faculties. Support for this view, as I see it, comes from Zénon et al.'s (2014) findings that pupil dilation occurs not only as a result of mental exertion, but also in physical exertion: moving from simple to difficult mathematical calculations and moving from less intense to more intense physical activities both result in pupil dilation presumably because both require increased mental fortitude. Zénon et al., however, discount the possibility that an increase in mental effort accounts for why pupil dilation occurs during their test case of increasing grip strength, arguing that the relevant cognitive task during the physical activity, which was modulating grip strength based on a computer display, was not very challenging and was the same in the low and high effort task. However, Zénon et al. do not consider that performing both increasingly difficult calculations and increasingly difficult physical actions require increasingly higher levels of willpower, and because of this, increased pupil dilation in physical activities might be caused by the increased mental effort of exerting one's willpower to maintain the effort.

## Kinds of Subjective Mental Effort

Wendy Slater, a pianist, composer, and lyricist, told me that her best performances feel effortless; yet when I asked if she would be ready to do it all again immediately afterward, she said "of course not: I'm exhausted!" How are we to understand these claims? Are her best performances effortless, or, because they leave her exhausted, do they involve effort?

I think that the answer to this question depends on whether we are talking about mental effort in the sense of willpower, or mental effort in the sense of deliberating, predicting, planning, and so forth. A simple, boring activity might require mental effort in the sense that it requires willpower to keep you doing it. You need to exert your will to keep putting away the dishes, though the task itself is not mentally taxing; my ten-year-old son could do it (if I could only get him to). As I see it, certain expert-level activities require this sort of mental exertion, not because they are boring, but rather—as with perhaps racing in a marathon—because they are so painfully difficult that you need to use willpower to keep going. Other expert-level activities, however, may be so intrinsically enjoyable that one does not need to exert one's will to continue doing them (compare Norman and Shallice 1986).

When Slater says that she finds good performances effortless, yet that she is mentally exhausted afterwards, it seems likely that what is occurring is that she does not need to exert her will to perform, yet such performances are mentally taxing. Are proponents of the just-do-it principle correct then at least in their claim that expert performance does not require willpower? It seems likely that truly great actions do not occur when someone is so bored by an activity that it requires willpower to do it. Yet, I think willpower might be needed in expert-level performance for another reason, and that is to force oneself to do actions that require enormous amounts of physical or mental effort, or to force oneself to do actions that are physically painful (as expert actions sometimes are): one naturally desires to avoid such actions. The pounding ambition to win, to excel, to achieve something beautiful or profound might render willpower superfluous. Yet it seems that, even when performing at one's best, ambition might not always suffice to carry action along without willpower: sometimes one wants to succeed, but is too exhausted or demoralized to continue, and in such cases, having an iron will is a great attribute.

Even for something that would seem as spontaneous as improvisational theater, you need to exert mental effort. I had the opportunity to ask the multitalented actress, producer, writer, and comedian Tina Fey about what it is like for her to perform at her best. "One thing you learn," she told me, "is that you need to be open to what others are giving you," and that you need to avoid the experience of feeling as if you have been "removed from your body and are watching yourself from afar." But how, I wanted to know, do you do it? Do you simply let yourself be open to what others are giving you and then react, or do you need to monitor it in some way? She thought that monitoring was key in order to avoid falling into stereotypes, and she said that this is something you can do only after years of experience. As she described it, "you need to push past it." Pushing past stereotypical reactions sounds very much like what Bayne and Levy identify as the experience of effort, and indeed, when I asked her whether it was difficult to do this, the response was a resounding "Hell, yes!"

Apart from situations in which the only way to calm nerves is to take it easy (and even here you might need to *try* to take it easy), experts, when they want to perform at their best, aim to give 100 percent of what they have; anything less is an inferior performance. As a dancer, this idea was pressed upon me by directors: "Dancers, I want to see you give it your all tonight!" "It was OK, last night, but tonight I want to see more, more, more!" These comments wouldn't make sense if excellence is achieved without trying. The skilled dancers in Dugdale and Eklund's (2003) study are skilled at dancing, not balancing on a wobble board. And thus I take it as an open question whether wobble-board experts would be derailed by trying.

As I have argued, part of what makes experts excel is that they are never or at least rarely satisfied. As such, expert actions are going to involve trying (since they involve trying to get better) and sometimes effortful trying. When I raise my arm at the entrance to my favorite café to push open the door, I do not usually try to do this;

however, when I raise my arm in the Black Swan *pas de deux* from *Swan Lake*, in order to push away (yet tantalize) Prince Siegfried, I give it my all and try my hardest. Of course, this might not be a case of trying to raise my arm; and it certainly doesn't involve trying to exert as much muscular force as possible. However, in my case, at least, it involves trying my hardest to impart an idea, to create an aesthetically rich movement, and to repel yet tantalize at the same time.

## Does Expert Action Involve Neural Efficiency?

I mentioned in the Introduction to this book that some take neurological data to support the idea that the actions of the expert are objectively easier to perform than those of the novice since they place less demand on the brain. This, roughly, is the idea illustrated by what is called the *neural efficiency hypothesis*, which, as Del Percio et al. (2009) describe it, "posits that neural activity is reduced in experts" (p. 193). If experts exhibit neural efficiency, this would seem to be good evidence that experts perform their action with less mental effort, in an objective sense, than novices. Do experts, then, exhibit neural efficiency?

The neural efficiency hypothesis originates from psychometric research suggesting that, based on measurements of glucose consumption and electrical activity in the brain, individuals who perform well on intelligence tests as compared to those who perform poorly exhibit reduced neural activity (Deary and Caryl 1997). One group of researchers states it as such: "the more intelligent a person is, the fewer mental resources have to be activated" (Grabner et al. 2003, p. 89). Yet the psychometric research has been challenged. As Neubauer and Fink (2009) explain in a recent review of the literature on neural efficiency and intelligence, although neural efficiency may be found in easier cognitive tasks as well as in well-practiced cognitive tasks, "in very complex tasks more able individuals seem to invest more cortical resources resulting in positive correlations between brain usage and cognitive ability" (p. 1004). This resonates with my view about expertise: experts are able to perform without much effort or thought when the goal is an *adequate* performance. For Susan, a ballet dancer who has a highly anticipated date after her evening performance, the morning's 9 a.m. show for schoolchildren might be one of those times when an adequate job is good enough. An adequate performance is much easier than a stunning one, and on autopilot she can attain adequacy. But when the stakes are high, she will exert herself, both mentally and physically, to do the best job possible.

Of course, neural efficiency, in the above sense, is perhaps not of much relevance to the just-do-it principle, since high intelligence, if understood as primarily a product of nature rather than nurture, is not clearly expertise, which, as I am defining it, is attained only after deliberate practice. However, various researchers report evidence for reduced cortical activity (neural efficiency) in activities that individuals have been trained to perform (see, for example, Krings et al. 2000; and Haufler et. al. 2000). However, it seems that, as with the varied thought experiments examined in Chapter 4, tests of neural efficiency are open to the criticism they fail to be ecologically valid since, arguably, neither the tasks nor the motivation mirrors what one finds in the wild. And studies of neural efficiency face the further challenge of coming up with an ecologically valid task capable of being performed inside of a brain scanner.

It is also difficult to find experts who are willing to go through the necessary trials. Yet it is not impossible. For example, Krings et al. (2000) were interested in examining cortical activation in four motor areas of the brain in professional pianists compared to control subjects (piano novices) during a complex motor task requiring hand dexterity. To investigate this, they recruited four expert pianists and four novices to perform a complex finger movement sequence (touching the thumb pad to fingertip of each of the four other fingers, in a predetermined and well-rehearsed order of twelve touches) in an fMRI scanner. And what they found was that, compared to the control subjects, the scans of the expert pianists showed a reduced area of activation within the four motor regions of interest during task execution. Moreover, the professional pianists gave the motor task a lower subjective rating of difficulty than the control subjects (an average difficulty rating of 2.25 for the professionals versus 3.5 for control subjects, on a scale from 1 (very easy) to 5 (very hard), though both groups performed the task with similar accuracy (p. 190). The authors conclude that the professionals' smaller area of cortical activation in motor regions indicates that "a smaller subset of neurons that control the complex task was recruited [in the professionals] for the same [level of] performance" compared to the novices, or in simpler terms, "for the same movements [fewer] neurons have to be activated" (p. 192). Krings et al. surmise that the professional motor experience with the complex finger movements involved in piano playing has, over time, led to greater neural efficiency within the motor regions that enable and control such tasks. In other words, it seems that the professionals did not need to try as hard.

This is interesting, but performing a complex sequence of finger touches is significantly different from performing the Kreutzer sonata in a recital, and so there is at least some question whether experts exhibit decreased cortical activity during execution of precisely the motor tasks that they are experts at performing. Other studies compare the neural activity of individuals learning a task with the neural activity of these same individuals performing the task after they have mastered it. For example, both Tracy et al. (2003), who observed differences in brain activation before and after two weeks of practice tying a complicated knot, and Puttemans et al. (2005), who looked at differences before and after eight days of practice performing a bimanual coordinated wrist movement, conclude that one possible interpretation of the data is that practice leads to reduced cognitive demands. Here too, one might interpret this to mean that the practiced individuals did not need to try as hard. However, again, since there is no need to think much about your movements when you are doing something utterly predictable, for which you are competent, and have no interest in improving, the subjects of these studies did not need to effortfully try to tie knots or move their wrists.

Again, with practice, certain aspects of an expert's performance, like the cellist's griping the bow, do not require effortful trying for an expert. This leaves mental resources available for effortfully trying to accomplish other ideals, for the expert is always trying to do more.

Yarrow et al. (2009), in their review article on the brain of the elite athlete, conclude that "clearly expert and novice athletes use their brains differently, but precisely interpreting these differences in terms of their functional roles seems some way off at present" (p. 589). If this is correct, it may even be difficult to say what the results of the experiments on neural efficiency are supposed to show. Nevertheless, it would not be surprising if experts can perform at a higher level than novices, yet with less physical and mental effort, measured both subjectively and objectively. This is because their movements are more efficient so they are able to get more done with less physical force, and if they were to perform in this way, their actions would be experienced as easy. But, again, I think that there is little reason to accept the view that when they are performing they do not commandeer all of their resources. And when they commandeer all of their resources, they are typically trying harder than the novice in the sense of exerting, in both the subjective and objective sense, more mental effort.

## Can the Coach of Seventy-Four Winners be Wrong?

I have argued that effort is part of an expert's mental and physical landscape. And part of this argument depends on examples from the performing arts. But could athletic excellence demand a different set of mental attributes? Certainly, small mistakes seem to matter more in sporting events. Though there are dance competitions (such as the Prix de Lausanne), such competitions are not the mainstay of a dancer's performing life. Rather, for a dancer, if something doesn't go well one night, it is usually possible to try it again the next night. More might turn on performance in an athletic event, however; making a mistake in a World Series game that causes your team to lose can be heart-wrenching, and in some cases, there is also enormous prize money at stake. And the observations of Bob Rotella, who has coached numerous professional title-winning players, ought not to be discounted. However, even for Rotella (2012), it is not clear that that effortful trying per se is detrimental to performance. Rather, the problem seems to be that effortful trying can lead to insecurity and nerves, and it is that which is detrimental to performance. As he explains it:

I have worked with players who can play without conscious thought, but when they do so, they forget to react to their target. They tend to get loose and sloppy. They're much better if they can keep the target as part of their mental equation. It seems almost contradictory, I know. How can I not have conscious thoughts but at the same time remember to react to my target? All I can say is that good players do it when they're at their best. (p. 71)

Well, what's going on? Should players try to hit the ball in a certain way or not? It seems that what really needs to happen, according to Rotella, is that a player needs to think, but only in a particular way:

A player can have just one swing thought such as, *Release the putter blade toward the target* or *Take the club straight back along the target line*, or *Turn the button of my shirt toward the target.* The problem with this is most can't keep to just one. (p. 78)

And after one, he finds, the mind tends to go haywire:

Golfers, to play their best, have to have the mental discipline to turn off their conscious brains just when the analytical portion of their minds…starts silently screaming…*You're on the last hole of a match you'd dearly love to win and very much hate to lose. You've got a delicate pitch from a lie in the rough to a front-hole location. Everything is riding on it—the match, the long hours of preparation you've put in, the trophy. Don't mess it up.* (p. 69)

So it seems that for Rotella, it is not trying per se that ought to be avoided, but the barrage of anxious thoughts that might enter the mind in high-pressure situations. This barrage of thoughts may lead to a loss of confidence and excess nervousness, and it is this—not thinking itself—that interferes with performance. If the only way to staunch this barrage of thoughts is to turn off the conscious mind completely, then, if the thoughts are harmful enough, so be it. However, the best athletes can leave the conscious mind on since when they think in action, they think useful thoughts, not detrimental ones.

How does an athlete or performing artist think useful thoughts without opening the floodgates to anxiety? In Chapter 4, I quoted the former tennis pro David Breitkopf who spoke of the ameliorative effects of training attention on one idea, or phrase, that efficiently captures many aspects of his stroke. He explained that this phrase, which he repeats over and over again in his mind, "isn't just a phrase that calms you, but also is intrinsic to the stroke itself, and allows every other part of the stroke to work properly." John Toner, Aidan Moran and I speculate that focusing on a single thought or a cue word can help one to monitor and control movement (Toner et al. in progress; see also Toner et al. 2014 and Sutton et al. 2011). And perhaps, if one follows Breitkopf's advice, the floodgates are kept closed because the repetition of the one useful thought prevents the others from breaking through.

The repetitive single thought, the "mantra," however, is not for Breitkopf the final destination. It is the means to arrive at a state where thinking can be more fluid, a state of optimal performance, or what is frequently referred to as being "in the zone." As he explains:

When I was growing up as a tennis player, we used to call it "treeing": that is, you're playing above your head. When I was "treeing" I would certainly be thinking. I would be very aware of my surroundings, the score, the strategic situations I'd find myself in—but I would be extremely calm. Nothing could disturb or distract my focus. At these moments, I felt I had total confidence, total belief in all my strokes. I knew wherever I was I could return the ball and return it to a spot on the court that would be difficult for my opponent. (pers. comm.)

## Automatic and Effortless

You have to try to perform an action that you experience as difficult. And, as we have just seen, contrary to the just-do-it principle, there appear to be examples of how effortful trying is involved in expert action. Even Rotella's view is consistent with the idea that expert action involves effort—there is the effort of keeping the target as part of the mental equation and of keeping that one, and only one, swing thought in mind. Beyond this, as we've already seen in previous chapters, many experts do recount how difficult their work can be. And the examples are easily multiplied: the international best-selling author Haruki Murakami (2007), who produces writing that appears to flow effortlessly from his fingertips says, "to put it in the simplest possible terms, I find writing novels a challenge" (p. ix).[5] Dreyfus and Kelly (2011a) ponder whether David Foster Wallace's inability to get washed up in the flow of inspiration—to experience the "whoosh"—was not an element in his depression (p. 22). However, whether or not it was relevant to his psychological instability, Wallace, as Dreyfus and Kelly also recount, clearly found writing torturous; yet he produced great work. A financier once told me that in his line of work pain is sometimes used as an indicator of a good choice: when it starts to feel painful, you know you've found the sweet spot. Philosophy also uses pain as an indicator: if there is no pain, you probably haven't found something that is surprising, something that isn't immediately apparent to everyone else. In all of these examples, if you do not try to persevere, you are going to give up.

Nonetheless, one sometimes also hears experts say things that make it seem as if their work were not difficult: for example, golfer Byron Nelson reports that "[f]rom about 1937 on through the rest of my career, I didn't think about much while making a shot ... and [it] became pretty automatic and effortless" (quoted in Rotella 2012, p. 57). Did Nelson, then, not need to try? Although in viciously competitive activities—and ballet is an example of this—comments to the effect of "it's all easy" might occasionally be deliberate attempts to lead others onto the wrong path, there is no reason to think that this is the case here. Likely, Nelson did reach a point in his career where it seemed effortless. But it also could very well be that although his game was effortless in one sense–he may, for instance, have not needed to exert will power–he still might have put in effort in another sense. For example, perhaps he still might have tried his hardest to get the ball in the hole. That said, it may be that there are some experts for whom the process becomes easy. Maybe Nelson was one of those. But another possible explanation is that around 1937 he lost the motivation to improve. When one is already great, one still can perform amazingly well even without this burning desire.

The great ballerina Violette Verdy told me that she had one performance—only one—where she "wasn't even there," where the performance was absolutely effortless (pers. comm.). Hoping that she would tell me that this was a dull, lifeless performance,

---

[5] As Thomas Mann purportedly said, "a writer is somebody for whom writing is much more difficult than it is for other people."

I asked her, "Did the audience notice this?" "Oh, yes," she replied; "A close friend came backstage afterward and was overwhelmed [by how good the performance was] and wanted to know what happened." Rather disappointed, I was not sure what else to ask, but then she added, "I had, of course, been reading Eastern philosophy by that point." The Eastern philosophy may have taught her how to leave the mind behind, or it may have influenced how she interpreted her own mindful performance. Interestingly enough, she also told me that after that performance, she knew it was time to retire.

## The Impossibility of Trying Too Hard

Let me conclude this chapter with an attempt to make good on the promissory note offered by its title. I have argued that expert performance often (if not always) involves an element of effortful trying, be it exclusively mental or both mental and physical. But I have yet to say anything about why I think you can't try too hard. Hence, let me do so, since it seems that, clearly, you shouldn't try *too* hard!

It is of course unreasonable to deny, and I do not deny that there is a sense in which trying *too* hard interferes with performance. For example, as a ballet dancer, I was never any good at tap dancing. In ballet, you control your ankles, but some tap steps required relaxing your ankles; I never could do this since I was unable to relinquish control. So in a sense I was trying too hard. The great tennis player Billie Jean King (2008), although she emphasizes the importance of "bringing your full self" to every game, also notes that sometimes it is important to pull back:

I always care about the task at hand and try to follow through, but there are times when I find myself hitting a brick wall. There are times when trying softer can work better…It is the difference between letting it happen and making it happen. When we try too hard we can be too tense, with muscles rigid and anxiety skyrocketing, there will be no flow to what we are doing. (p. 74)

In some sense, these are examples in which trying interferes with performance. But in another sense, I think that they can be seen as examples of not trying hard enough. Despite Billie Jean King's testament to "letting it happen," it seems that tension and anxiety rather than trying, is the culprit. The want of flow in such situations is not a failure to achieve an empty state of mind, which is how Dreyfus and others sometimes understand the term "flow," but rather it is a lack of fluidity in movement. In order to achieve this fluidity, King needed to try harder to relax her muscles. And in tap dancing, I needed to try harder to relax my ankles. In one sense this is relinquishing control; however, reduced control in this respect could have allowed for a greater degree of higher-level executive control: with less muscle tension, my motor command to perform a time step may have actually resulted in a decent time step.

Is it paradoxical, as Edward Slingerland (2014) makes out in his book *Trying Not to Try*, to try to relax? It seems that as long as it is not the 'trying muscle'—that is, our will to perform an action—that one is trying to relax then there is no incompatibility between trying and relaxing. If, rather than the trying muscle, what one needs to relax is a bodily muscle (in the ankles, thighs, shoulders, for example), then thinking really hard about how to do this is perfectly compatible with doing it. Sam Chase (2016) likens trying to relax with trying to feed a wild animal: you can't force it to eat out of your hand, however, you can try to be very calm and still, appear at the right time with good food, and let the animal come to you. And if it's not working, just like in tap, you need to try harder.

Another example that comes to mind is ballroom dancing. In ballet, the woman often initiates the movement during partnering, but in ballroom dancing, it is the man who leads. With my background, I find it difficult to let my partner lead and when waltzing the night away sometimes end up trying to gain control. When this happens, am I trying too hard? In one sense, yes, since in ballroom dancing I should passively wait for my partner's hand on my back to cue the turn. But in another sense, I wasn't trying hard enough to wait for the cue.

It is also clear that one's effort can be greater than what is optimal for the action. For example, if you would throw yourself off-balance in a pirouette by pushing off with your maximal energy (and you almost certainly would), then you are "trying too hard" and ought not to push with so much force. However, when we understand "trying to pirouette", as trying to do the movements that lead to successful pirouetting, experts ought to and do try their hardest; in other words, they can't try too hard to do that. If there is a certain dance step that ought to be performed with utmost delicacy, more physical effort would ruin the effect. But when you exert more physical effort, you are not trying harder to make the move delicate. Similarly, there might be a sense in which you are trying too hard to write a paper if you look up all the nuances of every word you use in the *Oxford English Dictionary*; this, it would seem, would impede your ability to think about the ideas, to say nothing of ever getting the piece done. But were you really trying too hard to produce your best writing? In another sense, "no," for it seems that if you were, you wouldn't spend so much time looking up every word. In the sense of trying to do well, one can never try too hard.

Expert action, I conclude, involves trying, and often effortful trying. Nonetheless, as I shall go on in the next chapter to discuss, it often appears effortless.

# 8

# Effortlessness with Effort

It is absurd to suppose that purpose is not present because we do not observe the agent deliberating.

Aristotle (384–322 BCE)
*Physics*

Although we praise effort, we prize effortlessness. Successful expert actions, as I argued in the previous chapter, typically involve effort. Nonetheless, such actions may appear effortless and, for many, it is this effortlessness that in part makes watching expert action aesthetically pleasurable. Yet what are we appreciating when we admire a dancer's effortless technique, precision, or presence? Why is it that when the renowned Alicia Markova "finishes her effortless variation, with the turn of its final phrase rounded off meticulously to the fraction of a beat, it is no wonder the house burst into applause almost as an automatic reaction" (Martin 1941, p. 15)? But what makes something effortless, be it effortless bodily movements, effortless speech, or even effortless objects aesthetically valuable? We may praise effort, but if aesthetic effortlessness is not to be an instance of the just-do-it principle, I need to argue that the effortless performance that we prize is compatible with the performer exerting a great deal of effort.

The concept of aesthetic effortlessness is rarely discussed in academic circles today, particularly in analytic philosophy. Moreover, in the art world, effortlessness, though still highly valued by some, has generally gone the way of the two related qualities of beauty and grace, with many contemporary artists more interested in creating works that are provocative, powerful, beleaguered, or shocking, than in creating works that are effortless. The choreography of Pina Bausch, is aesthetically valuable because it expresses frustration, alienation, brutality, and pain—not because it expresses effortlessness. And although the cellist Jascha Heifetz is admired for his calm, cool effortless playing, it was, in part, the palpable effort and verve of Jacqueline du Pré's playing that made her great.

Though unpopular in academic circles today, it cannot be denied that effortlessness captures us, and its aesthetic appeal seems to be more immediate, more bodily, and less cerebral than our interest in the conceptually charged work of artists such as Pina Bausch. Moreover, the idea of effortlessness has drawn the attention of many great thinkers in the past. To look at just a few examples, the ancient Chinese Taoist thinkers

Laozi and Zhuangzi have been interpreted by some scholars as exalting effortless action or *wu-wei* (literally translated as "no action"), in both the artisan and the political leader (Slingerland 2007). The Italian Renaissance theorist Baldassare Castiglione's (1528/1975) *Book of the Courtier* inspired the artists of his day to, as he puts it, "practice in all things a certain nonchalance which conceals all artistry and makes whatever one says or does seem uncontrived and effortless" (p. 67). And, arguably, one aspect of what Kant (1790/2007) meant when he said that "the fine arts must not seem purposeful, although they are purposeful" and that they "must be able to be considered as nature," is that fine art must appear to be merely a product of nature, that it must appear to be effortless (p. 135).

The concept of effortlessness and the closely related concept of grace also garnered the attention of the late nineteenth- and early twentieth-century thinkers Henri Bergson and Herbert Spencer, with Bergson (1889/2008) describing the impression of grace as "the perception of a certain ease, a certain facility in the outward movements" (p. 11), and Spencer (1907) claiming that "truly graceful movements...are those performed with comparatively little effort [and that] a good dancer makes us feel that...an economy of effort has been achieved" (p. 383).

Today, though the concept of effortlessness is largely passed over by tough-minded academics, the media chastises politicians for their lack of it, for displaying "what appear to be laboriously studied moves rather than anything that comes naturally" (Fallows 2012), and it adulates athletes, artists, and artworks that embody it: the ballerina Natalia Osipova's grand jetés, for example, are extolled for their effortless elevation, soaring "through the air with so little effort that the sight of her lithe form hanging high above the stage is a shock every time" (Kourlas 2012, July 7); the opera singer Beverly Sills is described as being able to "dispatch coloratura roulades and embellishments, capped with radiant high Ds and E-flats, with seemingly effortless agility" (Tomasini 2007); and of cellist Yo-Yo Ma, the novelist Mark Saltzman says, "his playing was so beautiful, so original, so intelligent, so effortless that by the end of the first movement I knew my cello career was over" (quoted in Weschler 2000, p. 78).

Effortlessness, it seems, can be ascribed to bodily movements, to intellectual insights, to poetry, prose, and paintings. Even the Golden Gate Bridge has been extolled for its "seeming effortlessness," being likened to "Grace Kelly in *Rear Window*" (John King and Anthea Hartig, respectively, interviewed in Christensen 2012). Indeed, perhaps one reason the topic of effortlessness does not have a foothold in analytic aesthetics is this multifariousness. There is something to be said in favor of this stance: trying to figure out what it means for a portrait to represent a person is difficult enough; ought we really to confuse things further by trying to understand what it is for a bridge to represent effortlessness? I appreciate such methodological scruples.[1]

---

[1] For example, in my work on physicalism, I have frequently advocated that we should not bother trying to understand whether the mind is physical until we have understood more basic ideas, such as what it means to be physical. See Montero (1999); (2001); (2005); (2016).

However, even in a work as long as this one, it is impossible to cover everything, so let me dive straight into the thicket.

What, then, is it for an action to be effortless? What are we appreciating when we admire Castiglione's effortless courtier, a dancer's effortless leaps, a basketball player's effortless shot, or even a seagull's effortless soar? For Castiglione effortlessness or *sprezzatura* in the ideal courtier was primarily a social value, for it enabled individuals to gain recognition, approval, and promotion to higher political positions in the royal court. And the type of effortless action associated with the ancient Chinese concept of *wu-wei* is, arguably, primarily a political virtue, capturing an ideal expressed in the *Analects* (a work generally thought to have been compiled by the followers of Confucius in the centuries after his death, assuming a settled form during the third century BCE), wherein the exemplary ritualistic ruler is described as one who need not rule by force nor decree nor even speak, but merely "made himself reverent and took his position facing south, that is all" (Confucius and Waley 1938: 15.5); the ruler is able to do this, it is thought, because *wu-wei* is said to engender *de*, which is an especially powerful form of charisma or, as it is well named, magnetism.[2] Whether the actions of the courtier or the ruler were done with ease was presumably not at issue. What was important for these purposes was to give off the air of effortlessness.

Though no less relevant to politics in the present than it was in the past, my concern in this chapter is primarily with the aesthetic value of effortlessness in works of art.

## Medium, Representation, Process

In appreciating a work of art such as a dance, a sculpture, a painting, or a musical performance, the accolade "effortless" may apply to three aspects of a work, what I shall call the "medium," the "representation," and the "process." The *medium* encompasses the relatively lower-level entities, properties, practices, and relations that the work comprises. For a dance, this might be bodily movements; for a painting, this might be the array of paint. The *representation* is, quite simply, what the work depicts or represents. For example, John Ward's sculpture of William Shakespeare represents the great author in a pensive, yet effortless pose; the representation is as of William Shakespeare. And the *process* is what goes into creating the work, as it appears in the work (rather than, say, the hours in the rehearsal room). Perhaps a few examples will help clarify these distinctions:

The painting is of an effortless figure (*the representation is of an effortless figure*).

The painting looks as if the painter created it effortlessly (*the process seems effortless*).

---

[2] As such, *wu-wei* need not involve effortlessness, though it does involve acting noncoercively. For a discussion of *wu-wei* as a form of influence or power see Lambert (2016).

The brush strokes seem effortless (*the medium is effortless*).

She played a piece representing a carefree dance (*a representation of effortlessness*).

It sounds as if the pianist plays effortlessly (*the process of playing seems effortless*).

The piano sonata sounds effortless (*the medium, the sound produced, is effortless*).

What are the relationships between these forms of effortlessness? Can we have one without the others? Or are some sorts of effortlessness invariably connected? It seems that we can readily differentiate the representation of effortlessness from the other two forms of effortlessness. That is, we may appreciate represented effortlessness—of the sculpted torso, painted hand, or a poetic description of a stream, and so forth—without necessarily feeling either that the process of creating the representations is effortless or the medium itself is effortless. Consider Michelangelo's *David* standing in a relaxed *contrapposto*: hip protruding slightly, he effortlessly bears his weight on one straight leg while the other rests, gently bent. The statue represents an effortless figure. Yet the statue might very well appear to have been effortfully created, and the shapes of the marble might not be perceived as effortless. Or consider Raphael's *Portrait of Pope Leo X with two Cardinals*. The painting represents an effortless figure, yet one can reasonably see both the process and the medium as effortful. With dance, the connection is tighter, yet perhaps still possible to pull apart. A dancer performing the female lead in the ballet *La Sylphide*, for example, may represent an effortless winged being, who is both enticing and unattainable, yet it might not seem that she is effortlessly coming up with her movements. And perhaps one even need not see the movements themselves as effortless, though I imagine that the best representations of effortless creatures in dance also evince effortless movements (effortlessness in the medium).

Also, though the idea here may be somewhat elusive, it seems that one can also at least sometimes identify effortless mediums without identifying effortless processes or representations. The Golden Gate Bridge may appear effortless—perhaps because it seems to be doing something so difficult yet with such little effort—yet it does not appear to have been created effortlessly, nor even less does it represent something effortless; for example, it certainly doesn't represent Grace Kelly. (Might it represent effortlessness or freedom or some other property, a property which is itself effortless? I leave this footnote to Plato aside.) A rock garden may appear effortless (perhaps because the curves suggest an effortless way of bodily movement), while also appearing to have been created with great care; and a Glenn Gould performance of *Art of the Fugue* may sound effortless, but not represent effortlessness.

Again, other times the connection among these three elements may be tighter: Marc Chagall's ceiling mural in the Palais Garnier might seem to be simply thrown together, in part because of the effortless individuals it represents; good writing, as Somerset Maugham put it, may appear "a happy accident," but in seeing a piece of poetry or prose as a happy accident, one both attributes an effortless process and feels the writing itself to be effortless. Moreover, one is more likely to experience such happy accidents in writing that represents effortless characters than in writing that portrays struggle, in T. S. Eliot's *Old Possum's Book of Practical Cats* (1939), rather than in *The Waste Land* (1922/2005b). (Though is this merely because the authors have chosen to match their writing style to their subject matter, or does the subject matter itself affect our attributions of effortless style?) It may also be that our attribution of effortless style influences our attribution of effortlessly represented subjects. And in many, or perhaps most cases when we ascribe effortlessness to bodily movements, we understand the movements as being both effortlessly created and effortless themselves. Fred Astaire, the king of effortlessness in dance, seems not only to move effortlessly, but also to come up with his ideas about how to move, or about which steps to do, effortlessly (and this may be apparent, despite his following set choreography).

## Bergson on Effortlessness and Grace

On Bergson's (1889/2008) view, effortlessness, which he closely aligns with grace, is the spilling of one movement right into another.[3] With effortless movements, according to Bergson, you expect what is going to happen next: "perception of ease in motion passes over into the pleasure of mastering the flow of time and of holding the future in the present" (p. 12). Music that accompanies dance adds to this effect. As he says, "the rhythm and measures. . . . [allow] us to foresee to a still greater extent the movements of the dancer" (p. 12).

This is an appealing idea, for many of the bodily movements we think of as effortless have a smooth, flowing, predictable quality, and, conversely, many of the movements we think of as smooth, flowing, and predictable, we dub as effortless. For example, when we think of the effortlessness of great athletes or dancers, we might imagine a smooth (perhaps even slow-motion) picture of their movements, and when we see individuals walking in an even, perfectly coordinated way, we understand their gait as effortless. Additionally, smooth actions not only appear to be effortless, but also generally take less effort to produce than sharp ones, which require a burst of energy at each start and stop.

However, although many actions that we understand as effortless do appear smooth and flowing, it is not clear that all effortless movements are like this. A breakdancer's movements, for example, may appear effortless yet include at least some sharp, jerky movements, and in fencing, a riposte may be quick, sharp, brilliant, and effortless.

---

[3] I am not sure that the connection between gracefulness and effortlessness is as tight as Bergson sees it since, as I shall explain later, I understand our attributions of effortlessness to depend in part on our knowledge of the difficulty of the movement; it is not clear that our attributions of gracefulness depend on this, or at least depend on this to the same degree. Clearly, there is much more to say about the relationship between effortlessness and grace, yet I shall, for the most part, pass over this, as there is already too much to say about effortlessness and its relation to other, perhaps less difficult concepts.

And although Michael Jackson's breakdancing was preternaturally fluid, arguably, even he could include a sharp, effortless pop or lock now and again. If these examples are accurately described—and there is room to question them—not all effortless actions are smooth. In addition, the sharp accents or quick ripostes, though effortless, may not be predictable from looking at the current movement.

Perhaps more apparent, not all fluid movements look effortless. For example, if one notices a tense expression on a performer's face, a smooth and flowing movement might appear effortful. Or if a movement is smooth, yet extraordinarily slow— not slow as seen on a slow-motion film, but physically slow—it might look effortful. This is especially evident in the Japanese dance form Butoh, in which performers often move at a glacial pace. Butoh can be smooth and beautiful, yet look extremely effortful. Moreover, effortful actions, such as Butoh, might also contain, as Bergson saw it, the future in the present. You might know, for example, that a Butoh dancer is going to fall, in an excruciatingly painful and protracted way, to the bottom of a staircase.[4] Yet you may also feel that this fall takes all the dancer's effort, and then some. Predictability might also occur without either smoothness or effortlessness. A toddler's steps do not appear effortless, yet, an observer often knows what is coming next; and a parent might sometimes rush over to get ready to catch before the fall has even started.

Thus, though often found together, it seems that smooth, flowing, predictable actions are neither necessary nor sufficient for effortless actions. Nonetheless, it may be that smooth, flowing movements, done at a normal pace without any facial signs of effort, at least often seem effortless. But why might we attribute effortlessness to a sharp movement, and why do glacially slow, yet smooth movements appear effortful?

## Spencer on Effortless Bodily Movements

For Spencer (1907), grace is exemplified by movements "performed with comparatively little effort" (p. 381). And in line with this view, it does seem that in praising the effortlessness of a dancer or athlete's movements, we are noting, among other things, an apparent reduction in bodily effort. We may not see his or her movements as requiring *little* bodily exertion—it would be hard to explain all that sweat if that were the case. Rather, we perceive the movements as efficient. As Spencer notes: "after calling to mind sundry confirmatory facts," he concludes that "grace, as applied to motion, describes motion that is effected with economy of force." "A good dancer," he tells us, "makes us feel that . . . an economy of effort has been achieved" (pp. 381, 383). Effortless bodily movement seems to use just the muscles necessary for the job.

---

[4] As does the Swiss Butoh dancer, Imre Thormann, in his 2006 performance at Hiyoshi Taisha Shrine in Japan. See <www.youtube.com/watch?v=9ms7MGs2Nh8> for a video excerpt of this remarkable event. Accessed April 6, 2012.

But it is not entirely straightforward how to explain what this is. The tennis player Roger Federer has been noted for (among other things) his effortless playing. He may be putting 100 percent of his energy into a game, but his playing appears to have no wasted movements. For example, other players, when they run for a ball, might end up taking a number of small steps at the end to get right where they need to go; Federer gets there with the minimum number of steps. Spencer, if he were to have had the opportunity to watch Federer play, would likely have held that it was because of this efficiency we marvel at his effortless games.

However, in dance, the efficiency equation is a bit more complicated, for in dance sometimes many little steps, as in a *pas de couru* (which involves many fast, tiny steps) are exactly what is called for. Or consider a *pas de cheval*, a movement in which the foot moves from a standing position, to an embrace around the ankle and then, after a slight lilt, is extended from the body and lowered down to the floor. Clearly this is not the most direct way to get from point *A* to point *B*. Efficient bodily movements in dance, then, cannot be understood as involving the minimum number of motions or as bringing one the most direct way possible from one point to another. Rather, in this context, it seems that an efficient movement is one that involves no superfluous muscle tension. Raised shoulders, for example, will not help one to perform a *pas de cheval* better, so raised shoulders while doing this step would typically indicate superfluous muscle tension. (Of course, sometimes a raised shoulder is an important part of the movement, such as if one is trying to portray coquettishness. But here the movement would not be superfluous.)

Perhaps the idea that effortless movements do not involve superfluous muscle tension helps explain some of the apparent counterexamples to the Bergsonian view of effortlessness as involving smooth, predictable flowing movements. Perhaps the breakdancer's sharp movements might seem to evince no excessive effort, that is, no superfluous muscle use. On the other hand, glacially slow, yet smooth movement may appear effortful, because we sense both the performer's effortful will power and her bodily control.

## Effortlessness and Difficulty

What else must be present if we are to understand a work of art as effortless? When we attribute effortlessness to bodily movements in dance, it seems that, at least in many cases, we also see the work as, in some sense, difficult; we see it as difficult, yet appearing easy. Natalia Osipova's effortless leaps are certainly difficult. In classical music, as well, we often attribute effortlessness to pieces that are technically challenging; that is we attribute effortlessness to the medium—the notes played—in light of an underlying difficulty. Even the Golden Gate Bridge seems to accomplish something very difficult—the longest span—with ease.

This seems to be part of what we love: accomplishing something difficult with ease, or at least apparent ease. But in what sense is it difficult? I said that we can, at times, separate our attributions of an effortless process from both an effortless medium and representation. For example, we might see a painting as representing an effortless individual, yet not think that the process was effortless. Yet, it may be that if the individual who is observing a work of art is positively convinced that the process is difficult for an artist, then the appearance of effortlessness (at least effortlessness of medium, and perhaps even of representation) may be lessened or destroyed, for effortlessness, it seems, is highly cognitively penetrable: our beliefs about it affect how we experience it.[5] Upon listening, you might experience Glenn Gould's music as effortless (that is, the product is effortless), yet after watching him play and seeing that it appears difficult for him (or at least uncomfortable, given his odd posture) you might not hear it in quite this same way. Even our perception of effortlessness in an artist's representation might be affected by our beliefs about how difficult the work seemed to produce. The Renaissance artists held this view and kept their toils hidden so as to not destroy the effortlessness of their represented figures. And although I seem to be able to see the Golden Gate Bridge as effortless (medium) yet not having been created effortlessly, perhaps an engineer who fully understands the difficulty of such an accomplishment would not even be able to see the bridge itself as effortless. So we find difficulty in effortlessness in as much as we see the process as difficult; however, if we understand extremely well just how difficult the process really is, this may lessen or destroy our ability to perceive the medium as effortless.

Yet what are we to say of the movements of dancers who are dancing in pieces choreographed using everyday movements? Such movements would not be difficult for us to perform. Do we, then, not appreciate the effortlessness in such movements? The Judson Dance Theater, for example, was known for creating dances out of everyday movements, sometimes even taking untrained individuals to perform the movements.[6] In cases when the individual is untrained, I would say that the value of the dance has nothing to do with its effortlessness. Though there may be conceptual interest in a dance performance that consists of, say, people off the street moving furniture on stage, we typically do not appreciate the effortlessness of the "dancers'" movements in such a performance. Of course, the movements themselves might not have required effort (if the movement was walking, for example, rather than moving heavy furniture); nonetheless, the movements were not aesthetically effortless.

Or at least, such movements do not typically evince effortlessness: for there are those charmed individuals who, without any training, seem to embody aesthetic effortlessness in the way they move about in everyday situations. But even here perhaps we can identify some way in which the movement is difficult, for they are moving

---

[5] Whether this is a veritable example of cognitive penetrability is certainly open to question and depends quite a bit on what counts as the purely visual element of such a perception. For discussion of cognitive penetrability see Fodor (1983); Pylyshyn (1999); Susanna Siegel (2012); Macpherson (2012); and Stokes (2012).

[6] See Kourlas (2012, Dec. 21).

in a way—so smoothly and evenly—that would be difficult for us.[7] The seagull spreads its wings and effortlessly soars. It's not hard for the seagull to do this, but it is an impossibility for us, and so we see it glide unencumbered.

In other cases, where everyday movements performed by dancers compose a dance, we might value the effortlessness of such dances. Yet such dances involve difficulty as well. For example, it would be quite difficult to perform the everyday sorts of movements that show up in some of Merce Cunningham's work in the way his dancers perform them; the movements may be ordinary walking or running, but the dancers perform them in an extraordinary way.

## Objective, Apparent, and Intentional Ease

Effortlessness involves an element of difficulty, or so I have argued, but what is it that we admire about this difficulty? In certain cases of natural effortlessness, such as the seagull's effortless soar, the action is not difficult to perform for the one who is performing it, yet we are in awe that it can be done at all, and with such ease. However, how are we to understand the effortlessness of actions that require long hours of deliberate practice to perfect? In particular, when we admire the effortlessness of a dancer or athlete, do we marvel at the fact that someone has mastered a movement to such a high degree that it has actually become easy for her to perform? Or is it that we value the apparent ease of the movement—that is, the artist's or athlete's ability to make what is difficult for her appear easy? In most sports, athletes do not deliberately try to make their movements look easy (exceptions might be gymnastics, figure skating, and other such endeavors). However, even in basketball, one can still ask: do we cherish the actual ease of the athlete's movements or the (unintentional) appearance of effortlessness in movements that are, for the athlete herself, extremely difficult to perform? Finally, in cases where there is a deliberate attempt to create effortlessness, do we, in addition to treasuring the beauty of the apparent effortlessness of the movement, treasure the ability to create the guise of effortlessness?

I proposed earlier that our attributions of effortlessness to the medium (such as the bodily movements of a dancer) depend on our familiarity with how difficult the action is to perform. And if you fully understand that a movement is difficult for the performer to execute, you may be inclined to not see the movement as effortless. But sometimes, even if you sense the difficulty, you may be able to perceive it as (merely) apparently effortless. Or at least, this is what my own experience suggests. With familiar movements that I know are difficult, I am less likely to think that the movements have actually become easy for the performer, though I still may relish the apparent ease

---

[7]  If this is correct, those who walk effortlessly should not see or appreciate the same kind of effortlessness (as opposed to merely smooth even movement) in the gait of others, for they do not see it as anything that would be difficult for them to do. Or at least they would not see it to the same extent as those who are not endowed with such grace. Whether this is true, however, I do not know.

of those movements. Similarly, sports journalists, who I assume frequently have practical knowledge of the endeavors they write about, often couple their praise of an athlete's effortlessness with an acknowledgment that the effortlessness is only apparent. For instance, the 2012 U. S. Women's Open golf champion Na Yeon Choi was lauded for her "easy swing that makes her game look effortless;" "yet," it is pointed out, "it was anything but" (Manoyan 2012). It seems that what is being noted in such cases is not that the athlete's movements are easy for her to perform, but rather that they *appear* easy. Thus, it might be that the more one knows about a type of highly skilled movement being observed, the less likely one is to see it as actually easy, rather than as merely appearing easy.

It may be that in thinking about the effort of one's own movements, we place more weight on whether a task requires effortful willpower than, say, on whether it requires great muscular strength, and thus our judgment that an action requires great effort will often turn on whether we judge it as requiring great willpower. And whether we determine that an action requires great willpower often depends, it seems, on whether the action is pleasurable. Doing the dishes, though in some objective sense an easy task, is an activity I find unpleasant (especially when I have waited until midnight); thus it requires willpower to do, and thus I judge it as effortful. A dancer, in contrast, may perform something that is in some objective sense effortful; nonetheless, in watching him I might think of his movements, not as presenting the guise of effortlessness, but as truly effortless (with regard to the will) if I assume that the movement is pleasurable and thus requires little willpower.

Over and above the appreciation of apparent ease is the appreciation of the guise of ease, that is, the deliberate creation of ease. Castiglione held that a courtier's manner should not only appear effortless, but also give no indication of the great pains the courtier must take in order to create this appearance, for it was believed by him that the courtier's effortlessness or *sprezzatura* would be destroyed by any hint that the process of creating an effortless manner itself required effort. The great artists of Castiglione's time, influenced by his work, believed this as well and kept their labors carefully hidden from view in order to preserve the *sprezzatura* of their paintings.[8] No doubt, there is something correct about this; as I have been emphasizing, our background knowledge seems to affect our attributions of effortlessness. However, it might be that one can see a bodily movement as effortless, even while also seeing it as produced by mental effort or willpower; we might call this a "studied effortlessness." Yet, distinct from this, at times one might appreciate the guise itself—that is, not the effortlessness of a movement, but the difficult process of making an action appear (to those not in the know) effortless.

---

[8] The effortlessness in these works is in the representation. Raphael's portrait of Pope Leo X, for example, reveals a man in tranquil thought, with his hands so smooth and delicate that they appear not only to be utterly relaxed as they rest, but to never have engaged in manual labor at all. Similarly, Raphael's portrait of the great Castiglione himself reveals an individual who embodies the ideal described in the *Book of the Courtier*.

The writer Edna O'Brien's (1979) short story "Violets" depicts an individual who presents a facade of effortlessness. A woman has agreed to a visit by a married man, and the reader is privy to her inner thoughts and turmoil while she prepares for his arrival: Will he show up? Maybe he will cancel? The clock has not chimed yet; perhaps it is broken. Finally, he knocks. Her mind racing, she is barely able to reach the door and by the time she does, it is almost too late. But once in his presence, she presents an outward appearance of nonchalance. "We like it," she says in response to his comment on her apartment; "keep him wondering," she thinks. Here, what we appreciate is not how easily she is able to engage in badinage; rather, although her gentleman caller falls for her effortlessness, the reader appreciates the guise.

Is the woman in O'Brien's short story an expert in my sense, or does she merely exhibit everyday expertise? Although wooing a mate is typically not something one is explicitly coached in some might put heart and soul into developing their courting prowess and so they might count as experts in my sense of the term. In any event, O'Brien paints a picture of a character who was performing at her best, apparently effortlessly, yet whose mind was working effortfully all along.

Slingerland (2014, p. 190) says that effortlessness is "unfakeable," however, the protagonist of "Violets" was consummately faking effortlessness; and as a professional ballet dancer, faking effortlessness was something I got paid to do.

## The Perception and Pleasure of Effortlessness

How is it that we perceive effortless movement? Most simply, while an effortless piano cadenza is heard, an effortless bodily movement is seen. But is there something special about the way we see effortless movement? Bergson (1889/2008) thought that our perception of grace had to do with "physical sympathy": we feel, in watching a graceful movement, that our body, though stationary, is in some way attuned to the body of the graceful individual (p. 13). As I understand this, it is the process by which upon watching someone else move, one feels as if one were moving in a similar way oneself. One might call this "proprioceptive sympathy," and what I have elsewhere called "proprioceiving another's movement" Montero (2006a; 2006b). Is proprioceptive sympathy relevant to our perception of effortlessness?

It does seem that part of the experience of watching effortless dance involves an experience in the observer of bodily ease. However, while knowing that someone is putting large amounts of effort into a movement reduces the appearance of effortlessness, the more practically familiar you are with the movement you are seeing, the greater your proprioceptive sympathy with the movement. In watching a ballet dancer, for example, I am less likely to sympathetically proprioceive her bodily movements as effortless—since I know from practice how difficult they are—than I am when watching a basketball player. Nonetheless, in watching a dancer, I may feel a strong proprioceptive sympathy with her movements. So proprioceptive sympathy would appear to be only part of the story.

For Bergson (1889/2008), however, proprioceptive sympathy accounts, at least in large part, for our pleasure in watching what he thought of as "higher grace" (p. 13). Such movements were effortless, but not *just* effortless. We take pleasure in them because of their "affinity with moral sympathy," and, in criticizing Herbert Spencer for claiming that what we appreciate when we appreciate grace is merely reduced effort, he tells us that we identify grace in another person when we are "able to detect…some suggestion of a possible movement towards ourselves," when we experience "a virtual and even nascent sympathy" (p. 13). How could Spencer account for why grace affords us such pleasure, Bergson wanted to know, if grace is nothing more than the saving of effort?

I think Spencer's (1907/2008) view, however, might have something to recommend it. If the movements we dub as effortless are movements that would be difficult for us to perform, yet appear to be performed with reduced effort, then part of the reason why effortless action is attractive could be that it reveals a superfluity of fitness. Of course, proprioceptive sympathy could be part of the reason we admire effortless movement as well. Whether or not this is in part because proprioceptive sympathy makes us feel as if we were attuned to our fellow human beings, as Bergson seemed to think, it does seem that upon watching effortless movement, one of the things we enjoy is the feeling of performing difficult movements in a smooth, coordinated, efficient way (and this, perhaps, can be experienced even if we know great work was put into creating this coordinated efficiency).

But perhaps most importantly, effortless movements are pleasurable because they are beautiful. And it may be that we recognize them as beautiful because we both sympathetically proprioceive them and see them as revealing a superfluity of fitness.[9]

---

[9] Parts of this chapter overlap with Montero (2011 and 2016). Many questions, both here and there, remain. For example: Is every attribution of effortlessness normative? Is effortlessness necessarily an aesthetic attribute? Or might there be cases in which we attribute it but do not intend to make an evaluative judgment?

# 9

# The Pleasure of Movement and the Awareness of the Self

> Those friends that have it I do wrong
> When ever I remake a song
> Should know what issue is at stake,
> It is myself that I remake.
>
> William Butler Yeats (1865–1939)
> "Preliminary Poem"

In a paper entitled "The Way of the Wanton" (2008), philosopher David Velleman posits that we achieve excellence only when we are "transcending reflective agency" (p. 182). What he means by this is that, although reflective agency—that is, thinking about and deliberating over our actions as they unfold—is a stepping-stone to developing expertise, we perform at our best when we attain what he refers to as "self-forgetful spontaneity," or "flow" (p. 187). Expressing a version of the view I have been referring to as the "just-do-it principle," he tells us that in highly skilled actions, "the capacity to monitor...performance, to consider how it falls short of an ideal, and to correct it accordingly...is no longer exercised" (p. 188). Rather, after the requisite training, according to Velleman, "evaluative judgment is suspended," and experts act "without deliberate intention or effort" (p. 185).

In previous chapters, I have argued for the importance of monitoring, evaluation, and effort in expert action. And in doing so, I have also been supporting the idea that self-awareness is not necessarily detrimental to, and is often a component of, optimal performance since, as I see it, conscious monitoring, evaluation, and effort go along with a sense of the self: when you are consciously monitoring or evaluating your actions, there is a sense that it is *you* who is doing the monitoring or evaluating; when you are conscious of making an effort to perform an action, you have a sense of effortfully exerting yourself.[1] However, in this chapter, I want to scrutinize two further ideas that seem to motivate the just-do-it contention that the self is absent in expert performance. This is the idea that the pleasure of movement "washes away the self" and the idea that the loss of self in expert movement is at least in part responsible for

---

[1] Or at least this is true, barring (as I shall do) any general worries about whether we even have a sense of the self at all.

the pleasure one experiences in expert movement. Although some who talk about the loss of self in expert action hold only one of these two positions, others seem to hold the "reciprocal pleasure principle": in expert action, pleasure washes away the self and a loss of self is a mainspring of pleasure.

Some of my thoughts on this topic have been inspired through a collaboration with the clinical neurophysiologist Jonathan Cole, which resulted in a paper on the pleasure of bodily movement, entitled "Affective Proprioception" (Cole and Montero 2007). Jonathan is a leading researcher on proprioception and I have learned a great deal both from my collaboration with him and from his insightful and engaging books and papers. However, I now think that some of what we said may have been beholden to just-do-it. In particular, if you were wondering who it is that holds the reciprocal pleasure principle, let me now tell you that in addition to finding shades of it in popular accounts of the phenomenon known as "flow," it seems to have been in the background of my work with Cole. We started with the premise that highly skilled bodily movement is often pleasurable—a view I still agree with, even though I would now place more emphasis on the fact that it can often be painful, as well. We were then interested in identifying what makes it pleasurable: in highly skilled movement, we argued, one is sometimes blissfully unaware of the self. And we also saw the pleasure of movement as conducive to a kind of bodily immersion which at least might be interpreted as a loss of the self. I now think that the more accurate description of those moments during which, as we put it, the self dissolves is this: there is an *aspect* of the self that is lost, but not the self *entirely*. And it is this partial loss of self that can help explain the pleasure of expert movement and also stand as the effect of pleasurable bodily immersion. Hence, I would like to take this chapter as an opportunity to both recount some of my work with Jonathan, as well as to amend aspects of it that I now think may have been under the thrall of just-do-it. And I thank Jonathan for allowing me to do so.

## The Pleasure of Movement

Central to the reciprocal pleasure principle is the idea that the exercise of expert-level physical skills can be pleasurable. But Cole and I were more concerned with the general claim that not only expert physical actions, but many forms of physical activity or exercise, can be pleasurable: although many people exercise for instrumental reasons—in order to improve their health, perhaps, or to get from one place to another—some find exercise simply intrinsically rewarding. In other words, it feels good to expend physical energy; indeed, it may be that, as the nineteenth-century anatomist and neurologist Sir Charles Bell (1833/2009) held, the exercise of the muscular frame is the source of some of our chief enjoyments.[2]

[2] This, as well as the health benefits of exercise, was a topic of great interest to both my parents. See, for example, J. C. Montero (1966); and J. C. Montero and D. Montero (1966).

Cole and I surmised that numerous possible factors might account for this. For example, sometimes a physical activity is pleasurable in part because it facilitates other pleasures. Going to the gym, playing tennis, and taking a ballroom dance class are all social activities, and so one might derive pleasure from the interpersonal interactions such activities afford. Other activities enable distinct pleasures, such as the pleasure of spending time in nature (for example, in mountain climbing or kayaking), while taking a ballet class allows you to enjoy listening to the live musical accompaniment (typically on the piano, though I have taken class with cello accompaniment). And while some physical activities may leave you feeling as if you've been run over by a truck, one may also take pleasure in the aftermath of bodily movement, especially physical fatiguing movement. Bell refers to this as an "almost voluptuous" feeling, a feeling, as he points out, that is "diffused throughout every part of the frame" (pp. 205–6). Then there is the so-called "runner's high."[3] But as Cole and I pointed out, there is also something pleasurable in the experience of bodily movement itself. And it is this pleasure of movement, some think, that an athlete or dancer (or other physically skilled expert) can get "lost" in, a pleasure, some think, that washes away the self.

Perhaps not everyone experiences pleasure in movement. And some philosophers might feel that they get enough exercise simply working their brains. However, my concern here is not with the philosopher's pleasure in movement, but with the pleasure that is experienced by someone who is an expert in physical activities, such as the expert dancer, athlete, or musician. Though expert skills can be painful—to close out a game in the world of professional tennis, for example, is likely going to hurt—they can also be pleasurable; the dancer Fergus Early (Lansley and Early 2011) explains: "I find considered movement deeply pleasurable. I always have and I continue to—movement that has a purpose, that I think about. That's one of my great pleasures in life" (p. 181).

Cole and I speculated that activities such as dance and yoga, which are more internally focused, may be greater sources of pleasure in movement than sports which are more focused on external objectives, such as making a goal, catching a ball, or winning a point. Since I can barely throw a football, to say nothing of throwing one with a perfect spiral, this is something I do not know from first-person experience. However, putting aside the question from the end of Chapter 6 about whether it is possible for an expert in the heat of the moment to attend fully to more than one target, it does seem that attending to external goals, would compromise one's ability to spotlight one's own bodily movements and the pleasurable feeling that they bring. That said, more externally focused expert activities, as I have maintained in previous chapters, may also encompass an internal focus. And this may be pleasurable: one high jumper told me that she enjoyed the "harmonious shape" of her body during a good jump.

Though Cole and I were interested in the pleasure associated with bodily activities, one can also find pleasure in acts of mental expertise, such as chess or poetry. The thrill of coming up with a surprising checkmate, or a keen poetic phrase, can be pleasurable.

---

[3] See, for example, Kolata (2008).

One even finds pleasure in those rare moments when one seems to have identified a surprising necessary condition for something (such are the thrills of the analytic philosopher!). Yet, as with bodily expertise, often there is also a considerable amount of pain involved in such activities; sometimes one perseveres merely because it will be such a relief to be done.

There are possible evolutionary explanations for why the exercise of bodily prowess should be, as Bell puts it, rewarded by pleasure. Obviously, escaping from danger sometimes requires fleetness of foot. Since being physically fit is conducive to such fleetness, it would seem that those who find pleasure in activities that promote physical and mental fitness are more likely to practice them. Thus, a selective advantage would accrue to those who find pleasure in challenging physical activities. Yet evolutionary explanations for the existence of a trait are notoriously easy to come by, so let me leave this issue aside. Besides, my concern is not with the evolutionary explanation of why certain movements are pleasurable, but rather with the reciprocal pleasure principle: what is it about such movements that makes them pleasurable—in particular, does it involve a loss of the self? And does the pleasure of being fully engaged or immersed in the movement lead to a loss of the self?

The philosopher Julia Annas, in her book *Intelligent Virtue* (2011), tells us "we lack a vocabulary for explicating just what is enjoyable about the exercise of expertise" (p. 81). I think that this is true to a degree; however, although we may not be able to say "just what is enjoyable about [it]," I also think (and likely Annas would agree) that it is possible to say *something* informative about it. For example, the writer David Foster Wallace (2006) captures an aspect of this enjoyment when he writes about tennis star Roger Federer: "Rather like certain kinds of rare, peak-type sensuous epiphanies (I'm so glad I have eyes to see this sunrise! etc.), great athletes seem to catalyze our awareness of how glorious it is to touch and perceive, move through space, interact with matter." I think Wallace expresses something correct here: expertly moving through space and interacting with matter can be glorious. But again, one should not forget that it can be sheer hell as well. This may be especially true of tennis, which does not have the sorts of dynasties one finds in other athletic endeavors—professional tennis players apparently do not want their children to follow in their footsteps. Could this be because profession-al-level tennis, as Andre Agassi's (2009) autobiography makes abundantly clear, is remarkable not just for its peak-type sensuous epiphanies, but also for its excruciating pain? Ballet can also be excruciatingly painful, yet, in my memory—which, admittedly, is often rosy—the pleasures outweigh the pain (though Kirkland's (1986) book, *Dancing on My Grave* is the ballet world's analog to Agassi's autobiography).

Although Wallace (2006) captures something correct about expert movement, some of what he says hints at a view that I oppose. In speaking of the amazing physical-ity of Federer's playing, Wallace—and this is one reason why Dreyfus and Kelly cite him approvingly—seems to understand Federer's adroitness as bestowed upon him from the outside. "It's hard to describe," Wallace says, "and one wouldn't want to make too much of it . . . [b]ut the truth is that whatever deity, entity, energy, or random genetic flux [that] produces sick children also produced Roger Federer." However, while a deity, entity, flow of energy, or random genetic flux may be the primary causal force behind birth defects and illness in children, the primary causal force behind Roger Federer—that is, Federer's athletic prowess—is Roger Federer himself. It may at times be glorious for Federer to interact with matter and to touch, perceive, and move through space. But, as I shall argue, this glory, this pleasure, does not invariably dissolve the self. Furthermore, positing a partial loss of the self explains the relevant pleasure of movement just as well as positing total annihilation.

## Does Bodily Immersion Dissolve the Self?

When the pleasure of expert skill does outweigh the pain, one way that dancers (and likely others) experience this pleasure is in "bodily immersion," that is, in the feeling of being in contact with every point of one's body.[4] Britt Juleen, a dancer with Dutch National Ballet, explained that during a performance she aims to engage fully in the quality of her bodily movements. In her words, the goal "is to be totally immersed in the feeling of my body moving" (pers. comm.).

The relevant sense involved in Juleen's experience of being immersed in the feeling of her body moving is, I submit, proprioception, our nonvisual sense of our bodily movements and position by means of receptors in joints, tendons, muscles, skin, and ligaments. Juleen is feeling, for example, her arms lifting, her upper back arched, her fingers extended. In contrast to Fitts and Posner's view about expert action, according to which experts ignore kinesthetic information, far from ignoring such information, she is deeply aware of it.

I, too, felt that my best performances typically involved being immersed in the feeling of movement. I am not sure if this was the most important aspect of a good performance for me, since the experience of being in dialog with the music was also crucial as well as pleasurable (Juleen also commented on how she loved the experience of dancing to music), as was the intimate form of communication one has with one's partner or fellow dancers. Nonetheless, the experience of bodily immersion was certainly highly important. Some of the pleasure comes from the bare quality of abstract movement itself, but sometimes an idea behind the movement facilities the experience. For example, during the White Swan pas de deux (from *Swan Lake*), the ballerina's partner wraps the ballerina's arms around her as he embraces her. The movement itself feels sensuous, and the idea of the embrace adds to the sensuality. When all is going well, I claim, a dancer will often feel immersed in this experience of movement. And such an experience, as New York City Ballet principal Wendy Weelan put it, is "like heaven" (Harss 2014).

---

[4] One might even say that in highly skilled movement, one experiences a pleasurable unity of mind and body, not through any philosophical argument, but through experience. However, it is not clear that fewer philosophers would be dualists if they were highly skilled in a physical activity. Plato, for example, advocated gymnastic training, yet dualism was prevalent in ancient Greece.

Musicians also become immersed in their bodily movements. Charles Rosen (2002), a philosopher as well as professional musician, talks about the sheer pleasure of moving his hands, going so far as claiming that one cannot become a professional pianist without having a deep enjoyment of the physical movements of one's fingers on the keys:

Pianists do not devote their lives to their instrument simply because they like music: that would not be enough to justify a dreary existence of stuffy airplanes, uncomfortable hotel rooms, and the hours spent trying to get the local piano technician to adjust the soft pedal. There has to be a genuine love simply of the mechanics and difficulties of playing, a physical need to contact with the keyboard, a love and need which may be connected with a love of music but are not by any means totally coincident with it. (p. 10)

This love and need, if not constitutive of, is at least accompanied by pleasure. "Part of the pleasure of playing the piano…is purely muscular," Rosen writes, and "in general[,] pianists neither have to look at nor listen to themselves" (p. 34). But in this instance and in Juleen's experience of bodily immersion, we need not be led to the view that the pianist's or dancer's mind or self is not there. Rather, the mind, it would seem, is on the feeling of movement, and this experience of movement is at least compatible with a sense of self. Perhaps in overwhelming pleasure (or pain) the self does get annihilated; for what is an overwhelming pleasure save for one that overwhelms all other experiences? However, the pleasure of dancing, at least, while great, is typically not so great that it prevents the dancer from attending to other things. For example, Juleen might be aware that someone on stage is slightly behind the music. And even in cases where the only thing on one's mind is the feeling of movement, it seems that this feeling can in part comprise a sense of the self. In other words, there seems to at least be no direct path from bodily immersion to the loss of self.

## The Self in Flow

The psychologist Mihaly Csikszentmihalyi, who has done extensive research into the concept of "flow," which is variously described as full immersion, or complete enjoyment or absorption in one's activities, or simply as peak experience, uses the term "autotelic" to refer to action that is rewarding in and of itself and is done at least in part because it is rewarding in this way (Nakamura and Csikszentmilhalyi 2002). Certainly, there is an autotelic element in what Juleen describes as being immersed in movement, but, again, I do not think that such an element implies that there is no experience of the self: when one is fully immersed in an action, it can be the self that is fully immersed.

David Velleman (2008), however, calls upon Csikszentmihalyi (1990) to support his own view that peak performance involves the suspension of evaluative judgment and that in expert performance the self dissolves. On the suspension of evaluative judgment, we are given this:

In normal life, we keep interrupting what we do with doubts and questions. "Why am I doing this? Should I perhaps be doing something else?" Repeatedly we question the necessity of our actions, and evaluate critically the reasons for carrying them out. But in flow there is no need to reflect, because the action carries us forward as if by magic. (Velleman 2008, p. 186, quoting Csikszentmihalyi 1990, p. 54)

And in support of his view that in expert action awareness of the self disappears, we are told:

One of the most universal and distinctive features of optimal experience [is that] people become so involved in what they are doing that the activity becomes spontaneous, almost automatic; they stop being aware of themselves as separate from the actions they are performing... [This involves] a loss of consciousness *of* the self. (p. 186, quoting Csikszentmihalyi 1990, p. 53)

But does Csikszentmihalyi's research—research based on the "experience sampling method," which prompts subjects at random times to write down what they are doing and what they are thinking about and then rate their state of consciousness—show that expert action is typically unreflective and involves no awareness of the self?

As Csikszentmihalyi (1990) himself makes clear, his research is not an investigation into peak performance, but rather an investigation into peak experience. And these two might not always line up. First off, in contrast to autotelic actions, expert actions are sometimes not rewarding in and of themselves, but are performed because they might lead to a future reward, such as winning a tournament or simply doing better than ever before. Second, as I have been emphasizing throughout the book, expert action does not and should not carry us forward as if by magic. When responses need to be nearly immediate, there is not much time to ponder "why am I doing this?" and "should I be doing something else?" (though as we've already seen in Chapter 5 and will see again in Chapter 11, even in high-speed actions, typically there is some time to think and ponder). However, pondering such questions seems to be a very important part of many forms of expertise, such as those that encompass actions that may need to be justified (as I discussed in Chapter 5) as well as one that Velleman is very adept at: writing. "Why am I putting this idea here?" "Might it not be better in an earlier section of the paper?" "Should I be giving a definition here rather than simply an illustration?" Repeatedly questioning the necessity of our actions, in this way, and critically evaluating the reasons for carrying them out is helpful in creating a good piece of writing, and perhaps this is why writing is particularly un-autotelic.

Dreyfus and Kelly (2011a) mull over whether part of the reason David Foster Wallace was unable to find meaning in his life was that he was incapable of simply standing back and letting things happen, and in particular, whether it was due in part to his incessantly analyzing his writing. I'll return to the topic of the meaning of life in Chapter 12; however, for now I simply point out that although, as Dreyfus and Kelly speculate, Wallace's tendency to incessantly analyze his writing may have interfered with his optimal experience of life, far from interfering with his ability to write optimally, I submit that it was conducive to it.

Of course, if what Csikszentmihalyi means by "interrupting what we do with doubts and questions" is wondering why we should be doing this at all—for example, if I were to start wondering whether I should train to be a pastry chef rather than trying to write a book—this is probably not conducive to optimal performance or to optimal experience. However, the types of doubts that lead to revising one's work are often quite conducive to optimal performance. Flaubert purportedly said he once spent the entire morning inserting a comma and the entire afternoon removing it.[5] If this is true (and not merely exaggerated for comic effect), perhaps such extreme doubts can be unproductive. But then again, if that's what it took to write Madame Bovary, perhaps it was worth it.

In flow, Csikszentmihalyi (1990) tells us, actions are spontaneous, and—like Yeats's dancer *becoming* her dance in his poem "Among School Children"—one stops being aware of the self as separate from the action. However, although it may be that some of our most intrinsically pleasurable actions involve such spontaneity (even if afterwards you might look back and say, why didn't I think before I acted!), I do not think that this melding of the self into the action is necessarily characteristic of expert performance. The cello player Inbal Segev I quoted in Chapter 4, told us that she was trained to avoid letting the music lead her, but instead to direct it. The direction, she further explained, should be integrated with what you have done; it has to follow from or be connected to what has gone on prior to that point (pers. comm.). The control, in other words, should not be oppressive, but nonetheless it is the self controlling the actions. And this is true of ballet as well: perhaps the audience can't tell the dancer from the dance, but the dancer knows. I wonder if Yeats ever tried a pirouette?[6]

Moreover, even when experts are in what Csikszentmihalyi (2014) characterizes as flow, they still seem to be engaging their minds, for as Csikszentmihalyi sees it, "intense concentration [is], perhaps the defining quality of flow" ( p. 92). And intense concentrate is neither thoughtless nor effortless. Jackson and Csikszentmihalyi (1999), argue that skilled athletes in flow are often deeply aware of their movements as they are executing them in performance situations and, moreover, they suggest that "without self-awareness an athlete misses important cues that can lead to a positive change in performance" (p. 105). So, even ignoring the fact that Csikszentmihalyi's concept of flow applies to optimal experience rather than optimal performance, he does not seem to think that individuals in flow are performing in an unminded way.

## Does the Loss of Self Account for the Pleasure of Bodily Movement?

In being totally immersed in the feeling of movement, I suggest, one is consciously attending to, or focusing on, on one's movement. The self is present in such an experience

---

[5] This quote has been variously attributed to Flaubert, Oscar Wilde, and Mark Twain.
[6] He most certainly did write, however, and in that activity he seemed to see the self as central (see the excerpt from "Preliminary Poem" in the epigraph for this chapter).

not in the sense that you feel as if you are outside your own body and watching your actions from afar, but rather in the sense of being the locus of focus from the inside. This is not because you see yourself (in your mind's eye) performing them (though I suppose this may occasionally happen) but rather simply because you are experiencing them. However, in my work with Cole (Cole and Montero 2007), we suggested that in bodily immersion, the self disappears. Here is what we said:

> When absorbed in movement there may even be what might be described as a loss of self, a feeling that, at least as a locus of thought, one hardly exists at all. And of course the best performances are those where one is not thinking about the steps at all but is rather fully immersed in the experience of moving itself. (Indeed, thinking about the steps may lead to "blanking out" and forgetting the steps.) (p. 304)

But not thinking about the steps—in the sense of not trying to remember the choreography—is different from not thinking about the movement at all. Doing the right steps is really a small part of any dance performance; it's how you do them that matters. Moreover, in contrast to what I claimed with Cole, now I believe, as I argued in Chapter 4, that a good way to avoid blanking out is to make sure that the steps are accessible to conscious reflection. Yes, one shouldn't think "what comes next?" in the *de dicto* sense of thinking the very phrase "what comes next?" (this only occurs when you don't know what comes next); however, it is fine to think about what comes next in the *de re* sense of thinking about the next action you are going to do.

On the supposition that sometimes one does not really appreciate something until it's gone, Cole and I also supported our view (that in skilled movement one loses the self) by referring to comments made by some individuals who have lost their ability to move. We quoted Robert Murphy (1987), a professor of social anthropology, who became quadriplegic as an adult. Murphy, who used to be very able-bodied, claimed that "a quadriplegic's body can no longer speak a 'silent language' ... the thinking activity can no longer be dissolved into motion, and the mind can no longer be lost in an internal dialogue with physical movement" (p. 101).

How should we understand these claims? Cole and I commented that what Murphy seems to miss is having "one's mind—in the sense of oneself as a reflexive thinking agent— dissolve in the movement" (Cole and Montero 2007, p. 312). This we saw as an important element of the pleasure of movement, and we said that when it results from sufficient mastery, it may even be that "attention to movement is no longer required at all even though movement continues" (p. 312). It seems we were accepting the reciprocal pleasure principle: the type of pleasurable, immersed skilled activity that was no longer available to Murphy is conducive to a loss of self and this loss of self is conducive to pleasurable skilled activity. What led us to this view?

When Cole and I were thinking about what occurs in pleasurable movement, we noticed that it can stop you from thinking painful thoughts, or worrisome thoughts, or simply the same old thoughts that tend to crowd your mind. Indeed, it is not uncommon to hear in the life story of a professional athlete or performing artist that part of the reason why they dedicated themselves so fully to practice was that they wanted to block out disturbing aspects of their lives (and that was certainly a motive for me in ballet). So unmitigated attention to one's craft—what Steve Blass claimed he lost after developing his control problems, as I explained in Chapter 4—does prevent some types of unpleasant thoughts, but it is the self that is attending to the activity. In other words, although there may be pleasure in "losing the self" in movement in the sense of not worrying about death, taxes, and other necessary evils, this does not mean that, for an expert, the self dissolves in the awareness of the movement.

If we go back and look at what Murphy says, it seems at least possible that this is what he was commenting on as well. He says not simply that now for him "the mind can no longer be lost" (p. 102), but that it can no longer be lost "in an internal dialogue with physical movement" (p. 101); that is, his mind, before the injury, was in dialogue with movement and, it was that, he felt, that silenced the unwanted worries. If this is correct, then it is not that the self is lost but that one type of mental activity ceases while another more pleasurable type takes over.

Now it may be that for someone who has reached a certain level of competency and is no longer pushing to improve, their sense of self in expert movement may disappear altogether. Such individuals might just do it and not recall what occurred. But for the type of experts that I am concerned with, experts who are continuously pushing themselves to improve (and I take it that most of those who are at the top of their game are like this), this manner of performance would at least not be typical and would not be the manner of performance at which they aim. Of course, sometimes when an athlete is interviewed after an amazing game, he or she might comment, "I don't know what I did." For example, in an interview with Alex Zolbert, tennis champion Maria Sharapova claims that she has no idea what happened when she beat Martina Navratilova, going so far as to say, in response to Zolbert's comment that without such knowledge, she is lucky that her groundstrokes didn't go into the net, that "maybe they were in the net"; she didn't know.[7] But I think it is possible that such remarks have more to do with wanting to get the interview over or with not wanting to go into details when one is exhausted from a game than with a lack of autobiographical memory. And even if this is an example of when autobiographical memory disappears, there are numerous examples of experts who appear to remember every aspect of their amazing performances. As I pointed out in Chapter 4, the baseball player Pete Rose was known for this. As Steve Blass explains it, "regardless of what one thinks of Pete Rose, he knows the game. And he doesn't just remember every hit he ever got but probably every pitch he ever saw... He had total recall of his career" (Blass and Sherman 2012, p. 7).

Velleman (2008) tells us that "forgetfulness [of external goals, evaluative judgments, and the self] is necessary because spontaneous action is inhibited by distinctions between good and bad, right and wrong" (p. 185). Yet, although it may be that distinguishing

---

[7] This is from the transcript of an interview on CNN: <http://transcripts.cnn.com/TRANSCRIPTS/1210/19/ta.01.html>.

good and bad does inhibit spontaneous action, an inhibition of spontaneous action is, as I have been arguing, compatible with if not conducive to expertise. Spontaneous action might produce actions that are good enough in certain situations, but experts usually do not settle for "good enough." And not only that, spontaneity can also lead you to do things you'll later regret.

## Proprioceptive Awareness

I claim that experts may be both present and immersed in the experience of movement. And the means by which the experience of bodily immersion occurs, I would now like to tender, is via proprioception. I shall have a good deal more to say about proprioception in the next chapter. But here let me say a few words about why we should accept the idea that we have proprioceptive awareness in the first place since some have argued that proprioception is not a form of conscious experience.

If part of the pleasure of movement, as I have argued, comes from a sense of being immersed in movement, and if proprioception is the sense by which we experience such immersion, I am committed to the view—in as much as the pleasure is conscious—that such experience is conscious. But is it? Proprioception is a relatively little studied sense among both scientists and philosophers, and among those who do talk about it, a number of philosophers claim that we are rarely aware of proprioceptive information.[8] For example, according to Brian O'Shaughnessy (1998), "proprioception is attentively recessive in a high degree, it takes a back seat in consciousness almost all of the time" (p. 175). And Gallagher (2003) tells us, "when I am engaged in the world, I tend not to notice my posture or specific movements of my limbs" (p. 54). Are expert athletes and performing artists, then, not attending to proprioceptive input?

I question whether proprioception is typically more recessive than any of our other senses. While working at your computer, your attention is typically not on your posture, but neither is it on any sensory information; rather it is on the content of what you may be writing or reading. So O'Shaughnessy and Gallagher may not be correct, if they mean that proprioception is more recessive than our other senses. Nonetheless, proprioception (along with all other sensory information) may be typically recessive, and if so, the perception of the expert, on my view, is often atypical.

There is also a rather knotty debate in the philosophy literature about whether proprioception is perceptual at all. According to Elizabeth Anscombe (1957/2000), when we know where our limbs are without looking, we know this without the benefit of sensory feedback; nothing shows us, she tells us, the positions of our limbs (pp. 13–14). This knowledge, on her view, is analogous to the knowledge possessed by the director of a building project who may know what a finished building will look like: she knows this not because she has observed it, but because she has designed it. Others have argued

---

[8]   However, see Fridland (2011).

that although we can be conscious of proprioceptive input, we are only conscious of it when the motor command fails to match the proprioceptive input; thus, when all is going well, there is no sensory aspect to proprioception. For example, according to Anthony Marcel (2003), "awareness of a voluntary action appears to derive from a stage later than intention but earlier than movement itself" (p. 71). And Patrick Haggard (2003) claims "awareness of movement appears to be less related to the actual motor production than to the preparatory process" (p. 121).

I shall return to Anscombe's argument in the next chapter; however, for now let me simply state that I understand proprioception as a sense, which is sometimes conscious and which plays a crucial role in awareness of one's own movement. It may be that in everyday movement, one primarily notices mismatches between motor command and proprioceptive input, but I think that experts in bodily movement are often intent on monitoring proprioceptive input. Moreover, one must remember that such experts have a much higher standard for what counts as a match; because of the self-critical nature of dancers, for example, mismatches are common.

In accepting that proprioception is a sense, I follow Hannah Pickard (2004) who tells us that "just as we perceive the world through the five senses, we perceive our own bodies 'from the inside'" (p. 210) as well as standard physiology textbooks, such as Patton (2009).[9]

It seems that when proponents of the just-do-it principle warn against propriocep-tive awareness, they typically have in mind sensory knowledge from the inside. But Anscombe's "director's knowledge" comes under fire as well, if we understand it as knowledge of our movement based on consciously directing our bodies to move. When expert dancers experience pleasure in bodily immersion they have sensory awareness from the inside. This, I claim, can be conscious and can involve a sense of self: you are consciously experiencing yourself as moving in a certain way via propri-oception. However, I also believe that Anscombe's director's knowledge may be part of expert action as well, and underpin another form of pleasure in movement, for as Cole and I also speculated, part of the pleasure of movement arises from a close cou-pling between intention and movement. Director's knowledge tells you what you are doing without the benefit of sensory feedback observation, and proprioception fur-nishes awareness of what you are doing via sensory feedback; when these two line up, one has a sense of harmony.[10]

But does the coupling between intention and movement implicate a loss of the self? Cole and I had said that given sufficient skill, "attention to movement is no longer required at all even though movement continues" (Cole and Montero 2007, p. 312). And this is true inasmuch as an expert can often perform certain actions in her domain

---

[9] For in-depth discussions of the nature of proprioception see Bermùdez (1998; 2010), Fridland (2011), and Gallagher (2003).

[10] Some might balk at the use of the term "knowledge" in "director's knowledge," since sometimes so-called "director's knowledge" is mistaken. If so, the term "knowledge" in this context should be thought of as in scare quotes.

of expertise without attention to her movements. Yet such actions are not necessarily done best without such attention. Moreover, when one has total focus on one's movement, other mental processes subside, but this does not mean that the mind is absent, for it is the mind that is focused on the movement.

## The Debate Over the Loss of the Self in Nineteenth-Century Germany

At the turn of the nineteenth century in Germany, one finds a discussion about whether the self is present in expert action that mirrors some of our present concerns.[11] At that time, there was a fairly widespread conception of consciousness comprising three parts: an awareness of an object, of the self, and of the self's representation of the object. Karl Reinhold (1790) referred to this as the "principle of consciousness," which he stated as follows: "in consciousness representation is distinguished through the subject from the subject and object and related to both" (p. 167). Among other things, then, consciousness was thought to contain a representation of the subject, or what I would say, the self.

This tripartite model of consciousness was seen as a general model of consciousness, not simply a model of consciousness in expert action. However, an objection voiced to it at the time was that in expert action, there is no awareness of the self, because we sometimes get "lost," in thought, sensation, or action. James Messina (2011) points out that this objection was made by Johann Schwab (1791), who, commenting on Reinhold's principle of consciousness, asks: "Is there not a consciousness where we do not distinguish ourselves from the object; and is this not the case when we lose ourselves, as one says, in a sensation?" (Schwab, 1791, p. 335, quoted in Messina 2011). For example, when we are engrossed in a philosophical problem and making progress (which may happen occasionally), are we not lost in thought? And, when all is going well, might not the self disappear in running a marathon, or dancing *Swan Lake*?

The contemporary philosopher Uriah Kriegel (2003), who has a conception of consciousness that is similar to the nineteenth-century tripartite model, addressed such objections by making the awareness of the self in conscious experience implicit, rather than explicit. On Kriegel's view, "in your auditory experience of [a] bagpipe [for example] you are aware primarily, or *explicitly*, of the bagpipe sound [the object]; but you are also *implicitly* aware that this auditory experience of the bagpipe [your representation of the bagpipe] is *your* experience [the self]" ( p. 104) But one need not concede as much, since, as I have already suggested, a more accurate description of such situations is not that one gets lost, but rather all those uninvited worries that have been crowding your mind vanish. The self is there when movement flows and you feel lost, but it is a self unencumbered by distractions. For similar reasons, we can question the idea that

---

[11]  I discuss the ideas in this section in more detail in Montero (2015).

the self gets lost in intellectual endeavors. Does one really lose the self, or does one experience oneself as focused on a particularly engaging topic? Again, as with bodily movement, I would say that intense thought can be an escape, not because one loses the self in it, but because it prevents one from thinking unpleasant thoughts.

Schwab voiced another objection to Reinhold's model of consciousness, and in particular to the idea that the self is always present in consciousness, and this was that we lose the self in overwhelming bodily pain. But is it true that when we experience overwhelming pain, the only thing present to our minds is the pain? Since expert action only rarely involves excruciating bodily pain, the case of the self getting lost in pain is tangential to my concerns. Indeed, when one does proceed with broken ribs, bullet wounds, or bloody toes, the situation might be so intense or captivating that such injuries go unnoticed.[12] But what about cases where one does experience overwhelming pain? Is the self absent in such an experience? Someone who accepts Kriegel's view can allow for the presence of self even here by making awareness of the self implicit. And if, as is sometimes the case, that one doesn't remember much about the experience of extreme pain, perhaps this is as much room for the self that such an experience will allow, unless, of course, one has the experience, *I* am in pain, in the moment, and then forgets.[13]

## From Sensuous Pleasure to Aesthetic Pleasure

I have been exploring the idea that expert action involves an experience of pleasure in movement, and that such pleasure need not dissolve the self nor be explained in terms of a loss of the self. That is, I have been arguing that the reciprocal pleasure principle is false. But what exactly is this pleasure in movement? In part, as we have seen, it is that voluptuous, sensuous feeling of movement whereof Bell speaks. However, there is another way in which certain bodily movements may be pleasurable to perform, and that is that they may effect aesthetic pleasure, not merely for the observer of such movements, but for the originator of them as well. This is the topic of the next chapter.

---

[12] Interestingly enough, in some situations focusing on pain reduces it more effectively than distracting oneself from it. See Johnston, Atlas, and Wager (2012). This leads one to wonder whether focusing on pleasure, might actually mitigate it. I'm assuming that in many cases, it doesn't. However, since I do not know if there is empirical research either confirming or refuting this assumption. I return to the topic of focusing on pleasure in Chapter 12.

[13] For a discussion of the difficulty of differentiating a lack of conscious experience from a lack of memory, see Dennett (1991).

# 10

# The Aesthetic Experience of Expert Movement

Your very flesh shall be a great poem and have the richest fluency not only in its words but in the silent lines of its lips and face and between the lashes of your eyes and in every motion and joint of your body.

Walt Whitman (1819–1892)
*Leaves of Grass*

The idea for writing a book on the role of thought and effort in expert action was prompted by an objection made by the philosopher and avid golfer Bob Child after a talk I had given on the idea of proprioceiving aesthetic properties. I was arguing that proprioception—the sense by which we acquire information about the positions and movements of our own bodies, via receptors in the joints, tendons, ligaments, muscles, and skin—is an aesthetic sense, that is, a sense by means of which we experience beauty, grace, and other aesthetic properties. Child wanted to know how a dancer on stage could have the aesthetic experience of her own movement, since focusing on highly skilled movements obstructs their performance. If experts are to perform at their best, he averred, they can't attend to what they are doing and thus they cannot have the sorts of aesthetic experiences I attribute to them. This objection stumped me at the time, and, indeed, as it was presented during an interview for a position at Child's college, I can see that in retrospect I was lucky to have got the job. However, I now have the answer I would have liked to have given.

Philosophers like to say that a man's *modus tollens* is a woman's *modus ponens*—well, perhaps not exactly this, but it is close enough—and although Child thought my view that dancers experience aesthetic pleasure proprioceptively must be wrong because experts cannot focus on their own bodily movements, I now hold that one reason to think that experts or at least expert dancers, focus on their movements rather than just doing them, is that via proprioception they experience various aesthetic properties of their movements—that is, they experience their movements and positions as beautiful, graceful, powerful, precise.[1] In other words, Child noticed that if the thesis of my talk is correct and dancers are aware of aesthetic properties of their

[1] What exactly are aesthetic properties? This is a controversial topic among aestheticians (see, for example, Sibley 1965; Cohen 1973; Kivy 1975; and Zangwill 2001), however, I shall try to sidestep it as much as

THE AESTHETIC EXPERIENCE OF EXPERT MOVEMENT 193

own movement via proprioception, then they are consciously attending to their movements. Yet, as he saw it, since attending to one's movements as they occur interferes
with expert performance, the thesis of my talk must be false. That was his *modus
tollens*. Child, I now think, was wrong. Because expert dancers are consciously aware
of aesthetic properties of their movements via proprioception, some experts do attend
to their movements—my *modus ponens*.

## Perceiving Aesthetic Properties

For Dreyfus and Dreyfus (1986), an expert's skill has become "so much a part of him
that he need be no more aware of it than he is of his own body" (p. 30). This may be
correct, but not for the reason Dreyfus and Dreyfus think it is correct. They make this
claim because they think experts are generally not aware of their own bodies. However,
if we consider dance, sports, musicianship, and other forms of expertise in which the
quality of one's actions depends on the quality of one's bodily movements, it may be
that experts are no more aware of their skills than they are of their own bodies simply
because they are highly aware of their bodies.

I provided an example of bodily awareness in Chapter 9, where we met Britt Juleen,
a dancer with the Dutch National Ballet, who spoke of how her best performances
involved being immersed in the feeling of her movement. There I argued that bodily
immersion was not an example of losing the self, but rather an example of where
unpleasant thoughts are washed away with pleasant, skill-directed thoughts and experiences. What I would like to add now is that such experiences may have an aesthetic
dimension: in being immersed in bodily movement via proprioception expert dancers
experience an array of aesthetic qualities of their own movements. Not only is this
contrary to the strongest incarnations of just-do-it that castigate any form of attention
to unfolding action, but it also opposes weaker forms of just-do-it according to which
conscious and/or conceptualized thinking and attention interferes with action. I argue
that via proprioception dancers have a conscious, conceptualized experience of the
aesthetic properties of their own movements: an experience of their movements as
beautiful, or graceful, or powerful, and so forth. Moreover, such an understanding of
their movements can ground deliberations over their actions. For example, based on
her perception of the aesthetic qualities of her bodily movements and positions, a
dancer may decide to cover more space or to bend at the elbow just a bit more. In other
words, in contrast to just-do-it's counsel, Juleen, and professional dancers in general,
seem to conceptualize their proprioceptive experience of movement in aesthetic terms
and make aesthetic judgments based, at least in part, on such conceptualization.
Indeed, much of a dancer's work involves constant aesthetic refinement of movement
qualities based on proprioceptive input.

---

possible by focusing merely on examples of properties that most everyone take as aesthetic, such as being
beautiful, being graceful, being powerful, and being precise.

Of course, proprioception during dance serves a number of functions besides providing aesthetic information for a dancer. For example, proprioception is important for guiding a dancer's movement, or informing a dancer that her movement is off, or that her strength is waning. And I have already argued in other chapters that once you become an expert in a physical domain, then you can be consciously aware of technical details of movement. Gallwey (1974), for example, speaks of being aware of his shoulder muscles rather than his forearm powering his best backhands and how during his forehand he is particularly aware of his triceps when his racket is below the ball (p. 112). Yet it may be that the most salient features of what experts are aware of in movement are often very high-level aspects of movement, and in dance such aspects are the aesthetic elements of their movement.

I should also note that although I claim that the experience of expert dancing involves an awareness of one's own bodily movements via proprioception, I certainly do not think that it involves only that. For example, it also encompasses focusing on the music and on what the other dancers on stage are doing. However, even these predominantly nonproprioceptive modes of awareness may incorporate proprioception in a significant way. Musicality—that is, the ability to dance in dialogue with the music—requires monitoring proprioceptive input and auditory input in creating an interesting conversation between the two. And one's awareness of other dancers gives one clues as to how one should move oneself, and such movement may involve proprioceptive awareness. Sondra Fraleigh (1987) puts it well in her book *Dance and the Lived Body: A Descriptive Aesthetics*: "When I move not merely in contrast to my partner... but to complement his movement, I am aware of my movement against his and equally aware that I am related to and bound up with him, in polar (equal and opposite) tension and attraction" (p. 201). Beyond this, I would add that one way in which we are aware of the movements of others on stage is by experiencing some sort of motor resonance in our own bodies.[2] Dance may not be proprioceptive through and through, but proprioception is an integral part of it.

A proponent of a restricted just-do-it principle that admonishes bodily awareness might say that maintaining an internal, proprioceptive focus during a performance would trammel movement, that the mind should not be on the body, but on the music and when this happens, the body will follow. And, from what I know, there is something to this: sometimes all one wants to and needs to think about is the music. Of course, this does not mean that a less restricted version of just-do-it—one that precludes thought about what you are doing—is correct. For in such a case you are still consciously aware of and, arguably, thinking about the music and your relation to it. And it might also be the case that in some contexts, certain movements are done better with less proprioceptive attention. When a dancer is nervous about holding a balance, for example, this might be well advised, for awareness of a slight wobble might increase

---

[2] To call such resonance a form of proprioception is clearly stretching the term. However, see Montero (2006a) for an argument suggesting that we should see it as such.

nervousness, which will make one wobble more. In such a case, it might make sense to attend to the music rather than the wobble. Moreover, it could be that awareness of said wobble could induce negative thinking—*I'm really going to fall*—which takes one's mind off of what really matters. Though at the same time, if you are very good at and confident about balancing, an acute proprioceptive awareness may help one to balance (a view that is consonant with studies on circus performers' balance by Wulf 2008; see also Montero, Toner, and Moran 2018).

## Countering the Idea That the Bodily Senses are Excluded from the Aesthetic Realm

Regardless of whether a dancer occasionally might want to turn her mind away from her body, one reason to reject forms of just-do-it that warn against bodily awareness, or proprioception, is that dancers, in line with the cognition-in-action principle, are often proprioceptively aware of aesthetic aspects of their movements and that one way they evaluate the aesthetic qualities of their movements is by *feeling* (that is, proprioceiving) what is right. Ask a dancer why he changed a certain movement to make it cover less space, or decided to move his wrist just so, and the answer will sometimes be, "I can feel that this particular way of movement is better than the other way;" and by "feel," he means feel proprioceptively. Via proprioception the dancer is aware that it is more exciting, or graceful, or brilliant, or any other number of aesthetic qualities that bodily movements can manifest. This is a common sentiment among dancers and I take it as my central piece of data that such experiences occur.

Can we believe what dancers say? In accord with the methodological principle of taking first-person reports of experience as defeasible evidence for the truth of such reports, I take such reports as defeasible evidence that expert dancers are proprioceptively aware of aesthetic properties of their movements. Accordingly, if there are no countervailing arguments to the effect that proprioception cannot be an aesthetic sense, we can take first-person reports as evidence for the view that dancers experience aesthetic properties proprioceptively, and correlatively, as evidence against the just-do-it principle. However, there are apparent countervailing arguments, which I now need to address.

The first, of course, is the big one that Child expressed: dancers cannot experience the aesthetic qualities of their own movements proprioceptively since this would interfere with performance. The intention of the overall argument in this book, an argument which aims at showing that experts focus on their movements and that when they do, this does not stymie their skills, is to counter this view. But there are also arguments specifically targeted at the idea that proprioception is an aesthetic sense, so let me address the reasons philosophers and others have given for why a sense such as proprioception could not ground aesthetic judgments.

The view that proprioception is an aesthetic sense—a sense through which we are able to experience aesthetic properties—is in part controversial because a long tradition of theorizing about aesthetics takes the aesthetic senses to include only those that are capable of focusing our attention beyond our own bodies. Aesthetic experience, it is thought, while sensuous (depending on sense experience), is not sensual pleasure (is not pleasure in our own bodily sensations). Rather, as D. W. Prall (1929) puts it, "experience is genuinely and characteristically aesthetic only as it occurs in transactions with external objects of sense" (pp. 28, 56). Or, in the words of George Santayana (1955), in aesthetic experience "the soul ... is glad to forget its connection with the body" (p. 24). Given this legacy and given that the very function of proprioception is to provide information about and awareness of our own bodies, one might wonder how proprioception could be an aesthetic sense.

Traditionally, the only two senses thought of as aesthetic are vision and hearing. As Francis Hutcheson (1725/1973) points out, "the ancients observe a peculiar dignity of the senses of seeing and hearing that in their objects we discern the *kalon* [beautiful], which we do not ascribe to the objects of the other senses" (p. 47). And according to Hegel (1835/1975), "art is related only to the two theoretical senses of sight and hearing, while smell, taste and touch remain excluded from the enjoyment of art" (p. 38). And if Hegel had considered it, he presumably would have excluded proprioception, or as Oliver Sacks puts it, "the inner sense by which the body is aware of itself" (Sacks 1995: p. x), from the enjoyment of art as well.

In questioning the privileged status of the visual and the aural, however, I am not alone. As others have argued, many of the features that supposedly make vision and hearing worthy of grounding aesthetic judgments are also features of other senses.[3] The ability vision and hearing afford us to distance ourselves, both physically and psychologically, from the object of awareness is a good example. The light waves that bounce off a painting must come in contact with one's eyes no less than the molecules wafting away from the perfume bottle must come in contact with one's nose. Moreover, while one must eat to survive, once the edge of appetite is taken off, one can distance oneself from one's needs and dine without the practical purpose of fending off hunger. Indeed, in some respects, a proprioceptive aesthetics may be less controversial than an aesthetics based on the so-called lower senses, namely, taste, touch, and smell. For, in the words of Thomas Aquinas (1960), "we do not speak of beautiful tastes and beautiful odors"—or, at least, if we do it is with a bit of awkwardness (p. 27). However, it is natural, at least for dancers, to talk of experiencing beauty proprioceptively. A dancer during a rehearsal onstage—a situation in which there are no mirrors from which to glean visual feedback—may claim that a certain movement or position is beautiful or, since dancers tend to be a self-critical lot, complain that the beauty, or whatever other aesthetic quality he or she is aiming at, is lacking. "The movement is too abrupt," "The line is ugly," "I'm not feeling the connections," are all phrases that roll naturally off a dancer's tongue.[4]

---

[3] See, for example, Carolyn Korsmeyer's *Making Sense of Taste: Food and Philosophy* (1999) and Dominic McIver Lopes's work on the aesthetics of touch (2002).

[4] This is not to say that dancers always know where their limbs are. Dancers rotating and turning upside down in a quick lift might need to watch a video in order to determine what they are doing. The video here, as I see it, helps them to experience the movement proprioceptively.

The aesthetic senses are also sometimes thought to be insatiable; in Bernard Bosanquet's (1915) words, "the aesthetic want is not a perishable want, which ceases in proportion as it is gratified (p. 4)." And this is thought to preclude some of the exteroceptive senses (senses that typically inform us about the external world) from being aesthetic senses. For example, gustatory taste might seem to satiable since eventually the pleasures of eating chocolate and other delicacies turns to disgust. And, one might argue, proprioception is satiable as well since if one kept on dancing one would collapse with exhaustion. However, it is not clear that this line of thought excludes either gustatory taste or proprioception from the aesthetic realm. While one becomes sated by food, it may be that the pleasure of eating, if it could be prolonged without actually ingesting anything, is insatiable. And although one gets physically exhausted while dancing, as one might get physically exhausted in looking at paintings in a museum (or physically stuffed by eating), one seems to never tire of the experience of moving in aesthetically valuable ways.

## Proprioception as Bodily yet Corrigible

Another challenge to the idea that proprioception can be a means of aesthetic experience is that aesthetic senses seem to require a distinction between the object one senses and the bodily sensation itself, a distinction that can be made with sight, smell, taste, touch, and hearing, even when these senses are directed at our own bodies. As Merleau-Ponty (1945/2005) tell us, we perceive our bodies as both subject and object, both as the locus of sensory awareness and as the object of such awareness: when one hand touches the other, he explains, it is possible to move back and forth between noticing the tactile experience of touch and what one is having an experience of (p. 130–131). To highlight this idea, consider an artist who creates beautiful shapes with her hands; she sculpts not only with her hands but also sculpts her own hands. If she created a representation of a bird in flight with just her left hand, she could, by representing her body both as subject and as object, experience the soft curves and strong lines of her creation by touching and exploring her left hand with her right; such an action would effect both a subjective tactile experience (the tactile experience in her right hand) and, intimately intertwined with this, an experience of an object: her left hand. Yet, unlike touch, which has both an objective and subjective element, it might seem that proprioceptive experience is entirely subjective and private. As such, it might seem impossible for proprioceptive experience to ground true disagreement rather than differing opinions, which was a requirement that Immanuel Kant (1790/2007) insisted on for aesthetic judgment when he argued that the object of aesthetic judgment must be shareable.

The difficulty with taking proprioception as an aesthetic sense thus seems to arise because of the particular nature of proprioception and the way it allows one to perceive one's own body. For proprioception may seem to direct one's attention primarily and perhaps exclusively not simply to one's own body, but to the sensory itself. Thus, the difficulty in thinking about proprioception as an aesthetic sense, one might argue, is that, as opposed to even the "lower" sense of touch, proprioception does not represent objects, but rather is merely a sensory experience and, correlatively, does not allow for a distinction between the object one senses and the bodily sensation itself. Yet the aesthetic senses, in contrast to our sense of pain, for example, do not provide us with merely sensory information but are directed to objects in the world, or at least it is thought that they must be if correct aesthetic judgments based on such sensations are to lay claim to intersubjective validity.

Is proprioception a mere sensation, more similar to pain, for example, than vision, or is proprioception representational?[5] Representation, as opposed to mere sensation, allows for misrepresentation, and I think that it is not too difficult to see that proprioception does as well. One way vision can misrepresent the world is that it can represent *p* as *q* when *p* is not *q*. When I look at a field and see it as covered with snow when it is actually covered with clover in bloom, my visual experience is misrepresenting the field. Proprioception can similarly misrepresent the world. Choreographers, ballet masters, rehearsal directors, and dance teachers, for example, often see dancers make mistakes based on such misrepresentations: a dancer might proprioceptively experience his or her knee as perfectly straight, when it is in fact bent or a leg as directly behind, when it off to the side. More dramatic proprioceptive mistakes occur with amputees who have phantom limbs; in this case, they may represent their right leg as bent, when they no longer have a right leg. Of course, even pain judgments can be mistaken in this more dramatic sense: with phantom limb pain, one can feel foot pain without having a foot. Yet, arguably, judgments of pain are not mistaken in the former sense: if a pain appears sharp, then it is sharp. However, like vision, which represents actual objects in the world as being a certain way and is capable of misrepresenting them, proprioception seems to represent one's body as being in a certain way and is capable of misrepresenting it: one's limb may proprioceptively appear straight when it is bent.

Does proprioception, then, like vision, represent something in the world? Although there is a sense in which one's own body is not part of the world, this is not the relevant sense here; rather, the relevant contrast here is between one's body and one's bodily sensations, between the positions and movements of one's limbs and the sensations one has of these positions and movements, between body as subject and body as object; proprioception admits such a contrast.[6] Proprioception may be a type of self-perception, but the self in question is not merely sensory. Thus, proprioceptive experience, it seems, need not be doomed to exist solely in the realm of the mere agreeable, which, according to Kant (1790/2007), is entirely subjective and appeals only to the senses (§ 7–8).

## Is Proprioception Private?

Despite the aforementioned similarities between vision and proprioception, there still seems to be a significant difference between the two cases: the ballet master uses vision to correct the proprioceptive judgments of dancers, yet when we disagree

---

[5] Of course, there are representational accounts of "pain" as well. For example, see Harman (1990).

[6] This is consonant with the view put forth in José Bermúdez (1998), *The Paradox of Self-Consciousness.* See also Wittgenstein's (1958) distinction between the body as "object" and the body as "subject."

about the snow on the field, we are disagreeing about properties in the world that are visually presented to us both. And one might wonder how proprioception could give us access to properties that ground this type of disagreement. Even tactile perception allows for such disagreement: the artist feels her left hand with her right, but another person could also reach out and touch the artist's hand. The possibility of genuine disagreement based on information via a sense modality indicates that that sense modality does not provide purely subjective information.

Is it possible for there to be disagreement not just differing opinions about properties that are presented to two individuals proprioceptively? Or is if not, proprioception akin to sensory systems that preclude such disagreement, such as nocioception (our sensory system that detects pain)? The problem is this: although an individual painting can be seen by many people, it seems that (just as only I can feel my own pain), only I can proprioceive my own movement. You may be able to experience the same type of *developpé* as the one I am performing—one, say, that begins with the foot wrapping around the ankle of the supporting leg, slowly proceeding up the calf to the knee, moving more quickly first into a short and then a longer *attitude*, and finally slowing down for the final extension of the knee—but you cannot experience the same *token developpé*, that is, the *developpé* done by my right leg at time *t*. It seems that a movement-token (a particular bodily movement at a certain time) can be proprioceived only by one individual, the person performing the movement. Or, in other words, the proprioceived movement-token seems to be private. It is not merely that the proprioceptive experience seems private, since, arguably, there is a sense in which all experience is private. Rather, it is that the object of experience appears to be private: the object of visual experience, a painting, can be experienced visually by many observers, while the object of proprioceptive experience, one's own body, can be proprioceived only by oneself. Yet, if Kant is correct, the object of aesthetic experience needs to be shareable. To be sure, conjoined twins who share an arm, for example, each proprioceive the same movement-token, that is, the movement of the shared arm.[7] However, if proprioception is to be a veritable aesthetic sense, it should be capable of grounding aesthetic experience in others besides conjoined twins.

So let us ignore this case and turn to the typical situation. The question, then, is whether the (typical) privacy of proprioception bars it from being an aesthetic sense. I don't think that it does since it seems that if a similar privacy accompanied our auditory perception of music, we would still allow hearing to ground our aesthetic experience of music. To see this, imagine a world that had a convention by which musicians were allowed to play music only while alone in soundproof rooms. There would be no recorded music, no chamber music, no orchestras, no Riot Grrrl bands (definitely a sad situation), but I could enjoy the Goldberg Variations by playing them on the piano in a soundproof room and you could do the same. In this situation, are we barred from sensing the aesthetic properties of the music we play? It seems to me that we are not. An indication of this is that after our isolated sessions, you and I could discuss the aesthetic value of the piece. Of course, in order to discuss the auditory qualities of the piece *as performed*, we would need to determine

---

[7] Thanks to Steven Jacobson for this point.

whether our techniques are similar enough to produce similar sounds. Without being able to hear each other, this would be difficult, since the mere fact that we both followed the same score would not suffice to determine that we produced significantly similar sounds, but it would not be impossible. I could watch a (silent) film of you playing, we could discuss our interpretations, and so forth. Barring, of course, the problem of other minds, once we have determined that our interpretations of the piece are close enough, we can assume that we are talking about different tokens of the same type of musical performance, which in the imagined situation seems sufficient to ground discussion of, and not just differing opinions about, the aesthetic qualities of the performance. In other words, audition would still be the means by which we experience the aesthetic properties of music, even if token musical performances are always private.

The situation with proprioception, though (typically) private by nature and not merely by convention, is similar to the private music room example—the "Beatles in a box" example—in the relevant respects: a dancer might proprioceive only his or her own movements, but by talking to others and watching others, dancers can judge whether they are moving, more or less, in the same way.[8] If a dancer says, "the movement is beautiful," I should not respond "to each his own; you find it beautiful, I do not, there is no standard, nor even 'to each her own.'" Rather, barring vagueness and assuming that we are not relativists about aesthetic properties in general, if the movement does not feel beautiful to me, it would be most reasonable to assume that either there are significant differences in the way we are executing the movement (which may be dependent on our interpretations of the movement, our different technical abilities, or simply on our physiques), or that one of us is mistaken in our aesthetic judgment.[9] This is what would occur in the odd music community, as well: after exiting our soundproof rooms, if I claim that the first variation is tranquil and you deny this, we will not turn relativistic but will instead assume either that one of us was playing the piece in a different way or that one of us is mistaken. If this is correct, the type of privacy involved in proprioception does not preclude proprioception from being a means by which we experience aesthetic properties.

In fact, dancers with similar training and abilities often do agree on the proprioceptive qualities of certain movements, with some steps feeling awkward, others graceful, some dynamic, some dull, indicating that such aesthetic judgments not only command the sort of "subjective universality" that Kant thought was required of aesthetic judgments, but seem to possess it as well.

---

[8] Credit for the phrase, "Beatles in a box," which alludes to Wittgenstein's (1953) "beetle in the box" thought experiment (§293), goes to Josh Weisberg.

[9] It is an interesting question, discussed by Alpert (in progress) whether different physiques tend to result in significant different experiences of the same movement or whether the same movement is not possible given different physiques.

# Proprioceiving Someone Else's Movements

A dancer's aesthetic experience of movement via proprioception also seems shareable in a more significant way since, though this might sound strange, observers can "proprioceive" a dancer's movements. That is to say, sitting motionless in a darkened theater, audience members can sense in their own bodies or have a "motor-perception" of the movements of the dancers behind the proscenium arch.

That there are neural underpinnings for at least the sub-personal components of such motor-perception is suggested by a large body of neuroscientific research which indicates that certain areas of the brain—areas that have been variously referred to as the "human mirror system," the "action-observation network," and the "action resonance circuit"—exhibit increased activity during execution and observation of the same or similar movements (Rizzolatti and Craighero 2004 for a review). Behavioral studies have also supported the idea that visual impressions of movement in some sense resonate in the observer's body. For example, it has been shown that subjects in perceiving static photographs of an individual in motion are more likely to mistake the position of the individual as being further along in the action than as being in a position prior to the one depicted in the photograph, indicating that even in perceiving static images, we can represent dynamic information (Frede 1983). Moreover, subjects tend to perceive geometrical figures in a way that is consistent with how that figure is naturally drawn. For example, if subjects see a circle being traced by a point of light which speeds up along the top and bottom of the circle and slows down along the sides, subjects tend to perceive an ellipse rather than a circle (Viviani and Stucchi 1989). Since we slow down in drawing sharp curves, one explanation of what is going on here is that our understanding of the circle is not entirely visual; we also understand its shape by feeling what it is like to draw it. When we watch a shape being drawn, the motion of drawing resonates in our own bodies.[10]

But perhaps the strongest reason to hold that proprioception is shareable, and not only shareable but also capable of grounding conscious aesthetic experience—comes from observing how dance critics talk about dance. For example, though he prefers to use the term "kinesthesia" rather than "proprioception," dance critic John Martin (1972) tells us that in order to appreciate dance fully one must make use of "kinesthetic sympathy" (p. 15). In his words, "not only does the dancer employ movement to express his ideas, but, strange as it may seem, the spectator must also employ movement in order to respond to the dancer's intention and understand what he is trying to convey" (p. 15). "The irreducible minimum of equipment demanded of a spectator," Martin tells us, "is a kinesthetic sense in working condition" (p. 17). Accordingly, his reviews of dance were rife with references to the qualities of dance appreciated via kinesthetic sympathy or motor-perception. For example, he speaks of the dynamic variation in a dancer's

---

[10] The idea that one can have a conscious motor-perception or proprioceptive-like experience of someone else's movement is also suggested by virtual reality wherein when watching an image of your arm reach out across the Hudson over to New Jersey, it seems that you are proprioceiving a virtual arm.

movement that gave it a "rare beauty and a powerful kinesthetic transfer," or "[a] gesture which sets up all kinds of kinesthetic reactions," or even a dancer who "leaves you limp with vicarious kinesthetic experience." If proprioception grounds not only judgments about the aesthetic qualities of one's own movement but also about the movement of others, the objects of proprioception would then easily meet the aesthetic bar.

Edwin Denby (1998) is another critic who frequently emphasizes the relevance of motor-perception in his writings. For example, in a review of a performance of *Afternoon of a Faun*, he mentions the bodily feeling that results from imitating the depictions of people on Greek vases and bas-reliefs: "The fact is that when the body imitates these poses, the kind of tension resulting expresses exactly the emotion Nijinsky wants to express" (pp. 34–5). He continues: "Both their actual tension and their apparent remoteness, both their plastic clarity and their emphasis by negation on the center of the body (it is always strained between the feet in profile and the shoulders en face)—all these qualities lead up to the complete realization of the faun's last gesture" (34–5). Denby is characterizing something kinesthetic: something that we come to understand not through our visual experience alone. Through motor-perception, Denby feels the tension of the dancer's bodily torque.

Denby illustrates how kinesthetic qualities provide insight into what are commonly called the "expressive qualities" of the work. Expressive qualities reveal the emotion represented in a work of art, and Denby's contention in the review cited above is that Nijinsky expresses discomfiting emotions via the strained and twisted comportment of the faun. In a piece such as this, the dancer's movements, among other things, also represent some of the expressive qualities of the Debussy score. As such, it is in part via motor-perception that audience members—especially those with dance training—experience both the expressive qualities of a dancer's movements and, more indirectly, the expressive qualities of the music. Yet the role of motor-perception in aesthetic judgment, as I see it, is not limited to the judgment of expressive qualities since part of the value of watching dance has to do with the motor-perceptual experience of aesthetic properties—such as beauty, precision, fluidity, and grace—that are not emotions. In watching a dancer, we not only experience the beauty of her movements visually, but we may experience it motor-perceptually as well.

There are numerous other critics who also understand motor perception as a means by which we come to understand and experience aesthetic qualities. Alastair Macaulay (2008), for instance, frequently alludes to motor perception—in one review telling us that Fredrick Ashton's choreography is "more kinesthetically affecting than any other ballet choreographer's," and that in "watching [it], you feel the movement so powerfully through your torso that it is often hard to sit still in your seat." Similarly, Louis Horst describes the "lyric beauty" of a dance choreographed by Anna Sokolow as having "*a direct appeal to kinesthetic response*" (Horst 1954, as quoted in p. 114 of Warren 1991). And Michael Wade Simpson (2005) describes the finale in a piece by Helgi Tomasson as "satisfying musically, kinesthetically and emotionally." But are such critics correct in their kinesthetically loaded assessments?

There are two questions here: how do we know that such critics really have the sorts of experiences they claim to have? And why should we think that such experiences could be aesthetically relevant? With respect to the first question, I return to my methodological principle: although it is common knowledge that one may misidentify what one is experiencing, the default position with regard to whether we are accurately identifying any particular experiences must be that we are. Unless there is good reason to think that Sally is not having a visual experience of red, feeling pain, feeling jealousy, or, for that matter, experiencing kinesthetic sympathy, we should believe what Sally tells us about her inner life. Similarly, unless there are good reasons to think that these dance critics are not experiencing what they write about, then we should accept that they are having kinesthetic experiences when watching dance. Are there any such reasons?

As I pointed out in the previous chapter, Anscombe (1957/2000 and 1962) argues that we come to learn of the positions of our limbs (nonvisually) without having any sensory awareness of where they are, without what she refers to as "observation" (since she holds that there are no specific proprioceptive sensations). And some see this as discrediting the type of kinesthetic sympathy I am attributing to critics, the idea being that if the typical case of proprioceiving your own movements and positions is not based on experiential data, the purported case of a critic having a motor perceptual experience of a dancer is nullified (see, for example, McFee 1992). I am, however, neither fully persuaded by Anscombe's argument that proprioception is nonobservational, nor do I think it is entirely clear that being nonobservational would make such knowledge incapable of grounding aesthetic judgments.

Why does Anscombe think that our knowledge of our own movements and positions is not observational? She argues that if we were to have observational knowledge of bodily movements and positions, this knowledge would need to be based on what she calls "separately describable" sensations. A separately describable sensation, as I understand her, is an identifiable sensation of merely one part of an entire movement. In having our legs crossed, Anscombe (1962) tells us, we can (nonseparately) describe the associated sensation as the sensation of having our legs crossed, but we can't describe the individual sensations that would need to provide a sufficient basis for our knowledge that our legs are crossed, if we were to have observational knowledge of them. Propriocpetion, she thinks, does not provide information about separately describable sensations. Thus proprioception can't ground knowledge of the positions and movements of our limbs. (See Bermùdez 2010 for a more detailed explanation as well as a defense of this argument.)

I question this argument for two reasons. The first is that I think it is possible that a nonseparately describable sensation of having my legs crossed could be the basis of my knowledge that my legs are crossed. To be sure, if one rejects self-grounding (which not everyone does; see, for example, Wilson 2014: 570–5) then one might claim that the knowledge that my legs are crossed can't ground the knowledge that my legs are crossed; however, it would still seem possible for the sensation to ground the knowledge.

The second reason for why I question Anscombe's argument is that I also think that there are more separable sensations (though perhaps not fully describable) than

Anscombe makes out and that these may suffice to ground or at least partially ground our knowledge of our movements and positions. For example, I think that it is possible to come to understand where your arm is in space by noticing proprioceptive sensations in your shoulder and elbow.

Anscombe arrives at her view via the premise that we do not acquire proprioceptive knowledge by noticing particular sensations: it is not as if we know that our legs are crossed, she tells us, because we notice a pressure on our thighs and a tingle in the knee, for example. Rather, according to Anscombe (1957/2000), we know that our legs are crossed because we have directed them to cross (p. 14). Just as an architect might know what a completed building looks like without seeing it, we can know where our limbs are without having sensations of them. But is this how we come to understand our bodily positions and movements? Anscombe is correct that information from tingles, pressure, touch, and so forth are not normally sufficient for us to know such things.[11] However, just because we do not arrive at knowledge of our bodily positions via those sensations does not mean that we never arrive at this knowledge via the sense of proprioception itself, for proprioception is not the sense of pressure or the experience of a tingle. To be sure, Anscombe's example of having one's legs crossed works in her favor since this is something to which we rarely pay attention. And thus in thinking about what it is like to have your legs crossed, it may be that not much comes to mind. However, the ballet dancer's experience of an *arabesque penchée* will encompass many separable proprioceptive sensations: the experience of the leg stretching upward, the arms extended, the knee taut, and so forth. They may not all be capable of being fully described, yet it seems that a dancer's awareness of them can be at least part of the basis for her knowledge that she is performing a *penchée*. A dancer may also know where her limbs are because she has directed them to go there. But given that we can have knowledge of entirely passive movements as well as bodily movements that fail to match our intended movements, director's knowledge cannot be the entire story. It seems then that Anscombe's argument that proprioception is not based on sensory experiences does not provide us with a reason to think that dance critics are mistaken in their claims to powerful kinesthetic responses to certain works of dance; proprioception at least gives us information about our own bodily movements and positions.

We have found no reason to doubt dance critics' claims that they enjoy kinesthetic experiences on watching dance. Let us (based on the methodological principle) therefore, accept that they do have such experiences. The question now is whether such experiences are aesthetically relevant. Here's an analogy. It seems reasonable to understand scientific knowledge as providing the best picture of what sorts of things exist in the world. Or at least, it seems reasonable to say that if something is theorized by scientists to exist, such as atoms and cells, or if something is classified by scientists in a certain way, such as a whale being classified as a mammal, it is reasonable to think that these things

---

[11] The case of Ian Waterman, discussed by Cole (1995), suggests that if an individual suffers a loss of proprioception (from the neck down), the individual can sometimes learn to nonvisually know where his or her own body is in space via other sensory processes, but it takes a tremendous amount of work to do so.

do exist and that these classifications are accurate, unless we have very strong arguments to the contrary. (For example, some might take Bas van Fraassen's (1980) argument for constructive empiricism to show that some of the posits of science actually do not exist.) I think that our attitude towards the posits of art critics, when they are writing in their area of expertise, should be analogous to our attitude towards the posits of scientists when they are writing in their area of expertise. That is, if art critics generally accept something as a work of art (such as a Duchamp readymade), it is reasonable to accept it as such unless one has good arguments to the contrary. Correlatively, if dance critics generally accept the aesthetic relevance of kinesthetic sympathy, it is reasonable for us to accept it too, unless there are good arguments to the contrary.

Do dance critics generally accept the aesthetic relevance of kinesthetic sympathy? As I have indicated, at least a good number of prominent ones do. Thus, we have more support for the idea that the objects perceived via proprioception are not private in the way that would preclude proprioception from being an aesthetic sense. We might not want to go as far as Alastair Macaulay (2012) and claim that watching dance may be "less visual than kinesthetic," but we seem to have good grounds for the claim that conscious motor-perception is one pathway to the aesthetic experience of dance.[12]

## The Interdependence of the Proprioceptive and the Visual

I have been trying to defend the antecedent of my *modus ponens*, that is, I have been trying to argue, contrary to just-do-it, that dancers are proprioceptively aware of the aesthetic properties of their own movements during performance. A large part of this task has involved defending the view that dancers are aware of specifically aesthetic properties of their own movements via proprioception, and to do this I have spent a great deal of time defending the view that proprioception is an aesthetic sense. Of course, to counter just-do-it, it would suffice if they were aware of any sort of properties regardless of whether they met the aesthetic bar. However, as the idea for writing this book was born out of my need to respond to an objection raised by Bob Child when I presented my argument for proprioception being an aesthetic sense, indulge me while I complete making my case for the view that proprioception is an aesthetic sense.

For proprioception to be a sense by means of which we are able to experience aesthetic properties, it seems that the judgment one makes that a certain movement quality is beautiful, for example, must be based on proprioceptive information. However, one might object that proprioception only gets its purchase on the aesthetic by informing us about what is beautiful visually. Although a dancer might make

---

[12] If Macaulay is correct, then people who have been diagnosed with a degraded sense of proprioception might not fully appreciate dance. Do they? Anecdotally, I know one individual who has been so diagnosed and he claims to have no appreciation of dance or sports, though he does, he said, like the rules of baseball. There is also the question of whether dance training affects one's aesthetic appreciation of dance (see Montero 2012; 2013).

proprioceptive certain qualities of aesthetically graceful movements, this alone, one might argue, does not show that proprioception is an aesthetic sense, since it might be the case that proprioception in these situations merely serves as a guide to the visual. In other words, if proprioception grounds aesthetic judgments about movement only in as much as it allows us to picture what the movement looks like, then it would be vision and not proprioception that is aesthetically relevant in such cases. It is difficult to counter this objection definitively. However, except for the theoretical considerations against proprioception being an aesthetic sense, which I have addressed, there is little reason to think that a translation of proprioceptive information into visual imagination *always* occurs when making such judgments. Proprioception can and sometimes does provide us with a platform on which visual imagination can work. However, since my claim is that we can make aesthetic judgments based on proprioceptive input, it is consistent with proprioception sometimes being merely grounds for visual imagination.

Now, if aesthetic judgments can be based on proprioceptive information without that information being translated into visual information, then it should be possible for blind dancers to have proprioceptive aesthetic experiences. Is this possible? Though I imagine that it is, this is a question for future investigation. In any event, for the sighted, presumably, the visual and the proprioceptive are interdependent, with proprioceptive aesthetic sensibility being in part informed by visual aesthetic sensibility and visual aesthetic sensibility being informed in part by proprioceptive aesthetic sensibility.[13] To be sure, in some cases, one might proprioceptively judge that a movement is beautiful because one knows that the movement, if seen, would look beautiful. But in other cases, one might visually judge that a movement is beautiful because one knows that if proprioceived, this movement would feel beautiful.

The partial dependence of the visual on the proprioceptive may not even be confined to the realm of bodily movements and positions. We speak as if we are visually aware of aesthetic properties, such as the grace of a curve in a statue or painting, but perhaps in this case our judgment of grace may be based on our sense that if we were to move our arm in such a way, the movement would feel graceful. The suggestion here is not just that some visual judgments may depend in part on proprioceptive input but, moreover, that they depend in part on proprioceptive, aesthetic input.[14] Why is the Mona Lisa's smile so captivating? Certainly, it is visually captivating, but it is also proprioceptively captivating: when we observe the smile we feel what it is like to smile in that way. If this is correct, there seems to be no reason to claim that visual experience is necessarily more fundamental than proprioceptive experience. Rather, the visual and

---

[13] Other senses are relevant too: the way a foot sounds as it glides across the floor, the way a hip feels pressed into a partner's hand, for example, can inform one's proprioception of these movements and positions.

[14] If a degraded sense of proprioception or no sense of proprioception interferes with one's appreciation of dance, might it also interfere with one's appreciation of some forms of visual art?

the proprioceptive may feed each other: I take my own bodily movements to be proprioceptively graceful, in part because I judge that if seen, these movements would look graceful, and I take certain bodily movements of others to be *visually* graceful, in part because I judge that if I were to move in this way, these movements would feel graceful.

## Beyond Dance

Although from my perspective as a former dancer, dance seems to present the clearest case of experts focusing on aesthetic properties of their movements via proprioception, I think it is likely to occur in other performing arts as well. And it might be that other types of performing artists would see their own art as presenting the clearest case of proprioception facilitating aesthetic experience.

To return to Charles Rosen, whose views on playing the piano we looked at in the prior chapter, we find he also highlights the idea of proprioceptively appreciating the aesthetic qualities of a piece of music in his discussion of what he calls "Chopin's ruthlessness" (1987). Chopin, he tells us, makes no concession to any technical limitations of pianist. In his words:

[t]he Etudes generally begin easily enough—at least the opening bars fit the hand extremely well. With the increase of tension and dissonance, the figuration quickly becomes almost unbearably awkward to play. The positions into which the hands are forced are like a gesture of exasperated despair.... The performer literally feels the sentiment in the muscles of his hand. This is another reason why Chopin often wanted the most delicate passages played with the fifth finger alone, the most powerful cantabile with the thumbs. There is in his music an identity of physical realization and emotional content.

Rosen is illustrating a proprioceptive aesthetic experience of playing; through an awareness of his body the pianist experiences the emotional content of the music: in the unbearably awkward figuration of the hands one finds an aesthetics of exasperated despair. Here proprioceptive awareness—contrary to the just-do-it principle—does not interfere with performance: if anything, it seems conducive to it. Or at least it does, if pianists do not get so immersed in their proprioception that they fail to pay attention to other relevant aspects of their performance. And according to Rosen (2002), sometimes they do fail to do this, for he comments that pianists are so attentive to their movements that they may forget to listen to themselves; indeed, as he explains: "many pianists developed the habit of recording themselves on tape, in order to hear what they were doing" (p. 36). This practice, however, as he sees it, "is a disastrous one, [and instead] we need to increase our awareness of what is taking place at the moment of performance."

It may even be that athletic performance occasionally involves proprioceiving aesthetic properties of one's own movements—and not merely in sports such as gymnastics, which have dancelike elements, but even in sports such as baseball, soccer, and hockey (see Cohen 1991). Perhaps the beauty or graceful feeling of a movement can even be a guide to what works in sports. Rather than thinking about the movement on a muscular level, perhaps sometimes the best way to assure a slam dunk is to focus on the aesthetic qualities of the movement.

## Proprioceptive Illusions

One final possible objection to my claim that proprioception is an aesthetic sense for both dancers and audience members is that the aesthetically relevant qualities of movement depend on the visual illusion—the appearance of floating on the stage during a *bourrée*, of suspending oneself in the air in *grand jeté*, and so forth—produced by the movement. In other words, what is aesthetically relevant is how a movement (deceptively) looks, not how it actually feels.

Certainly, some aspects of how a movement actually feels are aesthetically irrelevant. Performing certain steps, such as a *pas de couru* (if you have blisters), or a difficult lift (if you have bruises), can be painful, yet the experience of pain is typically not aesthetically relevant for either the dancer or the observer. Moreover, the aesthetic value of bodily movements at least sometimes depends on how they appear illusorily. Ballet, in particular, is based on the creation of visual illusions: leaps that appear to defy gravity, limbs that appear elongated, and so forth. Yet if all aesthetic judgments of bodily movements depend on the illusory image produced by the movement, and if proprioception only tells us how the actual movement feels, there is little, if any room left for a proprioceptive aesthetics. I think, however, that neither condition is satisfied. Not all aesthetically valuable movements are intended to create visual illusions; sometimes, especially outside the realm of ballet, a movement is supposed to be seen for what it is. A ballet dancer's beveled foot at the end of an arabesque is intended to create a longer line by drawing the eye out and up, while a modern dancer might leave the foot relaxed in order to show the body in a more natural state. But, more significantly, it seems to me that one can proprioceive an illusory movement. When one performs a "gravity-defying" leap by further extending one's limbs at its height, one has a proprioceptive sensation of being suspended mid-air, and the same goes for watching such a leap: what in part makes watching a dancer leap aesthetically satisfying is that we feel the flight. Indeed, I would claim that one of the wonders of dancing—one of the reasons why dancers will put up with the pain it often involves—is that dance allows one to experience the impossible.

If one can proprioceptively experience a gravity-defying leap, this means that there are proprioceptive illusions. That there are such illusions is widely accepted: pilots in flight and in-orbit astronauts may experience proprioceptive illusions related to their position in space, and artificial muscle vibration can create the proprioceptive illusion that one's limb is bent at a certain angle when it is not (Goodwin et al. 1972; Previc and Ercoline 2004). These sorts of illusions may be more robust than the proprioceptive illusion one experiences in dance, but at the same time the Mueller-Lyer illusion, for example, is more robust than the visual illusion one has of seeing a dancer defy gravity. So, while the illusory element of the aesthetics of bodily movements cannot be over-looked, we can proprioceive, as well as see illusory movement.

## The Proprioceptive Counter to Just-do-it

I have argued that there is no reason to think that proprioception must be excluded from the real of the aesthetic senses. Moreover, I have claimed that expert dancers (and others) are aware and consciously so of the aesthetic qualities of their movements via proprioception and that such awareness enables dancers to judge whether their move-ments are graceful, awkward, beautiful, or banal. Expert dancers perform at their best, not when they are performing automatically without focusing on their movements, but when they are aware of their bodily movements via proprioception. What this means, Professor Child, is that the well-worn idea that focusing on your movements as they occur impedes expert skill is wrong. That's my *modus ponens*.

# 11

# Intuition, Rationality, and Chess Expertise

> Truth derives its strength not so much from itself as from the brilliant contrast it makes with what is only apparently true. This applies especially to chess, where it is often found that the profoundest moves do not much startle the imagination.
>
> Grandmaster Emanuel Lasker (1868–1941)
> *Common Sense in Chess*

One might think that chess, a game sometimes referred to as "the gymnasium of the mind,"[1] is an obvious example of the cognition-in-action principle, for it would seem that contrary to just doing it, chess experts are engaged in effortful, deep strategic thought. However, although I do think it is an example of cognition-in-action, the obviousness of this is debatable since in the philosophical literature on expertise, chess (especially speed chess) is used to illustrate how one's best actions are not even in part the result of rational thought, but are rather instances of simply seeing straightaway what to do and doing it. For example, in line with the extreme form of just-do-it, which tells us that expert actions simply happen to the expert, Hubert Dreyfus argues that although in suboptimal situations analysis and deliberation play a role, the best moves made by chess players at the international master or grandmaster level involve neither analysis nor deliberation, nor even conceptualizing the board. Rather, Dreyfus (2013) tells us that "after much experience, the chess master is directly drawn by the forces on the board to make a masterful move" (p. 35). High-level chess, on Dreyfus's view, is bred neither in the heart nor in the head, but out there on the sixty-four-square board.

I think that this view is mistaken, and in this chapter shall critically analyze Dreyfus's view that when chess players are at their best, they do not think, but rather simply move. Dreyfus's position contrasts with John McDowell's view that reason or at least conceptualization plays a necessary role in all of our actions: it is concepts all the way down for McDowell (2013). However, when it comes to speed chess, McDowell's view presents merely a less extreme version of the just-do-it principle, proscribing not all mental processes, but just explicit thoughts, or thoughts that are expressible in words.

---

[1] Phrase attributed to Adolf Anderssen.

On McDowell's view, although high-level chess players have implicit or not consciously accessed conceptual knowledge about what they are doing as they are playing, in a very fast game such players "do not explicitly think its content... unless the flow is broken" (p. 46). To be sure, even if chess is the gymnasium of the mind, it is reasonable to think that during a one-minute game, there is no time for thought. However, I shall argue that experts at speed chess do think explicitly about their actions. Of course, chess players, speed or otherwise, do not deliberate over every possible move; rather, as Dreyfus emphasizes, they "zero in" on a limited number of possible moves. Nonetheless, contra Dreyfus, I shall also argue that there is a sense in which such zeroing in is both conceptual and rational.

Many of the ideas expressed in this chapter are based on work I have done with philosopher and national master chess player Cory A. Evans (Montero and Evans 2011), and I am grateful to him for all he has taught me about chess, and his generosity in granting me permission to recount some of our work here.

## Setting the Stage With the Example of Driving

On Dreyfus's view, we perform best when we neither think nor even do, but rather merely let ourselves be drawn into action. This happens, as he sees it, when we adeptly perform our everyday activities, such as opening familiar doors or climbing the stairs, as well as when professionals who are considered experts in their fields perform optimally in their domain of expertise. For Joe Smith opening the door to his house, as well as the expert musician, chess player, or nurse engaged in domain-related activities, years of practice have hewn their actions into smooth, seamless wholes that can be performed—and indeed are best performed—without the actor reflecting on or deliberating over what is to be done; indeed, in some sense without the individual doing anything at all. As Dreyfus and Dreyfus (1986) explain, beginners "make judgments using strict rules and features, but with talent and a great deal of involved experience, the beginner develops into an expert who sees intuitively what to do without applying rules and making judgments at all" (p. 253).

For Dreyfus (2007a), experts, in line with the descriptive component of just-do-it, proceed intuitively. Moreover, in line with the principle of interference, he holds that "mindedness [thought, reflection, deliberation, attention, and so forth] is the enemy of expert coping," by which he means not that mindedness prevents you from being an expert at coping, in the sense of being an expert at doing merely OK (as in "I'm coping"), but rather, that mindedness prevents an expert from being able to perform in a smooth, efficient, effortless, and highly accurate manner (p. 355). Although Dreyfus holds that expert coping, or what he also refers to as "involved" or "absorbed" coping, is hindered by mindedness, he does not think that an expert's actions are always nonminded. For example, he does not deny that world-class chess players deliberate over their moves in situations when their expert intuition—which he sees as immediate and unreflective—fails to provide the right move (Dreyfus and Dreyfus 1986). However, in their moment of glory, grandmaster chess players, according to Dreyfus, deliberate no more over what move to make than you do over which lace to place on top when you tie your shoes.

One of Dreyfus's (2004) favorite examples of expert coping is the familiar activity of driving.[2] In work with Stuart Dreyfus, he describes the actions of the expert (in his sense of "expert," which covers everyday expertise) as follows:

> The expert driver, generally without any attention, not only knows by feel and familiarity when an action such as slowing down is required; he knows how to perform the action without calculating and comparing alternatives. He shifts gears when appropriate with no awareness of his acts. On the off ramp his foot simply lifts off the accelerator. What must be done, simply is done. (p. 253)

Dreyfus makes a number of related points here, all of which individually could be seen as supporting various restricted versions of the just-do-it principle: experts proceed without attention to what they are doing; experts neither calculate nor compare alternatives; experts are arational[3] (they are not in a position to justify their actions); they act spontaneously (they proceed without deliberation); and they rely on neither rules nor standards to decide on or justify their actions. To add to this, he also claims that experts act "intuitively," which for Dreyfus (1986) involves "the understanding that effortlessly occurs upon seeing similarities with previous experiences" (p. 28 and throughout), and that "expert coping [is] . . . direct and unreflective," which he takes to be the same as "nonconceptual and nonminded" (2007a, p. 355). Taken together, these points add up to a fairly extreme version of just-do-it.

To address Dreyfus's argument that expert action is nonminded (and is hindered by mindedness), as well as McDowell's more moderate view that expert action is not explicitly minded (and is hindered by explicit mindedness), specifically, to address these arguments with respect to chess expertise, let me categorize the central questions as follows:

(1) Can expert chess players proceed just as well when they are not attending to (focusing on) the game?[4]

(2) Do expert players rely on neither rules nor standards to decide on or justify their actions?

(3) Do they proceed, as Dreyfus holds, without deliberation and thought (for example, without calculation, comparing of alternatives, reflection)? Or is such deliberation and thought, as McDowell holds, typically only implicit?

---

[2] Where Dreyfus lives in California's San Francisco Bay Area, most everyone is familiar with driving.

[3] As Gobet (2012, p. 238) points out, since the word "arational" combines a prefix from ancient Greek and a root from Latin, a better term might be *agnomic* (since the perhaps preferable term "alogic" already has a technical meaning). But for consistency's sake, I employ Dreyfus's terminology, as does Gobet.

[4] When I speak of "expert chess players," I mean chess players who have practiced chess deliberately and intensely for at least around ten years and are still intent on improving. In particular, I am not referring to the United States Chess Federation's (USCF) title, Expert, given to players with a USCF rating from 2000–2199.

(4)  Are their actions based on intuitive, arational responses to a situation (that is, are their actions effortless, nonconceptual, arational responses that occur upon seeing similarities to previous experiences)?

Affirmative answers to these questions support an array of just-do-it principles, while negative answers tell against such principles.

In sum, the answers I provide are as follows:

(1)  Dreyfus has not made a convincing case for the view that expert chess players proceed just as well, if not better, when they do not attend to the game.
(2)  The rules of the game are usually not consciously present, yet sophisticated heuristic rules may be consciously employed; moreover, contrary to Dreyfus's suggestion that the rules are not in the mind at all, chess players can readily access them.
(3)  Experts deliberate, often explicitly, even in speed chess, but not over everything.
(4)  Their best actions are not grounded in intuitive responses, if intuitions are seen as arational and nonconceptual. However, if intuitive responses are seen as both rational and conceptual (though not necessarily declarative), expert-level chess involves not only thought and deliberation, but also intuition.

## Attention

What is the relevance of attention to chess? Do high-calibre chess players attend to the game? By "attention," I understand Dreyfus to mean focusing on what you are doing (in the sense of paying attention to it as opposed to merely being immersed in the sensation of doing it). This is a weaker notion than deliberation, which I shall address in response to question 3, and which involves thinking about what you are doing. Dreyfus (2007b) certainly rejects the stronger claim that expert chess is thoroughly reflective, but he also seems to reject the weaker claim that it involves attending to the game, for as he says, in support of the principle of interference: "in general paying attention to ... [what one is doing] leads to a regression from expertise to mere competence" (p. 374).

As I have stressed, I think that, in Dreyfus's favor, it often does seem that attending to and analyzing your everyday actions hinders their execution. Ask yourself, for example, why you lift your feet approximately 1.3 inches above each stair as you climb? Although there is a reason for doing this—much less lifting might lead to bumping into the step, and much more might lead to fatigue—this reason is not in your mind guiding your behavior as you ascend a staircase. You don't need to think about it; you just do it. Many, though not all everyday actions seem to proceed in this way: thinking about how to type in my password does seem to interfere with typing it, but I can think quite carefully about tying my shoes without any interference, perhaps because it was not so long ago I taught my children how to do this. Focusing on what you are doing when you are doing it does seem to interfere, then, with some everyday expert performance.

However, as the arguments in prior chapters suggest, there is a significant difference between how attention affects rote skills, and how it affects the skills exhibited by professional-level experts. The expert emergency room nurse, the professional ballet dancer, or tennis player, I have argued, when in the thick of things, often do and should pay attention to or focus on what they are doing.

Dreyfus, however, argues that when performance proceeds well in high-level chess, attention, at a minimum, does no good. And he cites his mini-experiment that pitted international chess master Julio Kaplan against a slightly weaker player in a game of lightning chess (where each player has one minute to play the entire game), during which Kaplan was orally presented with addition problems, at a rate of about one per second, and had to present the answer aloud as quickly as possible. The result, he tells us, is that "even with his analytic mind completely jammed by adding numbers, Kaplan more than held his own against the master in a series of games" (Dreyfus and Dreyfus 1986, p. 33). This experiment, he seems to think, indicates that attending to one's moves is not important or essential to chess expertise. "Deprived of the time necessary to see problems or construct plans," Dreyfus tells us, "Kaplan still produced fluid and coordinated play" (p. 33).

Does Kaplan's performance indicate that attending to the game is not necessary for expert performance? Certainly, he still played well, but did the lack of attention cause him to play less well? It is difficult to say since the experiment is underdescribed. We don't know, for example, how much weaker the "slightly weaker" player was than Kaplan. Maybe Kaplan was distracted, but because of the ability differential was still able to hold his own. Moreover, we don't know whether "holding his own," means winning. If Kaplan lost to the slightly weaker player, the experiment would seem to indicate that attention is important to the game. But even if Kaplan had won, it may be that he was still attending to the game, for it may be that calling out the answer to addition facts was so automatic for Kaplan that this didn't interfere significantly with his attention. And there have been some studies indicating that when chess players are asked to perform even very simple but not automatic tasks (tasks that involve generation rather than mere reaction) they do interfere with chess performance. For example, when Robbins et al. (1996) asked master-level chess players to solve chess problems while generating random letters, it resulted in a 33 percent decrease in ability, and when they asked them to reproduce board positions that they had just seen while doing this, they found it resulted in a 66 percent decrease in ability. Both experiments indicate that attention is important in chess.[5] Finally, since Kaplan was adding numbers out loud and playing his opponent face-to-face, it is possible that this distracted his opponent, and it was this that made it easier for Kaplan, even if distracted himself, to hold his own.

---

[5] See also Saariluoma and Kalakoski (1998) for an illustration of how the Brooks's letter task, which involves counting the corners on block letters, degrades chess performance. For a view quite similar to the view I present here on awareness in chess, see Gobet and Chassy (2008) and (2009).

To try to better understand the Kaplan experiment, I ran two informal experiments of my own (in a public but fairly quiet spot). In the first, I had two master-level players, both of whom are experienced lightning players, each play master level opponents online (via the Internet Chess Club) while giving the answers out loud to single-digit addition problems. I had written down a series of problems, and I would fire one off about one second after I had heard an answer to the previous one. In line with Dreyfus's results, both felt that they played as well as they usually did (and both happened to win). However, both also stopped adding when things got difficult, with one, for example, taking quite a long time (about 15 seconds) to add 8 plus 1, while the other made some arithmetic mistakes right at the beginning. Neither observed the other or spoke to the other about the experience before they had both completed the experiment, but both said that, far from their analytic minds being jammed by the addition task, they focused almost entirely on the chess and let the addition proceed automatically. The one who made the arithmetic mistakes at the start said "I'm a cribbage player, so once I figured out that you were giving me all single-digit numbers, I can do that all automatically." The other commented that the addition task "was like a fly buzzing around my ears; I concentrated on the game and brushed away the questions as you called them." This suggests that at least part of the reason Kaplan held his own was that he was still fully or nearly fully attending to the game.

In the second informal experiment, I tried to jam up the analytic mind a bit more and had a (retired) international master play lightning chess with the same set-up, but this time adding double-digit numbers. He performed the addition correctly—though at one point pausing for around five second before giving an answer—but he lost the game and was not at all pleased with his performance. In response to my question "How do you feel you did?" he replied: "What do you mean, how do I feel? How do you think I feel? I'm playing an IM [international master] while adding double-digit numbers. I'll tell you how I feel: I'm going to go back to the cabin right now and slit my wrists."[6] Fortunately, he didn't follow up on his plan, nevertheless, I learned that really good chess players hate to lose, and in fact, it was only the one retired player that was willing to try this experiment. Of course, part of the reason this subject lost was that he was playing against a player rated at nearly the same level as he was (and, moreover, he said he hadn't noticed this initially and was thus perhaps not putting his all into the game at first). Still, his perception was that adding the numbers significantly interfered with his performance.

Of course, presumably even Dreyfus would say that chess players would not perform just as well no matter how distracted they are. A serious enough interference would presumably, on Dreyfus's account, interrupt absorbed coping. However, that the Kaplan experiment is open to other reasonable interpretations suggests that Dreyfus has not even shown that a minor distraction fails to interfere with the game,

[6] He, of course, didn't do this, but it makes you see the wisdom behind the need to acquire institutional board approval even for such chess experiments, which I did do (IRB File #2015–0216).

for we don't know that he played optimally in the experiment and we don't know whether the addition task was able to be performed automatically (and was thus, in a sense, not distracting at all).

If you consider generating random letters a minor distraction, the Robbins et al. experimental data indicates that a relatively simple distraction is enough to significantly degrade chess performance.[7] And a glimpse into the world of chess, where full attention is considered essential to expert-level play, indicates this as well. For example, high-level players demand absolute quiet in tournament halls so that they can concentrate; and many players go to great lengths to avoid hearing any music before games, out of fear that a tune will get stuck in their heads and distract them from the game. Focus, it seems, is paramount. That said, I should mention that there is at least one exception to my claim that chess players avoid listening to music prior to tournaments: the Dutch player Daniël Stellwagen would always listen to music before his games, and sometimes (using a headset) during his games. But, as Cory Evans (who asked Stellwagen about this and subsequently told me) explained, the reason why he did this was that the classical music he listened to had neither a bass line nor a steady melody, and thus could not get stuck in his head; indeed, it even prevented him from getting music stuck in his head—something which used to happen to him frequently, before using classical music in this way. So in this case, a player listened to music during games precisely to avoid getting music stuck in his head!

As another illustration of expert coping without attention, Dreyfus (2005) cites Charles Taylor's example of a man flawlessly navigating a path up a hill while his mind is totally absorbed in anticipating an ensuing difficult conversation (p. 56). In cases such as these, Dreyfus thinks, we do not pay attention to what we are doing at all. Rather, we just do it. But what counts as cases such as these? It seems that although one may scale a hill without attention, chess is more like the difficult conversation (and the data on texting during driving makes it seem that driving should be as well).

## Rules

Let me move on to the second question: Do experts proceed without relying on rules or standards to decide on or justify their actions? In chess, as Dreyfus explains, one can distinguish two kinds of rules: on the one hand, there are rules of the game, which govern how the pieces move, specify time limits, when draws will occur, and so forth; on the other hand, there are heuristic rules, which advise one as to general strategy, such as to control the center and make even trades when you are ahead. Consciously following the rules of the game or heuristic rules counts as a rational

---

[7] Furthermore, there are some kinds of tasks that seem to interfere with chess performance more than others. For example, it is thought that chess performance is degraded by tasks that interfere with visuospatial processing and executive processing more than tasks interfering with verbal processing (Saariluoma 1992; Robbins et al. 1996).

action, since such rules provide one with a reason to act. But according to Dreyfus, the expert does neither of these. Indeed, according to Dreyfus, the expert does not even follow the rules unconsciously: the beginner learns the rules, and the competent player relies on them, but the expert abandons them, just as accomplished bicyclists set aside their training wheels: "To assume that the rules we once consciously followed become unconscious," Dreyfus (2005) tells us, "is like assuming that, when we finally learn to ride a bike, the training wheels that were required for us to be able to ride in the first place must have become invisible" (p. 52). The rules of the game for an expert, it would then seem on Dreyfus's view, are not in the mind at all, not even invisibly so.

Although Dreyfus (2005) argues that the rules of the game are not "stored in the mind," he nonetheless holds that they function "as a landscape" on the basis of which the game is played (p. 53). Whatever it means exactly for the rules of the game to function as a landscape yet not be stored in the mind, it seems to at least imply that the rules of the game are not in the foreground of the expert's mind. This, I think, is generally true. But it means more than this since unconscious rules would not be in the foreground of a player's mind, yet for Dreyfus, the rules of the game are not unconscious, for they are not in the mind at all. Dreyfus goes so far as to say that "even if [the expert] can't remember the rules, they nonetheless govern his coping," and "he normally can be led to remember them," from which it seems reasonable to infer that normally expert chess players do not readily remember them. Yet expert chess players do not need to be led to remember the rules; they just remember them, and are able to teach them quite readily.

Or rather, this is true of the basic rules of chess. Sometimes a very complicated situation may arise during a tournament, and even a grandmaster might need to consult the rule book. Be that as it may, some players seem to have the entire rulebook stored in their minds. A vivid example of this occurred during the 1994 Intel Rapid Chess Grand Prix in New York. In one much talked-about game in the chess world, Grandmaster Vicktor Korchnoi made an illegal move against Grandmaster Anatoly Vaisser. In the televised match, Korchnoi indicated that he was unclear on the precise penalty and he proceeded to ask the arbiter for the rulebook. That proved unnecessary, as Vaisser immediately recited the entire half-page rule, word-for-word. Perhaps Dreyfus would claim that Korchnoi's illegal move prompted Vaisser to remember the rule and that during the game it had been forgotten. Certainly, it does seem that Korchnoi's illegal move prompted Vaisser to explicitly think of the penalty. However, it also seems reasonable to say that during the game it was never actually forgotten.

The rules of the game then, if not typically at the forefront of a player's mind, do seem to be in the mind to some degree. Beyond this, very occasionally a rule might figure explicitly in a player's deliberations, such as when a player might deliberate over and decide not to enter the dreaded rook-bishop versus rook ending, despite knowing it was a win, because he or she fears that the fifty-move rule might come into play (this rule states that if you make fifty moves without a pawn moving or a piece captured, the game is declared a draw). So in stating that the rules of the game are not "stored in the mind," Dreyfus is at least overstating his case.

What about heuristic rules? Again, it seems that basic heuristic rules, such as "move your knight before your bishop", and "capture towards the center," are not explicit targets of thought. But, again, contrary to Dreyfus, it also seems that they are not out of the mind entirely since even when they are not consciously consulted, most good players can rattle them off quite easily.[8] Again, this is a basic skill chess coaches (who are often themselves superb players) manifest.

Heuristic rules, since they frequently conflict, are not adhered to as firmly as rules of the game. And when they do conflict, this leads to deliberation, which is my next topic. However, what might be thought of as advanced heuristic rules, which are specific to particular positions (and which rarely conflict) are sometimes at the forefront of an expert's mind, consciously guiding high-level play and serving as justifications for moves. For example, when contemplating particular kinds of sacrifices, International Master Larry Evans first considers, then follows the following rule: "In the Maroczy Bind with the bishop on g7, don't sacrifice the two knights for the a-pawn, the d-pawn, and the exchange, unless you also either win the b-pawn or can force off a lot of material" (pers. comm.). Evans says he learned this rule from Julio Kaplan (yes, the very same Kaplan who participated in Dreyfus's experiment) in the 1970s, when Kaplan was training him for international play. And though he admittedly often can't remember what he ate for breakfast, he has remembered this rule ever since.

That great chess players engage in high-level, rule-based conscious thinking is also suggested by the comments of Grandmaster Patrick Wolff, whom the psychologist Christopher Chabris interviewed in 1991 (Chabris 1999). Wolff later became two-time US champion, and for a period occupied a position as one of the top one hundred players in the world. Chabris (in a very nonleading question) explained to Wolff that when playing chess, he "hardly ever think[s] of any overarching recommendation," and wanted to know whether Wolff "[knew] of any strong players who ever actually thought in general terms during a game ... as opposed to just seeing variations" (p. 16). Wolff responds as follows:

*I* think in general terms during the game ... I would be very surprised if there were a single very strong chess player who did *not* think in general terms. It's just that it depends what one means by "general terms" ... (Chabris 1999, p. 16)

Chabris clarified that by general terms he means something along the lines of "now I want to think about ideas of how to get my rook onto the seventh rank." Wolff, in stark

---

[8] Though this is generally true, very modern, very young chess-playing prodigies are sometimes so computer-driven that they never have to learn these rules. However, this is exceedingly rare. For a discussion of how players rely on computers in contemporary chess, see Hartmann (2008), especially his analysis of how the use of computers in pre-game preparations has led some chess theorists to describe chess as "rule-independent," and based more on calculation (pp. 55–6, fn. 21).

contrast to Dreyfus and Dreyfus's (1986) view that, when making a brilliant move, a great chess player "does not even think," responds:

Oh yes, sure, absolutely. And I think it's something that all strong grandmasters have to learn how to do. It's one of the things that separates chess players of a certain class. I'm sure that one of the very things that separates the strongest players from the not-so-strong players is the strength and clarity of that thinking. (Chabris 1999, p. 17)

To be sure, not all specific heuristics are conscious, or at least not all are consciously represented in words, such as those Evans used to describe the specific heuristic above; as Gobet (2012) puts it, specific heuristics "do not need to be encoded declaratively" (p. 241). Rather, as he points out, many are learned through extensive practice and study of the game and form a "perceptual chunk," which is an action-perception pathway that associates patterns on the board with a small number of possible chess moves, and is stored in memory as one unit (2012, p. 246).[9] This is where specific heuristics shade into a form of zeroing in; yet, as I shall argue in my discussion of expert-level chess intuition, zeroing in may still be rational and conceptual.

Although grandmasters may sometimes beat weaker players without ever relying on anything beyond heuristics, it is times when specific heuristics are flouted which decide who wins in games between grandmasters.[10] For example, in the famous game Botvinnik versus Capablanca (in the AVRO 1938 International Chess Tournament), Botvinnik, a future world champion, defeated Capablanca, a former world champion, by breaking a heuristic rule and subsequently coming up with a winning move. In their particular position, Capablanca used an advanced heuristic rule to justify capturing a stray pawn. But Botvinnik, after prolonged thought, brilliantly allowed this. He broke the rule, it seems, because he consciously realized that in that particular rare position, Capablanca would not be able to retreat his pieces in time. In general, rules are of no help in truly novel positions with no themes (that is, positions totally dissimilar from any past games with which the expert is familiar) and highly tactical positions (that is, in highly complex positions where broad plans are less important than trying to figure out exactly what is happening). Here, then, Botvinnik's brilliant move is not an example of following rules, though it is an example of cognition-in-action.

Dreyfus (2005), however, argues that expert play must not rely on heuristic rules, since "if one followed the reconstructed rules articulated by an expert[,] one would not exhibit expertise but mere competence" (p. 54). But the consequence does not follow: although merely learning a grandmaster's repertoire of heuristic rules may not turn a competent player into a grandmaster, this does not mean that the grandmaster never relies on heuristic rules when deciding on a move. Rather, the reason why this would

---

[9] See also Gobet and Waters (2003); Campitelli et al. (2007); Wan et al. (2011).
[10] In Montero and Evans (2011), we said that "although grandmasters can usually beat international masters or weaker players without ever relying on anything beyond heuristics, it is times where specific heuristics are flouted which decide who wins in games between grandmasters." Gobet (2012) points out, however, that even a top grandmaster would risk losing against an international master without relying on tactical thinking (p. 240, fn. 3). This is a good point and we stand corrected.

not turn a competent player into an expert is that in addition to employing heuristic rules, experts also calculate the consequences of moves, and have an ability to zero in on a few extremely good moves. This brings us to the topics of the next two sections.

## Deliberation

Do experts proceed without deliberation (that is, without calculation, comparing alternatives, or reflection)? In an essay on the art of chess, the philosopher Stuart Rachels (2008), who is an international master, emphasizes how, as he sees it, "chess cognition is mostly unconscious" (p. 214). For example, he tells us, "in studying a position, a master may quickly understand that there are three viable possibilities for the player on move" (p. 214). And when a player does deliberate, he tells us, "there is typically little inner dialogue," and that "chess thinking is rarely linguistic" (p. 214). Yet, at the same time, in a footnote, he tells us that "individual players do, however, have their little habits," and cites an example of one professional player who, even when he was certain to win, would always ask himself before each move whether he should offer a draw (p. 223). And as for himself, Rachels says that when he had to choose between two moves, one which he wanted to play and one which he "feared was better," he would "deliver a silent lecture" to see if he could convince himself that his preferred move was superior (p. 223). So which is it? Is there typically little linguistic thinking or are players silently talking to themselves all the time? Rachels seems caught between black and white.

Dreyfus (2007a) isn't torn. His view is that the best moves are not the result of deliberation. And in chess, as elsewhere, he also upholds the principle of interference: namely, that thinking interferes with expert performance, or as he puts it, "the enemy of expertise is thought" (p. 354). Rachels apparently does not accept the principle of interference, for if he did, he would likely find a way to break the habit of lecturing to himself. Though he does not discuss this, he might hold that deliberation is somewhat epiphenomenal in chess-playing, that is, it occurs yet has no effect on the outcome of his game. Dreyfus (2005), however, goes further, claiming that it is harmful, or at least that it is harmful when a chess player's intuition is in top form. As he tells us:

When a[n] [expert] has to deliberate in chess or in any skill domain, it's because there has been some sort of disturbance that has disrupted her intuitive response. Perhaps the situation is so unusual that no immediate response is called forth. Or several responses are solicited with equal pull. (p. 57)

Such deliberation, as he sees it, is rare:

Fortunately, the expert usually does not need to calculate. If he has had enough experience and stays involved, he will find himself responding in a masterful way before he has time to think. (p. 58)

However, this does not seem to happen. Although in simple positions, play may be guided entirely by heuristics, typically, as Rachels suggests, even in such cases a player will briefly deliberate to verify that there are no tactical errors. And as soon as the game gets complicated, experts start to deliberate in earnest—as readily confirmed by many players, as well as by a number of verbal protocol studies, which ask players to chose the best move while voicing their thoughts.[11] A complicated position does not necessarily mean that something has gone wrong and even in such situations one intuitive response may stand out as preferable; nonetheless, deliberation, according to players' first-person reports and as indicated by verbal protocol studies, does occur.

Dreyfus, however, takes chess-playing to illustrate the view that humans at their best do not decide rationally (or even decide at all) to act, but rather find themselves immediately responding to environmental cues. As Dreyfus sees it, this view flows out of the work of his philosophical ancestors, Martin Heidegger and Maurice Merleau-Ponty. On their phenomenological accounts, Dreyfus (2007a) tells us, "what we are directly open to is not rational or even conceptual... [rather,] it is the affordance's solicitation—such as the attraction of an apple when I'm hungry—to which I am directly open" (p. 357). But the problem with this picture for chess is that the very attractive apple is often poisoned. In these cases, letting yourself be pulled along by the forces on the board leads you right into your opponent's trap.

Why, then, does Dreyfus think otherwise? And, moreover, why does he think that deliberation would hinder expert play? As with attention, it does seem that there are times when deliberating over your everyday actions impedes performance. Going back to the example of climbing the stairs, if you try to figure out whether you should raise your foot just like so, or a little more, or perhaps a little less, you had better take the elevator. And I think that beyond inspiration from his philosophical ancestors, Dreyfus's theory of expertise is also motivated by situations such as these. But as I have emphasized, there is a significant difference between everyday actions and expert actions, and while deliberation may hinder the former, there is no reason to think that, in general, it hinders the latter. Dreyfus and Dreyfus (1986) liken seeing a great move to recognizing faces: Kaplan's phenomenal ability to play lightning chess while responding to addition problems, they tell us, falls into the same general category as most everyone's ability to recognize and respond to familiar faces without deliberation and even while attending to other matters. However, an experienced chess player's knowledge of positions on the board is relevantly different from our typical knowledge of faces. Although you may spend hours studying your beloved's posted selfies, you do not explicitly analyze them the way chess players analyze games; you are not, for example, thinking, these eyes are better than my ex's eyes because the pupils are 68 millimeters apart rather than 62; though because they are blue-green rather

---

[11] As Gobet (2012) has commented, the empirical evidence for this is overwhelming. See, for example, De Groot (1946/1978); Charness (1981); Gobet (1986), (1998); Saariluoma (1995); Campitelli and Gobet (2004); and Bilalić et al. (2009).

than green-blue, perhaps they are not quite so good as my friend's lover's eyes; let me test that hypothesis, and so on. Chess players, however, analyze their beloved positions with a vengeance. Thus, the analogy to face recognition provides little reason to think that deliberation would interfere with a chess player's ability to choose the best move.

Of course, chess is not the only example Dreyfus calls forth in his argument for the principle of interference. Another favorite example, as we have seen in Chapter 4, is the case of New York Yankees former second baseman, Chuck Knoblauch, who suddenly developed severe throwing problems (Dreyfus 2007a, pp. 354–5). I argued, however, that Dreyfus's claim that deliberation was the cause of any of Knoblauch's problems is unsubstantiated. Neither Knoblauch nor a number of other players who have been afflicted with similar problems seem to believe that thinking or deliberating precipitated their performance decline, and the few investigations into this suggest or hypothesize distinct etiologies.[12] In chess, however, it seems that we do not even have an analogue of a Knoblauch-type problem. Of course, when a player learns a new strategy or opening, thought may increase while performance at first takes a plunge. But, just as I argued in Chapter 6, in discussing examples of performance slumps when athletes first change their technique or equipment, there is little reason to think that the slump is due to thinking; deliberate practice makes perfect and such individuals have simply not yet engaged in enough deliberate practice.

Looking exclusively at standard chess played on a long clock, it seems obvious that deliberation is a component of play—what else could they be doing during those long periods of silence?—and even a component in making the best moves: great moves in tournaments are typically preceded by at least a moderate period of silence. Dreyfus's view about chess, however, seems to be highly influenced by how he understands the game of lightning chess, arguing that since grandmasters are able to play lightning chess so well (that is, at a master level) without deliberating, deliberation is similarly nonessential for making great moves in chess, quite generally (2005, p. 53).[13] But I see three problems with this argument.

First of all, the ability to play chess at the master level during lightning games is extremely rare, with perhaps currently only two players able to do this. Master-level chess is often more or less blunder-free, and certainly the loss of major pieces (such as the queen) to two or three move combinations is exceedingly unlikely. Yet even among most of the top lightning chess players, these results are common. Only the very best lightning chess players achieve consistently blunder-free play. Grandmaster Hikaru Nakamura, who plays online as "Smallville," and Grandmaster Roland Schmaltz, who plays online as "Hawkeye," are the two best lightning chess players in the world (at the time of writing this chapter), as measured by overall ratings on the Internet Chess Club

---

[12] The one exception I know of is Weiss and Reber (2012) who base their hypothesis entirely on Dreyfus's work.

[13] Also see Gobet and Simon (1996a), who present data that illustrates that stronger players are able to perform well against weaker players even when their time is limited.

network.[14] (This is the best site for high-level online chess play, and virtually all serious lightning chess is played online—otherwise the pieces would fall over!) Nakamura and Schmaltz do occasionally play master-level games, or, at least, they are able to defeat chess computers that are rated as master level (and because computers move almost instantly, chess computers are extremely strong opponents in lightning chess). No other players today can consistently beat master-level computers, and even Nakamura and Schmaltz occasionally make serious blunders that would not be seen at master-level standard time-control chess, especially against each other and other very strong lightning players. So at best, Dreyfus is making a point about a very small number of grandmasters.

Second, there is an enormous difference between grandmaster and master chess ability; if a master and a grandmaster play a hundred games, the master would be very lucky to beat the grandmaster even once. So with less time for deliberation, the decline in ability is quite significant. One way in which this decline in ability is illustrated is by comparing openings during standard games and lightning games. In modern slow-time play, it is unheard of for top players to vary significantly from leading opening theory.[15] For example, all of the openings from the 2010 world championship match are extremely solid lines. However, when lightning games are played, you see all sorts of bizarre openings.[16]

Finally, Dreyfus (2005) assumes that lightning chess is played too quickly to allow for deliberation:

When the Grandmaster is playing lightning chess, as far as he can tell, he is simply responding to the patterns on the board. At this speed he must depend entirely on perception and not at all on analysis and comparison of alternatives. (p. 53)

But according to a number of expert lightning players, this is not so. Cory Evans, who has been rated over 2700 at lightning chess on the Internet Chess Club server, which, at the time, placed him clearly among the top ten players on the server, explains that as he sees it, even though lightning chess is highly guided by heuristics, deliberation (albeit very fast deliberation) still occurs at crucial junctures. Whereas in a normal game one might deliberate over, say, the advisability of launching an attack and the appropriateness of a certain sacrifice, in lightning chess, according to Cory, one tends to deliberate more over the simple brute tactical details of the game, such as "does Nxf7 win a rook

---

[14] Accessible at <http://www.chessclub.com/> Accessed Jan. 4, 2011.

[15] According to Cory Evans, at the time of writing this chapter, Alexander Morozevich is probably the lone counterexample.

[16] During the 2010 world championship, for example, we witnessed Grunfeld Exchange, Catalan, Slav, Catalan, Slav, Catalan, Slav, Catalan, Nimzo-Indian, Grunfeld, English, Lasker Defense. The only one of these that is not considered the absolute height of orthodox opening theory is the Grunfeld, and for this reason was considered a risky choice by Anand, even though it is still a perfectly respectable opening. However, when lightning-time control is involved, you see a variety of unsound openings such as the Albin Counter-Gambit, hyperaggressive lines in the Dutch, and a lot more speculative Sicilian variations. There are also a number of psychological studies supporting the idea that time-pressure impedes performance (e.g. Chabris and Hearst 2003).

with a two move combination?" When Cory played lightning chess daily, part of his training included rapid-fire analysis of positions, with an aim at completing deliberations in fewer than 5 seconds. The point of this drill, it seems, was to teach him not to just-do-it.

When Cory asked Grandmaster Hikaru Nakamura about this, Nakamura also claimed to calculate when playing lightning chess. Of course, with far less time, far less deliberation occurs. For example, while he might see as far as fifteen or twenty moves ahead in a tournament format, he'll rarely see beyond three moves ahead in lightning. And, if this is correct, it would seem relevant to why he plays lightning at only master, not grandmaster level. Also, Gobet (2012), himself a (retired) international master, has said that these accounts conform to his own experience playing lightning chess, commenting that "although I do not think there is experimental evidence on this, this conclusion fits my own experience of playing such games, and I would guess that this must be even more the case with top-level grandmasters" (p. 241).

Do Evans, Nakamura, and Gobet really calculate when playing so quickly? Again, in line with my methodological precept, I take their descriptions of such calculations as defeasible evidence for their truth. However, I decided to conduct an informal experiment of my own to test both Dreyfus's view that in playing very fast games, high-level chess players would not be able to "say anything at all about [their] reasons for making a particular move," and that "the master could only respond to the demand for a reason by saying 'I made the move because I was drawn to make it'" (Dreyfus 2013, p. 35) and also McDowell's weaker claim that speed chess does not involve explicit deliberation, and that "if one compels a [chess master] to *say* what he thus knows in response to the question 'what are you doing[?]' one will break the flow" (McDowell 2013, p. 46).[17] I had four chess players—two masters, one national master and one (retired) international master—report, to the best of their ability, the thoughts that occurred to them as they played a lightning game online against similarly ranked players. Before trying the experiment, they all doubted that they would be able to do this, not since they felt that lightning chess was all perceptual responses, but rather that stating their thoughts in words would slow them down too much. However, surprising all of us, every player was able to say quite a bit, nonstop and very rapidly, with comments such as "If I play B6, he plays F3; is that the idea? B6, F3; what about C5, D5—D5? D5? If he plays D5 I get into a Leningrad-y thing; but I don't want a Leningrad-y thing...", and "Oh I can't really play knight there; knight here maybe; he'll just take the queen," and "I want to attack on the king's side but nothing's happening;

---

[17] Compare Wayne Martin's (2008) use of lightning chess as an illustration of a situation in which, although one makes a judgment, one does not explicitly review the evidence for one's judgment. Citing his own experience, he writes that when playing speed chess, "I make judgments—I reach a conclusion that is in some sense responsible to evidence—even though I don't undertake any conscious deliberation and I experience my judgment as issuing more-or-less instantaneously" (p. 2). As (I assume) Martin is not making a claim about highly skilled lightning-chess players, my conclusions are consistent with his view.

I guess I'll just go here because I think he might castle queen's side."[18] And not once did this task seem to interfere with their performance, neither in terms of the outcomes of the games (three won, one lost) nor in terms of their own personal evaluations of the game: they all thought that they played at least as well as they usually do, with one commenting, "I think it actually helped my game." The international master, in response to my question of whether he played well, said "I never think I play well, but I played like I play."[19] Thus, even if—as some defenders of just-do-it like to say to me in response to this experiment—such thoughts are an artifact of the request to verbalize what is going on in their minds, it would seem that, contrary to the principle of interference, such thoughts are compatible with (and perhaps even conducive to) expert performance.

Dreyfus, recall, relies on lightning chess to illustrate the insignificance of deliberation in chess with normal time controls, arguing that because chess players can still play stupendously well without deliberating during one-minute-per-side games, deliberation (though it may occur) is not of great import during longer games. Yet, the considerations I have canvassed indicate that high-calibre players actually do deliberate during lightning chess. And they deliberate even more when they have time to think before each move. A five-minute-per-side "blitz" though longer than a one-minute-per-side lightning game still goes by quickly, and sometimes Dreyfus uses blitz to make his point about the paucity of deliberation in chess, so I also ran some informal blitz experiments on the same group of expert chess players I had play one-minute games and found that even with just four more minutes, the deliberation was much more extensive, with players sometimes engaging in a bit of that

---

[18] I recorded all sessions and listened to them and transcribed selections of them myself (remember, philosophers are supposed to be the bargain for the university).

[19] Of course, lightning chess also relies significantly on pattern recognition, and since as pattern recognition allows players to see a good move or a limited number of candidate moves basically instantaneously, or to focus on only certain lines of search, it seems likely that pattern recognition is more important in speed chess than is calculation. However, there is some indication, albeit very weak, that in speed chess, a player's ability to deliberate quickly is actually more important than his or her ability to recognize patterns on the board. At the time of writing this, all of the world chess championships that have been decided by a five-minute game have been won by the younger player. Since (as suggested by Charness's 1981 study) younger grandmasters rely more on calculation than older grandmasters, it could be the younger players' superior ability to quickly calculate that is decisive in these outcomes. No doubt, other factors might fully explain the outcome. For example, it may be that the younger players have simply practiced more speed chess than the older players (the popularity of speed chess seems to have increased dramatically so even though older players have had a longer lifetime during which to play than younger players, it is not at all clear that older players have been playing speed chess for a longer time than younger players). Reflex time may be relevant as well (though in a five minute, as opposed to a one minute or quicker game, this may not be decisive). And as the number of chess matches at issue is very small, it is not even clear that there is a real phenomenon here to uncover. So at best, we have a very weak indication of the relative importance of deliberation over pattern recognition in speed chess, and ultimately, as I explain in the section on intuition, I leave open the question of the relative importance of deliberation versus pattern recognition in expert chess playing quite generally.

"silent lecture" that Rachels mentions, though (of course, for the purposes of the experiment) out loud.[20]

To get a sense of both the extent and relevance of deliberation during a normal time control game, which can extend for hours and hours, consider an explanation international master Larry Evans gives of his deliberations during one such game (Evans-Allen, Philadelphia International 1977, published in *Informant* 22). This is what the board looked like (see Figure 11.1):

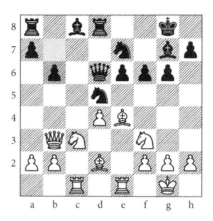

**Figure 11.1**

And here is Evans's description, given after the game, of what he thought about (understanding chess notation is not necessary to get the idea that the processes involves deliberation):

This position is an isolani-a middle-game trade-off where White has an isolated center pawn (bad) which simultaneously gives him space and attack (good). If given one more move, Black will consolidate his position with 1...Bb7, after which he is at least equal. Therefore, I knew it was now, or never. The fight in this position is over the square d5, so I looked at ways to control d5 through a combination. I therefore knew immediately to avoid the attractive looking Nb5, which moved away from the strategic fight. I considered first 1.Bxd5, but after 1...Nxd5 2. Nxd5 exd5 it did not look like White had an advantage. So, I looked at reversing the sequence by playing first 1.Nxd5. After 1.Nxd5 Black can play one of two moves (A) 1...exd5 or (B) 1...Nxd5. If (A) White can play 2.Bb4 followed by 3.Bxe7 Qxe7 4.Bxd5+, winning. So, Black must play (B). After 1.Nxd5 Nxd5 white needs a combination. After carefully analyzing I discovered the winning sequence, reproduced below:

1.Nxd5 Nxd5 2.Bb4! Qd7 (if 2...Nxb4 then 3.Bxa8 and if 2...Qxb4 3.Bxd5!) 3. Be7!! Re8 (3...Qxe7 4.Bxd5) 4.Rc7! Qxc7 5.Bxd5 exd5 6.Qxd5+ Be6 7.Qxe6+ Kh8 8.d5+/−

Was this exactly what was going on in his mind? Probably not; however, Larry Evans has said that this is basically how he was thinking, and if anything, it would seem that,

---

[20] See also Gobet and Simon's (1996a) paper on Kasparov's simultaneous matches against national teams.

as Gobet (2012) points out, "based on the extant scientific literature," the "careful ana-lyzing" that led to Evans's winning sequence was "no trivial matter and demanded extensive search in the jungle of possible moves and counter moves" (p. 242, fn. 4).

To go one step further, one might consider the role of deliberation in the 1999 "Kasparov versus the world," game in which Garry Kasparov played a two-days-per-move game against a "world team" headed by a handful of grandmasters in consultation with over 50,000 people. Kasparov, a long-time advocate for the importance of intuition (though not necessarily Dreyfus's style of nonminded intu-ition) in chess play, claimed that not even was that the best game he ever played, but that "it is the greatest game in the history of chess." Yet with not just minutes, nor even hours, but two days per move, he (and his team) definitely had time for delib-eration, as well as for effort, for he also claims to have never exerted more effort during a game.

Are there times when the clock is running out and a player needs to move without thought? Perhaps. But when there is time, even a miniscule amount of time, expert players think, and they do so apparently beneficially. Moreover, just like the soldier's description in Chapter 5 of how, ideally, soldiers avoid situations where one must sim-ply respond without considering what to do, ideally, chess players avoid situations where they need to respond without considering the move. Expert chess players, then, deliberate if it is at all possible, and perhaps sometimes even when it might seem impossible, for according to Cory, expert lightning players do not get themselves in a situation where deliberation is impossible in part because, as he states it, "I can still think even if I have half a second left."[21]

## Intuition

I have argued that chess players deliberate and calculate not only when, in Dreyfus's (2005) words, "there has been some sort of disturbance that has disrupted [their] intu-itive response" (p. 57), but even when all is going well and they are about to go in for the kill. Yet not every idea can be the result of deliberation. Some ideas must simply arise in chess players' minds so that they have something to initially deliberate over. And typically when a highly skilled chess player looks at the board after the opening, certain ideas for moves do seem to simply come to her—some which may be rejected immediately, and

---

[21] Dreyfus also argues more generally against chess ability being a particularly analytic skill by suggest-ing that grandmaster chess players are not especially mathematical. He quotes his brother, who was the captain of the chess team at Harvard, who claims that his analytic approach to chess stymied his progress: "while students of mathematics and related topics predominate in the population of young people enthu-siastic about chess, you are as likely to find a truck driver as a mathematician among the world's best players. You are more likely to find an amateur psychologist or a journalist" (Dreyfus and Dreyfus 1986, p. 25). Is this correct? To be sure, the very best players are as likely to be mathematicians as truck drivers, since the very best players are invariably professional chess players, and thus neither mathematicians nor truck drivers! Nonetheless, de Groot's (1946/1978) data on grandmasters' occupations indicates that among the best players that do have careers outside chess, they are disproportionately attracted to mathe-matical careers (pp. 364–6).

others, the "candidate moves," which are deemed worthy of consideration. The set of initial moves that comes to a player, as well as those that may present themselves during the process of deliberation, do not themselves arise out of deliberation. Moreover, in their deliberations over candidate moves, experienced players do not deliberate over every possible line of play, and this ability to home in on a few lines that need to be examined is also not the outcome of deliberation. As Gobet (2012) explains, "pattern recognition [or intuition] and search are not an either/or question, but are interleaved," and that "[d]uring look-ahead search, pattern recognition suggests possible moves not only with respect to the current board position, but also with respect to the positions that are anticipated" (p. 245). In general, the range of possibilities over which deliberation occurs is highly limited, and although deliberation leads a player to reject certain moves, the array of possibilities itself is not a result of deliberation.

Dreyfus calls the phenomenon of certain moves presenting themselves "zeroing in," and zeroing in, at least some sense, can be understood as a form of intuition, for as I just explained, the moves a player zeros in on, rather than arising from deliberate thought, suggest themselves. It is difficult to know what exactly guides a player's zeroing in; however, it seems reasonable to think that it is, as Dreyfus describes the phenomenon of intuition at one point, the result of what "occurs upon seeing similarities with previous experiences" (Dreyfus and Dreyfus 1986, p. 28). This form of intuition seems important to chess play, and when understood as a type of pattern recognition, has been widely studied in the empirical literature (see, for example, Simon and Chase 1973; Gobet and Simon 1996a, 1996b). But Dreyfus has a very particular picture of intuition: not only is it what separates the chaff from the wheat among chess players, but it is also nonmental; like the reflexive wave hello you may give to someone when you recognize their face, the grandmaster's play occurs in the movements of the arm, rather than in the movements of the mind. Is this type of intuition at play in high-level chess?

As I have said, I hold that some type of intuition is characteristic of all chess play. Since a computer must perform a humanly impossible amount of searching in order to play grandmaster-level chess, it seems clear that one factor that differentiates computer chess from human chess is our ability to narrow down the tree of possible moves. But is it primarily superior intuition that separates the great from the very good human players? Although all proficient players zero in on initial possible lines of play, grandmasters are better at this than weaker players, for grandmasters are better able to identify lines which are relevant and lines which are not (de Groot 1946/1978, pp. 317–20). But is zeroing in more important to grandmaster skill than deliberation, which involves long chains of tactical thinking? The psychological data on the relative importance of intuition over tactical thinking for high-level chess appears inconclusive. De Groot's (1946/1978) seminal research is sometimes cited as showing that while grandmasters are much better than lesser players at zeroing in on good candidate moves, chess players of different strengths are equally good at tactical thinking—as Dreyfus puts it, that "players at all levels of skill have been shown to be equally good at this"

(Dreyfus and Dreyfus 1986, pp. 37, 198). However, de Groot's work shows no such thing, since he studied exclusively very good players. Rather, what de Groot claims to have found was that there were only very small differences in the macrostructure of the searches among candidate masters and grandmasters. More recent studies have magnified these differences. For example, data collected by Charness (1981), also based on a think-aloud protocol, indicates that the best players search both wider and deeper than less skilled ones, and a reanalysis of de Groot's original data by Reynolds (1991) suggests that there are differences unnoted by de Groot between grandmasters and less skilled players in terms of their tactical thinking. And van Harreveld et al. (2007), who looked at the relative effect of time pressure on players of differing strengths, conclude that if we assume that time pressure affects slow processes such as calculating more than fast processes such as zeroing in, calculating is at least important for the strongest players as it is for weaker players. To be sure, as van Harreveld (2007) points out (p. 595), "playing with faster time controls induces a lot of 'noise' [such as the importance of dexterity and increased stress] into a game" (p. 591).[22] Nonetheless, it may be that at least some grandmasters shine because of their relative superior tactical thinking.[23]

Part of the difficulty of determining the importance of deliberation versus intuition in very high-level chess play is that it could be that top chess players do not push themselves to their tactical limits during psychology experiments—or at least not during experiments where they are not engaged in an actual game against a real opponent. De Groot (1946/1978) himself was well aware of this possibility, and claimed that if pressed, there is no doubt that the grandmaster can calculate deeper; as he put it, "it is certainly easier for [the best players] to calculate to a depth of five, six or seven moves, to analyze a certain situation, systematically to work out an intricate plan, or even to digest multibranches networks or variations" (p. 320; see also Hearst 1977). Deep tactical thinking, as opposed to pattern recognition, is painfully effortful, and while there is great motivation in an actual tournament to put up with the pain, when grandmasters are merely presented with a position from a game and asked to think aloud while choosing the best move, this motivation will be lessened significantly.

That said, as I pointed out, it is also true that numerous studies have emphasized the importance of pattern recognition in chess. De Groot himself held that pattern recognition and the ability to connect the patterns to possible moves was the more

---

[22] See also Holding and Reynolds (1982) and Saariluoma (1990). Not only is the data mixed, but there is considerable disagreement as to how to interpret some of it. For example, Gobet and Simon (1996a) argue that because Kasparov's chess rating drops from 2,750 to 2,646 when playing a simul which restricted the amount of time he had on each move, limiting a player's time for calculation has little effect on quality of play, as a 100-point decrease in rating is "slight." However, van Harreveld et al. (2007) take the same decrease to be "a significant decrease," pointing out that at the time they were writing the paper, such a drop in rating would place Kasparov, who was then the strongest player in the world, at somewhere around sixtieth place (p. 572, fn. 1). To put this in perspective, today a 2650 FIDE might be able to make about $40,000 a year playing chess; a 2750 player could easily make over $200,000 per year.

[23] As mentioned in footnote 18, How important tactical thinking is for a grandmaster may depend on the players' age, for according to Charness (1981), "two players possessing the same rating may vary greatly in chunking pattern if one is young and the other comparatively old" (p. 30).

important factor in chess expertise based, not so much on his protocol study, but on a study in which he tested players of varying ability for their recall of chess positions after a brief exposure to them. Finding that grandmasters' ability to reproduce the positions on a different board was almost perfect while amateurs' made numerous mistakes, de Groot reasoned that grandmasters must chunk the pieces into meaningful units or patterns, and he concluded that superior pattern recognition is the defining feature of chess excellence. Chase and Simon (1973a; 1973b; see also Simon and Chase 1973) replicated this experiment and additionally found that grandmasters and novices did not differ significantly in their ability to memorize randomly arranged pieces (in contrast to how they would be arranged if they were in a game). (However, more recent studies have shown that given sufficient exposure time, high-level players are better than novices at recalling random positions.)[24] But although grandmasters' unrivaled ability to memorize chess positions suggests that superior pattern recognition is *a* defining feature of chess excellence, it is not clear that it suggests that it is *the* defining feature of chess excellence; as such, since pattern recognition, being immediate and effortless, is reasonably counted as an intuitive process, it is not clear that it suggests that intuition is the defining feature of chess excellence.

Be that as it may, let me leave open the question of whether it is primarily intuition that differentiates strong players from weaker ones and move on to the question of whether intuition (in the form of zeroing in as well as intuitive choices between positions) is a nonminded process—in particular, to the question of whether it is arrational and nonconceptual—for even if intuition is what separates the chaff from the wheat in high-level chess play, if it is rational and conceptual, it fits into my cognition-in-action principle, which states that experts on their mettle frequently engage their minds, that doing so does not necessarily or even generally interfere with expert performance, and that experts should not, in general, avoid doing so. Indeed, even the existence of nonmental intuition is consistent with this principle since just as I can accept, for example, that many aspects of a tennis player's serve are not thought about, guided by, or monitored by the mind, I can, consistently with cognition-in-action, accept that zeroing in is an aspect of chess performance that is, as Dreyfus holds, not mental at all. As I have been emphasizing throughout the book, I do not think that all components of expert performance are conceptualized, are done for a reason, are conscious or are, in some way or other, mental; rather I think that, generally, when experts perform at their best the mind is engaged and that such engagement does not hinder expert performance and need not be avoided. However, what seems to be in tension with cognition-in-action and illustrative of just-do-it in its most extreme form is Dreyfus's idea that the best moves by top chess players are entirely intuitive and that intuition is entirely nonmental, or "nonminded," as he puts it. Of course, since I have already argued that deliberation is generally essential to high-level chess

---

[24] Gobet and Simon (1996a) confirmed a skill difference in the random position condition with a meta-analysis of thirteen studies. Also see Hartston and Wason (1985) and de Groot (1946/1978).

play, I could make the existence of such nonminded intuitive actions consistent with my view by arguing that they only occur occasionally. But whether or not this is correct, this approach strikes me as rather pedantic. World-class chess players sometimes make brilliant moves without apparently being able to express a reason for why they made them (Gobet 2012). And such actions seem to have a very strong just-do-it flavor. So what is going on? Are these actions in some sense guided by the mind or are they simply, as Drefyus sees it, reactions to forces on the board?

In apparent support of Dreyfus's position, one might cite how Bobby Fischer used to walk by a game, glance at a board position which others had long been struggling to analyze, and immediately see the best move. It seems that he instantly and automatically zeroed in on one move and knew it was the best one. How did he do this? In contrast to Dreyfus, who would see this ability as an arational process, I would like to suggest that chess intuition is rational: similar to how one is acting rationally when one sees a familiar flaw in a philosophical argument and is able, right away, to say what is wrong with it, so too is rationality involved in Fischer's ability to immediately see the best move.

In line with Dreyfus, I take an action to be rational if you can articulate what you are doing and you are able to justify your action, in the sense of providing a reason for and not just the cause of your action, even if the articulation is rather minimal and the justification incomplete. Both finding a familiar flaw in a philosophical argument and seeing the key move on a board often seem to satisfy those criteria. For example, you might say "in his argument for dualism, I instantly saw that he was using a mistaken definition and thus I rejected the argument" or "I saw that the position was a Dragon Sicilian Yugoslav Attack, and so I instantly saw that sacrificing on the h-file would lead to checkmate, as it inevitably does in those kinds of positions." Here we seem to have both an articulation of what is being done and a reason for why it is being done.

Gobet (2012) emphasizes, however, that not all of what is contained in chess-related insights can be expressed. In the Dragon Sicilian Yugoslav Attack, as he points out:

sacrificing on the h-file sometimes works, and sometimes does not. The reason might be clearly verbalizable (e.g. the black king can escape), can be ascertained only after analyzing numerous variations to great depths, or can even sometimes rely only on the player's "gut feelings" (intuition). (p. 245)

But what are these gut feelings? Do they not also incorporate the judgment, for example, that sacrificing on the h-file was the right thing to do in the given situation (even if this judgment turns out not to be correct)? If they do incorporate judgments, they would seem to enter the realm of the rational (in at least the weak sense mentioned above). Gobet (2012) claims that the Dragon example "beautifully illustrates the idea that perception, and hence intuition, precedes conceptualization, since it twice uses 'I saw,' indicating an immediate and perceptual act" (p. 245). And my example of finding a familiar flaw in an argument is expressed as a type of "seeing" as well. But, although both judgments may be immediate isn't it more accurate to see them as illustrating not that perception precedes conceptualization but, as Gobet (2012) himself puts it so well, that in such situations, "the two areas of thinking and perception are hardly ever separable, and in many cases even indistinguishable" (p. 245)? It might be that in such situations concepts without perception lose the game, but perception without concepts doesn't do any better.

Rationality, for Dreyfus, also implies conceptualization. And one way he emphasizes the arational nature of expertise is by arguing that in situations where expert chess players just see what to do, they do not conceptualize what they are doing. Yet to see the position as a Dragon Sicilian Yugoslav Attack, or as an isolani (as Evans did in the Evans versus Allen game), involves conceptualization at least in the sense of seeing the board in a certain way. And such examples are easily multiplied.

Dreyfus (2005), however, thinks that zeroing in is arational. He tells us:

> the master may make moves that are entirely intuitive and contrary to any preconceived plan. In such instances, when asked why he did what he did, he may be at a loss to reconstruct a reasoned account of his actions because there is none...Nothing about the position need be nameable and thinkable as a reason for moving. (pp. 54–55)

On this picture, there is no reason in the player's mind for why she made a certain move—not merely no *good* reason, but none at all. Does this happen?

As Gobet (2012) points out, there are examples in the technical literature of times when players do not explain the reasons for their final choice among the possible moves that they deliberated over (p. 244).[25] This is not an example of zeroing in on one or a few initial moves, but is an example where the choice among candidate moves is intuitive, that is, not the result of deliberation. But are such times examples of when there is no reason at all guiding play? Or might there be one, albeit a very thin one—for example, the simple reason that that particular move seemed to cinch the mate? Recall, that on Dreyfus's view, if a player was able to express the reason for why she made a great move which was guided entirely intuitively, entirely by the forces on the board, all she could say was "I was drawn to move." But in most of these cases that Gobet mentions, I presume that a player would still be able to say something like what Kasparov said in response to a question about how during the final game of the 1990 chess world championship he was able to see a certain move so quickly: "I didn't need to calculate...I saw that that would win."[26] This, it seems, is a reason: namely, that he made the move because he saw that it was a winning move. (For thoughts on how such conceptualization may work, see Stanley's 2011 discussion of demonstrative conceptualization, pp. 167–73.)

Occasionally, a player might not be able to provide even this type of justification for a move. But, still, in some such cases, there may be explanations for the player's actions other than that she was simply drawn to move. For example, perhaps the grandmaster

---

[25] For this point, Gobet cites O'Kelly de Galway (1963), Tals (1997), and Beliavsky and Mikhalchishin (2002).

[26] See <https://www.youtube.com/watch?v=SMe-hvCwTRo> Accessed June 20, 2012.

chooses move A over move B, merely because A and B were the only serious options and, failing to find a reason to pick one over the other, she merely chose the simpler move. But relative simplicity is not a good reason to choose a move, so to save face, she claims that she had no reason. In such a case, it would be luck rather than forces on the board that is responsible for the move being the right one. Emotions, as Gobet points out, are also springs of action (even in high-level chess play), and although desire, fear, and lust for blood may causally explain an action, they do not seem to provide a reason for action why one move was chosen over another. Moreover, it may be, as Hume thought, that emotion underpins all action. However, I assume that in at least most cases the desire to demolish your opponent leads to rook to e3 rather than knight to e3 because you conceive of the one move as being in some way better than the other.

There is still, however, the fact that a chess player may not have words to describe why she made a certain move. Gobet sees this as a reason for thinking that good moves are sometimes not conceptualized. However, if one accepts that concepts need not be verbally specifiable and that some spatial concepts fall into this category, a reason for a move might depend on concepts even if it is not expressible or fully expressible in words. As I mentioned in Chapter 2, that there are such concepts is controversial. However, whether one wants to call it "conceptual thought," or just "thought" it does seem that some reasoning takes place in a nonverbalizable or at least not fully verbalizable realm. For example, some areas of mathematical reasoning seem to depend on spatial though not fully verbalizable concepts, or thought. Though it is generally accepted that every proof in math must be presented in words, it is arguable that some spatial reasoning is only cumbersomely translated into words and might be much more elegantly presented as a picture.[27] The blackboard is an essential aspect of teaching math, not only to write down concepts and proofs, but also to illustrate spatial ideas visually. Gobet (2012) is working with a notion of concepts according to which concepts must be declarative, as well as with the idea that all conscious thought is declarative. But I leave open the possibility that some chess thinking, reasoning, and conceptualization is both conscious and nondeclarative.

## Intuition as Conceptual

There is a more general argument for the view that exemplary chess play—even the aspect of play that involves merely "seeing the right move," or making an unexplained choice among possible moves—is conceptual. This argument was made perhaps most elegantly by Alfred Binet in 1893 (1893/1966). Though Binet was not much of a chess player himself, he became fascinated with chess at the Café de la Régence in Paris, which in the nineteenth century was the center of the chess world. Binet was impressed by how chess players could remember their games so well, and concluded that a game

---

[27] For a discussion of the role of proofs without words in mathematics see <http://mathoverflow.net/questions/8846/proofs-without-words> Accessed July 3, 2012.

is memorable not because the individuals' moves are memorable, but because the underlying reasoning is memorable. "For the good player," Binet (1893/1966) wrote, "memorizing famous games...is no more difficult than reciting a bit of poetry. The logical sequence of moves links them together in memory as are the verses by their cadence" (p. 151).

Binet emphasized the difference between conceptualized chess memory and non-conceptualized sensory impressions:

When a person memorizes a long string of numbers, the ephemeral quality of such memories seems to indicate that they are like simple sensations...the numbers he tries to retain are meaningless and uninteresting. They are nothing but sensory impressions on his ear; meaning-less associations, they represent chance, chaos, they are without rhythm or reason; this is why they cannot be fixed firmly in mind. (p. 151)

And indeed, mnemonists, who fix an extraordinarily long string of numbers into memory, do assign meaning or images to the numbers. And this allows the number to enter long-term memory. (I tried this myself, and found that with just a bit of concep-tualization—for example, there is a sequence of groups of numbers that all end in "9" that I think of as the 9s—I was quickly able to place pi to the 100th decimal into my long-term memory.[28] Memorizing significantly longer bits, however, calls for a more systematic and well-worked out system of assigning meanings to the numbers.) Binet tells us that, in contrast to those who simply memorize a string of numbers without meaning—like you might do to remember a phone number, simply for the purposes of dialing it immediately—and subsequently forget it, chess player Paul Morphy (the greatest player of Binet's era) dictated to his publisher ten games he had played eight months earlier. The great chess player's memory, Binet says, "is not a memory of sensa-tions but a memory of ideas" (p. 151). These are the ideas the player had during the game, and such ideas would seem to be conceptual and also rational, in as much as they provide some reason (though not necessarily a complete one) for the player's actions.

As I see it, the research on pattern recognition in chess, which I mentioned earlier, and which illustrates how experienced players (but not weaker players) can correctly set up a board position from the middle of a well-played game after seeing the position briefly, supports this view. The pattern is encoded in memory, and it is a memory not merely of unconceptualized sensations, if indeed there could be such a thing. Not only does this contrast with how we remember a string of (relatively) unconceptualized numbers, which fly out of our heads fairly rapidly, but, to return to face recognition, it also contrasts with how the majority of us recognize and remember faces. Although you will recognize a familiar face, unless you are an artist, you will likely not be able to draw it, or even say in much detail what it looked like once out of view; experienced chess players' study of games provides them with the conceptual tools to recreate the relevant drawing.

---

[28] For proof, feel free to watch my pi dance: <https://www.youtube.com/watch?v=jepS-z_-gGc[youtube.com]>

Gobet (2012) tells us that "the standard explanation for the experiments on chess memory recall is that players use perceptual chunks, which are not necessarily verbalizable and conceptual" (p. 246). He writes:

Having been my own and only subject in an experiment where the aim was to memorize as long a sequence as possible of briefly presented chess positions, and having memorized about 1,800 positions in total, I do have some expertise on this subfield of chess skill (Gobet and Simon 1996b; Gobet 2011). While some positions clearly can be conceptualized (e.g. a "Dragon Sicilian Yugoslav Attack with opposite castles," to use our old friend), and while some can even be fully recognized as part of a known game, other positions simply cannot be coded that easily. And even when they elicit a concept, this concept sometimes characterizes the position so poorly that it becomes essentially useless. Thus, the claim that intuitions are rational and conceptual is not defensible empirically. (p. 246)

But again, I wonder if Gobet would understand the outcome of this experiment differently if he had a less strict notion of conceptualization, one that allows for some concepts to be nondeclarative. Gobet and Chassy (2009) point out that high-level chess players "show nearly perfect recall with a presentation as short as 5s…[yet] even though their task is to memorize the position, they also understand its meaning fairly well at the end of the presentation" (pp. 152–3). Part of the reason for this could be, as with Gobet's own experiment on himself, that they have conceptualized the positions declaratively. (And of course, the request to memorize the position may motivate the players to conceptualize the situation more than they might otherwise.) However, it may also be that in certain cases these players and Gobet himself understand the positions because they conceptualize them spatially; as such, they are able to see positions in a certain way and categorize and reidentify them, though not necessarily fully, or even usefully verbalize them.

The details of truly unconceptualized, automatic actions, such as Charles Taylor's example of a man flawlessly navigating a path, do not leave memory traces, or at least not long-lasting ones. When all goes well with such actions, the particulars of how they were accomplished are either quickly erased from the mind, or were never imprinted there to begin with. In such situations, it does seem that there are no whys and wherefores; the body takes over, leaving the mind free to contemplate something else. Perhaps this is why the memory of the sensory feeling of severe pain fades so much with time. You might remember that you were in serious pain, but after a couple of months, your memory of the exact feeling dims and after a couple of years, while you still remember that a certain occurrence was painful, the sensation itself is a blank. The pain, it seems, lacked the necessary conceptual content. For grandmaster chess players, however, the moves have conceptual hooks, which produce long-lasting memories.[29]

---

[29] Beilock and Carr (2001) have done some interesting work on so-called "expert-induced amnesia," which indicates that college golf team players do not remember as much about the mechanisms of their movements as novices. However, they remembered many more higher-level aspects of their movements. Mapping this onto chess, we would not be surprised to find that novices recall thinking about the basic rules and basic heuristics much more than experts, who may expect to recall thinking about the broader plans used in the game, and any novel opening themes they encountered.

The baseball player Steve Blass, who in his memoir speaks of his own "massive recall," describes Pete Rose as having even greater conceptual hooks on his game (Blass and Sherman 2012):

He knows the game. And he doesn't just remember every hit he ever got but probably every *pitch* he ever saw . . . He has total recall of his career. (pp. 6–7)

If expertise is like navigating a path without any conscious awareness of its twists and turns, then why is it that some experts remember every tortuous detail?

## The Gymnasium of the Mind

I have argued that expert chess players attend to their games and deliberate, though not over everything. The actions that do not result from deliberation are intuitive, in the sense that they are based on experiences of similar situations in the past. But such intuitions, I argued, are rational (minimally, they are seen as good moves) and conceptual (for example, they may be conceptualized as good moves, and may contain spatial conceptual content). Of course, as with other areas of expertise, a grandmaster chess player could approach a game as if it were a flight of stairs to surmount, and still beat most of us mere mortals—but, if my arguments are correct, this is not the approach grandmasters take when playing their best. Chess (even lightning chess, when played at a high level) in no way supports the idea that experts just do it, but rather is, as has oft been said, "the gymnasium of the mind."

# 12

# Sex, Drugs, Rock and Roll, and the Meaning of Life

A little theory must succeed practice: it is the means to make a perfect discipline.

Marquis de Sade (1740–1814)
*Philosophy in the Bedroom*

When we first began this journey, I mentioned that I organized the chapters so as to facilitate nonlinear reading. For those who have subsequently arrived here directly, let me summarize what has happened in the intervening pages.

My primary goal has been to argue that the view that experts perform best without thinking about what they are doing—an idea I refer to as "the just-do-it principle"—is mistaken. As I attempted to show, this principle or something similar to it, has been upheld in sundry forms by diverse thinkers both historically and today, and I stated the archetype of this view as follows:

**The just-do-it principle.** For experts, when all is going well, optimal or near-optimal performance proceeds without any of the following mental processes: self-reflective thinking, planning, predicting, deliberation, attention to or monitoring of their actions, conceptualizing their actions, conscious control, trying, effort, having a sense of the self, or acting for a reason. Moreover, when all is going well, such processes interfere with expert performance and such mental processes should be avoided.

I have criticized this extreme view, but I have also questioned weaker just-do-it positions, such as those that proscribe just one or some of these mental processes during expert action. And, at the risk of verbicide, I have been using (and shall continue in this chapter to use) the word "thought" to cover the gamut of mental modes that might be taken to fall under the just-do-it heading.

The view that I hold, and which I think is closer to the truth—a view which many of my arguments have been converging on—is this:

**The cognition-in-action principle**: For experts, when all is going well, optimal or near optimal performance frequently involves some of the following conscious mental processes: self-reflective thinking, planning, predicting, deliberation, attention to or monitoring of their actions, conceptualizing their actions, controlling their movements, trying, effort, having a sense of the self, and acting for a reason. Moreover, such mental processes do not necessarily or even generally interfere with expert performance and should not generally be avoided by experts.

Both of these principles employ the term "expert," but what do I mean by expert? I argued that for my purposes, I take this term to mean someone who has spent around ten years or more engaged in deliberate skill-related practice (which is practice with the specific aim of improving) and is still intent on improving. Not all domains of expertise admit a practice/performance distinction. Yet I argue that for endeavors that fall into this category, one can think of practice as any type of domain-relevant activity that is done with the aim of improving, or desire to do better than before. This specification of "expert" lines up (to a degree) with what we mean when we talk about professionals versus amateurs (and I sometimes use this terminology as well).

My critical task has been aimed at tearing down certain pillars of support for the just-do-it principle. For example, I argued that a battery of psychological experiments that purportedly provide evidence for it are open to other reasonable interpretations. To give one (simplified) instance, it may be that because the "expert" subjects in psychology experiments are typically of intermediate skill (indeed, in one study of golfers 35 percent of the more highly skilled participants had never even taken a golf lesson) they have not developed the appropriate conceptual tools that enable experts to think while in action. I also found little support for just-do-it from the argument that because expert action can be extremely fast, there is no time for thought. Expert action may be fast, but I argue that—except perhaps for the most extreme cases, such as hand-to-hand combat—thought in action and sometimes prior to action is possible and beneficial. Beyond this, I argued that the idea that the self is lost in expert movement would be better understood as the idea that certain aspects of the self—worries, doubts, and so forth—are washed away, and I also suggested that attributions of effortless movement to an expert may be reasonable, even if the expert is exerting a great deal of effort.

In a positive vein, I have supported the cognition-in-action principle by, among other means, arguing that because experts train thoughtfully, experts can think and even aim to improve while performing. And it is in part this training that distinguishes every day, well-worn actions—such as instantly recognizing a familiar face despite being unable to say very precisely what it looked like once out of view—from expert actions. I also argued for the importance of trying and effort in expert action, based on the idea that experts are highly motivated to do their best in situations that matter (that is, the World Cup soccer tournament, rather than the psychology experiment), and that times where trying appears to interfere with expert performance are not obviously times when trying per se is detrimental, but rather when not trying might be one means to reduce nerves: in such a case, it is the nerves, not the trying that is detrimental to performance. Moreover, I argued that qualitative studies of expert athletes indicate that players regularly cope with pressure by increasing their concentration on what they are doing.

My interest in the topic of whether thinking interferes with doing was kindled by a question Bob Child asked me after a talk I gave, in which I upheld the view that proprioception—our nonvisual sense of the movements and position of our bodies—is an aesthetic sense (that is, a sense by means of which we experience beauty, grace, and other aesthetic properties). Child thought that the idea of a proprioceptive aesthetic sense was misguided since he held that if a dancer were to focus on how she was moving, she wouldn't be able to perform well. That was his *modus tollens*. At long last, I have now presented my *modus ponens*, which is the argument that because dancers focus on their movements proprioceptively, this shows that focusing on one's own bodily movements does not interfere with expert skill. Finally, as we have just seen (for those of us who have not simply skipped right ahead to this chapter), I argued that despite the fact that chess does involve what might be called "intuition," this intuition is still rational and conceptual and, at least when it matters—in a tournament rather than a test—is accompanied by analytical thought. Though I am well aware that none of the considerations I have brought up show conclusively that the cognition-in-action principle is right and just-do-it is wrong, my hope, as I mentioned at the outset, has been that when taken together, they lend my theory of effortful expertise what William Wimsatt (2007) sees as a criterion for being the best explanation for the available data, namely, robustness.

However, there are a few lingering concerns I would now like to address. For example, I claim to take the words of experts seriously, but experts at times say things that suggest just-do-it. Dave Hill, we ought not to forget, quipped that a golf swing is like sex, because you can't be thinking about the mechanics of the act while doing it. How do I explain this? I should point out that not all of the loose ends I shall take up fall under the heading of "sex, drugs, rock and roll, and the meaning of life," though some do; be patient (or, if you must, skip ahead).

## Why Have So Many Accepted the Just-do-it Principle?

As we saw in Chapter 1, effortlessness and automaticity are not only guiding mantras in many popular books on expert action, but the idea that expertise is effortless and automatic also has deep roots in history, both in the East and in the West. Furthermore, experts themselves sometimes endorse it, if not by using the expression "just-do-it" or George Balanchine's "don't think, dear; just do," then with, say, the oft-touted phrase in the world of jazz music, "when you're thinking, you're stinking," or the comment that "you have to get in the groove," where it is the groove and not your conscious mind that is thought to be directing one's actions. Why, if I am correct and expert action is thoughtful and effortful, do many claim otherwise?

No doubt, part of the reason why just-do-it has captivated the general public turns on its role in the media and popular press. But why were the popular books written in the first place? And what accounts for the just-do-it acolytes among psychologists, philosophers, and others in the rather unpopular academy? One reason is that empirical research in psychology is seen as justifying just-do-it (which is a perception I have challenged). However, just-do-it was popular long before the existence of readily accessible, Googleable psychology research. And in any event, it sometimes seems that in this research, the experimenters are testing a view they already assume is correct. Whence did this idea arrive?

Just-do-it apostles sometimes aver that experts themselves say that when they are performing at their best, they are not thinking about what they are doing. I take this, as I explained in the Introduction, as a good *prima facie* reason to think that the just-do-it principle is correct. But do experts tend to make such claims? Or is the preponderance of anecdotal support in my favor? It is difficult to determine the answer to this question, at least without conducting a large-scale survey, and, of course, getting a random sample, asking neutral questions, and interpreting the data would pose a significant challenge. Besides, such studies are costly, and, as I pointed out in the Introduction, philosophers are supposed to be a bargain for the university. However, there are some who have aimed to conduct systematic investigations of the creative process. What have they found?

Csikszentmihalyi's (1996) ninety-one interviews with highly creative individuals, though still small-scale, reveals, as he lays it out, numerous examples of experts working in a state of what he calls "flow," which is sometimes described as complete enjoyment or absorption in one's activities. I mentioned in Chapter 9 that even though Csikszentmihalyi's earlier research that led to his concept of "flow" is sometimes taken (by, for example, Velleman 2008) as intimating that expert action involves attenuated effort and thought, that research was aimed at uncovering the nature of optimal *experience,* not optimal *performance.* This more recent work, however, targets creativity. As he sees it, creative discoveries or ideas require attention, but it is often effortless attention. Thinking, as Csikszentmihalyi sees it, is also essential, though he seems to value the "the mental activity that takes place backstage" more than deliberate, linear thinking, since, on his view, it leads to less predictable results (1996, p. 138). And when the creative idea arrives, he comments, it is sometimes in a flash. Most people interviewed, he tells us, though not all, recall "with great intensity and precision a particular moment when some major problem crystallized in their minds" (pp. 103–4). So these interviews, as he describes them, do provide some support for the claim that great ideas sometimes occur effortlessly. If this is common, it would be in tension with cognition-in-action, if it were not for the fact that, as he also points out, "most lovely insights never go any farther, because under the cold light of reason fatal flaws appear" (p. 104).

On Csikszentmihalyi's analysis of creativity, then, cold reason and lovely insights seem to work together. This does not run contrary to cognition-in-action, though I have tended to emphasize the cold more than the lovely. And there is some support for the idea that cold reason is the more important of the two. Albert Rothenberg (1990) who spent thirty-five years conducting and analyzing interviews with creative individuals, scrutinizing manuscripts and drafts of creative works, and performing empirical studies on creativity, finds little support for the idea that "lovely insights," play a significant role in the creative process, and although I shall not discuss his findings and methods in depth, let me nonetheless indicate his conclusion: quite contrary to the cultural stereotype of creative ideas arising via sudden inspiration, they are actually the result of "direct, intense, and intentional effort on the creator's part" (p. 9). And, in her review of poets' manuscripts from first to final draft, Phyllis Bartlett (1951) finds that initial drafts rarely show any signs that the poet was working from a sense of inspiration.

My own informal and entirely unsystematic interviews have led me to think that, in general, although some amateur athletes, musicians, or poets tell me that thinking interferes with doing, professionals in most areas (as well as the serious amateurs) are unlikely to say this. And when I ask the amateur athlete, musician, or poet who has just been trying to convince me of the truth of just-do-it whether she performs her professional activities best with thought and effort, she usually readily agrees that, of course, *my* work involves thought and effort.

A writer once told me that Gallwey's *The Inner Game of Tennis* (1974) changed his life, by which he meant that it changed (and, he felt, improved) his tennis game. In fact, he said that now, if he really needs to win a point, he asks his opponent—feigning keen interest—whether she locates her racket more in the middle of her back or behind her left shoulder before she serves the ball. "It works every time," he told me: "They start thinking and they muff." I responded by saying that his opponent must not have been a very serious tennis player, and summarily told him that he must not have read very much of this book that changed his life, for if he had, he'd be working on developing a way to think about even the movements of his arm muscles as he plays, since, after paying homage to *Zen in the Art of Archery* (or what according to Shoji (2001) might better be thought of as "the myth of Zen in the art of archery"), Gallwey goes on to explain that thinking about the details of his arm movements is exactly what he does while playing. (Or rather, that is what I wanted to say in response; somehow I rarely am able to say what I want to say, and when I try to, it often comes out wrong—which may, of course, be the reason I write.)[1] This weekend tennis-playing author, however, told me that when he writes, it's pure blood, sweat, and tears.

So I am not convinced that reflection on optimal performance in one's area of expertise generally does lead one down the path to just-do-it. Nonetheless, perhaps part of the reason why so many accept just-do-it is they infer that because their avocation suffers under self-reflection, their vocation suffers as well. Others,

---

[1] This is related to the question of whether what one says without revision, without thought, is most indicative of one's true beliefs. I certainly hope that this isn't the case for me.

however, may draw conclusions about thought-in-action based on their experience of everyday activities. Thinking about what you are doing as you are doing it does at least sometimes seem to interfere with everyday actions, such as answering the phone or going down stairs. As I put it in Chapter 2, if you start thinking about how exactly you are supposed to initiate a telephone conversation, the recipient of your call will notice your heavy breathing and hang up. And it is easy to see how an evolutionary advantage could accrue to those who could think about more important things during, say, grooming. But, as I have argued, expert action is significantly different from everyday action, since not only have experts trained in an analytical manner but also for the performer on stage or the professional golfer on the green, there is nothing more important than the task at hand. Thus we shouldn't expect that because just-do-it applies to everyday actions, it applies to expert actions as well. When Dreyfus embarked on his investigation of expertise in the air force, he had never flown a plane during a military assault; indeed, he had never flown a plane at all. So he reflected on his experience of driving, and generalized from there. Yet, driving, for better or worse, is something one often doesn't put one's heart and soul into. It is a life-or-death matter, but unlike air force pilots, we do not treat it as such, and so would rather chat with the person in the passenger seat than give it our all. And apart from an initial learning period and the modicum of studying one does to renew a license, it is not something that we train to improve. For this reason, it is not well suited as a generalization base for the type of expert action I have been investigating. Dreyfus, on my view, does not count as an expert driver. Yet he is an expert philosopher; why didn't he start there?[2]

Now, as I explained in Chapter 1, certain just-do-it-like precepts may, nonetheless, be beneficial. For example, when drafting a novel, a writer might want to avoid ruminating over how it will be perceived by others. But this does not mean she is not thinking at all; for there are many other aspects of the process that require thought, not the least of which is figuring out how to be true to herself. An athlete might want to avoid thinking about the crowd on the bleachers, but this might be merely because it distracts her from focusing on other more important things. In sum, that certain kinds of thoughts are detrimental does not imply that thinking is detrimental.

What type of thoughts are detrimental? If I could answer this question, I actually might make some money. However, I can't since I believe that it differs from person to person. For example, while thinking a great deal about the opinions of others stifles me, some might find the elixir of motivation in that very thought. I also believe that what one finds unproductive depends in part on what aspects of performance one has

---

[2] Interestingly enough, I have heard that in the 1960s, there was an excellent driving manual published by the US Air Force, which makes one wonder whether applying knowledge of military piloting to driving has better results than the reverse. The main idea of the manual was that accidents result when you are too close to another vehicle, pedestrian, or obstacle. And so the book focused on strategies for keeping your distance.

been working on to improve. If you have been working on improving the movements of your right pinkie finger—you may think this a joke, but the precise position of one's fingers is highly aesthetically relevant in ballet—then thinking about your right pinkie finger will not impede performance. But aren't negative thoughts (thinking, for example, *I can't do this*) always detrimental? Given that some apparently successful coaching techniques seem to turn on making one feel terrible about one's abilities, I do not want to claim even that; coaching is not a one-size-fits-all endeavor.

In earlier chapters, I have suggested a number of other reasons for why the idea of effortless expertise may be deceptively attractive. For example, just-do-it may be appealing because expert action in some areas can erroneously appear effortless. Also, when one is performing poorly, one is often thinking in action. Yet rather than thinking causing the blunder, as the just-do-iters would have it, it may be that the blunder caused one to think about what is going wrong.[3] But let me close this section with one last possibility: it could be that some of the popularity of just-do-it is based simply on the apparent fact that most people prefer ease to hard work. Books such as *Zen in the Art of Archery* and all of its spin-offs may very well turn upon this tendency. Perhaps they reach the status of bestsellers for the same reason that diet books that advocate the idea that you can eat as much as you want as long as you don't eat one somewhat arbitrary category of food are popular: not because they work, but because they are easy to follow.

## You Don't Need to Conquer the World

I have just argued that people may be drawn to accept the just-do-it principle for a number of reasons other than insight into its truth. And once propounded, the principle is perpetuated because introspection is susceptible to suggestion. Nonetheless, as a matter of psychological fact, not thinking, or at least not thinking much about what you are doing might, for some, help ease nervousness or prevent one's unproductive thoughts from multiplying out of control. Although it may be that the best performers keep nerves and unproductive thoughts in check and are able to effectively think in action, for some, occasionally suspending the thinking processes might be a useful means of conquering psychological demons. Something similar can be said about suspending the will to achieve.

Dancer David Hallberg commented in an interview (Barry 2011) that once, when he was practicing turning before going on for Act II in *Giselle*, the floor was slippery, and he "just kind of lost the feeling of being up on the leg and turning"—whereupon, Hallberg recounts, the director of the Bolshoi Ballet (the company he was dancing

---

[3] Of course, on my view, since thinking is a regular component of expert action, experts are always thinking in action; however, thinking about what is going wrong, because of its unpleasantness, may be an especially memorable event. Moreover, one might try to save face by saying, "I was thinking too much" rather than "I wasn't paying attention?"

with at the time) said, "You don't have to emote. Just calm down, relax, and just go for the pirouette calmly." Hallberg tells us that, "in essence—he didn't say this, but in essence—he's saying you don't have to conquer the world, just do a pirouette. You know, just go around three times." And this fixed the problem.

In this situation, thinking less and trying less (or perhaps not at all) may have been beneficial. But, again, this does not mean that trying or thinking, in and of itself, is detrimental, as Hallberg's further comments indicate: "sometimes when things aren't working you get yourself into a stupor. You start to panic a little bit and then it just gets worse and worse." The problem, then, seemed not so much that he was thinking or trying too hard, but that his suboptimal practice session led him to thinking in an unproductive way, namely, to panic, and panic, no doubt, should be avoided. What fixed the pirouette, according to Hallberg, was that he "calm[ed] down and let it happen." But perhaps the key was the calmness, rather than the let-it-happenness.

Of course, if your goal is to conquer the world, then (in line with the argument I presented in Chapter 7, "You Can't Try Too Hard") in order to achieve this goal, you should try your best to conquer the world. (Whether conquering the world is a worthwhile goal is another question). However, as I indicated, there are different shades of "trying," and when "trying" means simply exerting more force, then sometimes you can very well try too hard—if not when your goal is conquering the world, then at least when it is performing a pirouette—for if you push off with a great deal of force, especially if the floor is slippery, you may fall. And despite the fact that Balanchine used to say that he likes dancers who fall, one prefers to avoid it oneself, if possible. That excess force is unwarranted, as I argued, does not mean one should not try or put effort into one's expert actions. There is a balance between force and control: too much force will lead you to lose control. Thus one needs to *try* to find just the right balance.

Some might find that trying produces unwanted tension. Yet again, this does not mean that the trying in itself is problematic. If I am right, there is no necessary connection between trying and tension and, as I suggested, the best course of action is to learn to try your best without getting tense. What is more, the experience of trying is most pronounced when you are doing your best, yet still fail. Alas, that sometimes occurs, but so does lamentable trying to do your best and succeeding.

## Not All Ideas Arrive in the Shower

That expert action is effortless is a seductive idea, but might there also be some truth to it? Ideas occasionally *do* seem to come up when you least expect them, such as when you are in the shower: without any noticeable effort, you figure out the answer and rush out of the bathroom to jot it down before you forget, leaving a trail of water behind you. Such things happen. So I need to say something about how they fit into my account of effortful expertise.

First off, not all ideas are like this; experts occasionally get out of the shower. And when they do, thinking may involve quite a bit of effort. Of course, some stay in the shower, as it were, longer than others, by engaging in activities that promote a similarly relaxed state of mind and body. The peripatetic philosophers were probably on to something in practicing ambulatory philosophy. The mathematician Russell Miller told me that he takes cross-country train trips for the sole purpose of working. And the physicist Freeman Dyson talks of a "Eureka experience" coming to him in the middle of Kansas, while on a Greyhound bus from California to Princeton: "suddenly the whole picture [of a solution to a problem with quantum electrodynamics] became clear" (quoted in Csikzentmihalyi 1996, p. 42). Both on the train and on the trail, hard work also occurs: one struggles away as the scenery flies by. Yet occasionally when you simply look out the window—when you see the trees, rivers, or endless strip malls—the idea comes to you, pop, just like that. What is going on in such cases?

One thing that may be going on is that with relatively few distractions, one can really think in the shower! It is not as if washing up takes much attention. Indeed, given that wireless networks have permeated every cranny of our waking lives, including train and bus travel, the shower might be the last bastion of undistracted thought. Yet perhaps on a less extreme just-do-it account that denigrates only conscious thinking, this is just what is needed for an idea to pop into your head since the fully formed idea arises, on this picture, only after the unconscious mind has been churning away. And what could be more conducive to unconscious churning than warm water?

The phenomenon of an idea coming to you after prolonged unconscious cerebration is significantly different from the phenomenon of chess intuition that I referred to as "zeroing in." Such chess intuition is immediate: the grandmaster looks at the board and immediately zeros in on a few possible moves, whereas in the shower the idea might not arise until the strawberry crème rinse. If this is the correct description of what goes on in that steamy sanctuary, it does not support the radical just-do-it position, which holds that optimal expert action is entirely nonmental, for unconscious churning is mental churning nonetheless. However, I wonder if such times should be described as involving exclusively unconscious thought. Could it be that such ratiocination is better described as involving conscious, yet calm thought? Or is it most aptly described as a time during which peripheral conscious thought is shining? The best way to see a faint distant object is via peripheral vision; peripheral thought might be the best way to penetrate faint ideas. And aren't many of the ideas we encounter in philosophy faint?[4]

---

[4] See Chapter 11, footnote 18 for a comment on studies of unconscious processing by Dijksterhuis et al. (2006) Dijksterhuis and van Olden (2006) and their relevance to just-do-it.

## The "Aha!" is Overrated

Moments of inspiration where an answer appears to come to you in a flash are often prized more than the effort which is part and parcel of bringing such moments to fruition. That such "aha" moments exist is undeniable; they are preceded by intense conscious thought, but, as they are often described, they seem to involve a leap which causes one to suddenly see something in a new light. But here are two questions: is this type of insight significantly different from slower, unsurprising, ordinary thought? And are the "aha" insights the most important aspect of the creative process: are they what differentiates truly brilliant ideas from ordinary ones?

In answer to the first question, Simon Blackburn (2014) defends Robert Weisberg's (2006) model of creativity as "business as usual," by, among other things, pointing out, and I think quite reasonably so, that although aha insights are typically characterized as moments where inspiration comes from nowhere, in our typical cogitations we similarly often do not know whence our ideas arise. As Blackburn puts it, "all this shows is that consciousness is not built to be privy to the causal antecedents of its own materials" (p. 151).

I am more interested in the second question: regardless of whether sudden insights are significantly different in kind from business as usual, are these unbidden insights the golden key to brilliance? Or is it that, generally, ideas that arrive via sudden insights are equally valuable as ideas that arrive via methodological plodding? Or could it be that although some ideas arise via effortless thought, these ideas are relatively insignificant to expert performance? In philosophy classes, one sometimes finds undergraduates effortlessly coming up with views that in essence are the same as those that philosophy's greats have pondered. And one is shocked, amazed, and perhaps even a bit disheartened that they could do this. But it may be that what makes the greats great in philosophy (and elsewhere) is what they have done with these ideas: the effortful elucidation, revision, reevaluation, and frequent rejection.

That the "aha" moment is relatively insignificant to expertise is suggested by Ray Bradbury's method of composition (Bradbury, 1990). In the early days of his writing career, Bradbury used to wake up and first thing jot down an idea, out of which he would subsequently craft a story. He used to feel that those early morning "ahas" were incredibly important. But then he realized that the specific ideas didn't much matter, and that he could get the same results by simply taking as his starting point a couple of words chosen at random from the dictionary. One needs to begin somewhere, and where one begins is not the result of thoughtful deliberation, but at least for Bradbury, arriving at these starting points was not a significant aspect of his expertise.

The graphic artist Dan Fallon told me a story about the early days of his career, which illustrates in a different way how the content of the aha insight can be arbitrary:

[When] I was an art director in the early 90's at Young & Rubicam...I quickly found there are many ways to be creative, and I saw first-hand how a seasoned pro could creatively sell the most uncreative idea and look like a hero in the process. I remember one such incident at the end of a very large, pressure-filled creative presentation. In meetings such as this, the agency's client service people and creative director will carefully study the clients' faces during the lengthy presentation. Every smile, wince, and peek at the clock is carefully noted. On this day, the long meeting was not going well...[, however, the Creative Director] began an impressive impromptu creative presentation by...sketching out his "concept" on a small white paper napkin...When he was finished, everyone was elated. The Creative Director had saved the meeting, the business, and the relationship, with a scribble on a lunch napkin. I'll never remember what was on that napkin, nobody will—but I'll never forget the smiling, back-slapping clients loading into the elevator, fully assured of our competence and creative ability...[T]he napkin idea never saw the light of day, and the truth was it never mattered. (pers. comm.)

The artists' long-worked-out concepts had failed to impress, yet the creative director's "aha" won the contract. But the napkin-concept itself was irrelevant; the creative director won the contract not because of his ability to come up with a mind-blowing graphic concept on the spot, but because of his ability to read his clients and know that presenting an impromptu idea might win them over. This insight was no "aha," but was rather the result of careful, deliberate study.

I know one mathematician, Joel David Hamkins—in fact, I happen to be married to him—who claims to have faith in his "aha" moments. He thinks that great ideas can come to him in a flash of inspiration. However, I observe him at work, and over the course of an evening there may be numerous "aha, I've got it" acclamations, each followed by a half-hour or so of effortful thought, whereupon I hear him sigh and lament that, alas, maybe he hasn't quite got it after all. Of course, his "ahas" are not just random, but come to him because he has extensive knowledge of the subject, something like a chess player's ability to zero in on a few candidate moves. However, appropriating international chess master Willy Hendriks' (2012) comment that "the opposite of moves that have proven to be successful coming to mind automatically, almost randomly, are moves that come to mind much less easily, though they may be the strongest in the given situation" (p. 42), it could be that the opposite of great theorems coming to mind automatically, almost randomly, are theorems that come to mind much less easily, though they may be the strongest in the given situation. Moreover, in stark contrast to the lonely ahas are the long hours mathematicians spend talking to one another, figuring things out. Is it possible that this is valuable in part because thinking aloud in this way facilitates conscious thinking?

And then, of course, there is the famous bath-inducing "aha" of Archimedes, who, according to legend, suddenly realized how to determine whether the king's gold crown had been speciously mixed with silver: understanding in a flash that displaced water can serve as an exact measure for the volume of a submerged object, it struck him that if the crown were mixed with the lighter metal silver, it would displace more water (since silver is lighter than gold, a fraudulent crown would need to be bulkier, if it were to weigh the same as a pure gold crown). And, as the story goes, so taken was he by this sudden discovery that the jubilant Archimedes jumped out of his bath and ran naked through the streets shouting, "Eureka!" It is a captivating story, but it is doubtful that it ever occurred (Biello 2006). The tale is first described by the Roman writer Vitruvius nearly 200 years after the event was said to have taken place, and numerous scientists, including Galileo, have thought it much more likely that Archimedes would have evaluated the crown by using the law of buoyancy (the upward buoyant force on a submerged object is equal to the weight of the fluid that the object displaces—a law that Archimedes discovered) and an accurate scale, which is something that was far more common during Archimedes' time than a precise pycnometer that would have been needed to accurately measure the minuscule difference between the volume of a pure gold and an amalgam crown (Hidetaka 2010). Of course, Archimedes may have made discoveries in the bath. And it would be an apposite setting for discovering the law of buoyancy. However, the baths of ancient Greece were good places, not to await the lonely "aha," but to think and discuss one's ideas: scrubbing up wasn't a solitary affair back then and, in the communal baths, as Plutarch (*c*.75/1906) records, Archimedes "used to trace geometrical figures in the ashes of the fire and diagrams in the oil on his body" (p. 257).

Yet why do we place so much value on "aha" moments? The mathematician Miha Habič suggested that it is because they are the only chance we have to see a result as surprising (pers. comm.). Sometimes when we work slowly and linearly, by the time we have arrived at the final result, though it may be astonishing to others, it may seem obvious to us. But it is possible that the conclusions one arrives at in a slower, more deliberate manner may at least sometimes be more surprising (to others) than any which came about via sudden insight—and perhaps also more likely to be correct.

## The Poem Arose During an Opium-Infused Dream

Can drugs be used to attain effortless inspiration, to put one in a state where one need not think or struggle to come up with ideas, but where insight just comes unbidden? Stories of individuals who have made great achievements under the influence of mind-altering substances are countless, especially when the category of mind-altering substances includes alcohol, nicotine, and caffeine, but let me consider just three cases of individuals whose achievements have been seen as both especially noteworthy and, at least in the first two cases, occurring under the influence of drugs rather stronger than espresso.

Perhaps the quintessential example of the effortless creation of a great piece of work that supposedly arose under the influence of drugs and without conscious thought is Samuel Taylor Coleridge's creation of *Kubla Khan*. Coleridge, who was an opium addict, claims in the 1816 preface to the poem that no less than "two or three hundred lines" came to him in a "profound sleep" during which the images of the poem "rose up before him as *things*, with a parallel production of the correspondent expressions" (1816/1912). In Lawrence Hanson's (1962) words, the composition of *Kubla Khan* is "the supreme example in English literature of the workings of the creative subconscious, unhelped—or unhindered—by conscious composition" (p. 260). Of course, that Coleridge was able to remember so clearly what he had purportedly dreamt suggests that such a dream would, in some sense, be conscious; still, Coleridge's description of the images rising before him indicates that rather than creating the poem himself, he only had to take opium and let it happen. Is this correct?

There is some doubt that the event occurred in the manner Coleridge describes in the 1816 preface. As John Spencer Hill (1983) points out, although in the 1816 preface to *Kubla Khan*, Coleridge claims that the poem came to him during a profound sleep, in an earlier handwritten manuscript, the Crewe Manuscript, he claims that the poem was "composed in a sort of Reverie brought on by two grains of Opium" (p. 149). Being *composed* in a sort of reverie has much less of a just-do-it flavor than arriving in a profound sleep. So even if Coleridge composed *Kubla Khan* after taking opium, it may be that he, and not simply the opium, was doing the work. Furthermore, the differences between the 1816 publication and the earlier written Crewe Manuscript indicate that the poem was revised before publication. (Furthermore, even if the poem did in some sense come to him in a reverie, it did not arise out of nowhere since, as he explains in the preface to the poem, immediately prior to the dream he had read a passage from a 1626 work that began, "In Xamdu did Cublai Can build a stately Palace . . . and in the middest thereof a sumptuous house of pleasure." Coleridge's poem begins, "In Xanadu did Kubka Khan/ A stately pleasure-dome decree.")

Another impressive example of an individual arriving at a brilliant idea while on drugs is the chemist Kary Mullis's experience with LSD. Mullis claims that taking LSD was integral to his invention of the polymerase chain reaction technique, for which he won a Nobel prize; LSD, as he explained it, allowed him to "sit on a DNA molecule and watch the polymers go by" (Nutt 2012, p. 258; see also Lovering 2015). But here, too, this does not seem to be an example of where the drugs inhibited thought, or even conscious thought, but merely altered it. (Mullis, who had been a student at Berkeley, also claims that taking LSD was "certainly much more important" than any courses he ever took; however, one can't but wonder if perhaps he ought to have placed a bit more importance on his coursework: in his 1998 autobiography, he not only denies both that HIV causes AIDS and that the ozone is being depleted, but also claims to believe in astrology and to have once encountered—while not on LSD—a glowing green talking raccoon.)

Lastly, let me mention the case of Paul Erdős, who was one of the most prolific mathematicians ever, and also a coffee-and-other-stimulant addict. I don't think that anyone would say that stimulants inhibit thinking (though they may make one think in a different way). Yet perhaps caffeine and other stimulants (before one becomes resistant to their effects) make it easier to be motivated to work hard and to concentrate, and thus make one's actions relatively effortless, in the sense that they lessen the need to exert great willpower, or in the novelist Honoré de Balzac's words, when one drinks coffee, "one's ideas advance . . . like battalions of the Grande Armée . . . [b]rilliant notions join in the combat as sharpshooters . . . the characters don their costumes, the paper is covered with ink" (quoted in Gerson 1972). But while stimulants, perhaps, can lessen the need for grit they can also inspire effort in another sense—besides being addicted to coffee and stimulants, Erdős was also addicted to work. There may be some truth to the witticism that "a mathematician is a machine for turning coffee into theorems" (widely attributed to Erdős yet actually first said by another Hungarian mathematician Alfréd Rényi), but the machine is a thinking one.[5]

I leave aside the question of whether alcohol in any way enables experts to just do it, rather than merely removing certain inhibitions to thought, or, indeed, just helping them to cope with the agony of continually striving to do better than before.[6]

## Do Musicians Just Do It?

I wrote in Chapter 4 that the classical cellist Inbal Segev, following the wisdom of Pablo Casals, believes that it is important to not be led by the music, but to consciously direct it. Do nonclassical musicians also guide their music, or do they tend to follow it where it leads them?

Charlie Parker famously said, "You've got to learn your instrument. Then, you practice, practice, practice. And then, when you finally get up there on the bandstand, forget all that and just wail" (quoted in Petras and Petras 2011). Trey Anastasio, the guitarist from the band Phish, explains that in improvisatory performance, "There's a lot of preparation and discipline that goes into it just so that, when you're in the moment, you're not supposed to be thinking at all" (Simonini 2001). It is, as I have mentioned, sometimes difficult to know what is going on in your own mind, but if I take seriously the claims of experts who say that they think in action, I need to take seriously the claims of those who say that they don't. So let me ask: in music improvisation, do musicians turn off the thinking mind?

Neuroscientists have weighed in on this question by having musicians improvise on a custom-built, non-ferromagnetic piano inside a functional magnetic resonance imaging (fMRI) scanner (for example, Limb and Braun 2008). And, in line with just-do-it, one thing some of these studies show is that in comparison to playing a memorized arrangement, such as a scale, professional musicians improvising in the scanner exhibit reduced activity in executive control areas associated with conscious self-monitoring. (Liu et al. 2012 find similar effects in rap artists.) This suggests that contrary to Casals's advice to direct the music, improvisers let the music lead them. As such, this research challenges my cognition-in-action account as applied to conscious self-monitoring during music improvisation.

There might be reason to question whether the conclusion we should draw from these studies is that executive control is diminished during improvisatory music

---

[5] After buying coffee with the money he received from a publisher's representative in exchange for some math textbooks, Berkeley mathematician Ken Ribet purportedly said, "now I'm turning theorems into coffee."

[6] See the chapter entitled "The Muse in the Bottle" in Rothenberg (1990) for a discussion of this issue. "Faulkner," he points out, "had long periods of abstinence, or virtual abstinence, during his working life, and it was during these periods that his great novels were produced."

performance. A recurrent theme in this book has been, as I put it in the Introduction, that controlled laboratory experiments destroy expertise. Clearly, there is something peculiar about playing a keyboard while lying down in an fMRI machine (for a critical analysis of the ecological validity of such experiments see McPherson and Limb 2013). Yet it would seem that this peculiarity would, if anything, make one need to exert more conscious control.

Something else, however, may be going on. Based on my understanding of dance, even though all improvisation is new to a degree, a dancer's improvised movements, when performed without conscious guidance, often have the same general look. When the look is good enough, perhaps one need not try to alter it. Twyla Tharp's choreography, which arises out of improvisation—indeed, I have been told by dancers from her company that she often does not even recall what she has done—is perhaps a case in point. To be sure, dancing or choreographing in the same style is unobjectionable and characteristic of the best choreographers, like Tharp. However, one wants to avoid the feeling of creating "the same old stuff." One way to do this in dance, and I would think in musical improvisation as well, is to engage the conscious mind. The same old stuff is fine for playing in the scanner, but not for playing on stage. (And even Tharp, who employs improvisation to arrive at ideas for her dances, meticulously sifts through her video-taped improv sessions: "[i]f I find thirty seconds of movement out of three hours, I'm happy;" moreover, in the battle over "some transcendent, inexplicable Dionysian act of inspiration . . . [versus] hard work," she says, "I come down on the side of hard work" (2003 p. 6).

Moreover, as I also suggested in Chapter 4, playing music often involves social interactions, not all of which are unconscious and automatic. Indeed, a recent neuroimaging study that examined the process of trading fours, in which musicians alternate four-bar solos, brings this point home (Donnay et al. 2014). In contrast to the earlier neuroimaging studies that looked at solo improvising, the researchers who undertook this study found that the improvisers displayed not reduced, but heightened activity in executive control areas of the brain (see also Berkowitz and Ansari 2008).

Songwriting, though it may employ improvisation to generate ideas, is typically not simply improvisation—though some rappers, such as the late Notorious B.I.G rely on it heavily (Lang 2007). And certainly, songwriting can be difficult work. I mentioned, for example, that the singer-songwriter Leonard Cohen spent at least four grueling years working on the song "Hallelujah." However, Cohen's employment of a cognition-in-action strategy seems to stand in stark contrast to Bob Dylan's apparent just-do-it compositional method. As Cohen tells in a 1992 interview:

Dylan and I were having coffee the day after his concert in Paris a few years ago . . . and he asked me how long it took to write ["Hallelujah"]. And I told him a couple of years. I lied, actually. It was more than a couple of years. Then I praised a song of his, "I and I," and asked him how long it had taken and he said, "Fifteen minutes." (quoted in Light 2012, p. 2)

This story, as Light (2012) points out, was clearly told for laughs. Nonetheless, Dylan did compose a prodigious number of songs in a relatively brief period of time. And some songwriters seem to work even more quickly: "I find you can write [most songs] in less time than it takes to sing them," Harry Nilsson confesses (Zollo 2003, p. 242); and in response to the question, "do you find your songs come in a flash, or do they come from the result of a lot of work," Yoko Ono answers, "it's always a flash" (Zollo 2003, p. 252).

To be sure, some musicians who cherish the flash also may hint that the process can involve work. Elsewhere Dylan tells of the novel he wrote, which he admits to having worked on for an extended period, and then explains songwriting: "It's like writing a novel; it just takes me a lot less time and I can get it done—done to where I can reread it in my head a lot."[7] Rereading sounds like thinking to me, and if writing the novel took effort, then it would seem that songwriting, given that it felt like an abbreviated form of novel-writing, may have taken some effort too. And Carole King, who claims that "You've Got a Friend" was one song that "wrote itself" also emphasizes the importance of novelty and how it takes effort to arrive at it:

There is a lot of hard work involved in songwriting...I like to be unpredictable... [Not] one song has a [recognizable structure]...And that's something I work at. (Zollo 2003, p. 142)

I said that not all ideas arrive in the shower. I didn't mention, however, that part of the reason for this is that with musicians, ideas seem to also come to them while driving. In Paul Zollo's (2003) interviews with songwriters, this was a theme: "you're driving a car or something," Dave Brubeck says, "and *pow*, it's there" (Zollo 2003, p. 58).[8] Chris Brown, guitarist for the band Dog, told me that many of his ideas also materialize "while driving, and not specifically thinking about music or trying to write anything" (pers. comm.). He explained: "I can labor at a song for a long time (this is when nothing gets written that I will keep, in general), until there is a flash of insight...and an idea will come to me." But again, just like in the shower, one might wonder how to understand the "pow." Why is it described in terms of ideas arriving unbidden, rather than in terms of thinking of ideas while driving? Perhaps it is that driving can be relaxing, and so—like in the shower—one is only thinking in a relaxed way, or in a peripheral way. And of course, it may be that driving is conducive to unconscious thought. Moreover, I wouldn't be surprised if some of these songs that come to musicians out of nowhere while driving "coinciden-tally" happened to be similar to what was playing on the radio a few miles back.[9]

---

[7] *Playboy* interview, part 1.

[8] Whether or not songs came to Brubeck this way, I cannot say, but it is known that the song he is most famous for, "Take Five," did not, for as he explains it, the melody was actually composed by his sax player Paul Desmond.

[9] Chris Brown told me that his radio has been broken for years. Nonetheless, see Samantha Grossman's (2014) article on the "Stairway to Heaven" lawsuit. All of this talk about songs coming to musicians while driving made me realize how different this phenomenon is from my experience with finding ideas for a dance, which, when, it comes to steps, was always done by doing the steps or some approximation of the steps myself and never while driving (though, to be fair, I should mention that I don't drive).

Then there is the famous story about Paul McCartney, who claims to have woken up one morning with the melody for "Yesterday" fully formed in his head (see Deezen 2014). Was the tune of one of the most-covered songs in music history an example of effortless mastery? While the melody, he claims, came to him in a dream, the lyrics apparently took a great deal of thought and effort. Indeed, McCartney was working so hard trying out various possibilities on a piano during the four or so weeks the Beatles spent shooting their film *Help!* that the director of the film threatened to have the piano removed unless he finished writing the song. And when he wasn't trying out various possibilities, he was often discussing the song with the other Beatles, which tried their patience: "Blimey," George Harrison opined, "he's always talking about that song. You'd think he was Beethoven or somebody" (Deezen 2014). Of course, it was the melody and not the lyrics that were dreamt, and I don't know how much, if at all, the melody of the song changed during the intervening two years from when it came to him to when it was first recorded, but one imagines that during those two years of struggle with the lyrics, the melody underwent at least some revisions.

Nonetheless, I think that the singer-songwriter might sometimes be, if not an example of an extreme case of just-do-it, then at least on the just-do-it spectrum. And, to conjecture a bit more, perhaps one reason for this is that many rock/folk/singer-songwriters do not have formal musical training and do not read standard musical notation. Although Carole King was classically trained, neither Leonard Cohen, nor Bob Dylan, nor Paul McCartney, read standard musical notation. This wouldn't be relevant to why composing lyrics was so apparently effortless for Dylan, and effortful (at least with "Hallelujah") for Cohen. But if in certain forms of music, the entire training process is less analytic than training in at least some other areas of expertise—if it proceeds less in terms of words that identify concepts, than in terms of "making, making, making," as Alex Craven explained it to me (see Chapter 5 in this volume)—this could account for the attenuated verbal thought process that, at least for some, facilitates composing the music. In other words, one important reason for why experts are able to think beneficially in performance is that they train in a thoughtful, analytic way; musicians who do not train in this way may be more likely to just do it.

Thought may enter the compositional process, even for less analytically trained musicians, but it may be thought in music rather than in words. What this really means, I as a nonmusician cannot fully fathom; however, it may be similar to how dancers do not have words to describe every significant aspect of movement, but nonetheless conceptualize their movement in various multitudinous ways. One is thinking, in such situations, in movement. Perhaps the jazz bass violinist Mike Fleming was alluding to thinking in music when he commented, "you got to hear the note before playing it" (pers. comm.), which, after all, is not so different from what a baseball player once told me: "you've got to know what to do with the ball before you catch it."

Of course, it might be that part of the appeal of some rock music, like the appeal of the blog, is that, though it may come about only after years of practice, the piece itself was created quickly and somewhat thoughtlessly. Less worked out and refined ideas can sometimes be grasped more readily than ideas which result from the output of many years of editing (of course, one need only think of Hegel, who wrote very quickly to see that this is not always the case). Some rock songs have immediate appeal, and if this is in part due to the fifteen-minute composition, it leaves a place for just-do-it.

Yet again, perhaps the degree of explicit, conceptual thought involved in musical composition simply differs among individuals.[10] In response to Zollo's (2003) question, "Is it possible that knowledge can get in the way of spontaneity?" Paul Simon says, "certainly in popular music and rock and roll, that's not the problem. The problem is that people don't know enough" (p. 113).

## Expert Action and the Meaning of Life

In "Saving the Sacred from the Axial Revolution," Dreyfus and Kelly (2011b) tell us:

the Homeric Greeks led the very opposite of nihilistic lives. They were filled with wonder at the way they were taken care of by a pantheon of shining Olympian gods. They lived intense and meaningful lives. Heroes, athletes, moods, and gods, were constantly welling up and drawing them in. Their world was a world of sacred, shining people and things. And the Homeric Greeks were grateful to everything that the gods drew them into—from sleep to heroic deeds, to overwhelming passions. (p. 198)

And they recommend that we:

cultivate the practices of opening ourselves to being overwhelmed by the power of moods and nature, and at the same time learn the practice of cultivating ourselves so that our routines are transformed into rituals that bring things out at their shining best. (p. 197)

This is connected to just-do-it since, for Dreyfus and Kelly (2011a), the key to a meaningful life also unlocks expertise: it is when we are open to external forces, when we allow things to happen rather than doing them ourselves, that we perform at our best—the greatest poets, they tell us, "speak from something beyond themselves," and, just like one falls asleep, the expert cannot perform her actions "by dint of effort and control" (pp. 198–9)—and it is when we are "taken over by the situation," that life "really shines and matters most" (p. 201). We find meaning, according to Dreyfus and Kelly, in those moments when your actions are the result of being carried away rather than the result of thought, effort, and deliberation.

The idea that meaningful lives are ones built out of passion more than deliberation is also found in Søren Kierkegaard's writings. What drains our lives of meaning, of even the ability to act, according to Kierkegaard (1846/1962) is deliberation:

---

[10]  I thank the musician Mike Errico for his insight on this topic.

Nowadays not even a suicide kills himself in desperation. Before taking the step he deliberates so long and so carefully that he literally chokes with thought…[I]t is really thought which takes his life. He does not die *with* deliberation but *from* deliberation. (p. 33)

Throughout this book, however, I have been arguing for the importance of effort, deliberation, thought, and control in expert action, and for the idea that experts do not merely let it happen, but actually make it happen. Perhaps it is sometimes psychologically useful to tell yourself "my actions are not up to me." And perhaps this is part of the reasoning behind programs such as Alcoholics Anonymous, which ask you to give yourself up to a higher power. There is some question whether these programs are effective (Dodes and Dodes 2014); nonetheless, it might be that when the idea of tackling an addiction on your own seems so overwhelmingly difficult that one feels that it is not worth even trying to do so, it is useful to think that winning the battle is not up to you. But my concern is experts not addicts and on the type of view that I defend, experts do not give themselves over to any external forces, but rather, with deliberate force and effort, take control of their own actions. Have I been leading experts into a life of nihilism and despair?

On my view, although experts do not embody the type of meaning that Dreyfus and Kelly claim to find in Homer's epic, they are paragons of another type of meaning: the meaning one finds in developing one's potential, what Immanuel Kant (1785/2012) speaks of in the *Groundwork for the Metaphysics of Morals* as our duty to cultivate our "predispositions to greater perfection"—a duty that can entail a struggle (p. 42).The life of extreme drug addiction lacks meaning, not because drug addicts fail to experience the "whoosh," which is the term Kelly and Dreyfus use to refer to the state of being carried away—the state, as they see it, in which you are grateful for something beyond your control, something that draws you to achieve at your best—but rather because they are failing to develop their brains and bodies; their potential is going to waste.[11] Now, how to make sense of this notion of potential, and why it is important to fulfill it in a world that is ultimately particles in the void, is a deep and difficult topic that I cannot address here (or likely anywhere).[12] However, as I hope my arguments throughout the book have shown, if living a meaningful life is about living up to your potential, then the idea that the expert should stand back and effortlessly let it happen, just isn't going to do it. Of course, living up to your potential should not involve working so hard at one thing, especially in youth, that one misses out on life's joys and is precluded from developing any other talents. Just how narrowly focused and determined we should allow our lives—and our children's lives—to become, however, is another one of those important questions I cannot answer.

Furthermore, I'm not sure if what Dreyfus and Kelly see as the Homeric ideal is worth fighting for—or rather, as they would have it, leaving one's self open to. At least,

---

[11] They also fail to experience the "whoosh" since whooshes, on Dreyfus and Kelly's view, come about only after prolonged training and lead one to achieve at one's best. My point is merely that their lack of experiencing the whoosh is not what robs their lives of meaning.

[12] See, however, Johnson (2010).

it is not the type of meaning I seek. In particular, I prefer not to leave myself open to "being overwhelmed by the power of moods" (Dreyfus and Kelly 2011b, p. 200). In the world Dreyfus and Kelly admire, people, events, and goals "shine," and they call on us to leave ourselves open to these shining things so that our moods will bring us under their thrall. However, I prefer a world that is more matte than shining, which allows me to rationally choose the course I wish to take, rather than being drawn into it by its glistening light. Of course, since Dreyfus and Kelly (2011b) allow in their picture of a meaningful life a role for "the philosophical aspiration to a mood-less mood" (p. 201), it is not clear that I am disagreeing with them here. "The mood of tranquility and clear-headed, rational decision that philosophers like Descartes have brought to the center of our world…has its place," they tell us (p. 201); but although tranquility may be a mood, it seems that when we classify clear-headed, rational decision-making as a mood, we've lost the distinction between moods and reason.

Dreyfus and Kelly also speak of the appeal of the Homeric "life of intensity," and tell us that "perhaps we can aspire to Dante's all-encompassing bliss" (p. 201). Yet, although I like bliss as much as the next guy, I wouldn't say that it is what I aspire to, at least if bliss is understood as something like the present experience of pleasure or joy. I am not sure I would not go so far as Kant (1785/2012) and claim that "devoting [one's] life to pleasure is morally forbidden" (p. 16), but I can say that it doesn't seem to give my life meaning. I get great blissy pleasure in taking yoga classes, but at the end of the day, I want something more to show of my life than toned triceps. I do aspire, however, to another ancient Greek ideal, and this is the ideal of living a life that allows one to look back and say, "I have lived my life well," this is a life conducive to what Greeks called *eudaimonia*. If all I were to see in that final backward glance is all-encompassing bliss, I would not have achieved *eudaimonia*.

A life lived well, for me, will be one in which have I developed my talents, but not only this; to develop my talents in a vacuum is also not something that I would retrospectively value. Rather, in reviewing my life, I also want to feel that I have affected others in a positive way. Gratitude seems to be a central source of meaning for Dreyfus and Kelly (2011b); it is by "opening ourselves up to the moods of wonder and gratitude at the root of Homer's sense of the sacred" that we may "recover and revive the intensity and meaningfulness that Homer's polytheists enjoyed" (p. 195). However, although I certainly take gratitude to be a positive emotion, it is not for me what matters most; it is not, for me, highly conducive to *eudaimonia*. Rather, I find more meaning in affecting other people's lives; I want to do something that warrants gratitude (whether or not the beneficiary of my actions actually ever give it) more than being a beneficiary of acts for which I shall be grateful.

## Is Sex Like Golf?

In Chapter 1, I quoted golfer Dave Hill's claim that "the golf swing is like sex. You can't be thinking about the mechanics of the act while you are performing." If, as I have been arguing, experts generally think in action, is Hill an exception? It is not at all clear that he is since saying that you can't think about the mechanics of the golf swing while performing is not the same as saying that you can't think about the swing while in action. Maybe for Hill thoughts about larger scale aspects of his swing were beneficial. His claim is also compatible with the idea that you can think about the mechanics of your swing prior to going through with it. Besides, Hill was known to make outrageous remarks, so perhaps he was simply trying to be provocative (Hill and Seitz 1977).

In any event, I prefer Tom Watson's description: "My golf swing is a bit like ironing a shirt. You get one side smoothed out, turn it over and there is a big wrinkle on the other side. Then you iron that one out, turn it over and there is yet another wrinkle" (quoted in Yong 2011, p. 4). Not very provocative and not at all sexy, but maybe true.[13]

One possibility of course, is that Hill and Watson simply have different views about what type of mental state is conducive to a good golf swing. However, even if Hill believed that the golf swing proceeds unencumbered by thought, it is not clear that he followed his own advice:

Experimenting is my nature, and I know it has cost me considerable prize money over the years. I overcomplicate the game, toy around with too many options, and try too many difficult shots when a simple shot could get the job done. (Hill and Seitz, 1977)

Hill's golf career overlapped to a degree with that of the legendary Jack Nicklaus and perhaps it is less demoralizing to say that you lose because you were trying too hard, experimenting, and overcomplicating things, than to say that the winning player was simply better.

Yet, enough conjectures about why Hill may have made the comments he did, for I imagine that you have arrived at this point in the book not merely to better understand Hill's motivation for saying what he did, but to find out whether cognition-in-action applies to sex; that is, you want to know whether when we do it, we should just do it. Assuming that golf allows one to think in action and is benefited by such thinking, you want to know: Is sex is like golf?

Sex is, assuredly, a complicated matter, and one relevant complication—though rather uninteresting in the larger scheme of things—is that it is not clear, outside the ranks of professionals in the sex trade, that sexually active adults should count as experts, in my sense of "expert."[14] Is the sex act something that we deliberately train to perform? Are we engaged in an ongoing quest to improve our actions in this area of our lives? Or might it be more like an everyday activity (if you're lucky enough)?

Let's put this issue aside as well and get to the interesting question. Regardless of whether sexually active adults count as experts in the relevant domain, and thus whether the topic of sex (outside the professional sex trade) is at all relevant to my

---

[13]  Or maybe it is sexy, see Cambridge Women's Pornography Cooperative's *Porn for Women*.

[14]  It has been pointed out to me that those who practice tantric sex might also count as experts in my sense of the term and that, moreover, they don't just do it. And my meticulous investigation of this issue in *The Complete Idiot's Guide to Amazing Sex*, 4th ed. backs up this contention.

main goal in this book, which has been to tear down just-do-it and fortify cognition-in-action, we can still ask: Is Dave Hill correct about sex? Does thinking interfere with doing it? And if so, should we refrain from thinking while thusly engaged?

None other than Aristotle (350 bce/2002) had something to say about this:

οἷον τῇ τῶν ἀφροδισίων· οὐδένα γὰρ ἂν δύνασθαι νοῆσαί τι ἐν αὐτῇ.

As with the pleasure of sex: no one could have any thoughts when enjoying that. (*Nicomachean Ethics* VII.11, 1152b17–18, trans. C. Rowe)

Sounds like support for Dave Hill. However, let us look at the larger context in which this remark occurs. This comment on sex is actually not presented by Aristotle as his own, but rather as the view of someone who objects to Aristotle's position that pleasure is good. That is, Aristotle is asserting that his opponent may hold that "pleasure is not a good at all" because, among other things, "pleasures are a hindrance to thought, and the more so the more one delights in them" (1152b16–17), and this is illustrated, claims his rhetorical opponent, by sex: he is not so much saying that thinking interferes with the pleasure of sex but rather that the pleasure of sex interferes with thinking. Aristotle disagrees and thinks pleasure is compatible with performing at one's best. So we should not understand this remark as Aristotle's endorsement of the view that thinking interferes with enjoying that.

What, then, would Aristotle say about whether one can think while delighting in sexual activity? Since his concern is with whether pleasure impedes thinking, rather than with whether thinking impedes pleasure, it is difficult to say. However, he does respond to his opponent by claiming that neither practical wisdom (*phronesis*) "nor any disposition at all is impeded by the specific pleasure deriving from it, but only by alien ones" (1153a20). For example, since the pleasure of learning is not alien to learning itself, the pleasure of learning, he tells us, does not impede learning, but makes us learn all the better. Aristotle's position is not that alien pleasures invariably hinder performance. For example, it would seem consistent with Aristotle's view that the pleasure of drinking tea is alien to the pleasure of learning yet conducive to it. Rather, his view is that if a pleasure is going to interfere with performance, then that pleasure will be an alien one. For example, though he does not explain what he means by "alien pleasures" (save for the comment that they are pleasures not derived from the activity at issue), he would (if he were teaching today) presumably say that the pleasure of texting (and certainly sexting) may impede learning from a classroom lecture, while the pleasure of listening to the lecture would not. Given, then, that Aristotle holds that only alien pleasures impede activities, one might speculate that he also holds that only alien thoughts impede pleasures, where an "alien thought" is one that does not concern the pleasurable activity. If so, his view would imply that while thinking about, say, mathematics during sex may very well hinder sexual pleasure (since thoughts about mathematics are alien to sexual pleasure), thinking about sex during sex would not hinder sexual pleasure but would make us enjoy it all the better.

Of course, regarding Aristotle's main concern, whether it is *only* alien pleasures that impede thinking may depend on the expert and the action; for although in Chapter 9 I spoke of the pleasure of bodily movement as compatible with expert dancing, we have, contra Aristotle, the testimony of comedian Steve Martin (2007):

My most persistent memory of stand-up is of…the mouth speaking the line, the body delivering the gesture, while the mind looks back, observing, analyzing, judging, worrying, and then deciding when and what to say next. Enjoyment while performing was rare—enjoyment would have been an indulgent loss of focus that comedy cannot afford. (p. 1)

Was this said disingenuously? Or did Aristotle perhaps not know what it was like to be funny?

In any event, a matter of far greater consequence remains: even if one can beneficially think about sex while doing it, can one think about the *mechanics* of sex while doing it? And what, precisely, are the mechanics of sex, anyway? These questions could be discussed in delightful detail; however, as we are drawing to a close, suffice it to say that a woman's anatomy is so exquisitely subtle that if her partner just does it without thinking about the mechanics, it is likely that nothing in the realm of optimality will obtain.

(Incidentally, I have found that women are much less prone to see the creative process as effortless; with their long nine months of pregnancy culminating in excruciating pain, women know that creating takes hard work; men, however, whose contribution involves little more than a mere fifteen seconds of ecstasy, are sometimes deluded.)[15]

## Don't Think; Just Do?

The writer Heinrich von Kleist (1810/1972) claimed that "grace appears to the best advantage in that human body structure that has no consciousness at all—or has infinite consciousness—that is, in the mechanical puppet, or in the God" (p. 26). For those who hold that expertise is spontaneous and effortless, experts are the marionettes: after they have honed their skills, they dispense with self-regulation and are simply drawn to act in ways that are no longer under their control. In this book, however, I have tried to make the case that rather than being pulled by God's strings, experts are today's gods who perform their exquisite skills with, if not infinite, than at least a great deal of thoughtful, attentive, and self-reflective conscious control.

Yet what about Balanchine's claim that his dancers shouldn't think? I asked Violette Verdy, one of the premier ballet dancers of the twentieth century, about this. Verdy was a principal dancer with New York City Ballet under Balanchine's direction for eighteen

---

[15] I'd like to thank John Krakauer for his extensive explanation of the precise timing of these matters. Let me also mention that there are of course numerous other ways in which one might develop the golf-is-like-sex analogy; for example, both are more fun when not engaged in alone. And while we are on the topic, it might be worth pointing out that, no matter how long it lasts, it wouldn't hurt to take a bit more time getting there. Perhaps Aristotle puts it best: "it is rarely that a godlike man is found" (*Nicomachean Ethics*, 1145a25). Fortunately, I'm married to one.

years, during which time he created many famous roles for her. But Verdy brushed off the question. "Oh that," she replied: "he only said that when a dancer was stuck, like an elevator between floors." And after thinking this over, I realized that it makes perfect sense. Unreflective, automatic action does play a role in performing. But quite contrary to the just-do-it-principle, it is when things go wrong, not when they go right, that we need it.

And isn't this also true of philosophy? When is it that you need to step back from thinking and just let your unconscious mind, or perhaps, simply your hand guide your writing? Precisely when you're stuck between floors. Yet it is not the thinking itself that gets you stuck; it is not as if the thinking is interfering with the action, and the unconscious mind alone will take you on a gilded path to success. Philosophy—like any other area of expertise for which room for improvement is endless—is challenging, which means you might get stuck between floors. And when you're really stuck—not just facing a challenging problem and finding flaws in all of your attempts to address it, which is the typical state of affairs in philosophy, but really stuck, in the sense of not being able to address it at all—just doing it may be useful. But then again, so might be not doing it at all. For even experts occasionally need to take a break.

# Bibliography

Abernathy, C. M. and Hamm, R. M. (1995). *Surgical Intuition: What It Is and How To Get It* (Philadelphia, PA: Hanley and Belfus).

Ackerman, J. M. and Bargh, J. A. (2010). "Two to tango: Automatic social coordination and the role of felt effort," in B. Bruya (ed.), *Effortless Attention: A New Perspective in the Cognitive Science of Attention and Action* (Cambridge, MA: MIT Press): 335–72.

Adler, C. H. (2007). "Sports-related task-specific dystonia: The yips," in M.A. Stacy (ed.), *Handbook of Dystonia* (New York: Informa Healthcare).

Agassi, Andre (2009). *Open: An Autobiography* (New York: A. Knopf).

Aglioti, S. M., Cesari, P., Romani, M., and Urgesi, C. (2008). "Action anticipation and motor resonance in elite basketball players," *Nature Neuroscience* 11: 1109–16.

Amiel, Henri Frédéric (1893). *Amiel's Journal: The Journal Intime of Henri Frédéric Amiel*, trans. H. Ward (2nd ed.) (London: Macmillan and Co.).

Anderson, John R. (1982). "Acquisition of cognitive skill," *Psychological Review* 89(4): 369–406.

Anderson, John R. (1983). "Acquisition of Proof Skills in Geometry," in R. S. Michalski, J. G. Carbonell, T. M. Mitchell (eds), *Machine Learning (Part Three)* (Berlin: Springer Berlin Heidelberg): 191–219.

Anderson, John R. (1993). "Problem solving and learning," *American Psychologist* 48(1): 35–44.

Anderson, John. R. and Lebiere, Christian J. (1998). *The Atomic Components of Thought* (Mahwah, NJ: Lawrence Erlbaum Associates).

Andersson, Astrid (2009). "Michael Phelps changes technique in bid for perfect stroke," *Daily Telegraph*, April 23. <http://www.telegraph.co.uk/sport/olympics/swimming/5205810/Michael-Phelps-changes-technique-in-bid-for-perfect-stroke.html> Accessed Nov. 5, 2015.

Annas, Julia (2011). *Intelligent Virtue* (Oxford: Oxford University Press).

Anscombe, G. E. M. (1962). "On Sensations of Position," *Analysis* 22/3 (1962), 55–8.

Anscombe, G. E. M. (1957/2000). *Intention* (2nd ed.) (Cambridge, MA: Harvard University Press).

Aquinas, Thomas (1960). *Summa Theologiae*, vol. 1 (New York: McGraw-Hill).

Aristotle (350 BCE/ 2002). *Nicomachean Ethics*, trans. C. J. Rowe, ed. S. Broadie (Oxford: Oxford University Press).

Aristotle (1990). *On the Generation of Animals*, trans. A. Platt (Raleigh, NC: Alex Catalogue).

Arnheim, Rudolf. (1966). *Toward a Psychology of Art: Collected Essays.* (Berkeley, CA: University of California Press).

Ashcraft, M. H. and Kirk, E. P. (2001). "The relationships among working memory, math anxiety, and performance," *Journal of Experimental Psychology: General* 130: 224–37.

Associated Press (2004). "Knoblauch's Throwing Troubles May Force Him to Play Left Field," *The Daily Texan*, August 6.

Attali, Yigal (2013). "Perceived hotness affects behavior of basketball players and coaches," *Psychological Science* Jul 1, 24(7):1151–6. doi: 10.1177/0956797612468452.

Audi, Robert (1993). *Action, Intention, and Reason* (Ithaca, NY: Cornell University Press).

Bahill A. T. and LaRitz, T. (1984). "Why can't batters keep their eyes on the ball?" *American Scientist* 72: 249–53.

Bargh, J. (1994). "The Four Horsemen of Automaticity: Awareness, Intention, Efficiency, and Control in social cognition," in R. S. Wyer and T. K. Srull (eds), *Handbook of Social Cognition, Vol. 1* (Hillsdale, NJ: Erlbaum): 1–40.

Barry, Ellen (2011). "It's official: American is now a Bolshoi dancer," *New York Times, ArtsBeat*, Nov. 9. <http://artsbeat.blogs.nytimes.com/2011/11/09/its-official-american-is-now-a-bolshoi-dancer/> Accessed Nov. 5, 2015.

Bartlett, Phyllis Brooks (1951). *Poems in Process* (New York: Oxford University Press).

Baumann, Michael (2013). "Rick Ankiel: The greatest story everyone's gotten bored with" *Grantland.com*. May 13. <http://grantland.com/the-triangle/rick-ankiel-the-greatest-story-everyones-gotten-bored-with/> Accessed Nov. 4, 2015.

Baumeister, R. F. (1984). "Choking Under Pressure: Self-Consciousness and Paradoxical Effects of Incentives on Skillful Performance," *Journal of Personality and Social Psychology* 6: 610–20.

Baumeister, R. F. (1995). "Disputing the Effects of Championship Pressures and Home Audiences," *Journal of Personality and Social Psychology*, 68(4): 644–8.

Baumeister, R. F. and Steinhilber, A. (1984). "Paradoxical effects of supportive audiences on performance under pressure: The home field disadvantage in sports championships," *Journal of Personality and Social Psychology*, 47: 85–93.

Bayne, Tim and Levy, Neil (2006). "The feeling of doing: Deconstructing the phenomenology of agency," in N. Sebanz and W. Prinz (eds), *Disorders of Volition* (Cambridge, MA: MIT Press): 49–68.

Becker-Cantarino, Barbara (ed.) (2005). *German Literature of the Eighteenth Century: The Enlightenment and Sensibility* (Rochester, NY: Camden House).

Beilock, S. L., Bertenthal, B. I., McCoy, A. M., and Carr, T. H. (2004). "Haste does not always make waste: Expertise, direction of attention and speed versus accuracy in performing sensorimotor skills," *Psychonomic Bulletin and Review* (11): 373–9.

Beilock, S. and Carr, T. H. (2001). "On the fragility of skilled performance: What governs choking under pressure?" *Journal of Experimental Psychology: General* 130(4): 701–25.

Beilock, S. L. and Carr, T. H. (2004). "From novice to expert performance: Attention, memory, and the control of complex sensorimotor skills," in A. M. Williams, N. J. Hodges, M. A. Scott, and M. L. J. Court (eds), *Skill acquisition in sport: Research, theory and practice* (New York, Routledge): 309–28.

Beilock, S. L. and Carr, T. H. (2005). "When high-powered people fail: Working memory and 'choking under pressure' in math," *Psychological Science* 16(2): 101–5.

Beilock, S. L., Carr, T. H., MacMahon, C., and Starkes, J. L. (2002). "When paying attention becomes counterproductive: Impact of divided versus skill-focused attention on novice and experiences performance of sensorimotor skills," *Journal of Experimental Psychology: Applied* 8: 6–16.

Beilock, S. L. and DeCaro, M. S. (2007). "From poor performance to success under stress: Working memory, strategy selection, and mathematical problem solving under pressure," *Journal of Experimental Psychology: Learning, Memory, and Cognition* 33: 983–98.

Beilock, S. L. and Gray, R. (2007). "Why do athletes 'choke' under pressure?" in G. Tenenbaum and R. C. Eklund (eds), *Handbook of Sport Psychology* (3rd ed.) (Hoboken, NJ: John Wiley and Sons): 425–44.

Beilock, S. L., Wierenga, S. A., and Carr, T. H. (2002). "Expertise, attention, and memory in sensorimotor skill execution: Impact of novel task constraints on dual-task performance and episodic memory," *Quarterly Journal of Experimental Psychology: Human Experimental Psychology* (55): 1211–40.

Beilock, Sian (2010). *Choke: What the Secrets of the Brain Reveal About Getting It Right When You Have To* (New York: Free Press).

Beliavsky, Oleksadr and Mikhalchishin, Adrian (2002). *Secrets of Chess Intuition* (London: Gambit).

Bell, Charles (2009). *The Hand. Its Mechanism and Vital Endowments as Evincing Design; Bridgewater Treatises* (Cambridge: Cambridge University Press).

Benner, P. (2004). "Using the Dreyfus Model of Skill Acquisition to describe and interpret skill acquisition and clinical judgment in nursing practice and education," *Bulletin of Science, Technology and Society Special Issue: Human Expertise in the Age of the Computer* 24(3): 188–99.

Benner, P., Tanner, C. A., and Chesla, C. A. (1992). "From beginner to expert: Gaining a differentiated clinical world in critical care nursing," *Advances in Nursing Science* 14(3): 13–28.

Benner, P., Tanner, C. A., and Chesla, C. A. (1996). *Expertise in Nursing Practice: Caring, Clinical Judgment, and Ethics* (New York: Springer).

Benner, Patricia (1982). "From novice to expert, *American Journal of Nursing* 82(3): 402–7.

Benner, Patricia (1984). "The Dreyfus model of skill acquisition applied to nursing," in *From Novice to Expert: Excellence and Power in Clinical Nursing Practice* (London: Addison Wesley).

Bereiter, C. and Scardamalia, M. (1993). *Surpassing Ourselves* (Chicago: Open Court Publishing Company).

Bergson, Henri (1889/2008). *Time and Free Will: An Essay on the Immediate Data of Consciousness* (New York: Cosimo).

Berkowitz A. L., Ansari, D. (2008). "Generation of novel motor sequences: The neural correlates of musical improvisation," *NeuroImage* 41: 535–43.

Bermúdez, José (1998). *The Paradox of Self-Consciousness* (Cambridge, MA: MIT Press).

Bermúdez, José (2007). *Thinking Without Words* (New York: Oxford University Press).

Bermùdez, José Luis (2010). "Action and Awareness of Agency," *Pragmatics and Cognition* 18:3, 584–96.

Bernier, M., Thienot, E., Codron, R., and Fournier, J. F. (2009). "Mindfulness and acceptance approaches in sport performance," *Journal of Clinical Sports Psychology* 4: 320–33.

Bernier, M., C. Trottier, E. Thienot, and J. Fournier (2016), "An Investigation of Attentional Foci and their Temporal Patterns: A Naturalistic Study in Expert Figure Skaters," *Sport Psychologist* 30, 3: 256–66.

Berry, D. and Broadbent, D. (1984). "On the Relationship between Task Performance and Associated Verbalizable Knowledge," *Quarterly Journal of Experimental Psychology: A Human Experimental Psychology* 36: 209–31.

Biederman, Irving and Shiffrar, Margaret M. (1987). "Sexing Day-Old Chicks: A Case Study and Expert Systems Analysis of a Difficult Perceptual-Learning Task," *Journal of Experimental Psychology: Learning, Memory, and Cognition* 13(4): 640–45.

Biello, David (2006). "Fact or fiction?: Archimedes coined the term 'Eureka!' in the bath," *Scientific American*, <http://www.scientificamerican.com/article/fact-or-fiction-archimede/> Accessed Nov. 4, 2015.

Bilalić, M., McLeod, P., and Gobet, F. (2008a). "Inflexibility of experts—Reality or myth? Quantifying the Einstellung effect in chess masters," *Cognitive Psychology* 56(2): 73–102.

Bilalić, M., McLeod, P., and Gobet, F. (2008b). "Why good thoughts block better ones: The mechanism of the pernicious Einstellung (set) effect," *Cognition* 108: 652–61.

Bilalić, M., McLeod, P., and Gobet, F. (2009). "Specialization effect and its influence on memory and problem solving in expert chess players," *Cognitive Science* 33: 1117–43.

Binet, Alfred (1966). *Mnemonic Virtuosity: A Study of Chess Players* (Provincetown, MA: Journal Press).

Bishop, Greg (2014). "Seeking bigger sweet spot, Roger Federer hopes his racket will grow on him," *New York Times*, Jan. 17. <http://www.nytimes.com/2014/01/17/sports/tennis/is-change-good-federer-with-new-racket-to-find-out.html?_r=0> Accessed Jan. 16, 2014.

Bishop, Paul (2010). "The unconscious from the Storm and Stress to Weimar classicism: the dialectic of time and pleasure," in A. Nicholls and M. Libscher (eds), *Thinking the Unconscious: Nineteenth Century German Thought* (Cambridge: Cambridge University Press) 26–55.

Blackburn, Simon (2014). "Creativity and not-so-dumb luck," in E. S. Paul and S. B. Kaufman (eds), *The Philosophy of Creativity: New Essays* (New York: Oxford University Press): 147–56.

Blakemore, S. J., Wolpert, D. M., and Frith, C. D. (2002). "Abnormalities in the awareness of action," *Trends in Cognitive Sciences* 6(6), 237–42.

Blass, Steve and Sherman, Erik (2012). *A Pirate for Life* (Chicago, IL: Triumph Books).

Borah, Woodrow (1983). *Justice By Insurance: The General Indian Court of Colonial Mexico and the Legal Aides of the Half-Real* (Berkeley: University of California Press).

Bosanquet, Bernard (1915). *Three Lectures on Aesthetic* (London: Macmillan and Co.).

Bradbury, Ray (1990). *Zen in the Art of Writing* (Santa Barbara, CA: Joshua Odell Editions).

Brandom, Robert (1994). *Making It Explicit: Reasoning, Representing, and Discursive Commitment* (Cambridge, MA: Harvard University Press).

Breed, Michael (2011). *The 3-Degree Putting Solution: The Comprehensive, Scientifically Proven Guide to Better Putting* (New York: Gotham Books).

Brennan, Christine (2007). "Lack of marquee teams doesn't mean viewers can't watch," *USA Today* Oct. 17. <http://usatoday30.usatoday.com/sports/columnist/brennan/2007-10-17-baseball-tv_N.htm> Accessed Nov. 4, 2015.

Bretherton, George (2012). "Dissecting Mark Sanchez's Postgame Demeanor," blog post, Oct. 22. <http://fifthdown.blogs.nytimes.com/2012/10/22/dissecting-mark-sanchezs-postgame-demeanor/> Accessed Nov. 4, 2015.

Broadbent, D. (1958). *Perception and Communication* (London: Pergamon Press).

Brogan, T. V. F. (1993). "Genius," in A. Preminger and T. V. F. Brogan (eds), *The New Princeton Encyclopedia of Poetry and Poetics* (Princeton, NJ: Princeton University Press): 455–56.

Brooks, David (2007). "Your Brain on Baseball," *New York Times*, March 18. <http://www.nytimes.com/2007/03/18/opinion/18brooks.html> Accessed Nov. 4, 2015.

Bryan, W. L. and Harter, N. (1899). "Studies on the telegraphic language: The acquisition of a hierarchy of habits," *Psychological Review* 6: 345–75.

Buchner, Axel, Funke, Joachim, and Berry, Dianne C. (1995). "Negative correlations between control performance and verbalizable knowledge: Indicators for implicit learning in process control tasks?" *Quarterly Journal of Experimental Psychology* 48(1): 166–87.

Burge, Tyler (1993). "Content Preservation," *Philosophical Review* 102: 457–88.

Buskell, Andrew (2015). "How to Be Skilful: Opportunistic Robustness and Normative Sensitivity," *Synthese* 5: 1445–66.

Bychkov, O. V., Sheppard, A. (eds) (2010). *Greek and Roman Aesthetics* (Cambridge: Cambridge University Press).

Camerer, C. F. and Johnson, E. J. (1991). "The process-performance paradox in expert judgment: How can the experts know so much and predict so badly?" in K. A. Ericsson, J. Smith (eds), *Towards a General Theory of Expertise: Prospects and Limits* (Cambridge: Cambridge University Press): 195–217.

Campitelli, G. and Gobet, F. (2004). "Adaptive expert decision making: Skilled chessplayers search more and deeper," *Journal of the International Computer Games Association* 27: 209–16.

Campitelli, G., Gobet, F., Head, K., Buckley, M., and Parker, A. (2007). "Brain localization of memory chunks in chessplayers," *International Journal of Neuroscience* 117(12): 1641–59.

Canby, Vincent (1984). "'Amadeus', Directed by Forman," *New York Times*, Sept. 19. <http://www.nytimes.com/packages/html/movies/bestpictures/amadeus-re.html> Accessed Nov. 4, 2015.

Carlson, Charles (2004). "Split second reactions," Feb. 1. <http://www.exploratorium.edu/baseball/biobaseball.html> Accessed Nov. 6, 2015.

Carpenter, William B. (2011). *Principles of Mental Physiology* (Cambridge: Cambridge University Press).

Carroll, Noël (1994). "Identifying Art," in Robert J. Yanal, *Institutions of Art: Reconsiderations of George Dickie's Philosophy* (University Park, PA: Penn State University Press): 12.

Carruthers, Peter (1998). *Language, Thought and Consciousness: An Essay in Philosophical Psychology* (Cambridge: Cambridge University Press).

Castaneda, B. and Gray, R. (2007). "Effects of focus of attention on baseball batting performance in players of differing skill levels," *Journal of Sport and Exercise Psychology* 29: 60–77.

Castiglione, Baldassare (1975). *Book of the Courtier*, trans. George Bull (original work published 1528) (New York: Penguin).

Chabris, C. F. (1999). *Cognitive and Neuropsychological Mechanisms of Expertise: Studies with Chess Masters*. Unpublished doctoral dissertation, Harvard University, Cambridge, MA.

Chabris, C . F. and Hearst, E. S. (2003). "Visualization, pattern recognition, and forward search: Effects of playing speed and sight of the position on grandmaster chess errors," *Cognitive Science* 27: 637–48.

Chalmers, David J. (1996). *The Conscious Mind: In Search of a Fundamental Theory* (New York: Oxford University Press).

Charness, N. (1981). "Search in chess: Age and skill differences," *Journal of Experimental Psychology: Human Perception and Performance* 7: 467–76.

Chase, S. (2016). *Yoga and the Pursuit of Happiness: A Guide to Finding Joy in Unexpected Places* (Oakland: New Harbinger Publications).

Chase, W. G. and Simon, H. A. (1973a). "The mind's eye in chess," in W. G. Chase (ed.) *Visual Information Processing* (New York: Academic Press).

Chase, W. G., and Simon, H. A. (1973b). "Perception in chess," *Cognitive Psychology* 4: 55–81.

Chi, M. T. H., Glaser, R., and Farr, M. (eds) (1988). *The Nature of Expertise* (Hillsdale, NJ: Erlbaum).

Christensen, Jon (2012). "The Color, Romance, and Impact of the Golden Gate at 75," *The Atlantic*, May 27. <http://www.theatlantic.com/technology/archive/2012/05/the-color-romance-and-impact-of-the-golden-gate-at-75/257721/> Accessed Nov. 5, 2015.

Christensen, W., Sutton, J., and McIllwain, D. J. F. (2015). "Putting pressure on theories of choking: Towards an expanded perspective on breakdown in skilled performance," *Phenomenology and the Cognitive Sciences* 14(2): 253–93.

Christensen, W., Bicknell, K., McIlwain, D. and Sutton, J. (2014). "The sense of agency and its role in strategic control in expert mountain biking," *Psychology of Consciousness: Theory, Research, and Practice* 2(3) 340–53.

Cioffi, J. (2000). "Nurses' experiences of making decisions to call emergency assistance to their patients," *Journal of Advanced Nursing* 32(1): 108–14.

Clausewitz, Karl von (1976). *On War* (Princeton, NJ: Princeton University Press).

Claxton, Guy (2000). *Hare Brain, Tortoise Mind: How Intelligence Increases When You Think Less* (New York: Harper Collins).

Cohen, Ted (1973). "Aesthetic/non-aesthetic and the concept of taste: A critique of Sibley's position," *Theoria* 39 (1–3): 113–52.

Cohen, Ted (1991). "Sports and Art: Beginning Questions," in J. Andre and D. N. James (eds), *Rethinking College Athletics* (Philadelphia, PA: Temple University Press): 258–304.

Cole, Jonathan (1995). *Pride and the Daily Marathon* (Cambridge, MA: MIT Press).

Cole, Jonathan and Montero, Barbara (2007). "Affective proprioception," *Janus Head* 9(2): 299–317.

Coleridge, Samuel Taylor (1816/1912). "Kubla Khan," in *The Complete Poetical Works* (Oxford: Clarendon Press).

Collins, D., Jones, B., Fairweather, M., Doolan, S., and Priestly, N. (2001). "Examining anxiety associated changes in movement patterns," *International Journal of Sport Psychology* 31: 223–42.

Confucius and Waley, A. (1938). *The Analects of Confucius* (New York: Random House).

Coope, Ursula (2007). "Aristotle on Action," *Aristotelian Society Supplementary* 81 (1):109–38.

Csikszentmihalyi, Mihaly (1990). *Flow: The Psychology of Optimal Experience* (New York: Harper and Row).

Csikszentmihalyi, Mihaly (1996). *Creativity: Flow and the Psychology of Discovery and Invention* (New York: Harper Collins).

Csikszentmihalyi, Mihaly (2014). "The Concept of Flow," in M. Csikszentmihalyi, *Flow and the Foundations of Positive Psychology* (Dordrecht: Springer) 239–63.

Danto, Arthur (1966). "Freedom and forbearance," in Keith Lehrer (ed.), *Freedom and Determinism* (New York: Random House) 45–63.

De Brigard, Filipe and Prinz, Jesse (2010). "Attention and Consciousness," *Wiley Interdisciplinary Reviews* 1 (1) 51–9.

de Groot, Adrian D. (1946/1978). *Thought and Choice in Chess* (rev. and trans. ed.) (Amsterdam: Amsterdam University Press).

Deakin, Janice. M. and Cobley, Stephen (2003). "A search for deliberate practice: An examination of the practice environments in figure skating and volleyball," in J. Starkes and K. A. Ericsson (eds), *Expert Performance in Sports: Advances in Research on Sport Expertise* (Champaign, IL: Human Kinetics): 90–113.

Deary, I. J. and Caryl, P. G. (1997). "Neuroscience and Human Intelligence Differences," *Trends in Neuroscience,* 20(8): 365–71.

Deezen, Eddie (2014). "'Yesterday': The most recorded song of all-time," *Neatorama* June 18. <http://www.neatorama.com/2014/06/18/Yesterday-The-Most-Recorded-Song-of-All-Time/#!btaL0D> Accessed Nov. 5, 2015.

Del Percio, C., Babiloni, C., Marzano, N., Iacoboni et al. (2009). "'Neural efficiency' of athletes' brain for upright standing: A high-resolution EEG study," *Brain Research Bulletin* 79(3–4): 193–200.

Denby, Edwin (1998). *Dance Writings and Poetry* (New Haven, CT: Yale University Press).

Dennett, Daniel (1991). *Consciousness explained* (Boston, MA: Little, Brown and Co.).

Descartes, René (1986). *Meditations on First Philosophy* (New York: Macmillan).

Devitt, Michael (2011). "Methodology and the Nature of Knowing How," *Journal of Philosophy* 108(4): 205–18.

Dewey, John (1997). *How We Think* (Mineola, NY: Dover).

Dickie, George (1969). "Defining Art," *American Philosophical Quarterly* 6: 253–56.

Dickson, Mike (2009). "Exclusive: Steffi Graf still striving for perfection," *Daily Mail Online*, June 12.<http://www.dailymail.co.uk/sport/othersports/article-1192647/EXCLUSIVE-Steffi-Graf-40--striving-perfection.html> Accessed Nov. 6, 2015.

Dijksterhuis, A., Bos, M. W., Nordgren, L. F., and van Baaren, R. B. (2006). "On making the right choice: The deliberation-without-attention effect," *Science* 311(5763): 1005–7.

Dijksterhuis, A. and van Olden, Z. (2006). "On the benefits of thinking unconsciously: Unconscious thought can increase post-choice satisfaction," *Journal of Experimental Social Psychology* 42: 627–31.

Di Nucci, Ezio (2014). *Mindlessness* (Newcastle upon Tyne: Cambridge Scholars Publishing).

Dodes, L. and Dodes, Z. (2014). *The Sober Truth: Debunking the Bad Science Behind 12-Step Programs and the Rehab Industry* (Boston: Beacon Press).

Donnay, G. F., Rankin, S. K., Lopez-Gonzalez, M., Jiradejvong, P., and Limb, C. J. (2014). "Neural substrates of interactive musical improvisation: An fMRI study of 'trading fours' in jazz," *PLoS ONE* 9(2): e88665.

Dreyfus, Hubert L. (2005). "Overcoming the myth of the mental: How philosophers can profit from the phenomenology of everyday expertise," *Proceedings and Addressings of the American Philosophical Association* 79(2): 47–65.

Dreyfus, Hubert L. (2007a). "The return of the myth of the mental," *Inquiry* 50(4): 352–65.

Dreyfus, Hubert L. (2007b). "Response to McDowell," *Inquiry* 50(4): 371–7.

Dreyfus, Hubert L. (2013). "The Myth of the Pervasiveness of the Mental," in J. K. Schear (ed.), *Mind, Reason, and Being-in-the-World: The McDowell-Dreyfus Debate* (New York: Routledge): 15–40.

Dreyfus H. L. and Dreyfus, S. E. (1986). *Mind Over Machine: The Power of Human Intuition and Expertise in the Era of the Computer* (New York: Free Press).

Dreyfus, H. L. and Dreyfus, S. E. (1991). "What is moral maturity? Towards a phenomenology of ethical expertise," in J. Ogilvy (ed.), *Revisioning Philosophy* (Albany, NY: State University of New York Press): 111–31.

Dreyfus, H. L. and Dreyfus, S. E. (2004). "The ethical implications of the five-stage skill-acquisition model," *Bulletin of Science, Technology and Society* 24: 251–64.

Dreyfus, Hubert and Kelly, Sean Dorrance (2011a). *All Things Shining: Reading the Western Classics to Find Meaning in a Secular Age* (New York: Free Press).

Dreyfus, Hubert, and Kelly, Sean Dorrance (2011b). "Saving the sacred from the axial revolution," *Inquiry* 54(2): 195–203.

Dugdale, J. R. and Eklund, R. C. (2003). "Ironic processing and static balance performance in high-expertise performers," *Research Quarterly for Exercise and Sport* 74(3): 348.

Duhigg, Charles (2012). *The Power of Habit: Why we do What we do in Life and Business* (New York: Random House).

Eagleman, D. M. and Sejnowski, T. J. (2000). "Motion integration and postdiction in visual awareness," *Science* 287(5460): 2036–8

Eagleman, David (2011). *Incognito: The Secret Lives of the Brain* (New York: Pantheon Books).

Eden, S. (2013). "Stroke of madness: How has Tiger Woods managed to overhaul his swing three times?" *ESPN* 2/12/2015 <http://espn.go.com/golf/story/_/id/8865487/tiger-woods-reinvents-golf-swing-third-career-espn-magazine> Accessed Nov. 6, 2015.

Einstein, Albert (1915/1998). "Letter to Walter Dallenbach" May 31, 1915, in *The Collected Papers of Albert Einstein, Volume 8: The Berlin Years: Correspondence, 1914–1918*, Doc. 87. (Princeton: Princeton University Press).

Ellis, P. (1977). "Processes used by nurses to make decisions in the clinical practice setting," *Nurse Education Today* 17(4): 325–32.

Eliot, T. S. (1939). *Old Possum's Book of Practical Cats* (London: Faber and Faber).

Eliot, T. S. (2005b). "*The Waste Land*," in R. Malamud (ed.), *The Waste Land and Other Poems* (New York: Barnes and Noble Classics).

Elstein, A. S., Shulman, L. S., and Sprafka, S. A. (1978). *Medical Problem Solving: An Analysis of Clinical Reasoning* (Cambridge, MA: Harvard University Press).

Elstein, A. S., Shulman, L. S. and Sprafka S. A. (1990). "Medical problem solving: a 10-year retrospective," *Evaluation and the Health Professions* 13: 5–36.

Epstein, David (2013). "Why Pujols Can't (and A-rod Wouldn't) Touch This Pitch," *Sports Illustrated*, July 29. <http://www.si.com/vault/2013/07/29/106348951/why-pujols-cant-and-a-rod-wouldnt-touch-this-pitch> Accessed Nov. 7, 2015.

Ericsson, K. A. and Charness, N. (1994). "Expert performance: Its structure and acquisition," *American Psychologist* 49: 725–47.

Ericsson, K. A., Krampe, R. T., and Tesch-Romer, C. (1993). "The role of deliberate practice in the acquisition of expert performance," *Psychological Review* 100(3): 363–406.

Ericsson, K. A., Prietula, M. J., and Cokely, E. T. (2007). "The making of an expert," *Harvard Business Review* 85(7–8): 114–21.

Ericsson, K. A. and Smith, J. (1991). "Prospects and limits in the empirical study of expertise: An introduction," in K. A. Ericsson and J. Smith (eds), *Towards a General Theory of Expertise: Prospects and Limits* (Cambridge: Cambridge University Press): 1–38.

Ericsson, K. A., Whyte IV, J., and Ward, P. (2007). "Expert performance in nursing: Reviewing research on expertise in nursing within the framework of the expert-performance approach," *Advances in Nursing Science* 30(1): E58–71.

Ericsson, K. A. (2006). "An introduction to *Cambridge Handbook of Expertise and Expert Performance*: its development, organization, and content," in K. A. Ericsson, N. Charness, P. J. Feltovich, and R. R. Hoffman (eds), *The Cambridge Handbook of Expertise and Expert Performance* (Cambridge: Cambridge University Press): 3–19.

Ericsson, K. A. (2008). "Deliberate practice and acquisition of expert performance: A general overview," *Academic Emergency Medicine* 15: 988–94.

Eriksen, J. W. (2010). "Should soldiers think before they shoot?" *Journal of Military Ethics* 9: 195–218.

Fallows, James (2012). "Slugfest," *The Atlantic Monthly*, Aug. 22. <http://www.theatlantic.com/magazine/archive/2012/09/slugfest/309063/?single_page=true> Accessed Nov. 5, 2015.

Fitts. P. M. (1964). "Perceptual-motor skill learning," in A.W. Melton (ed.), *Categories of Human Learning* (New York: Academic Press): 243–85.

Fitts, Paul Morris and Posner, Michael I. (1967). *Human Performance* (Belmont, CA: Brooks/Cole Publishing).

Flegal, K. E. and Anderson, M. C. (2008). "Overthinking skilled motor performance: Or why those who teach can't do," *Psychonomic Bulletin and Review* 15(5): 927–32.

Fodor, J. A. (1968). "The Appeal to Tacit Knowledge," *Journal of Philosophy* 65 (20): 627–40.

Fodor, J. A. (1983). *The Modularity of Mind: An Essay on Faculty Psychology* (Cambridge MA: Bradford Books, MIT Press).

Ford, P., Hodges, N. J., and Williams, A. M. (2005). "Online attentional-focus manipulations in a soccer-dribbling task: Implications for the proceduralization of motor skills," *Journal of Motor Behavior* 37(5): 386–94.

Ford, P. R., Ward, P., Hodges, N. J., and Williams, A. M. (2009). "The role of deliberate practice and play in career progression in sport: The early engagement hypothesis," *High Ability Studies* 20: 65–75.

Folkman, S. and Moskowitz, J. T. (2004). "Coping: Pitfalls and promise," *Annual Review of Psychology* 55: 745–74.

Fox, Allen (1993). *Think to Win: The Strategic Dimension of Tennis* (New York: Harper Perennial).

Fraleigh, Sondra Horton (1987). *Dance and the Lived Body: A Descriptive Aesthetics* (Pittsburg, PA: University of Pittsburg Press).

Frankl, Viktor E. (2006). *Man's Search For Meaning* (Boston, MA: Beacon Press).

Fraser, Chris (2007). "Review: On Wu-Wei as a Unifying Metaphor," *Philosophy East and West* 57 (1): 97–106.

Frede, J. (1983). "The mental representation of movement when static stimuli are viewed," *Perception and Psychophysics* 33 (6): 575–81.

French, Hal W. (2001). *Zen and the Art of Anything* (New York: Broadway Books).

Fridland, Ellen (2011). "The Case for Proprioception," *Phenomenology and the Cognitive Sciences* 10 (4): 521–40.

Fridland, Ellen (2012). "Knowledge-How: Problems and Considerations," *European Journal of Philosophy* 23(3): 703–27.

Fridland, Ellen (2014). "They've Lost Control: Reflections on Skill," *Synthese* 191 (12): 2729–50.

Fridland, Ellen (2015). "Automatically Minded," *Synthese*, Jan. 30, 2015.

Gallagher, Shaun (2000). "Philosophical Conceptions of the Self: Implications for Cognitive Science," *Trends in Cognitive Sciences* 4(1).

Gallagher, Shaun (2003). "Bodily self-awareness and object perception," *Theoria et Historia Scientarum* 7(1): 53–68.

Gallagher, Shaun (2007). "The Natural Philosophy of Agency," *Philosophy Compass* 2(2): 347–57.

Gallwey, W. Timothy (1974). *The Inner Game of Tennis* (New York: Bantam Books).

George, Alexander and Bennett, Andres (2005). *Case Studies and Theory Development in the Social Sciences*, Belfer Center Studies in International Security (Boston: MIT Press).

Gerson, Noel (1972). *The Prodigal Genius: The Life and Times of Honoré de Balzac* (New York: Doubleday).

Ghiselin, Brewster (1952). *The Creative Process* (9th ed.) (Berkeley, CA: University of California Press).

Gladwell, Malcolm (2000). "The Art of Failure," *New Yorker*, August 21/28: 84–92.

Gladwell, Malcolm (2005). *Blink: The Power of Thinking Without Thinking* (New York: Little, Brown and Co.).

Gobet, F. (1986). *Effets de l'incontrôlabilité sur la résolution de problèmes d'échecs [Effects of uncontrollability on chess problem solving]*, unpublished master's thesis, University of Fribourg, Switzerland.

Gobet, F. (2009). "Protocol analysis," in T. Bayne, A. Cleeremans, and P. Wilken (eds), *The Oxford Companion to Consciousness* (Oxford: Oxford University Press): 538–40.

Gobet, F. (1998). "Chess Thinking Revisited," *Swiss Journal of Psychology* 57, 18–32.

Gobet, F. and Chassy, P. (2008). "Towards an alternative to Benner's theory of expert intuition in nursing: A discussion paper," *International Journal of Nursing Studies* 45: 129–39.

Gobet, F. and Simon, H. A. (1996a). "The roles of recognition processes and look-ahead search in time-constrained expert problem solving: evidence from grandmaster level chess," *Psychological Science* 7: 52–5.

Gobet, F. and Simon, H. A. (1996b). "Recall of random and distorted chess positions: Implications for the theory of expertise," *Memory and Cognition* 24: 493–503.

Gobet, F. and Waters, A. J. (2003). "The role of constraints in expert memory," *Journal of Experimental Psychology: Learning, Memory, and Cognition* 29: 1082–94.

Gobet, F. (2012). "Concepts without intuition lose the game: Commentary on Montero and Evans," *Phenomenology and the Cognitive Sciences* 11(2): 237–50.

Gobet, F. and Chassy, P. (2009). "Expertise and intuition: A tale of three theories," *Minds and Machines* 19(2): 151–80.

Goldman, Alvin I. (2001). "Experts: Which ones should you trust?" *Philosophy and Phenomenological Research* 63(1): 85–110.

Goldman, M. and Rao, J. (2012). "Effort vs. Concentration: The asymmetric impact of pressure on NBA performance." Paper presented at the MIT Sloan Sports Analytics Conference, Boston, MA. <http://www.justinmrao.com/goldman_rao_sloan2012.pdf> Accessed Nov. 5, 2015.

Goodwin, G. M., McCloskey, D. I., and Matthews, P. B. (1972). "The contribution of muscle afferents to kinaesthesia shown by vibration induced illusions of movement and by the effects of paralysing joint afferents," *Brain* 95: 705–48.

Gould, Stephen Jay (2000). "The Brain of Brawn," *New York Times*, June 25. <http://www.nytimes.com/2000/06/25/opinion/the-brain-of-brawn.html> Accessed Nov. 5, 2015.

Grabner, R. H., Stern, E., and Neubauer, A. C. (2003). "When intelligence loses its impact: Neural efficiency during reasoning in a familiar area," *International Journal of Psychophysiology* 49: 89–98.

Grand, David and Goldberg, Alan S. (2011). *This is Your Brain on Sports: Beating Blocks, Slumps and Performance Anxiety for Good!* (Indianapolis, IN: Dog Ear Publishing).

Gray, G. and Wedderburn A. (1960). "Grouping strategies with simultaneous stimuli," *Quarterly Journal of Experimental Psychology* 12: 180–5.

Gray, J. R. (2004). "Integration of emotion and cognitive control," *Current Directions in Psychological Science* 13: 46–8.

Gray, Jeffrey A. (2004). *Consciousness: Creeping up on the Hard Problem* (Oxford: Oxford University Press).

Green, B. and Gallwey, W. T. (1986). *The Inner Game of Music* (London: Pan Books).

Grice, H. P. (1989). *Studies in the Ways of Words* (Cambridge, MA: Harvard University Press).

Groopman, Jerome (2007). *How Doctors Think* (Boston, MA: Houghton Mifflin).

Grossman, Samantha (2014). "Led Zeppelin Loses First Round in 'Stairway to Heaven' Lawsuit," *Time Magazine*, Oct. 21.

Gruen, John (1976). *The Private World of Ballet* (New York: Penguin Books).

Gucciardi, D. F. and Dimmock, J. A. (2008). "Choking under pressure in sensorimotor skills: Conscious processing or depleted attentional resources?" *Psychology of Sport and Exercise* 9(1): 45–59.

Guthrie, E. R. (1952). *The Psychology of Learning* (New York: Harper and Row).

Haggard, Patrick (2003). "Conscious awareness of intention and of action," in J. Roessler and N. Eilan (eds), *Agency and Self-Awareness: Issues in Philosophy and Psychology* (Oxford: Clarendon Press).

Haggard, P., Clark, S., and Kalogeras, J. (2002). "Voluntary action and conscious awareness," *Nature Neuroscience* 5: 382–5.

Hagura, N., Kanai, R., Orgs, G., and Haggard, P. (2012). "Ready steady slow: Action preparation slows the subjective passage of time," *Proceedings of the Royal Society of London B* 279: 4399–406.

Hammond, K. R. (2000). *Judgment under stress* (New York: Oxford University Press).

Hanfling, Oswald (2000). *Philosophy and Ordinary Language: The Bent and Genius of Our Tongues* (New York: Routledge).

Hanna, Robert and Maiese, Michelle (2009). *Embodied Minds in Action* (Oxford: Oxford University Press).

Hanson, Lawrence (1962). *The Life of S. T. Coleridge, The Early Years* (New York: Russell and Russell).

Hardy, Godfrey Harold (2012). *A Mathematician's Apology* (Cambridge: Cambridge University Press).

Harig, Bob (2010). "Tiger Woods to revamp swing," *ESPN.com.*, Sept. 8. <http://sports.espn.go.com/golf/news/story?id=5547968> Accessed Nov. 5, 2015.

Harman, G. (1990). "The Intrinsic Quality of Experience," in E. Villanueva (ed.), *Philosophical Perspectives: Action Theory and Philosophy of Mind.* (Atascadero: Ridgeview): 4.

Harss, Marina (2014). "Sweating Their Grace in Motion: Wendy Whelan, Tyler Angle and Others on Collaborating," *New York Times*, Dec. 27.

Hartmann, J. (2008). "Gary Kasparov is a cyborg; or What ChessBase teaches us about technology," in B. Hale (ed.), *Philosophy Looks at Chess* (Chicago: Open Court Press): 39–64.

Hartston, W. R. and Wason, P. C. (1985). *The Psychology of Chess* (New York: Facts on File).

Haufler, A. J., Spalding, T. W., Santa Maria, D. L., and Hatfield, B. D. (2000). "Neuro-cognitive activity during a self-paced visuospatial task: Comparative EEG profiles in marksmen and novice shooters," *Biological Psychology* 53(2–3): 131–60.

Hearst, E. (1977). "Man and machine: chess achievements and chess thinking," in P. W. Frey (ed.), *Chess skill in man and machine* (New York: Springer-Verlag).

Hegel, G. W. F. (1835/1975). *Aesthetics: Lectures on Fine Art, 2 vols*, trans. T. M. Knox (Oxford: Clarendon Press).

Hegel, G. W. F. (1807/1977). *Phenomenology of Spirit*, trans. A. V. Miller (New York: Oxford University Press).

Heidegger, Martin (1988). *The Basic Problems of Phenomenology* (rev. ed.), trans. A. Hofstadter (Bloomington, IN: Indiana University Press).

Hempel, Carl Gustav (1966). *Philosophy of Natural Science* (New York: Prentice-Hall).

Hendriks, Willy (2012). *Move First, Think Later: Sense and Nonsense in Improving Your Chess* (Alkmaar, Netherlands: New in Chess).

Herrigel, Eugen (1953). *Zen in the Art of Archery*, trans. R. F. C. Hull (New York: Pantheon Books).

Hidetaka, Kuroki (2010). "What did Archimedes find at 'Eureka' Moment," in S. A. Paipetis and M. Cedarelli, *The Genius of Archimedes—23 Centuries of Influence on Mathematics, Science and Engineering*, vol. 11 of the series *History of Mechanism and Machine Science*, 265–76.

Hill, David (ed.) (2003). *Literature of the Sturm und Drang* (Rochester, NY: Camden House).

Hill, Dave and Seitz, Nick (1977). *Teed Off* (Englewood Cliffs, NJ: Prentice-Hall).

Hill, Denise M., Hanton, S., Matthews, N., and Fleming, S. (2010). "A Qualitative Exploration of Choking in Elite Golf," *Journal of Clinical Sport Psychology* 4, 221–40.

Hill, John Spencer (1983). *A Coleridge Companion* (London: Macmillan Press).

Hobbes, Thomas (1651/2000). "*Leviathan*," in R. Ariew and E. Watkins (eds), *Readings in Modern Philosophy Vol. 1. Descartes, Spinoza, Leibniz and Associated Texts* (Indianapolis: Hackett): 128–42. )

Hock, Jonathan (dir.) (2013). *Play Without Thinking* [doc. film] (USA: Grantland).

Hogan, Ben (1957). *Five Lessons: The Modern Fundamentals of Golf* (New York: Barnes).

Holding, D. H. and Reynolds, R. I. (1982). "Recall or evaluation of chess positions as determinants of chess skill," *Memory and Cognition* 10(3): 237–42.

Homer (1961). *The Odyssey*, trans. R. Fitzgerald (Garden City, NY: Doubleday).

Hornsby, Jennifer (2015). "Acting and Trying to Act," in *Philosophy of Action: An Anthology*, Jonathan Dancy and Constantine Sandis (eds) (Malden, MA: John Wiley and Sons): 48–90.

Housman, A. E. (1933). "The Name and Nature of Poetry," Leslie Stephen Lecture, May 9, University of Cambridge, Cambridge.

Hume, David (1888). *A Treatise of Human Nature*, L. A. Selby-Bigge (ed.) (New York: Macmillan and Co).

Hunt, Earl (2006). "Expertise, Talent, and Social Encouragement," in Ericsson, K. A. et al. (eds), *The Cambridge Handbook of Expertise and Expert Performance* (Cambridge: Cambridge University Press): 31–8.

Hutcheson, Francis (1973). *An Inquiry Concerning Beauty, Order, Harmony, Design*, P. Kivy (ed.) (The Hague, Netherlands: Martinus Nijhoff).

Ivanhoe, P. J. and van Norden, Bryan W. (2005). *Readings in Classical Chinese Philosophy* (Indianapolis, IN: Hackett).

Jackson, S. A. and Csikszentmihalyi, M. (1999). *Flow in sports: The keys to optimal experiences and performances* (Champaign, IL: Human Kinetics).

James, William (1890/2007). *The Principles of Psychology, Vol. 1* (New York: Cosimo).

Johnson, J. G. and Raab, M. (2003). "Take the First: Option-generation and resulting choices," *Organizational Behavior and Human Decision Processes* 91: 215–29.

Johnson, Robert (2010). *Self-Improvement: An essay in Kantian Ethics* (Oxford: Oxford University Press).

Johnston N. E., Atlas, L. Y., and Wager, T. D. (2012). "Opposing effects of expectancy and somatic focus on pain," *PLOS One* 7(6): e38854.

Joint Commission (2014). "Facts about the Universal Protocol." <http://www.jointcommission.org/standards_information/up.aspx> Accessed Nov. 7, 2015.

Jowitt, Deborah (1989). *Time and the Dancing Image* (Berkeley, CA: University of California Press).

Kahneman, Daniel (2011). *Thinking, Fast and Slow* (New York: Farrar, Straus and Giroux).

Kant, Immanuel (1790/2007). *Critique of Judgment*, trans. J. C. Meredith, ed. N. Walker (New York: Oxford University Press).

Kant, Immanuel (2012). *Groundwork for the Metaphysics of Morals,*. M. J. Gregor and J. Timmerman (eds) (Cambridge: Cambridge University Press).

Kaptchuk T. J, Friedlander, E, Kelley J. M., Sanchez, M. N., Kokkotou, E., Singer, J. P., et al. (2010). "Placebos without Deception: A Randomized Controlled Trial in Irritable Bowel Syndrome," *PLoS ONE* 5(12): e15591. doi:10.1371/journal.pone.0015591.

Karz, Zippora (2011). *the Sugarless Plum* (New York: Harlequin).

Keele, S. W. and Summers, J. J. (1976). "The structure of motor programs," in G. E. Stelmach (ed.), *Motor Control: Issues and Trends* (New York: Academic Press): pp. 109–42.

Kekulé, F. August (1865). "Sur la constitution des substances aromatiques," *Bulletin de la Société Chimique de Paris* 3(2): 98–110.

Keys, Ivor (1980). *Mozart: His Music in His Life* (New York: Holmes and Meier).

Kimble, G. A. and Perlmuter, L. C. (1970). "The problem of volition," *Psychological Review* 77: 361–84.

King, Billie Jean (2008). *Pressure is a Privilege: Lessons I've Learned from Life and the Battle of the Sexes* (New York: Life Time Media Inc.).

Kirkland, Gelsey with Greg Lawrence (1986). *Dancing on my Grave* (Garden City, NY: Doubleday).

Kisselgoff, Anna (1981). "Ballet: Joffrey Stages Laura Dean's 'Night'," *New York Times*, Oct. 31. <http://www.nytimes.com/1981/10/31/arts/ballet-joffrey-stages-laura-dean-s-night.html> Accessed Nov. 7, 2015.

Kivy, Peter (1975). "What makes 'aesthetic' terms aesthetic?" *Philosophy and Phenomenological Research* 36(2): 197–211.

Kivy, Peter (2001). *The Possessor and the Possessed: Handel, Mozart, Beethoven and the Idea of Musical Genius* (New Haven, CT: Yale University Press).

Klämpfl, M. K., Lobinger, B. H., Raab, M. (2013). "Reinvestment—the Cause of the Yips?" *PLoS ONE* 8(12): e82470. doi:10.1371/journal.pone.0082470

Klein, Gary (2003). *Intuition at Work; Why Developing Your Gut Instincts Will Make You Better at What You Do* (New York: Currency).

Koethe, J. (2002). "Comments and Criticism: Stanley and Williamson on Knowing How," *Journal of Philosophy* 99: 325–8.

Kolata, Gina (2008). "Yes, running can make you high," *New York Times*, March 27. <http://www.nytimes.com/2008/03/27/health/nutrition/27best.html?_r=0> Accessed Nov. 5, 2015.

Kourlas, Gia (2012). "Elusive treasure; Object of a pirate's affections," *New York Times*, July 7, p. C2. <http://www.nytimes.com/2012/07/07/arts/dance/le-corsaire-american-ballet-theater-with-natalia-osipova.html?_r=0> Accessed Nov. 5, 2015.

Kriegel, Uriah (2003). "Consciousness as intransitive self-consciousness: Two views and an argument," *Canadian Journal of Philosophy* 33(1): 103–32.

Kriegel, Uriah (2013). "A hesitant defense of introspection," *Philosophical Studies* 165(3): 1165–76.

Krings, T., Topper, R., Foltys, H., Erberich, S., Sparing, R., Willmes, K., and Thron, A. (2000). "Cortical activation patterns during complex motor tasks in piano players and control subjects: A functional magnetic resonance imaging study," *Neuroscience Letters* 278: 189–93.

Lambert, Andrew (2016). "Rethinking disability through classical Daoist thought" in D. Schumm, and M. Stoltzfus (eds), *World Religions and Disability Studies: Making the Connections* (Waco, TX: Baylor University Press).

Lang, Holly (2007). *The Notorious B.I.G.: A Biography* (Westport, CT: Greenwood Publishing Group).

Langer, E. J. and Imber, L. G. (1979). "When practice makes imperfect: debilitating effects of overlearning," *Journal of Personality and Social Psychology* 37(11): 2014–24.

Lansley, Jacky and Early, Fergus (2011). *The Wise Body: Conversations with Experienced Dancers* (Chicago: Intellect).

Lay, B. S., Sparrow, W. A., Hughes, K. M., and O'Dwyer, N. J. (2002). "Practice effects on coordination and control, metabolic energy expenditure, and muscle activation," *Human Movement Science* 21: 807–30.

Leavitt, J. L. (1979). "Cognitive demands of skating and stick handling in ice hockey," *Canadian Journal of Applied Sport Sciences* 4: 46–55.

Lee, Steven L. (2010). "The extended surgical time-out: Does it improve quality and prevent wrong-site surgery?" *The Permanente Journal* 14(1): 19–23.

Lewicki, P., Hill, T., and Czyzewska, M. (1992). "Nonconscious acquisition of information," *American Psychologist* 47(6): 796–801.

Lieb, K. (2010). *Hirndoping—Warum Wir Nicht Alles Schlucken Soliten* (Dusseldorf: Verlag Artermis und Winkler).

Light, Alan (2012). *The Holy or the Broken: Leonard Cohen, Jeff Buckley and the Unlikely Ascent of "Hallelujah"* (New York: Atria Books).

Limb, C. J. and Braun, A. R. (2008). "Neural substrates of spontaneous music performance: An fMRI study of jazz improvisation," *PLoS ONE* 3(2): 2–9.

Liu, S., Chow, H. M., Xu, Y., Erkkinen, M. G., Swelt, K. E., Eagle, M. W., and Braun, A. R. (2012). "Neural correlates of lyrical improvisation: an fMRI study of freestyle rap," *Scientific Reports* 2: 834.

Lovering, Rob (2015). *What's Wrong with Getting Right? A Moral Defense of Recreational Drug Use* (New York: Palgrave Macmillan).

Lopes, Dominic M. (2002). "Vision, touch and the value of pictures," *British Journal of Aesthetics* 42: 87–97.

Lyyra, Pessi (2005). "Review of José Luis Bermudez: Thinking Without Words," *Psyche* 11.

Macaulay, Alastair (2008). "A spinning, twisting tribute to Ashton, with skaters and pigeons," *New York Times*, Dec. 22. <http://www.nytimes.com/2008/12/23/arts/dance/23asht.html?pagewanted=all&_r=0> Accessed Nov. 5, 2015.

Macaulay, Alastair (2012). "Works that are longer on style than on choreography," *New York Times*, May 9. <http://www.nytimes.com/2012/05/10/arts/dance/alonzo-king-lines-ballet-at-the-joyce-theater.html> Accessed Nov. 5, 2015.

McCrone, John (2000). *Going Inside: A Tour Round a Single Moment in Consciousness* (London: Faber and Faber).

McDowell, John (2007b). "Response to Dreyfus," *Inquiry* 50(4): 366–70.

McDowell, John (2010). "Brandom on Experience," in B. Weiss and J. Wanderer (eds), *Reading Brandom: On Making It Explicit* (New York: Routledge): 129–43.

McDowell, John (2013). "The Myth of the Mind as Detached," in J. K. Schear (ed.), *Mind, Reason, and Being-in-the-World: The McDowell-Dreyfus Debate* (New York: Routledge): 41–58.

McFee, Graham (1992). *Understanding Dance* (New York: Routledge).

McGrath, Charles (2012). "Two Different Reads on How to Putt Better," blog post, July 22. <http://onpar.blogs.nytimes.com/2012/07/22/two-different-reads-on-how-to-putt-better/> Accessed Nov. 5, 2015.

McLean, J. and Welty, C. (2004). "Woods' swing has a new look," *ESPN 4/7/2004* <http://sports.espn.go.com/golf/masters04/news/story?id=1776900> Accessed Nov. 8, 2015.

Macpherson, Fiona (2012). "Cognitive Penetration of Colour Experience: Rethinking the Issue in Light of an Indirect Mechanism," *Philosophy and Phenomenological Research* 84 (1): 24–62.

McPherson, M. and Limb, C. J. (2013). "Difficulties in the neuroscience of creativity: Jazz improvisation and the scientific method" *Annals New York Academy of Science* 1303, 80–3.

Mann, D. L., Spratford, W., and Abernethy, B. (2013) "The Head Tracks and Gaze Predicts: How the World's Best Batters Hit a Ball," *PLoS ONE* 8(3): e58289. doi:10.1371/journal.pone.0058289.

Manoyan, Dan (2012). "Doubt Lasts Only a Moment in an Open Win," *New York Times,* July 8. <http://www.nytimes.com/2012/07/09/sports/golf/na-yeon-choi-wins-us-womens-open-after-miscue-on-no-10.html?_r=0> Accessed Nov. 8, 2015.

Marcel, Anthony J. (2003). "The sense of agency: Awareness and ownership of action," in J. Roessler and N. Eilan (eds), *Agency and Self-Awareness: Issues in Philosophy and Psychology* (Oxford: Clarendon Press): 48–93.

Martin, John (1941). "Dolin work given by ballet group; 'Pas de Quatre,' patterned on London number of 1845, is added to repertory," *New York Times,* Nov. 29, p. 15.

Martin, John (1972). *Introduction to the Dance* (New York: Dance Horizons Inc.).

Martin, Steve (2007). *Born Standing Up: A Comic's Life* (New York: Scribner).

Martin, Wayne M. (2008). *Theories of Judgment* (New York: Cambridge University Press).

Masters, R. S. W. (1992). "Knowledge, (k)nerves, and know-how: The role of explicit versus implicit knowledge in the breakdown of a complex motor skill under pressure," *British Journal of Psychology* 83: 343–58.

Masters, R. S. W., Polman, R. C. J., and Hammond, N. V. (1993). "Reinvestment: A dimension of personality implicated in skill breakdown under pressure," *Personality and Individual Differences* 14: 655–66.

Maudsley, Henry (1993). *The Physiology and Pathology of the Mind* (London: Routledge/Thoemmes).

May, Larry (2007). *War Crimes and Just Wars* (Cambridge: Cambridge University Press).

Melcher, J. M. and Schooler, J. W. (1996). "The misremembrance of wines past; Verbal and perceptual expertise differentially mediate verbal overshadowing of taste memory," *Journal of Memory and Language* 35(2): 231–45.

Melcher, J. M. and Schooler, J. W. (2004). "Perceptual and conceptual training mediate the verbal overshadowing effect in an unfamiliar domain," *Memory and Cognition* 32(4): 618–31.

Merino-Rajme, Carla (2014). "A Quantum Theory of Felt Duration," *Analytic Philosophy* 55(3): 239–75.

Merleau-Ponty, Maurice (1945/2005). *Phenomenology of Perception* (London: Taylor and Francis Books Ltd.).

Messina, James (2011). "Answering Aenesidemus: Schulze's attack on Reinholdian representationalism and its importance for Fichte," *Journal of the History of Philosophy* 49(3): 339–69.

Mole, Christopher (2011). *Attention Is Cognitive Unison: An Essay in Philosophical Psychology* (Oxford: Oxford University Press).

Moul, C. and Nye, J. (2009). "Did the Soviets Collude? A statistical analysis of championiship chess 1949–1978," Journal of Economic Behavior and Organization, Elsevier, vol. 70 (1–2) 10–21.

Montero, Barbara G. (1999). "The body problem," *Nous* 33(2): 183–200.

Montero, Barbara G. (2001). "Post-physicalism," *Journal of Consciousness Studies* 8(2): 61–80.

Montero, Barbara G. (2005). "What is the physical?" in A. Beckermann and B. P. McLaughlin (eds), *The Oxford Handbook of Philosophy of Mind* (Oxford: Oxford University Press): 173–88.

Montero, Barbara G. (2006a). "Proproceiving someone else's movement," *Philosophical Explorations* 9(2): 149–61.

Montero, Barbara G. (2006b). "Proprioception as an Aesthetic Sense," *Journal Of Aesthetics And Art Criticism* 64 (2): 231–42.

Montero, Barbara G. (2010). "Does Bodily Awareness Interfere with Highly Skilled Movement?" *Inquiry* 53, pp. 105–22.

Montero, Barbara Gail (2011). "Effortless bodily movement," *Philosophical Topics* 39 (1): 67–79.

Montero, Barbara Gail (2012). "Practice makes perfect: The effect of dance training on the aesthetic judge," *Phenomenology and the Cognitive Sciences* 11(1): 59–68.

Montero, Barbara Gail (2013). "The Artist as Critic," *Journal of Aesthetics and Art Criticism* 71 (2): 169–75.

Montero, Barbara Gail (2015). "Philosophy of Mind in Nineteenth-century Germany," in *Oxford Handbook of German Philosophy in the Nineteenth Century*, M. Forster and G. Kristen (eds) (Oxford: Oxford University Press).

Montero, Barbara Gail (2016). "Aesthetic Effortlessness," in Sherri Irvin (ed.), *Body Aesthetics* (Oxford: Oxford University Press).

Montero, Barbara Gail and Evans, Cory (2011). "Intuitions without concepts lose the game: mindedness in the art of chess," *Phenomenology and the Cognitive Sciences* 10(2): 175–94.

Montero, Barbara Gail, Toner, J., and Moran, A. (2018). "Questioning the Breadth of the Attentional Focus Effect," in M. Cappuccio (ed.), *Handbook of Embodied Cognition and Sport Psychology* (Cambridge, MA: MIT Press).

Montero, J. C. (1966). "Physical fitness—Who needs it?" *Medical Tribune* 7(15).

Montero, J. C. and Montero, D. (1966). "Vanity is good for your health," *Veterans Administration Reports*.

Moore, James, Dickinson, A., and Fletcher Paul C. (2012). "Sense of agency, associative learning, and schizotypy," *Consciousness and Cognition* Sep. 20(3–2): 792–800.

Morgan, W. P. and Pollack, M. L. (1977). "Psychologic characterization of the elite distance runner," *Annals of the New York Academy of Sciences* 301: 382–403.

Morrone, M. C., Ross, J., and Burr, D. (2005). "Saccadic eye movements cause compression of time as well as space," *Nature Neuroscience* 8: 950–4.

Murakami, Haruki (2007). *Blind Willow, Sleeping Woman* (New York: Vintage International).

Murakami, Haruki (2008). *What I Talk About When I Talk About Running* (New York: Alfred Knopf).

Murphy, Michael and White, Rhea A. (1995). *In the Zone: Transcendent Experience in Sports* (New York: Penguin/Arkana).

Murphy, Robert (1987). *The Body Silent* (New York: Henry Holt).

Myers, David (2002). *Intuition: Its Powers and Perils* (New Haven, CT: Yale University Press).

Myopoulos, Myrto (2015). "Agentive Awareness is Not Sensory Awareness," *Philosophical Studies* 172: 761–780.

Nadal, Rafael and Carlin, John (2011). *Rafa* (New York: Hyperion).

Nakamura, Jeanne and Csikszentmilhalyi, Mihaly (2002). "The concept of flow," in C. R. Snyder and S. J. Lopez (eds), *Handbook of Positive Psychology* (New York: Oxford University Press): 89–105.

Nakayama, Tommy (1993). "The Japanese Vent Sexing Method," in J. L. Skinner and American Poultry Historical Society, *American Poultry History, 1974–1993 Vol. II* (Mount Morris, IL: Watt Publishing).

Naparstek, Belleruth (1998). "Extrasensory Etiquette," *Utne Reader* Nov./Dec. 1998. <http://www.utne.com/mind-and-body/intuitive-psychic-etiquette.aspx#axzz357Gn3OmL> Accessed Nov. 5, 2015.

Nathan, Amy (2008). *Meet the Dancers: From Ballet, Broadway and Beyond* (New York: Henry Holt).

Neisser, U. (1976). *Cognition and Reality* (San Francisco: Freeman).

Neubauer, A. C. and Fink, A. (2009). "Intelligence and neural efficiency," *Neuroscience and Biobehavioral Reviews* 33: 1004–23.

Newman, Barbara (1982). *Striking a Balance: Dancers Talk About Dancing* (Boston, MA: Houghton Mifflin).

Nicholls, A., Holt, N. L., Polman, R. C. J., and Bloomfield, J. (2006). "Stressors, coping, and coping effectiveness among professional rugby union players," *Sport Psychologist* 20(3): 314–29.

Nicholls, A. R., Holt, N. L., Polman, R. C. J., and James, D. W. G. (2005). "Stress and coping among international adolescent golfers," *Journal of Applied Sport Psychology* 17: 330–40.

Nicholls, Adam R. (2010). *Coping in Sport: Theory, Methods, and Constructs* (New York: Nova Science Publishers).

Nisbett, R. E. and Wilson, T. D. (1977). "Telling more than we can know: Verbal reports on mental processes," *Psychological Review* 84(3): 231–59.

Noë, A. (2005). "Against Intellectualism," *Analysis* 65: 278–90.

Noë, A. (2006). *Action in Perception.* (Cambridge, MA: MIT Press).

Norman, D. A. and Shallice, T. (1986). "Attention to action: willed and automatic control of behaviour," in R. J. Davidson, G. E. Schwartz, and D. Shapiro (eds), *Consciousness and Self-Regulation: Advances in Research and Theory* (New York, NY: Springer): 1–18.

Nutt, David (2012). *Drugs—Without the Hot Air* (Cambridge: UIT).

Nyberg, G. (2015). "Developing a 'somatic velocimeter'—the practical knowledge of freeskiers," *Qualitative Research in Sport, Exercise and Health,* 7: 109–24.

O'Brien, Edna (1979). "Violets," *New Yorker,* Nov. 5. <http://www.newyorker.com/magazine/1979/11/05/violets> Accessed Nov. 5, 2015.

O'Kelly de Galway, Alberic (1963). *Tigran Petrosian, Champion de Monde: 30 Parties* (Brussels: Marais).

O'Shaughnessy, Brian (1973). "Trying (as the mental 'pineal gland')," *Journal of Philosophy* 70 (13): 365–86.

O'Shaughnessy, Brian (1981). *The Will: A Dual Aspect Theory* (New York: Cambridge University Press).

O'Shaughnessy, Brian (1998). "Proprioception and the body image," in J. Bermúdez, A. Marcel, and N. Eilan (eds), *The Body and the Self* (Cambridge, MA: MIT Press): 175–204.

O'Shaughnessy, Brian (2009). "Trying and acting," in L. O'Brien and M. Soteriou (eds), *Mental Actions* (New York: Oxford University Press).

Onuma, Hideharu, DeProspero, Dan, and DeProspero, Jackie (1993). *Kyudo: The Essence and Practice of Japanese Archery* (New York: Kodansha America).

Oudejans, R. R., Kuijpers, W., Kooijman, C. C., and Bakker, F. C. (2011). "Thoughts and attention of athletes under pressure: skill-focus or performance worries?" *Anxiety, Stress, and Coping* 24 (1): 59–73.

Pacherie, Elisabeth (2007). "The Sense of Control and the Sense of Agency," *Psyche* 13 (1): 1–30.

Pacherie, Elisabeth (2008). "The Phenomenology of Action: A Conceptual Framework," *Cognition* 107 (1): 179–217.

Papineau, David (2013). "In the Zone," *Royal Institute of Philosophy Supplement* 73: 175–96.

Papineau, David (2015). "Choking and the yips," *Phenomenology and the Cognitive Sciences* 4(2): 295–308.

Pappas, Nickolas (1989). "Plato's 'Ion': The Problem of the Author," *Philosophy* 64(249): 381–9.

Parris, Kenneth E. (2011). "Drawing Dance: The Cunningham Company at Stanford," blogpost, Nov.7.<http://artsbeat.blogs.nytimes.com/2011/11/07/drawing-dance-the-cunningham-company-at-stanford/> Accessed Nov. 5, 2015.

Patton, Kevin (2009). *Essentials of Anatomy and Physiology* (New York: McGraw-Hill College).

Pavesse, Carlotta (2015). "Knowing a Rule," *Philosophical Issues* 25(1): 165–88.

Peacocke, Christopher (1992). *A Study of Concepts* (Cambridge, MA: MIT).

Petras, Kathryn and Petras, Ross (2011). *Dance First. Think Later: 618 Rules to Live By* (New York: Workman Publishers).

Pickard, Hanna (2004). "Knowledge of action without observation," *Proceedings of the Aristotelian Society* 104(1): 205–30.

Plato (*c.*380 BCE/1996). *The Dialogues of Plato, Volume 3: Ion, Hippias Major, Laches, Protagoras*, trans. R. E. Allen (New Haven, CT: Yale University Press).

Plato (2000). *The Trial and Death of Socrates*, J. M. A. Grube (trans.), revised by John Cooper (Cambridge, MA: Hackett Press).

Prall, D. W. (1929). *Aesthetic Judgment* (New York: Thomas Y. Crowell).

Pray, Doug (2009). *Art and Copy* (doc. film), produced by Jimmy Greenway and Michael Nadeau, Distributed by PBS/7th Art Releasing. Previc, F. H. and Ercoline, W. R. (2004). *Spatial disorientation in aviation* (Reston, VA: American Institute of Astronautics and Aeronautics).

Prince, Allison, Zhang, Yifan, Croniger, Colleen, and Puchowicz, Michelle (2013). "Oxidative Metabolism: Glucose Versus Ketones," *Advances in Experimental Medicine and Biology* 789: 323–8.

Prince, Joseph (2010). *Destined to Reign: The Secret to Effortless Success, Wholeness and Victorious Living* (Tulsa, OK: Harrison House).

Prinz, Jesse (2012). *The Conscious Brain: How Attention Engenders Experience* (Oxford: Oxford University Press).

Proctor, R. W. and Dutta, A. (1995). *Skill Acquisition and Human Performance* (Thousand Oaks, CA: Sage).

Pushkin, Aleksandr (1830/2002). *Mozart and Salieri* (repr. as *Mozart and Salieri: the little Tragedies*) (Chester Springs, PA: Dufour Editions).

Puttemans, V., Wenderoth, N., and Swinnen, S. P. (2005). "Changes in brain activation during the acquisition of a multifrequency bimanual coordination task: from the cognitive stage to advanced levels of automaticity," *Journal of Neuroscience* 25: 4270–8.

Pylyshyn, Zenon W. (1999). "Is Vision Continuous with Cognition? The Case for Cognitive Impenetrability of Visual Perception," *Behavioral and Brain Sciences* 22 (3): 341–65.

Quast, Christian (forthcoming). "Understanding the Nature of Expertise: A Minimalistic Approach to a Definition of Expertise," *Topoi*.

Rachels, Stuart (2008). "The reviled art," in B. Hale (ed.), *Philosophy Looks at Chess* (Chicago: Open Court Press): 209–25.

Ravn, S. and Christensen, M. K. (2014). "Listening to the body? How phenomenological insights can be used to explore a golfer's experiences of the physicality of her body," *Qualitative Research in Sport, Exercise and Health*, 6 (4): 462–77.

Reinhold, Karl Leonhard (1790). *Contributions to the Rectification of Misconceptions Hitherto Held by Philosophers*, Vol. 1 (Jena: Mauke).

Reynolds, R. I. (1991). "The application of a search heuristic by skilled problem solvers," *Bulletin of the Psychonomic Society* 29(1): 55–6.

Rietveld, Eric (2010). "McDowell and Dreyfus on Unreflective Action," *Inquiry* 53(2): 183–207.

Rizzolatti G. and Craighero, L. (2004). "The mirror-neuron system," *Annual Review of Neuroscience* 27:169–92.

Robbins, T. W., Anderson, E. J., Barker, D. R., Bradley, A. C., Fearnyhough, C., Henson, R., Hudson, S. R., and Baddeley, A. D. (1996). "Working memory in chess," *Memory and Cognition* 24(1): 83–93.

Roholt, Tiger (2015). "From the Author's Perspective: *Groove*," *American Society of Aesthetics Newsletter* 31(1).

Rosefeldt, T. (2004). "Is Knowing How Simply a Case of Knowing That?" *Philosophical Investigations* 27: 370–9.

Rosen, Charles (1987). "The Chopin touch," *New York Review of Books*, May 28. <http://www.nybooks.com/articles/archives/1987/may/28/the-chopin-touch/> Accessed Nov. 5, 2015.

Rosen, Charles (2002). *Piano Notes: The World of the Pianist* (New York: Free Press).

Rotella, Robert (2012). *The Unstoppable Golfer: Trusting Your Mind and Your Short Game to Achieve Greatness* (New York: Free Press).

Rothenberg, Albert (1990). *Creativity and Madness: New Findings and Old Stereotypes* (Baltimore, MD: Johns Hopkins University Press).

Rubin, Hanna (2011). "Teaching with the Stars, what it is like to step from the spotlight to the head of the class," *Pointe Magazine* August/September.

Saariluoma, P. (1990). "Chess players' search for task relevant cues: Are chunks relevant?" in D. Brogan (ed.), *Visual Search: Proceedings of the 1st International Conference on Visual Search* (London: Taylor and Francis Ltd.): 115–21.

Saariluoma, P. (1992). "Visuospatial and articulatory interference in chess players' information intake," *Applied Cognitive Psychology* 6(1): 77–89.

Saariluoma, P. (1995). *Chess Players' Thinking: A Cognitive Psychological Approach* (London: Routledge).

Saariluoma, P. and Kalakoski, V. (1998). "Apperception and imagery in blindfold chess," *Memory* 6(1): 67–90.

Sacks, Oliver (1995). "Foreword," in Jonathan Cole, *Pride and a Daily Marathon* (Cambridge, MA: MIT Press).

Saenz, Arlene and Friedman, Emily (2011)."Rick Perry's debate lapse: 'Oops'—can't remember Department of Energy." Blog article, Nov. 9, *ABC News, The Note*. <http://abcnews.go.com/blogs/politics/2011/11/rick-perrys-debate-lapse-oops-cant-remember-department-of-energy/> Accessed Nov. 8, 2015.

Salk Institute (2000). "We Live In The Past, Salk Scientists Discover," Salk News Release, March 16, 2000. <http://www.salk.edu/news/pressrelease_details.php?press_id=31> Accessed Nov. 6, 2015.

Salvucci, D. D. and Taatgen, N. A. (2008). "Threaded cognition: An integrated theory of concurrent multitasking," *Psychological Review* 115 (1): 101–30.

Sampras, Pete and Bodo, Peter (2008). *A Champion's Mind: Lessons from a Life in Tennis.* (New York: Crown Publishers).

Santayana, George (1955). *The Sense of Beauty* (New York: Modern Library).

Scarry, Elaine (2011). *Thinking in an Emergency* (New York: Norton).

Schiffer, Stephen (2002). "Amazing knowledge," *Journal of Philosophy* 99: 200–2.

Schlenker, B., Phillips, S. T., Boniecki, K. A., and Schlenker, D. R. (1995). "Championship pressures: Choking or triumphing in one's own territory?" *Journal of Personality and Social Psychology* 68(4): 632–43.

Schooler, J. W. and Engstler-Schooler, T. Y. (1990). "Verbal overshadowing of visual memories: Some things are better left unsaid," *Cognitive Psychology* 22(1): 36–71.

Schneider, Elisabeth (1945). "The 'dream' of Kubla Khan," Publications of the Modern Language Association of America 60(3): 784–801.

Schneider, W. and Shiffrin, R. M. (1977). "Controlled and automatic human information processing: 1. Detection, search, and attention," *Psychological Review* 84: 1–66.

Schwab, Johann (1791). "Review of volume 1 of 'Beiträge zur Berichtigung bisheriger Misverständnisse der Philosophen' ["Review of Contributions"], by Karl Reinhold," *Philosophisches Magazin* 4: 335.

Schwitzgebel, Eric (2011). *Perplexities of Consciousness* (Cambridge, MA: MIT).

Seiwert, Charles (2013). "Intellectualism, experience, and motor understanding," in J. K. Schear (ed.), *Mind, Reason and Being-in-the-World: The McDowell-Dreyfus Debate* (New York: Routledge): 194–226.

Shaffer, Peter (1981). *Amadeus.* (New York: Harper and Row).

Shakespeare, William (1973). *Hamlet: The Tragedy of Hamlet Prince of Denmark*, E. Hubler (ed.) (New York: Signet Classics).

Shanteau, James (1988). "Psychological characteristics and strategies of expert decision makers," *Acta Psychologica* 68(1): 203–15.

Shelley, Percy Bysshe (1840/1965). "A Defence of Poetry," in R. Ingpen and W. E. Peck (eds), *The Complete Works of Percy Bysshe Shelley* (London: Benn).

Shepherd, Joshua (2015). "Conscious Control Over Action," *Mind and Language* 30 (3): 320–44.

Sherman, Robert (1980). "Natalia Markarova," *Great Artists Series* (excerpted from a 1977 interview) (WNYC archives id: 70039).

Shoji, Yamada (2001). "The myth of Zen in the art of archery," *Japanese Journal of Religious Studies* 28(1/2): 1–30.

Shusterman, Richard (2008). *Body Consciousness: A Philosophy of Mindfulness and Somaesthetics* (New York: Cambridge University Press).

Shusterman, Richard (2012). *Thinking Through the Body: Essays in Somaesthetics* (New York: Cambridge University Press).

Sibley, Frank (1965). "Aesthetic and nonaesthetic," *Philosophical Review* 74(2): 135–59.

Siegel, Susanna (2012). "Cognitive Penetrability and Perceptual Justification," *Noûs* 46 (2): 201–22.

Simon, H. A. and Chase, W. G. (1973). "Skill in chess," *American Scientist* 61: 394–403.

Simonini, Ross (2001). "Trey Anastasio," *The Believer*, July/Aug. <http://www.believermag.com/issues/201107/?read=interview_anastasio> Accessed Nov. 5, 2015.

Simpson, Michael Wade (2005). "Dancers relay Robbins' gentler, reflective side in Chopin piece," *SFGate/San Francisco Chronicle*, April 9. <http://www.sfgate.com/entertainment/art-icle/Dancers-relay-Robbins-gentler-reflective-side-2687074.php> Accessed Nov. 5, 2015.

Slingerland, Edward (2007). *Effortless Action: Wu-wei as Conceptual Metaphor and Spiritual Ideal in Early China* (New York: Oxford University Press).

Slingerland, Edward (2014). *Trying Not to Try: The Art and Science of Spontaneity* (New York: Crown Publishers).

Sonas, Jeff (2002). "The Sonas Rating Formula—Better than Elo?" *Chess News* 0/22/2002 <http://en.chessbase.com/post/the-sonas-rating-formula-better-than-elo-> Accessed Nov. 7, 2015.

Spaethling, Robert (2000). *Mozart's Letters, Mozart's Life* (New York: W. W. Norton and Co.).

Sparrow, W. A., Hughes, K. M., Russell, A. P., and LeRossignol, P. F. (1999). "Effects of practice and preferred rate on perceived exertion, metabolic variables, and movement control," *Human Movement Science* 18: 137–53.

Sparrow, W. A. and Newell, K. M. (1998). "Metabolic energy expenditure and the regulation of movement economy," *Psychonomic Bulletin and Review* 5: 173–96.

Spencer, Herbert (1907). "Gracefulness," in *Essays: Scientific, Political, and Speculative, Vol. II* (New York: D. Appleton and Co.): 381–86. Retrieved from Google Books.

Stafford, William (1991). *The Mozart Myths: A Critical Analysis* (Stanford, CA: Stanford University Press).

Stanley, J. and Krakauer, J. W. (2013). "Motor skill depends on knowledge of facts," *Frontiers in Human Neurosciences* 7: 503.

Stanley, Jason (2011). *Know How* (Oxford: Oxford University Press).

Stanley, Jason and Williamson, Timothy (2001). "Knowing how," *Journal of Philosophy* 98: 411–44.

Steele, C. M. and Aronson, J. (1995). "Stereotype threat and the intellectual test performance of African-American," *Journal of Personality and Social Psychology* 69(5): 797–881.

Steinhardt, Arnold (1998). *Indivisible by Four: A String Quartet in Pursuit of Harmony* (New York: Farrar, Straus, and Giroux).

Stern-Gillet, Suzanne (2004). "On (Mis)interpreting Plato's 'Ion'," *Phronesis* 49(2): 169–201.

Stockton, Dave and Rudy, Matthew (2011). *Unconscious Putting: Dave Stockton's Guide to Unlocking Your Signature Stroke* (New York: Gotham Books).

Stokes, Dustin (2012). "Perceiving and Desiring: A New Look at the Cognitive Penetrability of Experience," *Philosophical Studies* 158 (3): 479–92.

Strawson, Galen (2003). "Mental ballistics or the involuntariness of spontaneity," *Proceedings of the Aristotelian Society* 103 (3): 227–57.

Styles, Elizabeth (1999). *The Psychology of Attention* (New York: Psychology Press).

Suss, J. and Ward, P. (2010). "Skill-based differences in the cognitive mechanisms underlying failure under stress," *Proceedings of the Human Factors and Ergonomics Society Annual Meeting* September 2010, 54 (14): 1062–6.

Sutton, J., Mcilwain, D., Christensen, W., and Geeves, A. (2011). "Applying intelligence to the reflexes: Embodied skills and habits between Dreyfus and Descartes," *Journal of the British Society for Phenomenology* 42: 78–103.

Tal, Mikhails (1997). *The Life and Games of Mikhail Tal* (London: Cadogan Chess).

Tharp, Twyla (2002). *The Creative Habit: Learn it and use it for Life* (New York: Simon and Shuster Paperbacks).

Toner, J., Montero, B. G., and Moran, A. (2014). "Considering the Role of Cognitive Control in Expert Performance," *Phenomenology and the Cognitive Sciences.*

Toner, J., Montero, B. G., and Moran, A. (2015)."The perils of automaticity," *Review of General Psychology* 19(4): 431.

Toner, J., Montero B. G., and Moran, A. (in progress). "Reflective and Pre-reflective Awareness in Bodily Action."

Toner, J. and Moran, A. (2009). "Technical adjustments and their influence upon the putting strokes of expert golfers," *12th World Congress of Sport Psychology*, Marrakech, Morocco (17–21 June).

Toner, J. and Moran, A. (2011). "The effects of conscious processing on golf putting proficiency and kinematics," *Journal of Sports Sciences* 29(7): 673–83.

Toner, J. and Moran, A. (2014). "In praise of conscious awareness: a new framework for the investigation of 'continuous improvement' in athletes," *Frontiers in Psychology: Cognition* 5: 769.

Toner, J. and Moran, A. (2015). "Enhancing performance proficiency at the expert level: considering the role of 'somaesthetic awareness,'" *Psychology of Sport and Exercise* 16: 110–17.

Tovée, M. J. (1994). "How fast is the speed of thought?" *Current Biology* 4(12): 1125–7.

Tracy, J., Flanders, A., Madi, S., Laskas, J., Stoddard, E., Pyrros, A., Natale, P., and Del Vecchio, N. (2003). "Regional brain activation associated with different performance patterns during learning of a complex motor skill," *Cerebral Cortex* 13(9): 903–10.

Treffert, D. (2013). "Savant Syndrome, a compelling case for innate talent," in S. B. Kaufman (ed.), *The Complexity of Greatness, beyond practice or talent* (New York: Oxford University Press): 103–18.

Treisman, A. (1964). "Selective attention in man," *British Medical Bulletin* 20: 12–16.

Tyson, Alan (1987). *Mozart: Studies of the Autograph Scores* (Cambridge, MA: Harvard University Press).

Tzu, Sun (513 BCE). *The Art of War* (public domain). Internet Classical Archive <http://classics.mit.edu/Tzu/artwar.html> Accessed Nov. 8, 2015.

U.S. Army Training and Doctrine Command (2008). "The U.S. Army Concept for the Human Dimension in Full Spectrum Operations—2015–2024 [TRADOC Pamphlet 525-3-7]," <http://www.tradoc.army.mil/tpubs/pams/p525-3-7-01.pdf> Accessed Nov. 6, 2015.

Valéry, Paul (1954). "Poetry and abstract thought," Zaharoff Lecture for 1939 at University of Oxford, trans. C. Guenther, *The Kenyon Review* 16(2): 208–33.

van Fraassen, Bas (1996). "Science, Materialism and False Consciousness," in J. Kvanvig, (ed.), *Warrant in Contemporary Epistemology: Essays in Honor of Plantinga's Theory of Knowledge* (Lanham, MD: Rowman and Littlefield).

van Fraassen, Bas (1980). *The Scientific Image* (Oxford: Oxford University Press).

van Harreveld, F., Wagenmakers, E. J., and van der Maas, H. L. J. (2007). "The effects of time pressure on chess skill: An investigation into fast and slow processes underlying expert performance," *Psychological Research* 71: 591–7.

van Valkenburg, Kevin (2009). "Different strokes for Michael Phelps," *Los Angeles Times*, July 07, 2009 <http://articles.latimes.com/2009/jul/07/sports/sp-phelps-swimming7> Accessed Nov. 6, 2015.

Vecsey, George (2010). "A Tournament Filled With Hope and Grace," *New York Times*, Sept. 11. <http://www.nytimes.com/2010/09/12/sports/tennis/12vecsey.html> Accessed Nov. 6, 2015.

Velleman, J. David (2008). "The way of the wanton," in C. Mackenzie and K. Atkins (eds), *Practical Identity and Narrative Agency* (New York: Routledge).

Viviani, P. and Stucchi, N. (1989). "The effect of movement velocity on form perception: Geometric illusions in dynamic displays," *Perception and Psychophysics* 46 (3): 266–74.

von Hartmann, Eduard. (1869/2002). *The Philosophy of the Unconscious*, Vol. 1, Part B (London: Living Time Press).

von Kleist, Heinrich (1972). "On the marionette theater," trans. T. G. Neumiller, *The Drama Review* 16(3): 22–6.

Wahl, Erik (2013). *Unthink: Rediscover Your Creative Genius* (New York: Crown Business).

Walker, Sidney C. (2004). *Trust your Gut: How to Overcome the Obstacles to Greater Success and Self-Fulfillment* (Houston, TX: High Plains Publications).

Wallace, David Foster (2006). "Federer as a religious experience," *New York Times*, Aug. 20. <http://www.nytimes.com/2006/08/20/sports/playmagazine/20federer.html?pagewanted=all> Accessed Nov. 6, 2015.

Wallace, H. M., Baumeister, R. F., and Vohs, K. D. (2005). "Audience support and choking under pressure: A home disadvantage?" *Journal of Sports Sciences* 23: 429–38.

Wallis, C. (2008). "Consciousness, Context and Know-how," *Synthese* 160: 123–53.

Wan, X., Nakatani, H., Ueno, K., Asamizuya, T., Cheng, K., and Tanaka, K. (2011). "The neural basis of intuitive best next-move generation in board game experts," *Science* 331(6015): 341–6.

Warren, Larry (1991). *Anna Sokolow: The Rebellious Spirit* (Princeton, NJ: Princeton Book Co.).

Weisberg, Robert (2006). *Creativity* (Hoboken, NJ: Wiley).

Weiss, Stephen and Rever, Arthur (2012). "Curing the Dreaded 'Steve Blass Disease,'" *Journal of Sport Psychology in Action* 3: 171–81.

Werner, Kenny (1996). *Effortless Mastery: Liberating the Master Musician Within* (New Albany, IN: Jamey Aebersold Jazz).

Weschler, Lawrence (2000). "The Novelist and the Nun," *New Yorker*, Oct. 2, pp. 74–86.

Wescott, Howard (2000). "The Courtier and the Hero: Sprezzatura from Castiglione to Cervantes," in F. L. R. Prado (ed.), *Cervantes for the 21st Century* (Newark, NJ: Juan de la Cuesta): 227.

Wiersma, L. (2014). "A Phenomenological Investigation of the Psychology of Big-Wave Surfing at Maverick's," *Sports Psychologist* 28 (2): 151–63.

Williams, Bernard (1985). *Ethics and the Limits of Philosophy* (Cambridge, MA: Harvard University Press).

Williams, John (2008). "Propositional Knowledge and Know-how," *Synthese*,165: 107–25.

Wilson, Jessica (2014). "No Work for a Theory of Grounding," *Inquiry* 57: 535–79.

Wilson, M., Chattington, M., Marple-Horvat, D. E., and Smith, N. C. (2007). "A comparison of self-focus versus attentional explanations of choking," *Journal of Sport and Exercise Psychology* 29(4): 439–56.

Wilson, T. D. and Schooler, J. W. (1991). "Thinking too much: Introspection can reduce the quality of preferences and decisions," *Journal of Personality and Social Psychology* 60(2): 181–92.

Wimsatt, William (2007). *Re-Engineering Philosophy for Limited Beings: Piecewise Approximations to Reality* (Cambridge, MA: Harvard University Press).

Wine, J. (1971). "Test anxiety and direction of attention," *Psychological Bulletin* 76: 92–104.

Winkly, Ira (2007). *Zen and the Art of Information Security* (Rockland, MA: Syngress).

Wittgenstein, Ludwig (1953). *Philosophical Investigations* (New York: Macmillan).

Wittgenstein, Ludwig (1958). *The Blue and Brown Books* (Oxford: Basil Blackwell).

Wordsworth, William (1862). "Preface to 'Lyrical Ballads,'" in H. Reed (ed.), *The Complete Poetical Works of Williams Wordsworth* (Philadelphia, PA: Troutman and Hayes): 660–71.

Wu, W. (2013). "Mental Action and the Threat of Automaticity," in Andy Clark, Julian Kiverstein, and Tillman Vierkant (eds), *Decomposing the Will* (New York: Oxford University Press): 244–61.

Wulf, Gabrielle (2007). *Attention and Motor Skill Learning* (Champaign, IL: Human Kinetics).

Wulf, G. and Lewthwaite, R. (2010). "Effortless motor learning? An external focus of attention enhances movement effectiveness and efficiency," in B. Bruya (ed.), *Effortless Attention: A New Perspective in Attention and Action* (Cambridge, MA: MIT Press): 75–101.

Wulf, G. and Prinz, W. (2001). "Directing attention to movement effects enhances learning: A review," *Psychonomic Bulletin and Review* 8: 648–60.

Yarrow, K., Brown, P., and Krakauer, J. W. (2009). "Inside the brain of an elite athlete: the neural processes that support high achievement in sports," *Nature Reviews Neuroscience* 10: 585–96.

Yarrow, K., Haggard, P., Heal, R., Brown, P., and Rothwell, J. C. (2001). "Illusory perceptions of space and time preserve cross-saccadic perceptual continuity," *Nature* 414: 302–5.

Yeats, William Butler (1908). "Preliminary Poem," *The Collected Works in Verse and Prose of William Butler Yeats*, Vol. II (London: Chapman and Hall Ltd).

Yocum, Guy (2002). "My shot: Sam Snead," *Golf Digest*, April. <http://www.golfdigest.com/magazine/myshot_gd0204> Accessed Nov. 5, 2015.

Yogis, Jaimal (2012). "I Think, Therefore I Choke," *ESPN The Magazine*, March 19. <http://espn.go.com/nfl/story/_/id/7649003/nfl-science-why-ravens-kicker-billy-cundiff-choked-afc-championship-game-espn-magazine> Accessed Nov. 8, 2015.

Yong, David (2011). *Breakthrough Power for Golfers: A Daily Guide to an Extraordinary Life* (Round Rock, TX: Wind Runner Press).

Zangwill, Nick (2001). *The Metaphysics of Beauty* (Ithaca, NY: Cornell University Press).

Zaslaw, Neal (1994). "Mozart as a working stiff," in James M. Morris (ed.), *On Mozart* (Cambridge: Cambridge University Press).

Zénon, A., Sidibé, M., and Olivier, E. (2014). "Pupil size variations correlate with physical effort perception," *Frontiers in Behavioral Neuroscience* 8: 286

Zollo, Paul (2003). *Songwriters on Songwriting: Revised and Expanded* (New York: Da Capo Press).

# Index

# K

Kahneman, Daniel 30, 34, 108
 and Amos Tversky 20
Kaizen xi, 128, 140
Kant 87, 197–200, 255–6
Kekule 28, 88
Kelly, Sean Dorrance *see* Dreyfus and Kelly
Kierkegaard, Søren 254–5
kinesthetic sympathy *see* motor resonance/
 perception
Kivy, Peter 23
Klein, Gary 30
Knoblauch, Chuck 18, 29, 102
Krakauer *see* Stanley
Kriegel, Uriah 8 n. 4, 190

# L

laboratory settings, pitfalls of 3–4, 63
Leavitt, J. L. 26

# M

Maiese, Michelle *see* Hanna, Robert and Maiese,
 Michelle
Mann, David 9
Martin, John 201
Masters, Richard 77
May, Larry 119
McDowell, John 25, 102, 210–12, 224
meaning of life 254–6
medical profession 112–13
Merleau-Ponty, Maurice 24, 104–5, 197
mindball 73 n. 18
mirror neurons 201
monitoring movement *see* attention
Moran, Aidan *see* Toner and Moran
motor control *see* control
motor control *see* control, conscious
motor resonance/perception 201–5
mountain biking *see* biking
Mozart 30–1, 88–9
musicianship 50, 60–3, 65 n. 15, 72, 91,
 100 n. 25, 113, 123, 129–30, 135–7, 141,
 143, 172, 183, 193, 199, 216, 250–1
 composing 28, 30, 32, 64, 89, 127,
  251–3
 piano 160, 173, 183, 199, 207, 250
 cello 156, 167, 185, 100–1
 guitar 99–100, 141, 143, 250–2
 singing 45, 143, 167
 bass 130, 133, 253

# N

Nadal, Rafael 19–20, 98
natural talent 30–1
neural efficiency 159–61
Nicholls, Adam 6, 20, 96–7
nursing 109–12

# O

O'Shaughnessy, Brian 148–53, 188

# P

Pacherie, Elizabeth 47
Papineau, David 18 n. 4, 75–6 n. 2, 119
paralysis-by-analysis *see* choking under pressure
Pavesse, Carlotta 56, 57 n. 8
Pickard, Hanna 189
planning 42
Plato 23
poetry 23
Poincaré, Henri: 28
politics 19, 168
practice 6, 64–8, 128–30, 141–2
 as striving to improve 134–5
 for an emergency 142–4
 for performance (or game) 130–4
predicting 42
principle of interference 37–8, 48, 75–105
Prinz, Jesse 144 *see also* De Brigard, Filipe and
 Prinz
proprioception 12, 188–90, 192–209
pupil dilation in relation to effort 155, 157

# R

race-car driving *see* driving
Rachels, Stuart 220–1, 226
radiology 115
Reinhold, Karl 190–1
Rietveld, Eric, 48 n. 7
risk taking 138–9
robustness *see* Wimsatt, William
Roholt, Tiger 65
Romanticism 23–4, 27–9
Rosen, Charles 183, 207
rugby 6, 96
running 60, 100 n. 26, 119, 156–7, 190

# S

Scardamalia *see* Bereiter and
 Scardamalia
Schiffer, Stephen 30–1
Schiller, Friedrich 28
Schooler *see* Wilson and Schooler
Schwitzgebel, Eric 8, 98
science
 in contrast to philosophy 1
 science of expertise challenges 2–4
Seiwert, Charles 121
self 22, 47
self-reflective thinking 41–2
sex 14, 256–9
Shakespeare *see* Hamlet
Shanteau, James 58
Shelley, Percy 23–4
Shepherd, Joshua 9